In the Image
of
YHWH

By
Dallas D. Stratman

In the Image of YHWH

by Dallas D. Stratman

Published by:
       AFJ Books LLC
       www.afjbooks.com

All Biblical text and references are from the King James Version (KJV).

Printed in the United States of America

ISBN 978-0-9834948-1-2

Library of Congress Control Number: 2013919682

Dedication

This book is dedicated to YHWH who makes all things possible and to my beloved wife Joyce for her support and patience.

Preface

The Holy Bible is the most significant book in mankind's history, and the book you are holding analyzes it in a way that has not been done before. The Holy Bible includes the Torah, and it is the only book ever written specifically to all mankind by YHWH, the sovereign creator God of the universe. YHWH is ancient Hebrew and contains no vowels. Thus, the original pronunciation with vowels included is uncertain but it was probably Yahweh. Today the word "god" has many different meanings to people. To avoid confusion, the God of the Holy Bible will be referred to as YHWH throughout this book.

The purposes of *In the Image of YHWH* are (1) to address the ways in which an individual is like YHWH; (2) to demonstrate quantitatively that the Holy Bible is YHWH's inspired word; and (3) to make everyone aware of the issues and decisions they will be confronted with in the near future when YHWH harvests the souls of all mankind.

The Holy Bible is the most amazing book in history. It contains specific revelation for today's generation. This is *time dependent revelation* in the form of specific numerical relationships and expressions that could not have been understood until after 1960 AD, when mankind attained the capability of digital computing and numerical analysis. *In the Image of YHWH* addresses significant historical and future events by applying these scientific analysis tools to the Holy Bible. The author refers to this approach as *Quantitative Theology*.

In the Image of YHWH will examine several widespread assumptions regarding the Holy Bible, and will also examine the following specific topics.

- The pre-creation universe.
- YHWH's BODY, SOUL and WILL,
- What it means to be made in the image of YHWH.
- YHWH's creation of the material universe starts the Anno Mundi (AM) calendar, which is the reference for the history of the world.
- The fall of man starts the Original Sin (OS) calendar, which is the reference for YHWH's planned reconciliation of man's sin.
- The requirements for an individual to have a good personal relationship with YHWH.
- Examples of YHWH's love, mercy and grace for mankind.
- The mystery of how a person's soul develops.
- YHWH's harvest of an individual's soul occurs when he dies, experiences the first-death, and no man knows the day or hour he will die.
- Today YHWH is in the process of preparing this generation for the seven year Tribulation Period, which is the harvest of all individual souls prior to His return in power and glory to initiate the Age of the Kingdom.

Preface

- YHWH's Age of the Kingdom or Millennium is a 1000 year period of His personal instruction from Jerusalem that ends with the Great White Throne Judgement.
- The Great White Throne Judgment where YHWH evaluates each individual's soul with respect to its type and individuals who have soul types in rebellion against YHWH shall experience the second-death, the Lake of Fire.

The analysis begins with a review of some assumptions, terms, processes, concepts, and then proceeds to the first book of the Holy Bible, the Book of Genesis, with an assessment of the pre-creation universe and YHWH's composition. It then continues throughout the biblical text, examining its significant historical events with respect to man's assumptions, decisions, and YHWH's merciful and gracious responses. The analysis concludes with a quantitative assessment of the seven types of souls identified by the seven churches as described in the last book of the Holy Bible, the Book of Revelation. This assessment is unique because it identifies the nature of the judgment that each church will experience and the season that YHWH's soul harvest will occur.

Also, the analysis is unique because it introduces several new concepts that are foreign to current theological though and Christian understanding. First, is the seven churches in the Book of Revelation are soul types and each soul type corresponds to a branch of the Menorah. Second, is the soul types are distributed across the world's population in accordance with a normal distribution. Third, is the relationship between and the functioning of the Body, Soul, and Will. The fourth, is the relationship between an individual's Will, Anxiety, Love, and Faith.

In the light of eternity, an individual's personal relationship with YHWH is literally the most important factor in any person's life. The hope is this book will help the readers better understand themselves and what they can expect in the future.

NOTE
Throughout this text the author's comments regarding any scripture reference is made using bold text within brackets.

Dallas D. Stratman

Table of Contents

Introduction

This introduction section provides some assumptions, terms, processes, and concepts that will apply to the subsequent analysis of the Holy Bible.

In the Image of YHWH is based on the understanding that YHWH gave the Holy Bible to all mankind incrementally starting with the Torah, followed by the remainder of the Old Testament, and subsequently the New Testament. The purpose of the Holy Bible is to provide a detailed history and chronology of the material universe, declare who YHWH is, define His expectations of mankind, and identify future events resulting from mankind's decisions.

Another assumption is that the Holy Bible includes information revealed by YHWH concerning what will happen to mankind, which was deliberately provided in a form not comprehensible to man until a given point in history. This is *time dependent revelation,* where YHWH uses the accumulation of mankind's knowledge with the passage of time to trigger the revelation of information hidden in the Holy Bible.

Today development of mankind's knowledge is referred to as science. The essence of the scientific method is the process of constructing a model for anything based upon a set of assumptions. The model or design is then tested to check how well it conforms to expectations, and the test results are published including all non-conformities. The test results and assumptions are reviewed and revised as required. This process is then repeated until the scientist's faith in his model is increased to a level that the model is considered a reasonable representation of the item being modeled.

The scientific method can be applied to anything, and the resulting models can range from the very simple to the very complex. A model may have many associated subordinate models. Depending upon the set of assumptions a model is based on, the results maybe very precise; however if the assumptions underlaying the model are faulty, the model will invariably be faulty also.

A scientist also has a responsibility to be ethical. Ethical science ensures that non-conforming test results are published so that others may understand and attempt to resolve the issues associated with the model. Identifying these issues allows other people to apply the model correctly, and may lead to future improvements or refinements of the model.

Unethical science conceals the non-conformities associated with a model. When a model is presented or taught without revealing its significant non-conformities, science is abandoned and indoctrination results. Indoctrination deliberately limits other's knowledge about a model in order to undermine their ability to accurately apply, evaluate, and refine it.

Today, science has produced an astonishing number of very high quality

1

models. These models have allowed man to land on the moon; explore other planets; communicate information with astonishing speed and efficiency; improve weather prediction; produce and use various forms of energy, medicines, medical procedures, foods, and many other advancements. The scientific process has immensely improved the length and quality of man's life. Ultimately, however, the science process is a method to improve and establish one's confidence in any model, whatever its application.

The scientific process can readily be applied to the Holy Bible. The basic assumption of the Biblical model for the universe is that YHWH created the material universe that we live in. The Holy Bible provides mankind (1) a description of the pre-creation universe, (2) who YHWH is, (3) YHWH's composition, (4) how YHWH functions, (5) how YHWH created the material universe, and (6) an accurate chronology of significant events past, present, and future.

Analysis regarding the pre-creation universe indicates that we exist in a universe composed of many dimensions. These dimensions are grouped together, typically in sets of three dimensions, to form what is referred to as a *component*. These are <u>not components</u> like nuts and bolts but are groups of dimensions. These components have units, which are bonded together to provide a particular function. We are most familiar with the material part of the universe, where we can easily observe at least three dimensions (x, y, z) and the unique dimension of time (t). We are less familiar with the Spirit, Soul, and WILL components of the pre-creation universe, which are also time dependent. Each of these components also likely have three dimensions. The Holy Bible also indicates there are several additional sets of dimensions associated with the three heavens. When totaled, the different dimensions in the entire universe could number as many as twenty-one, if not more.

YHWH in the Holy Bible's Book of Genesis introduces Himself as having BODY, SOUL, and WILL components and then describes how these components functionally relate to each other when YHWH addresses issues related to various historical events (such as the creation of the material universe, the fall of mankind, and the first murder).

YHWH describes how He is structured functionally because this allows Him to relate more readily to mankind in a manner they can understand. YHWH's BODY receives information from the universe and provides it to YHWH's SOUL. YHWH's BODY is described using terms such as "the Son," or "the Spirit of God," or "God saw." YHWH's SOUL contains all knowledge about every aspect of the universe and makes decisions based on this perfect knowledge. YHWH's SOUL is described using terms such as "the Father," or "the Glory of God." YHWH's

WILL implements any SOUL decision perfectly. YHWH's WILL is described using terms such as "the Holy Spirit," or "God said." The BODY, SOUL and WILL are characterized as individuals with each having its own responsibilities and interfaces.

As beings made in the image of YHWH, human beings are also composed of a Soul, Will and Body that are functionally related in the same manner. However, YHWH constrained a person's spirit body with a material mortal body. A person's soul, like YHWH's SOUL, contains all his accumulated knowledge of the universe and formulates decisions, but each individual's soul contains different knowledge and different quantities of knowledge depending upon his experiences. Once a decision is made, like YHWH, a person's WILL stimulates his body to act in some way to implement the decision. A person's Body, Soul and Will are infinitesimal compared to that of YHWH, who created man and the universe we live in.

Another important assumption is related to the seven churches in the book of Revelation. Some ignore completely or allegorize the entire book of Revelation. Other more realistic interpretations relative to the seven churches are:

1. *A literal letter was sent to each of the seven churches* that were in Asia minor by John the Apostle. If this assumption is valid, then one might expect the specific church leaders would be identified by name.

2. *The seven churches represent historical church ages.* This interpretation was introduced by Isaac Newton (1642 to 1727 AD) and is the generally accepted understanding today. The approximate ages are:
   a. Ephesus: The Apostolic Church Age from 31 to 96 AD.
   b. Smyrna: The Roman Persecution Age from 96 to 313 AD.
   c. Pergamos: The Age of Constantine from 313 to 538 AD.
   d. Thyatria: The Dark Ages from 538 to 1517 AD.
   e. Sardis: The Reformation Age from 1517 to 1739 AD.
   f. Philadelphia: The Missionary Age from 1739 to 1900 AD.
   g. Laodicea: The Age of Apostasy from 1900 to return of Jesus.

3. *Each church represents people with similar types of souls or natures.* All the seven churches, types of souls, are present at all times throughout history.
   a. Philadelphia: Individuals willing to die for YHWH.
   b. Smyrna: Individuals dedicated to YHWH.
   c. Ephesus: Individuals who place self above YHWH.
   d. Laodicea: Individuals who place self above all else.
   e. Thyatria: Individuals who place self above Satan.
   f. Pergamos: Individuals dedicated to Satan.
   g. Sardis: Individuals willing to die for Satan.

3

In the Image of YHWH

The interpretation that the seven churches are seven different types of souls is advanced in this book and is an example of YHWH's *time dependent revelation* in the Holy Bible. *Time dependent revelation* requires that mankind's knowledge must attain a specific level before a concept can be understood. Knowledge required in order to understand the literal meaning that the seven churches, types of souls, were not available until after 1960 AD with the advent of the digital computer and numerical analysis. This technology allowed the scientific process to be applied to characterize the seven churches, types of souls. The seven churches conform to a normal distribution across the world's population and the percentage of the people in each church is confirmed by the Holy Bible. Application of the scientific process to understand the significance of specific numbers in the Holy Bible is referred to by the author as *Quantitative Theology.*

Biblical *time dependent revelation* also places YHWH's personal stamp on the Holy Bible by including future events that were unknown at the time of the writing. Until these future events have become history, nothing can replace them, alter them, or supersede them. Thus the Holy Bible cannot be superseded by any other book or revelation until after YHWH's return to earth! This is particularly important to the generations alive as the time of YHWH's return approaches because many people during this time will distort or reject YHWH and the Holy Bible.

The Holy Bible also defines how each person is to relate to YHWH, to his or her self, to other people, and to the material universe. To accomplish this, the Holy Bible starts by revealing how YHWH created the material universe. Then YHWH proceeds to document how mankind misused the freedom YHWH had gave them, from the Garden of Eden through Noah's flood. This was followed by the rejection of YHWH at Mount Sinai and the resultant consequences of that sin. To relate with mankind at a human level, YHWH's BODY took on a mortal-material body, Jesus the Messiah, who was the perfect example of everything expected of mankind. He demonstrated everything that mankind will experience. This included the first-death. Every human being will experience the first-death and spend eternity with YHWH. But unfortunately there will be some who experience the second-death. Hence, an individual should not take his soul development lightly.

YHWH's Holy Bible is an inerrant account of history from the creation of the material universe, through the present and into the future after YHWH returns. YHWH should not be taken lightly because eternity is a very long time with respect to man's infinitesimal mortal-physical existence.

Do not ignore Genesis 1:1, YHWH's declaration that He created the universe. There is a danger associated with calling YHWH a liar because YHWH is also our judge.

4

I   YHWH Before Creation

Everyone who ever has existed and who will ever exist has developed some kind of model for how the universe functions and came into existence. These numerous models vary radically in complexity and type.

Some models assume that a person and the universe are one; or the universe is self's quantum thought; or the universe is god's imagination; or the universe is god's hologram. Other models for the universe assume only the existence of only a material universe. Typically these models include material dimensions x, y, z, and time and assume the universe came into existence by chance over a long period of time, typically millions or billions of years. Then human life eventually resulted from evolution, from the simple material to the complex. None of these models will be considered any further herein.

This book addresses the biblical model for the universe as detailed in the Torah and the Holy Bible. The Holy Bible opens with a very powerful declaration from YHWH in Genesis 1:1.

Genesis 1:1
*1   In the beginning <u>God</u> [**YHWH**], created the heaven and the earth.*

This statement leaves no doubt that YHWH solely created the heavens and earth, but there may be two possible structures for the universe:

1.   YHWH as an unknown first cause created Himself and the heaven and earth at the same time. Thus the universe includes only the heaven and the earth.

        or

2.   YHWH existed in a pre-creation universe prior to performing the creation event. Thus the heaven and the earth, the material universe we know today, is an addition to the pre-creation universe.

When one assumes YHWH existed prior to the creation event, then the Holy Bible shows YHWH created the material universe we live in as part of a very complex multi-dimensional universe. The Holy Bible also shows YHWH has remained actively involved in the development of the material heaven and earth since creation to accomplish His objectives. It is probable that YHWH's primary objective centers around a mystery—new soul development.

This chapter addresses the pre-creation universe, which YHWH existed in prior to performing the creation event as stated in Genesis 1:1.

In Genesis 1:2-3 YHWH continues to introduce Himself to mankind by describing the pre-creation universe's composition and its functionality as He prepares to perform the creation event.

Genesis 1:2-3
2   And the earth was without form, and void; and darkness was upon the face
    of the deep. And the *Spirit of God* **[YHWH's BODY]** moved upon the face of
    the waters.
3   And *God said* **[YHWH's WILL]**, Let there be *light* **[The light source was
    YHWH's SOUL]**: and *there was light* **[Observed by YHWH's BODY]**.

In Genesis 1:2-3 above YHWH first describes the initial state of the earth and
the material component of the pre-creation universe as non-existent. Thus from
YHWH's perspective as an observer in the pre-creation universe, there was no
form, the material dimensions ($x_{material}$, $y_{material}$, $z_{material}$) did not exist yet. The face
of the material universe appeared to YHWH's BODY as a void or a vast dark
emptiness.

It is very important to recognize that in Genesis 1:2 the "Spirit of God" is not
a reference to YHWH's Holy Spirit, but is YHWH's BODY that existed in the
pre-creation universe with spirit dimensions ($x_{BODY\text{-}Spirit}$, $y_{BODY\text{-}Spirit}$, $z_{BODY\text{-}Spirit}$). All
bodies including YHWH's that are in the pre-creation universe are spirit and the
word *spirit* implies invisibility for a human material observer.

But what is YHWH's BODY doing? The answer is contained in the next phrase
"moved upon the face of the waters."

The word *moved* is derived from the Hebrew word ***rachaph*** (OT:7363) [5]. It is
a primitive root meaning to brood, but it is typically translated as flutter, move, or
hover when used in the Holy Bible to support the concept of invisible wind being
associated with the "Spirit of God."

The word *upon* in Hebrew `*al* (OT:5919) [5] and means either upon or over
something.

The word *face* is translated from the Hebrew word ***paniym*** (OT:6440) [5] and
typically implies a surface being viewed by an observer.

The word *waters* is the Hebrew word ***mayim*** (OT:4325) [5]. Typically ***mayim*** is
translated as waters and is commonly referred to as the chaotic primordial waters
or the forming material for the universe. Euphemistically ***mayim*** may also reflect
the idea of semen/seed. As such it would reflect the conception of the material
component within the pre-creation universe.

When ***rachaph*** is translated as *to brood*; `*al* is translated as *over*; ***paniym***
is translated as *face* and ***mayim*** is translated as *semen* then the phrase would be
"brooded over the face of the semen." This pictures YHWH's BODY in the pre-
creation universe encompassing the semen or seed or the fetus of the new material
component of the pre-creation universe — like a hen sitting on a nest preparing to
hatch an egg. This picture is consistent with the material component of the universe
being created as an addition to the pre-creation universe. Also, it is consistent with

YHWH's BODY providing the external interface for YHWH's SOUL and WILL.

In Genesis 1:3, YHWH continues to introduce His WILL, God said, and SOUL, light. YHWH describes Himself in the pre-creation universe as being triune, having three sections, with a BODY, SOUL, and WILL. The BODY, SOUL, and WILL are bonded together operating as a single entity with each section having its own specific functions and responsibilities as shown in Figure I-1.

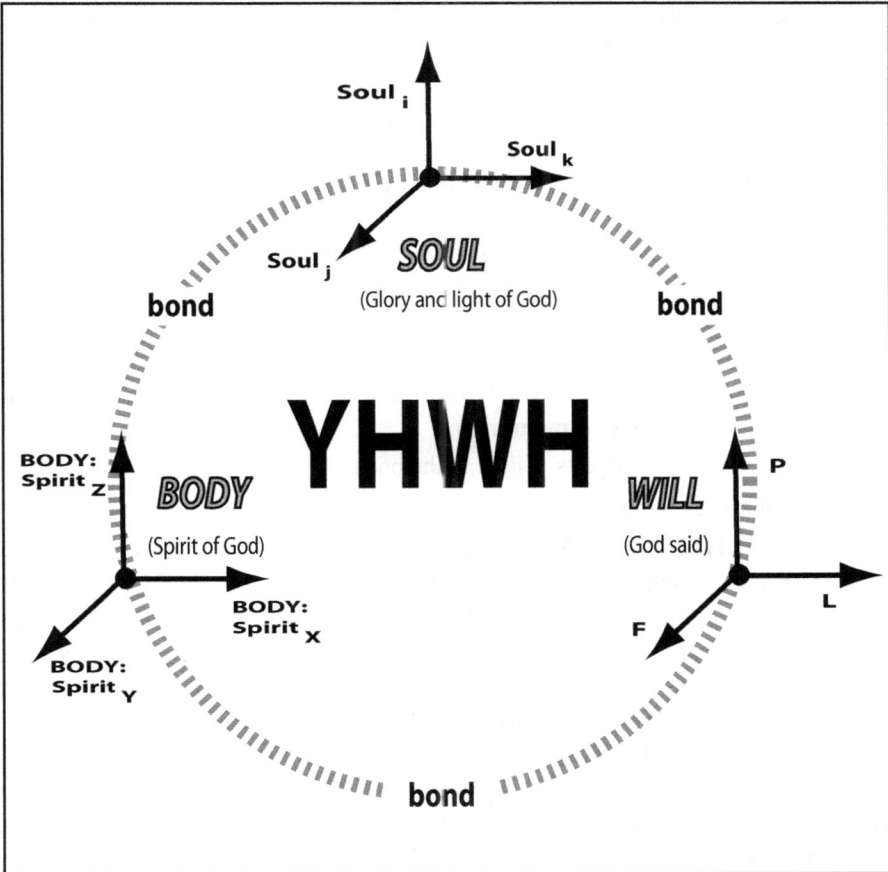

Figure I-1   YHWH in the Pre-creation Universe

YHWH's BODY, SOUL, and WILL are <u>not individual spirit people, or persons</u>. YHWH's BODY, SOUL, and WILL are often characterized as persons to illustrate how they interact with each other. This is YHWH's *self-talk*, which He uses for the benefit of mankind.

7

In the pre-creation universe in addition to the dimension of time (t) the BODY, SOUL and WILL each have an associated set of dimensions that have different functions, which are:

- **"Spirit of God" (YHWH's BODY)**

YHWH's spirit body exists in the spirit component of the universe, and His body has three orthogonal spirit dimensions ($x_{BODY:Spirit}$, $y_{BODY:Spirit}$ $z_{BODY:Spirit}$), which are consistent with biblical descriptions of YHWH's throne and spirit beings. The function of YHWH's BODY is to provide external communication to the entire universe and receive all inputs from the entire universe. YHWH's BODY takes in the current state information from the entire universe for use by YHWH's SOUL. Terms like **"God saw"** or **"it was so"** are used to describe the input of information. YHWH's BODY supports YHWH's WILL with outgoing communication using His voice.

Note that YHWH does not have a material body at this point in time because He has not created the material dimensions of the universe yet.

- **"Light" (YHWH's SOUL)**

Light both literally and figuratively represents YHWH's SOUL or the FATHER or His GLORY. Light has two meanings:

1. Light that makes objects visible to the body.

2. Light associated with YHWH's knowledge and truth.

YHWH's SOUL, His GLORY, appears in the pre-creation universe and in the future material component of the universe as visible light. In Exodus 33:17-23 YHWH provides a glimpse of the light of His GLORY to Moses. In I Samuel 4:18-22 YHWH's GLORY and truth are represented by the Ark of the Testimony. In Isaiah 60:19-20 and Revelation 22:5 when YHWH's GLORY is present the sun and moon are not needed just as during the first 3 days of creation.

The function of YHWH's SOUL is to contain all information or knowledge of the universe for all possible past, present, and future events. YHWH uses this perfect knowledge to establish perfect truth, which determines everything that will subsequently be implemented by YHWH's WILL.

YHWH's SOUL exists in the SOUL component of the pre-creation universe, and it has three orthogonal dimensions ($SOUL_i$, $SOUL_j$, $SOUL_k$) per Figure I-1.

In the Holy Bible's New Testament, YHWH's SOUL is referred to as the Father.

- **"God said" (YHWH's WILL)**

The function of YHWH's WILL, the Holy Spirit, is to implement or generate or provide what YHWH' SOUL has determined shall occur. WILL is expressed by speech and /or actions. YHWH's WILL is reflected by words like "**God said**," "**God called**," "**God made**," or similar statements.

YHWH has perfect WILL that exists in the WILL component of the pre-creation universe and WILL has at least three dimensions (*L, F, P*), which are *L*ove, *F*aith, and *P*ower.

The following information from the New Testament is included here to provide some additional insight into how the BODY, SOUL, and WILL function with respect to each other.

An algebraic word problem exists in I Corinthians 13:1-3, which illustrates the relationship between WILL, L and F only for YHWH's image, mankind.

> *1 Corinthians 13:1-3*
> 1 Though <u>I speak</u> **[WILL]** *with the tongues of men and of angels, and have not* <u>charity</u> **[Love = 0]**, *I am become as sounding brass, or a tinkling cymbal.* **[WILL = 0]**
> 2 *And though I have the gift of* <u>prophecy</u> **[WILL]**, *and understand all mysteries, and all* <u>knowledge</u> **[perfect soul]**; *and though* <u>I have all faith</u> **[Faith = 1]**, *so that I could remove mountains, and* <u>have not charity</u> **[Love = 0]**, *I am nothing.* **[WILL = 0]**
> 3 *And though I bestow all my goods to feed the poor, and though I give my body to be burned, and* <u>have not charity</u> **[Love = 0)**, *it profiteth me nothing.*

This algebraic word problem shows two of the three dimensions that form the WILL. These three orthogonal dimensions are related as a product. This understanding was first developed in the book, *Self's Destiny and Self,* [2] and yields the following expression.

$$WILL(t) = L(t) * F(t) * P(t)$$

Where all values for *WILL, L, F,* and *P* have magnitudes between the perfect number 1.0 and the null number 0.0. The magnitude of an item's *WILL, L, F,* and *P* are also time dependent as shown by *(t)*.

The term *L(t)* represents the magnitude of *L*ove, priority, that is associated with all items within one's soul. Love and priority are identical terms, which are interchangeable and reflect how important an item is to the individual. YHWH's *L(t)* is perfect and always has a magnitude equal to 1.0.

The term *F(t)* represents the magnitude of *F*aith, confidence, that is associated with all items within one's soul. Faith and confidence are also identical terms, which reflect an individual's certainty that an item will occur in time. *F(t)* has a very unique property whose source can come from self or someone else. For

9

example, if an individual is confronted with a task that he is personally responsible for, he knows the magnitude of his *F(t),* his confidence in his ability to perform the task. However, if the individual asks someone else to do the task the magnitude of his *F(t)* depends upon the other person.

The term *P(t)* represents the magnitude of *P*ower that is available to apply to any item within one's soul. This term limits the amount of power the WILL can exert while implementing a soul's decision.

YHWH is the only perfect entity that exists and the number of perfection is one. Thus when YHWH decides to do something, He does it using His perfect WILL, which can be expressed by:

$$WILL(t) = L(t) * F(t) * P(t)$$

YHWH's perfect WILL is   1   = 1   *   1   *   1

As one explores the Holy Bible, the power of YHWH's perfect WILL is incredible. He can create new dimensions in the universe. He can bond sets of dimensions together or separate them. It is the power of YHWH's perfect WILL that created the material component of the universe and gave mankind responsibilities with the ability to make his own decisions. Moreover, YHWH's perfect WILL controls the outcome of future events and there is nothing that it cannot do! Except, YHWH cannot contradict His own WILL.

What happens when YHWH asks an individual or mankind to do a task? YHWH's *F(t)* toward the task is now dependent upon the individual's or mankind's WILL to do the task because YHWH has created him with the ability to make his own decisions. The result is YHWH also has ANXIETY or WRATH.

$$ANXIETY(t) \ or \ WRATH(t) = [L(t) - F(t)] * P(t)$$

YHWH's is at *prefect peace* ,WRATH = 0 = [1 - 1] * 1, with all His perfect decisions even His decision to give the individual the ability to make his own decisions. However, YHWH's WRATH associated with any individual or group is:

$$WRATH_{individual}(t) = [1 - F_{individual}(t)] * 1$$

Where YHWH's $F_{individual}(t)$ is an individual's $Will_{YHWH}(t)$. An individual's $Will_{YHWH}(t) = L_{YHWH}(t) * F_{YHWH}(t) * P_{individual}(t)$ and is a direct measure of the individual's love for and faith in YHWH. YHWH justifies each individual by his faith in YHWH because it can only come from an individual's acceptance of YHWH's provision. Throughout the Holy Bible, YHWH deals with an individual or a group of people by first stating a command and the consequences for disobedience. Then the individual or group of people decide what will be done. If they are obedient to YHWH, He will bless them. If they are disobedient, sin, YHWH will discipline them to reconcile His WRATH toward them.

To differentiate between YHWH and man, YHWH's BODY, SOUL, and WILL will all be capitalized and man's Body, Soul, and Will will have the first letter capitalized.

Mankind will be created in the image of YHWH. However, each new individual soul is not perfect. YHWH with perfect wisdom will limit mankind's ability to influence the universe by making the term *P(t)* extremely small. An individual's limited Will is:

$$Will(t) = L(t) * F(t) * P(t) = 1 * 1 * tiny = tiny$$

Although the power of an individual's Will is extremely tiny and has no real affect on the material universe, it does accurately reveal the type of Soul and Will the individual possesses.

Prior to YHWH's creation of the material component of the universe, the pre-creation universe contained at least three components (soul, body, will) with each component having at least three dimensions plus time for a total of at least ten dimensions. A simple way of viewing YHWH's structure is to picture only three dimensions (one for the soul, one for the body, and one for the will) in Cartesian coordinates (x, y, z). For example, a cube having dimensions x, y, z. If any one dimension of the cube is not present then the cube ceases to exist. YHWH is one entity with a BODY, SOUL, and WILL.

YHWH's *self-talk* is YHWH's description of His own internal communication and interfaces between His BODY, SOUL, and WILL. YHWH's self-talk in the Holy Bible is often described as communication between persons. Particularly in the New Testament where YHWH's BODY, SOUL, and WILL are referred to as the Son, Father and Holy Spirit respectively. This communication includes phrases like God saw; God said; God made; it is not for me, the Son, to know but my Father; why has thou forsaken me; and many others.

YHWH very often uses self-talk between His BODY, SOUL, and WILL to help mankind to understand how He functions. A better understanding of how YHWH functions also helps one understand himself better. YHWH's BODY, SOUL, and WILL functional relationships and interfaces are depicted in Figure I-2.

YHWH is functionally triune with YHWH's BODY positioned on the right hand side of YHWH's SOUL and YHWH's WILL is on the left hand side. Current universe state information is received by the YHWH's BODY and passed to the YHWH's SOUL where it is processed and decisions are made based on perfect knowledge of all possibilities. Once a decision is made the YHWH's WILL implements all of it and states it to the universe using His BODY's voice.

PRE-CREATION UNIVERSE

YHWH

	YHWH's BODY	YHWH's SOUL	YHWH's WILL
Inputs →	*(SPIRIT of God)* *(God saw)* *(Son)*	*(GLORY of God)* *(Light of God)* *(Father)*	*(God said)* *(God made)* *(Holy Spirit)*
	Function The BODY recieves information from the universe and provides it to the SOUL. The WILL provides the BODY information to pass	**Function** The SOUL based on perfect knowledge of possibilities in the universe and current information from the BODY prefect decisions	**Function** The WILL implements the SOUL's decisions and informs the universe via the BODY.
Outputs ◀	on to the universe.	are made.	

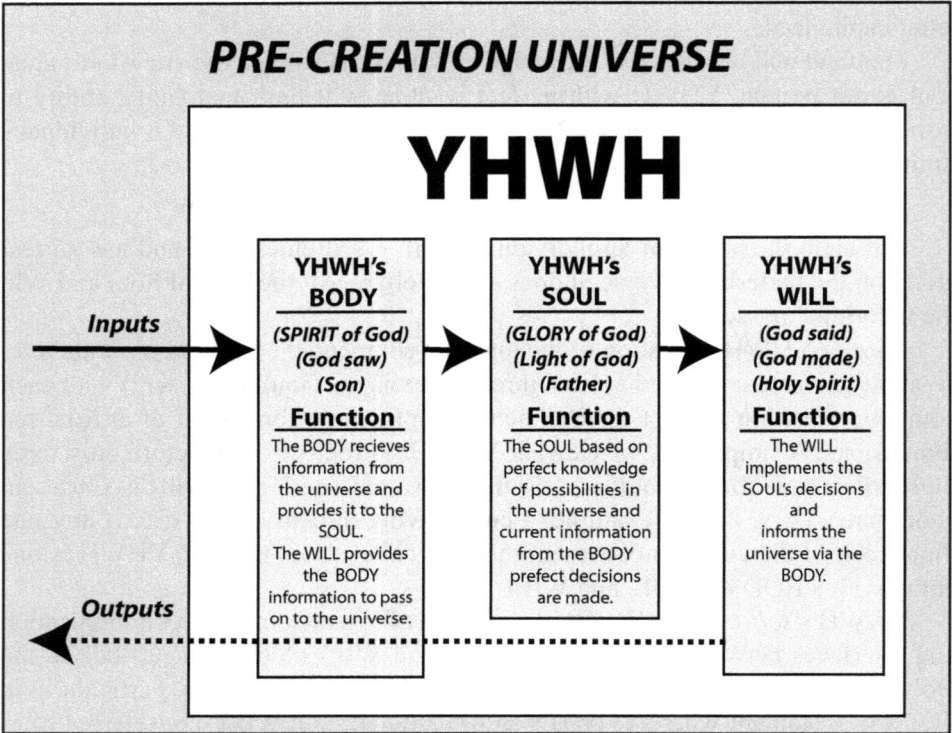

Figure I-2 YHWH's Functional Composition

No where in the Holy Bible or elsewhere does YHWH provide any detailed description with respect to how the pre-creation universe came into existence. This will remain a mystery forever because YHWH would never compromise Himself. However, mankind and Satan will continue to speculate.

The pre-creation universe must be extraordinary, having a least ten dimensions; SPIRIT: Body (x,y,z), SOUL (i,j,k), WILL (L,F,P), and time (t). Also, it contains structures like YHWH's throne, other spirit beings, and must have an infinite capacity. From this existing state YHWH adds the material part of the universe we are aware of today. During the creation of the material universe, YHWH proceeds to use His self-talk to describe how His BODY, SOUL, and WILL interacted to accomplish the task.

12

II   YHWH During Creation

The six 24 hour day creation event is described in Genesis 1:4 through 2:25. At the start of the creation process, the pre-creation universe consisted of at least ten dimensions, which were three soul, three spirit, three WILL, and time. YHWH is pictured brooding over the initial essence of His new creation or its waters, sperm, seed or a mass just like a mother hen hatching an egg. For simplicity the initial essence of the new creation or its waters, sperm, seed or a mass will now be referred to as *material*. This material is configured by YHWH to form a new material component within the pre-creation universe. It is important to note that the material component is an addition to the existing pre-creation universe. During the next six days, YHWH uses His self-talk between His BODY, SOUL, and WILL to describe the formation of the new material component to the pre-creation universe.

First Day of Creation – The Conception

The first day is described in Genesis 1:4-5.

Genesis 1:4
4   And *God saw* **[YHWH's BODY]** the *light* **[YHWH's SOUL , GLORY, shown over the void]**, that *it was good:* **[YHWH WILL]**
    : and *God divided* **[YHWH's WILL]** the light from the darkness.
5   And *God called* **[YHWH's WILL]** the light Day, and the darkness *He called* **[YHWH's WILL]** Night. And the evening and the morning were the **first day.**

YHWH's SOUL is providing the light source! From Chapter I we know the word "light" has two key properties.

The first property of YHWH's SOUL is light that is related to enlightenment, or knowledge. YHWH's self-talk is declaring that the concept, or plan, for the new material component of the universe is good.

The second property of YHWH's SOUL is light that provides visibility for an observer's body in the universe. This is similar to that described in Revelation 22:5 and Isaiah 60:19-20. It is this light property that YHWH uses to synchronize time between the pre-creation universe and the hatching new material dimensions.

YHWH uses the light from His SOUL to establish His time reference for the newly conceived material universe. The division between light and darkness occurs when YHWH's WILL implements YHWH's SOUL's plan. When light is visible it is *day*, or daytime, and the lack of light is darkness, or *night*. Then, YHWH's WILL starts the newly conceived material to rotate on its axis creating the evening and morning. He then defines the rotation to have a period time equal to one day. The result is complete time synchronization between the pre-creation universe and the new material addition as depicted in Figure II-1.

13

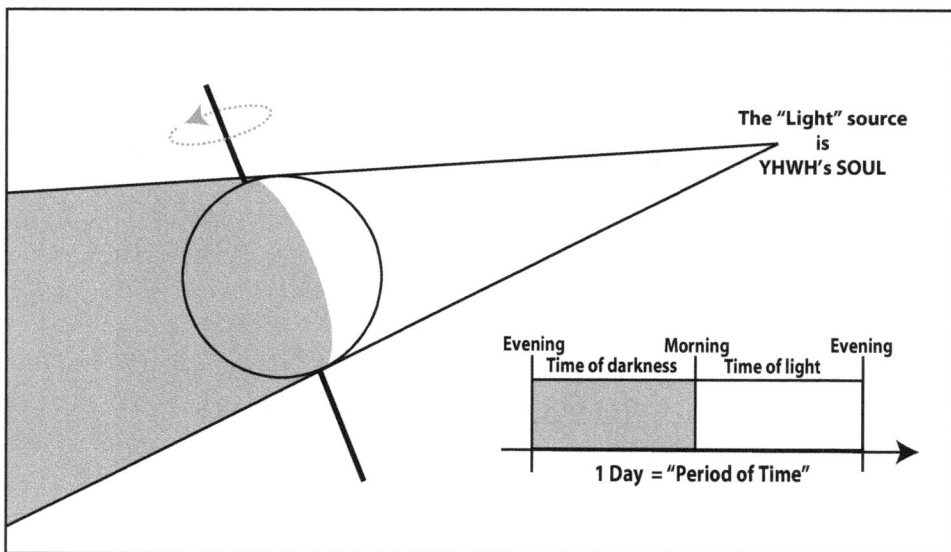

Figure II-1   Day 1 - Universe Time Synchronization

What are the implications of YHWH's activity during this first day? It is important to note that YHWH's first action was to synchronize time between what exists and what He has started to create. Time is an extremely significant dimension because the assumptions, or doctrines, related to it have a tremendous impact how people have viewed and continue to view YHWH and the material universe we live in. The following are some of the numerous assumptions different people have concerning YHWH and the properties of time:

- **Time does not exist:** Few people support this assumption, although some people may believe that everything in the universe is imagined.

- **Time duration of first day:** The time duration of the first day is dependent upon the assumptions of what the word *day* means.

  - If the word *day* is assumed to be a period of time having any length, then some assume the period time to be billions of years. This is referred to as long days. This type of model typically assumes that the universe is only material having dimensions x, y, z, and time. It also assumes the universe is developed by the process of evolution. The biblical model does not support evolution because death is present prior to the Original Sin and evolution does not adequately address the issue of kinds, For kinds to reproduce, the male and female must have come into existence at the same time, and in the same area.

14

- If the word *day* is considered to be a standard 24 hour period of time, then it is consistent with our present experience. YHWH's perfect WILL does not require billions of years to implement His SOUL's decisions. The 24-hour day is consistent with the historical record documented in the Bible, and according to this record, the material component as we know it is approaching 6000 years of age.

• **YHWH can move to any point in time past, or present, or future:** YHWH uses this capability to establish His desired outcome for the history of His universe. This is a basic assumption behind the concept of predestination. Where YHWH has predetermined all past, present, and future things. None of His creation has true freedom of choice. YHWH has predetermined His *elect*, those receiving eternal life, by name before creating the material component of the universe. This assumption is also the basis for the various ideas associated with time travel and time machines.

• **YHWH moves in time from the present toward the future:** YHWH only moves forward in time and knows all possible outcomes for all things at any point in time. YHWH allows people to freely decide what they will do. Then YHWH uses their present state to determine to bless them or not. YHWH also provides people with conditional agreements and subsequently holds them accountable for their decisions. YHWH, before creating the material component of the universe, predetermined His *elect* to be those who will decide to love and follow Him and this view is supported by this text.

• **Time has a constant velocity:** Time has a constant elapse rate of 1 second/second or 1 minute/minute or 1 unit/unit. Time, having a constant rate, provides a perfect reference for all events that have occurred, are occurring, and will occur in the future. If time were non-linear, the non-linearity must be fully known, or there would be no accurate history of the universe. The idea that time changes due to magnetic field strength or gravity or the relative velocities between different observers is based upon the assumption that the clocks used or the light path were not affected, but time experiences a rate change. The other possibility is that time retains a constant rate and the method of measurement or path length is altered so that time appears to be altered. The easiest way to compensate for this type of issue is to adjust the apparent time. The assumption that people will age at different rates depending upon the magnitude of velocity difference between them at this point in time has no empirical support because man has not flown near the speed of light.

Time is a unique dimension, and it probably correlates events between all components of the universe, material, spirit, soul, will, and with any other components that may exist.

As the first day concludes, YHWH has described His structure and initiated the addition of the material component, three new dimensions, to the pre-creation universe. YHWH started the initial material to rotate, which established or synchronized the time reference between the new material component and the pre-creation universe. YHWH's SOUL (GLORY) was the light source similar to that described in Revelation 22:5 and Isaiah 60:19-20.

15

<u>Second Day of Creation - The Birth</u>

The second day of creation is unique because it brings to mind the birth process where the fetus is separated from the mother's womb as the birth occurs. The mother's womb is like the pre-creation universe and the new fetus is like the new material component of the universe, which is to be birthed and then matured during the next four days. YHWH's WILL implemented the birth by expanding the material component of the universe. Keep in mind that YHWH's residence is in the pre-creation universe while adding the material component to it. The expansion process is described in Genesis 1:6-8

> *Genesis 1:6-8*
> 6   And <u>God said</u> **[YHWH's WILL]**, *Let there be a firmament* **[expanse or space]** *in the midst of the waters, and let it divide the waters from the waters.*
> 7   And <u>God made</u> **[YHWH's WILL]** *the* <u>firmament</u> **[expanse or space]**, *and divided the waters which were under the* <u>firmament</u> **[expanse or space]** *from the waters which were above the* <u>firmament</u> **[expanse or space]**: *and* <u>it was so</u> **[YHWH's BODY observed]**.
> 8   <u>God called</u> **[YHWH's WILL]** *the* <u>firmament</u> **[expanse or space]** <u>Heaven</u> **[sky]**. *And the evening and the morning were the **second day**.*

The meaning of the word *firmament* is translated from the Hebrew word *raqiya`* (OT: 7549) [5] and its root *raqa`* (OT: 7554) [5], which implies an expanse or to beat or make broad or spread abroad or expand or stamp or stretch. In this context YHWH's WILL has expanded or stretched the material to add a very particular space called heaven. The meaning of the word *heaven* is translated from the Hebrew word **shamayim** (OT: 8064) [5] meaning to be lofty. Typically it is assumed to reflect the sky or air around our planet. Thus heaven is equal to a space. The water above the space, heaven, is a layer of water vapor that forms a greenhouse that protects the mass below as shown in Figure II-2. The arbitrary axis is to show the earth is rotating.

At the end of the second day, the material center of the new planet is covered with water, and there exists a space between it and the new water vapor canopy above it.

It is important to note the word *heaven* as used here is the space above the earth and <u>not where a person goes when he dies</u>. When a person dies, being in the image of YHWH, he will cease to exist in the material universe and transition into the pre-creation universe as we shall see.

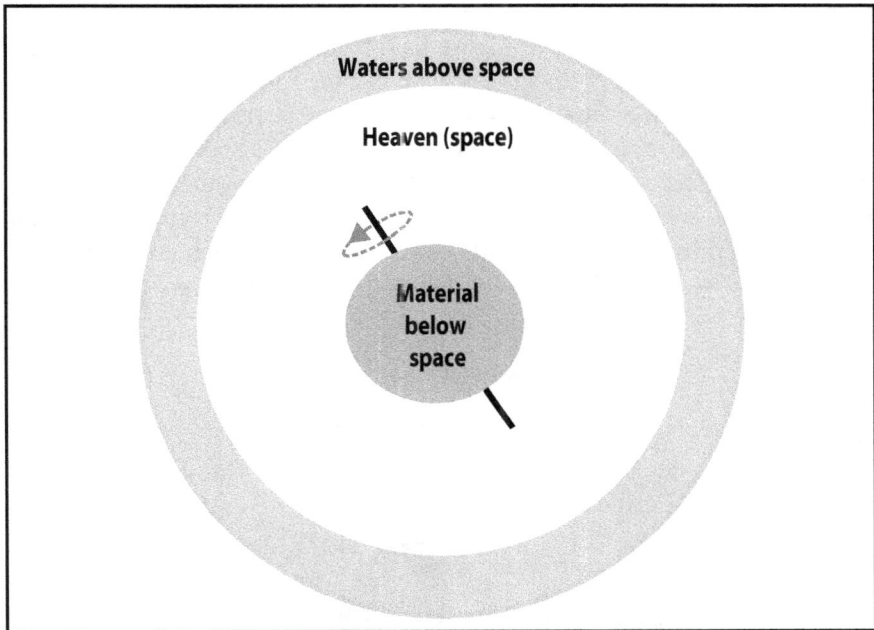

Figure II-2   Second Day of Creation - The New Planet

Third Day of Creation - The land and sea

At the start of third day, the protective water vapor shield is in place, and YHWH's WILL is focused on the material covered by waters, under the space called heaven.

In Genesis 1:9-13, the planned activity is described.

Genesis 1:9-13
9   And *God said* **[YHWH's WILL]**, Let the waters under the heaven be gathered together unto one place, and let the dry land appear: and it was so.
10   And *God called* **[YHWH's WILL]** the dry land Earth; and the gathering together of the waters called he Seas: and *God saw* **[YHWH's BODY]** that it was good.
11   And *God said* **[YHWH's WILL]**, Let the earth bring forth grass, the herb yielding seed, and the fruit tree yielding fruit after his kind, whose seed is in itself, upon the earth: and it was so
12   And the earth brought forth grass, and herb yielding seed after his kind, and the tree yielding fruit, whose seed was in itself, after his kind: and *God saw* **[YHWH's BODY]** that it was good.
13   And the evening and the morning were the **third day**.

17

In the Image of YHWH

YHWH's WILL now separates the material into water, sea, and dry land, earth. These changes are illustrated in Figure II-3. Note, there is one area for the sea and one area for the dry land, which is not at all like the rivers, lakes, oceans, mountains and continents that we know today. As we will see later, there are only four rivers, which all have the same source, the Garden of Eden. These four rivers all flow in different directions into the single sea. This suggests that the Garden of Eden was located near the center of the dry land at its highest point. From the Garden of Eden the land in all directions had a gentle slope to the sea, which encompassed it.

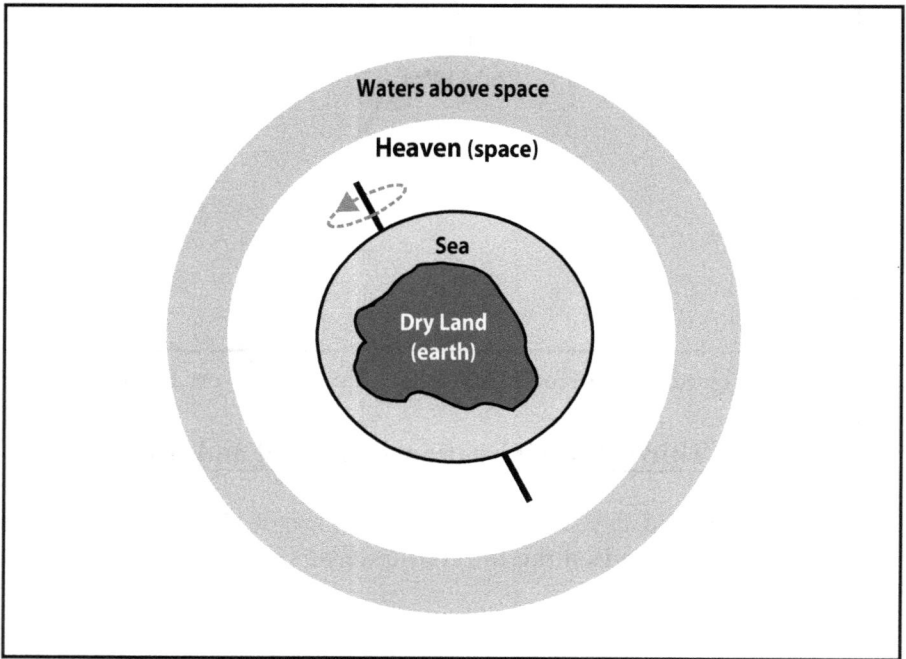

Figure II-3 Third Day of Creation - The Sea and Dry Land

Hence the landscape was totally different from what we experience today. The water vapor canopy would form a green house, which would provide a humid warm climate without the presence of any ice caps or frozen lakes and rivers as we are familiar with today.

With the dry land and the water vapor canopy greenhouse in place, YHWH populated the land with all the various "kinds" of vegetation — where all vegetation of the same *kind* can only reproduce with vegetation of the same *kind* and all seeds are unique to their *kind*.

By the end of the third day, the new planet was fully formed with all the various *kinds* of vegetation in place. The various forms of vegetation are mature and possess their kind of seeds for reproduction. Assuming the dry land was comparable to the total continental land mass of today, then it would have an area of approximately 57,000,000 square miles. If the dry land was circular in shape, it would have a radius of approximately 4260 miles. This land mass probably had a mixture of grass lands and forests designed for the convenience and the enjoyment of mankind. In Genesis 1:12, YHWH's BODY observes that it was good.

Here again YHWH's SOUL determines what will be done, then His WILL implements it, and then His BODY observes and/or informs what His WILL has done or will do.

Fourth Day of Creation – The space beyond the planet

YHWH's WILL now completes the implementation of the outer part of the material component of the universe as described in Genesis 1:14-19.

Genesis 1:14-19
14 And *God said* [**YHWH's WILL**], Let there be lights in the **firmament of the heaven** to divide the day from the night; and let them be for signs, and for seasons, and for days, and years:
15 And let them be for lights in the **firmament of the heaven** to give light upon the earth: and *it was so* [**YHWH's BODY**].
16 And **God made** [**YHWH's WILL**] two great lights; the greater light to rule the day, and the lesser light to rule the night: he made the stars also.
17 And *God set* [**YHWH's WILL**] them in the **firmament of the heaven** to give light upon the earth,
18 And to rule over the day and over the night, and to divide the light from the darkness: and *God saw* [**YHWH's BODY**] that it was good.
19 And the evening and the morning were the **fourth day**.

The phrase "firmament of the heaven" is the stretching or expanding of the heaven or material surrounding the earth to include the remainder of the material universe. The state of the material universe is depicted in Figure II-4.

The fourth day is unique because YHWH created sun, moon, and stars; and proceeds to place the earth in orbit about the sun and the moon about the earth. This also places our planet at or near the center of the material universe.

Also, the basic increment of time, the 24-hour day, established by the light of YHWH's SOUL is retained while adding seasons and years. It is not clear if YHWH stops using the light of His SOUL as the source of light for time on this day or waits until the seventh day.

YHWH performed the activity of this fourth day to make the Torah/Holy Bible completely incompatible with such man-made models or theories, which are based on a single event such as the big bang and a single source with evolution to form all life. The biblical model shows YHWH created the material component of the universe with all its parts being placed in their initial states during a single 24-hour day.

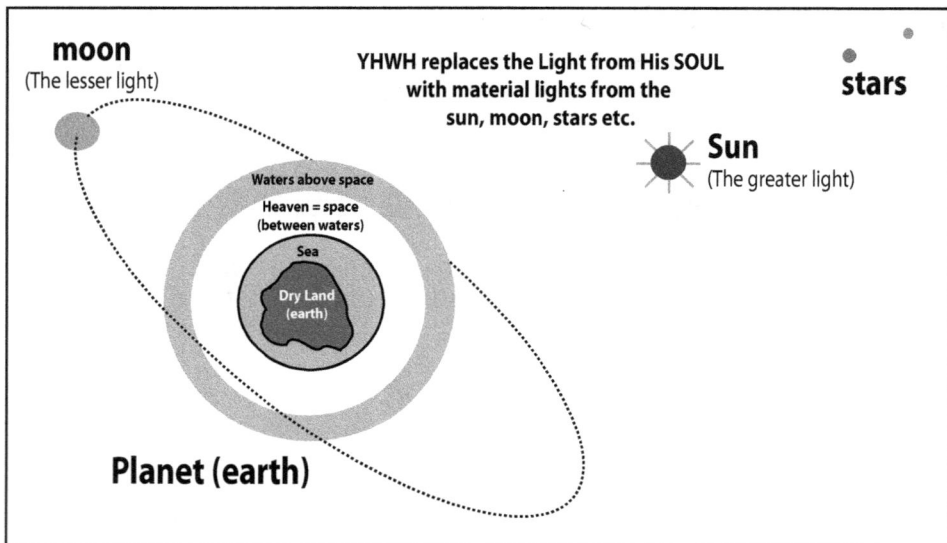

Figure II-4   Fourth Day of Creation - Moon, sun and stars

Empirical data relative to the moon tends to support the biblical model for the material universe being about 6000 years old. The data comes from the Lunar Laser Ranging Experiment that uses laser technology to measure the moon's orbit. The first successful tests were accomplished in 1962 by a team from the Massachusetts Institute of Technology that succeeded in observing reflected laser pulses using a laser with a millisecond pulse length. On July 21, 1969, the crew of Apollo 11, Neil Armstrong and Buzz Aldrin, were the first humans to land on the moon. During the mission, they installed a retroreflector array to improve the measurement accuracy of the Moon's orbit. Subsequent Apollo missions 14 and 15 added two more retroreflector arrays. As a result, the distance to the moon has been measured with increasing accuracy for more than 44 years. The distance to the moon, which averages about 238,897 miles, continually changes for a number of reasons. Most important is that the moon is spiraling away from earth at a rate of 3.8 cm per year. [4] It is interesting to note if the universe was created 6000 years ago, the expected change in the moon's orbit would have increased by .142 miles. However, if the moon was in orbit about the earth for over a billion years, like models based on evolution require, then one can ask, "Why does the earth still have a moon?"

YHWH also positioned the moon and sun so that they were visible to an observer on earth because they established days, months, and years; but they may have looked a little pale due to the water vapor canopy. The water vapor canopy may have obscured from view some of the stars that are visible today.

Here again, YHWH's SOUL determines what will be done, then His WILL implements it, and then His BODY observes and/or informs what His WILL has done or will do.

Fifth Day of Creation – Fowl and Sea Life

On the fifth day YHWH's SOUL has His WILL start the creation of birds and sea life.

Genesis 1:20-23
20 And <u>God said</u> **[YHWH's WILL]**, Let the waters bring forth abundantly the moving creature that hath life, and fowl that may fly above the earth in the open firmament of heaven.
21 And <u>God created</u> **[YHWH's WILL]** great whales, and every living creature that moveth, which the waters brought forth abundantly, after their **kind**, and every winged fowl after his **kind**: and <u>God saw</u> **[YHWH's BODY]** that it was good.
22 And <u>God blessed</u> **[YHWH's WILL]** them, saying, Be fruitful, and multiply, and fill the waters in the seas, and let fowl multiply in the earth.
23 And the evening and the morning were the **fifth day.**

YHWH created sea life and fowl by their *kind*. This means YHWH created the male and female parts having the complete genetic information for their kind. Any given kind cannot reproduce with any other *kind*. Thus the number of kinds would be relatively small, but a particular kind was abundantly created. Thus by the end of the fifth day, there was a number of mature fish, birds, whales inhabiting the air and sea.

Here again YHWH's SOUL determines what will be done, then His WILL implements it, and then His BODY observes and/or informs what His WILL has done.

In *the Image of YHWH*

<u>Sixth Day of Creation - Animal and Human life</u>

The sixth day of creation is special. Up to this point in time, YHWH has created the planet we live on with its vegetation. He has placed the moon in orbit around our planet, our planet in orbit about the sun, and added the stars. Then YHWH created sea life, and He is about to create animal life by its kinds as described in Genesis 1:24-25.

Genesis 1:24-25
*24 And <u>God said</u> [**YHWH's WILL**], Let the earth bring forth the living creature after his **kind**, cattle, and creeping thing, and beast of the earth after his **kind**: and <u>it was so</u> [**YHWH's BODY**].*
*25 And <u>God made</u> [**YHWH's WILL**] the beast of the earth after his **kind**, and cattle after their **kind**, and everything that creepeth upon the earth after his **kind**: and <u>God saw</u> [**YHWH's BODY**] that it was good.*

YHWH created land animals cattle, beasts, and those that creep by their *kind*. This means YHWH created the male and female parts having the complete genetic information for their *kind*. Any given kind cannot reproduce with any other *kind*. Thus the initial number of animal kinds was very small.

Then in Genesis 1:26-28 YHWH creates mankind in His own image and uses His personal self-talk between His functions to help us to understand His composition and our composition better.

Genesis 1:26-31
*26 And <u>God said</u> [**YHWH's WILL**], Let <u>us</u> [**YHWH's SOUL, BODY and WILL**] make man in <u>our image</u> [**having Soul, Body and Will**], after our likeness: and let them have <u>dominion</u> [**responsibility**] over the fish of the sea, and over the fowl of the air, and over the cattle, and over all the earth, and over every creeping thing that creepeth upon the earth.*
*27 So <u>God created</u> [**YHWH's WILL**] man in his own image, in the image of God created he him; male and female created he them.*
*28 And <u>God blessed</u> [**YHWH's WILL**] them, and <u>God said</u> [**YHWH's WILL**] unto them, Be fruitful, and multiply, and replenish the earth, and subdue it: and have dominion over the fish of the sea, and over the fowl of the air, and over every living thing that moveth upon the earth.*
*29 And <u>God said</u> [**YHWH's WILL**], Behold, I have given you every herb bearing seed, which is upon the face of all the earth, and every tree, in the which is the fruit of a tree yielding seed; to you it shall be for meat.*
*30 And to every beast of the earth, and to every fowl of the air, and to everything that creepeth upon the earth, wherein there is life, I have given every green herb for meat: and <u>it was so</u> [**YHWH's BODY**].*
*31 And <u>God saw</u> [**YHWH's BODY**] everything that he had made, and, behold, it was very good. And the evening and the morning were the **sixth day**.*

Man and woman are both created in the image of YHWH, and thus are different from all the other kinds of life created during fifth and sixth days. The image of YHWH was defined in Genesis 1:2-3 where YHWH states He has three members consisting of a BODY, SOUL, and WILL with each having a specific function as shown in Figure I-1. Being in the image of YHWH means that man has a body, Soul, and Will. However, is man's composition different from YHWH's?

First, man's body like YHWH has a spirit body ($x_{body:spirit}$, $y_{body:spirit}$, $z_{body:spirit}$). YHWH also constrained mankind by adding a bond from man's spirit body to a mortal-material body ($x_{body:material}$, $y_{body:material}$, $z_{body:material}$). The mortal-material body He created from the dust of the earth. That is YHWH created mankind mortal, which means mankind must have access to the Tree of Life to avoid death.

Second, like YHWH, man's soul contains all his knowledge of the universe. Man's Soul is bonded to his spirit Body and his Will, but not to his mortal-material body. Man's Soul and Will interface with his mortal-material body through the brain. The brain receives information for the soul to process and the brain manages the material body's actions in accordance with the man's WILL. YHWH also gave man dominion, responsibility, for the planet, which is a direct statement that man has freedom to make decisions and he is responsible for them. Mankind has freedom of choice and YHWH probably made mankind mortal as one means to control it. The structure of mankind is illustrated in Figure II-5.

How do both man and animals differ from vegetation? The various kinds of vegetation that exist are all composed of the material from the material component of the universe. Vegetation does not contain any blood like man, sea life and animals. All sea life, animal life and mankind are to use the vegetation for food.

Then how is mankind who is in the image of YHWH different from the various kinds of animals? Animals are composed completely from the three material dimensions of the new material component of the universe and they have a brain that manages their body activities including speech.

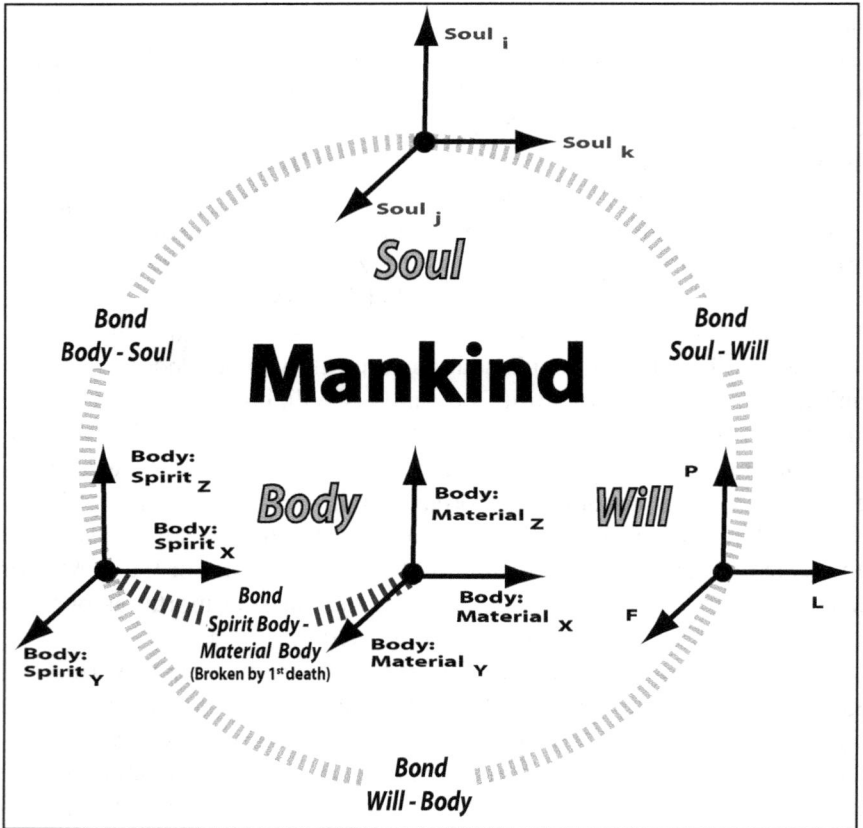

Figure II-5 Mankind's Composition

Whereas, mankind who is in the image of YHWH as shown in Figure II-5 has:

1. A soul, which is resident in the pre-creation universe.

2. A WILL, which is resident in the pre-creation universe.

3. A body that contains:

   A spirit body ($x_{body:spirit}$, $y_{body:spirit}$, $z_{body:spirit}$) from the pre-creation universe.

   A mortal-material body ($x_{body:material}$, $y_{body:material}$, $z_{body:material}$) from the new material component of the universe with a brain to interface with self's spirit body, soul and WILL.

The universe is very complex, having many components with each component having several dimensions, and these various components are uniquely bonded together. That is, man's material and spirit body are bonded together, and the *first-death* occurs when this bond is broken by killing, drugs, accident or old age. Moreover, the soul is bonded to one's spirit body, and one's WILL is bonded to one's soul.

Note that during creation <u>YHWH does not have a mortal-material body</u>, but His body/voice could interface with Adam and Eve. He did not take on a mortal-material body Himself until the birth of Jesus the Messiah.

YHWH did give Adam and Eve some knowledge for their souls concerning their responsibilities on the first day of their existence. They were to be responsible to care for the material component of the universe that YHWH had just created. Adam was responsible to name the *kinds* of life they coexisted with. That is, they are responsible to create knowledge themselves. They are responsible to be fruitful and multiply. They could eat any fruit except from the Tree of Knowledge of Good and Evil, which will cause them to die. Note, they were not told "good" is being obedient to YHWH's WILL and "evil" is not doing His WILL. Thus, good and evil are just an inherent property of YHWH's gift of freewill to man.

Via these preceding commands YHWH did give Adam and Eve the knowledge that He created them responsible to make their own decisions.

What was YHWH's purpose for creating mankind in His image? This question is part of the *mystery of soul development*, which will unfold as we progress through this book.

Seventh Day of Creation - Rest

The seventh day of creation is unique because it completes YHWH's creation activity. The number seven is composed of the number four, which represents the created, and the number three, which represents completion. The number seven is only divisible by seven or one and the number one is the only perfect number. Hence, it would be appropriate that creation would be complete by the seventh day as described in Genesis 2:1-3.

Genesis 2:1-3
1 *Thus the heavens and the earth were finished, and all the host of them.*
2 *And on the **seventh day** God ended his work which he had made; and he rested on the seventh day from all his work which he had made.*
3 *And <u>God blessed</u> [**YHWH's WILL**] the seventh day, and sanctified it: because that in it he had rested from all his work which God created and made.*

25

What happened on this day of rest?

1. Did YHWH move in and take control over the new material part of the post-creation universe?

2. Did YHWH make the sabbath for mankind?

Clearly creation was finished and YHWH rested. Then YHWH declared the seventh day a day of rest that is a Sabbath. To whom was this declaration for?

Did YHWH declare He would rest every seventh day? YHWH does not specifically state that He will rest every sabbath.

Did YHWH himself declare it was time for Him to take up residence in and control over His new creation? YHWH's residence is still in the pre-creation universe because the light of His GLORY (SOUL) would have eliminated the need for the sun and moon. (See Revelation 22:5 and Isaiah 60:19-20.) It is unlikely that YHWH was taking control over His creation because on the sixth day He gave dominion over the earth to Adam and the *Woman*.

The only people in existence at this time were Adam and the *Woman*, and YHWH created the seventh day for them and their descendents so that they could reflect on Him and the universe. This time of rest and reflection is needed by mankind to stabilize their souls and WILLs. [2]

Thus YHWH makes Sabbaths to help mankind align their souls and WILLs with His. This supports a close personal relationship with YHWH. YHWH's creation is complete, but what does the world look like and how does mankind function in this new world?

The Garden of Eden

YHWH proceeds to describe how the earth's structure appears and was populated in Genesis 2:4-25.

Genesis 2:4-14
4 ***These are the generations*** *of the heavens and of the earth when they were created, in the day that the Lord God made the earth and the heavens,*
5 *And every plant of the field before it was in the earth, and every herb of the field before it grew: for the Lord God had not caused it to rain upon the earth, and there was not a man to till the ground.*
6 *But there went up a mist from the earth, and watered the whole face of the ground.*
7 ***And the Lord God formed man of the dust of the ground, and breathed into his nostrils the breath of life; and man became a living soul.***
8 *And the Lord God planted a garden eastward in Eden; and there he put the man whom he had formed.*

26

9 *And out of the ground made the Lord God to grow every tree that is pleasant to the sight, and good for food;* **the tree of life also in the midst of the garden,** *and the* **tree of knowledge of good and evil.**
10 *And a river went out of Eden to water the garden; and from thence it was parted, and became into four heads.*
11 *The name of the first is Pison: that is it which compasseth the whole land of Havilah, where there is gold;*
12 *And the gold of that land is good: there is bdellium and the onyx stone.*
13 *And the name of the second river is Gihon: the same is it that compasseth the whole land of Ethiopia.*
14 *And the name of the third river is Hiddekel: that is it which goeth toward the east of Assyria. And the fourth river is Euphrates.*

The Garden of Eden is the head of four rivers that flow to the sea as shown in Figure II-6.

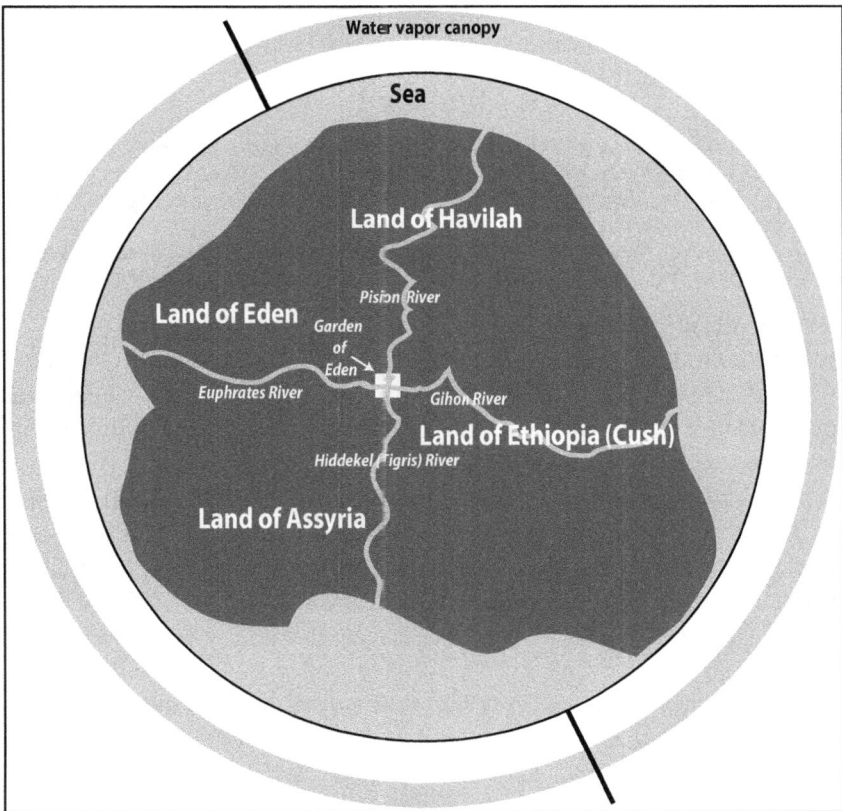

Figure II-6 The planet earth with the Garden of Eden

27

As mentioned previously, the single area of dry land on earth is large and probably about the same size as the land surface of today or about 57,000,000 square miles. If it is circular in shape, the land would have a radius of about 4260 miles with the Garden of Eden at the center. Eden must have been the highest point because it was the source of the four rivers that flowed to the single sea. Prior to Noah's flood there was no mention of mountains, valleys, or waterfalls. Therefore it is valid to assume, that the land did not have rough terrain and it gently sloped from the Garden of Eden to the sea. This was an environment that would support lush vegetation, grasslands, and forests designed especially to make life easy for mankind. The Garden of Eden was near the center of the land mass and was particularly lush and beautiful.

YHWH had created mankind mortal, from the dust of the earth. Therefore, man needed to eat from the Tree of Life located in the Garden of Eden to avoid the first-death. Then in Genesis 2:15-17, YHWH provides Adam with additional instructions.

> *Genesis 2:15-17*
> 15 *And the Lord God* **[YHWH's BODY]** *took the man, and put him into the garden of Eden* **to dress it and to keep it.**
> 16 *And the* <u>*Lord God commanded*</u> **[YHWH's WILL]** *the man, saying, Of every tree of the garden thou mayest freely eat:*
> 17 **But of the tree of the knowledge of good and evil, thou shalt not eat of it: for in the day that thou eatest thereof thou shalt surely die.**

When YHWH places Adam in the Garden of Eden, He gave Adam the responsibility to take care of the garden. What does responsibility mean?

First, Adam's job was to improve and maintain the garden. Thus, Adam was accountable to YHWH who owns the garden. Also, YHWH has the authority to tell Adam if he was doing an acceptable job.

Second, to improve and maintain the garden YHWH had to have given Adam the ability to reason and make decisions. Thus, Adam's Body received information about the state of the garden and passed it to his Soul. Based on the knowledge in Adam's Soul, he made decisions with respect to the garden, and had his Will implement those decisions. Adam processed information in a triune fashion like YHWH.

Also in Genesis 2:15-17, YHWH told Adam that he could not eat from the Tree of Knowledge of Good and Evil or he would die. From the tree's name, it must contain knowledge, and at that time Adam's soul was ignorant of what *good, evil,* and *die* meant. Do not eat from the Tree of Knowledge of Good and Evil could have been any command such as, don't swim in the river, don't climb the tree, or don't eat mushrooms. It was the command itself that was important!

The knowledge contained in this command was that one could choose to obey what YHWH commanded, *good*, or one could choose not to do what YHWH commanded, *evil*. Moreover, there will be consequences if one does evil and that is he will die.

Then YHWH continues to create *Woman* as described in Genesis 2:18- 25.

Genesis 2:18-25
18 *And the Lord God said, It is not good that the man should be alone; I will make him an help meet for him.*
19 *And out of the ground the Lord God formed every beast of the field, and every fowl of the air; and brought them unto Adam to see what he would call them: and whatsoever Adam called every living creature, that was the name thereof.*
20 *And Adam gave names to all cattle, and to the fowl of the air, and to every beast of the field; but for Adam there was not found an help meet for him.*
21 *And the Lord God caused a deep sleep to fall upon Adam and he slept: and he took one of his ribs, and closed up the flesh instead thereof;*
22 *And the rib, which the Lord God had taken from man, made he a woman, and brought her unto the man.*
23 ***And Adam said****, This is now bone of my bones, and flesh of my flesh: she shall be called **Woman**, because she was taken out of Man.*
24 *Therefore shall a man leave his father and his mother, and shall cleave unto his wife: and they shall be one flesh.*
25 *And they were both naked, the man and his wife, and were not ashamed.*

Then YHWH continues during the sixth day to create the *Woman* who was also mortal being made from Adam's rib, which was taken from the dust of the earth. The stage was now set because Adam and his wife, *Woman,* were in the Garden of Eden to care for the garden and to be fruitful and multiply.

The creation event that occurred during the first seven days of 0000 AM had been completed and the time had come for Adam and his wife, *Woman,* to enjoy and develop their new environment. It was also a time for each person to develop their personal relationship with YHWH. Also, it is unknown if YHWH required any fruit from efforts of Adam and his wife, *Woman.*

The Holy Bible is conspicuously silent with respect to the amount of time that passed between Genesis 2:25 and Genesis 3:1. Thus, the duration could be days, months, or years. YHWH purposely does not specify this period of time. and the reasons are developed later in this text.

Note in the Holy Bible, not all people or time durations are mentioned, but only those people involved in specific events that YHWH deems important for mankind to know about. Moreover, it is important to recognize that Adam and his wife, *Woman,* were real people, and they were not symbols representing mankind in general. They had children some of whom were specifically named.

Moreover, in the next chapter we will find that Adam and his wife, *Woman,* were obedient to YHWH's command to be fruitful and multiply. They had a family, which probably included grandchildren and great grandchildren all whom were present in the Garden of Eden prior to the Fall of Man.

III   YHWH During the Fall of Man, 0000 OS

Genesis 1 establishes a calendar that starts with YHWH's creation of the material component the universe also called the AM, year of the world, calendar. From the time of 0000 AM (creation) as time passed Adam and his wife, *Woman*, who were real people, began to have children. Sin is disobedience to any of YHWH's commands. Adam and his wife, *Woman*, were commanded to be fruitful and multiply, and failure to multiply was clearly not the cause of the Original Sin, the Fall of Man.

It is extremely unlikely that the serpent ran up to *Woman* and tempted her during the first few days, months, or even years because both she and Adam would not have had time to develop their relationship with YHWH to the extent that they wanted to be like or replace Him. YHWH is merciful and just, therefore it is equally unlikely that He would allow the serpent to tempt Adam and *Woman* before they have an opportunity to establish themselves in the Garden of Eden.

Assuming that Adam and *Woman* were obedient, then the population in the Garden of Eden would begin to increase at some rate. Consider the term for pregnancy is nine months. Then some conservative growth rate percentages (%) based on five year increments are provided in Table III-1, where Adam and *Woman* are represented by the *(2)*.

Table III-1 Possible Garden of Eden Population Growth Rates

Year (AM)	0.0 %	25 %	35 %	50 %	65 %	75%	100 %	125 %	150 %
0000	(2)	(2)	(2)	(2)	(2)	(2)	(2)	(2)	(2)
0005	(2)	3	3	3	3	4	4	5	5
0010	(2)	3	4	5	5	6	8	10	13
0015	(2)	4	5	7	9	11	16	23	31
0020	(2)	5	7	10	15	19	32	51	78
0025	(2)	6	9	15	24	33	64	115	195
0030	(2)	8	12	23	40	57	128	259	488
0035	(2)	10	16	34	67	101	256	584	1221
0040	(2)	12	22	51	110	176	512	1314	3052

Starting with the left hand column of Table III-1, the population growth rate is equal to 0.0 %, which represents complete disobedience for YHWH's command to be fruitful and multiply. The 100 % column represents a doubling of the population every five years. The right most column with 150 % represents *Woman* having one

31

child per year. By 0025 AM Adam and *Woman* certainly had grandchildren, and the Garden of Eden's population may have exceeded 100 people. By 0040 AM the population may have exceed 1000 people. Adam and *Woman* had children because they were obedient to all of YHWH's commands prior to the Fall of Man.

Keep in mind that in the Holy Bible, YHWH does not identify all people that exist, but only those people who were directly involved with significant events from YHWH's perspective. Adam and *Woman* were real people, and the Fall of Man was a real event.

Starting in Genesis 3:1 YHWH begins to describe the history of Adam, *Woman*, and their descendants. Also, Genesis 3:1-24 establishes a new calendar that starts with the Fall of Man, Original Sin, on 0000 OS. The Original Sin probably occurred between 20 to 50 years after 0000 AM, the creation event. The Original Sin is described in Genesis 3:1-24.

Genesis 3:1-15
1 Now the <u>serpent</u> **[Satan]** *was more subtil than **any beast of the field** which the Lord God had made. And he said unto the **woman**, Yea, hath God said, Ye shall not eat of every tree of the garden?*
2 *And the **woman** said unto the serpent, We may eat of the fruit of the trees of the garden:*
3 *But of the fruit of the tree which is in the midst of the garden, God hath said, Ye shall not eat of it, neither shall ye touch it, lest ye die.*
4 *And the <u>serpent</u>* **[Satan]** *said unto the **woman**, Ye shall <u>not surely die</u>:* **[Satan's lie]**
5 *For God doth know that in the day ye eat thereof, then <u>your eyes shall be opened</u>* **[No longer ignorant]**, *and ye shall be <u>as gods</u>* **[Satan's lie]**, *knowing good and evil.*
6 *And when the **woman** saw that the tree was good for food, and that it was pleasant to the eyes, and a tree to be desired to make one wise, she took of the fruit thereof, and did eat, and gave also unto her husband with her; and he did eat.*
7 *And the <u>eyes of them both were opened</u>* **[No longer ignorant]**, *and they knew that they were naked; and they sewed fig leaves together, and made themselves aprons.*
8 *And they heard the voice of the Lord God walking in the garden in the cool of the day* **[Note YHWH's pre-creation body is visible but it is not a mortal-material body.]** *: and Adam and his wife hid themselves from the presence of the Lord God amongst the trees of the garden.*
9 *And the Lord God called unto Adam, and said unto him, Where art thou?*
10 *And he said, I heard thy voice in the garden, and I was afraid, because I was naked; and I hid myself.*
11 *And he said, Who told thee that thou wast naked? Hast thou eaten of the tree, whereof I commanded thee that thou shouldest not eat?*
12 *And the man said, The **woman** whom thou gavest to be with me, she gave me of the tree, and I did eat.*
13 *And the Lord God said unto the **woman**, What is this that thou hast done? And the **woman** said, The <u>serpent</u>* **[Satan]** *beguiled me, and I did eat.*

> 14 **_And the Lord God said unto the serpent_ [Satan]**, *Because thou hast done this, thou art cursed above all cattle, and above every beast of the field; upon thy belly shalt thou go, and dust shalt thou eat all the days of thy life:*
> 15 *And I will put enmity between thee and the **woman**, and between **thy seed** and **her seed**; it shall bruise thy head, and thou shalt bruise his heel.*

The serpent is known throughout the Holy Bible by various names such as; king of the bottomless pit, Abaddon, or Apollyon (in Revelation 9:11); or great dragon, serpent, Devil, Satan (in Revelation 12:9); Lucifer, the fallen angel (in Isaiah 14:12). To be consistent the name *Satan* will be used throughout the remainder of this book.

What is *Satan's-seed* and the *Woman's-seed*? The word *seed* in Hebrew is **zera`** (OT:2232)[5], which figuratively, fruit, plant, sowing-time, or posterity. *Seed* can then be:

1. The part of a plant that can grow a new plant.

2. The part of an animal or human that results in reproduction or the offspring.

3. The source, origin, or beginning of anything [the *seed* of revolt].

It is clear that we are not concerned with plant seeds because the subject is mankind. Another possibility is the word *seed* is associated with the human reproductive process. This is not relevant because Satan is a fallen angel who is constrained as a beast of the field (Genesis 3:1). Thus, Satan is not a member of mankind and therefore cannot reproduce with humans. To be of mankind Satan would have had to be a child of Adam and *Woman*. Thus, Satan has no human descendents and all of mankind descends from Adam and *Woman*.

Thus, the word *seed* must mean the source, origin, or beginning of anything such as the seed of revolt. Hence *Satan's-seed* is prompting rebellion against YHWH among mankind, the descendents of Adam and *Woman*. Satan uses the knowledge of mankind's freedom to chose as a means to convince men to follow him in overthrowing YHWH and eventually replacing Him as god.

After eating of the fruit from the Tree of Knowledge of Good and Evil, *Woman* recognizes that Satan was lying because neither she nor Adam physically became as YHWH. Instead they both became aware that they were naked. *Woman* now detests Satan, and what he was for, she was against! She had learned her lesson about sin, repented, and now the *Woman's-seed* was promoting total obedience to YHWH's WILL. She now had tremendous enmity against Satan for taking advantage of her. Thus, people and societies who embrace *Satan's-seed* will abuse or enslave women. It should be noted *Satan's-seed*, evil, will cause man much trouble bruising his heel, but in the end those individuals who remain with YHWH will prevail and defeat Satan, bruising his head.

In summary *Satan's-seed* is evil or lying about YHWH's truth, and *Woman's-seed* is good or stating YHWH's truth. There is no indication in the Holy Bible that YHWH takes Satan's life before Noah's flood, when all but Noah's family dies. Thus Satan's mortal beast body does not die as a result of his beguiling *Woman,* and so he continues to influence mankind in the material component of the universe.

Genesis 3:15 is thought to be a direct reference to Jesus the Messiah, the Son, and this is true to the extent that YHWH's BODY added three mortal-material dimensions through the virgin birth in accordance with YHWH's SOUL and WILL. Jesus the Messiah is the perfect *seed* of YHWH's perfect truth and also has a mortal-material body that is truly a "Son of Man" or descendent of Adam and *Woman* just as we are.

> *Genesis 3:16*
> *16 **Unto the woman he said,** I will greatly multiply thy <u>sorrow</u> [**pain**] and thy conception; in <u>sorrow</u> [**pain**] thou shalt bring forth children; and thy desire shall be to thy husband, and he shall rule over thee.*

If Adam's wife *Woman* did not have any children prior to 0000 OS, it would be impossible for her to relate to the new increase in pain during child birth!

It is interesting that *Woman*'s unique consequence for her sin is physical body pain during childbirth, which will frequently refresh her knowledge that there are consequences for sin. Also, this will be a reminder to all women throughout every generation that there are consequences related to sin. In the future, *Woman*'s soul shall not have priority on becoming like YHWH, but she will be responsible to Adam so that Adam must decide when any evil fruit is to be accepted. Therefore, in the future Adam will be without any excuse for his sin because he is responsible to YHWH for any evil decision she brings to him. In the future Adam cannot blame his wife *Woman* for his own sin.

> *Genesis 3:17-19*
> *17 **And unto Adam he said,** Because thou hast hearkened unto the voice of thy wife, and hast eaten of the tree, of which I commanded thee, saying, Thou shalt not eat of it: cursed is the ground for thy sake; in sorrow shalt thou eat of it all the days of thy life;*
> *18 Thorns also and thistles shall it bring forth to thee; and thou shalt eat the herb of the field;*
> *19 In the sweat of thy face shalt thou eat bread, till thou return unto the ground; for out of it wast thou taken: for dust thou art, and unto dust shalt thou return.*

It is also interesting that Adam's unique consequence for his sin is that his physical body will hurt everyday as he works to get food. This will be a daily reminder that his mortal body will die and return to dust. This will be a reminder to all men throughout every generation that sin has consequences and it will cause all people to die.

The result of the Original Sin was so significant that on 0000 OS Adam's first act was to rename his wife from *Woman to Eve*.

Genesis 3:20
*20 And Adam called his wife's name **Eve**; because **she <u>was</u> the mother of all living.***

Genesis 3:20 is very significant because Adam renames his wife from **Woman** to *Eve*, because she was (past tense) the mother of all living human beings. This statement affirms that Adam and Eve's descendents were dwelling in the Garden of Eden at the time of the Original Sin, 0000 OS. Now *Eve* has given all the people in the Garden of Eden the knowledge good and evil. These people were the result of Adam and Eve's obedience to YHWH's command to be fruitful and multiple, and they would obtain knowledge of anything that occurred in the Garden of Eden.

Eve's-seed, obedience to YHWH, only appears after the Original Sin and indicates that both Adam and Eve had repented of their sin. However, their repentance does not remove the penalty they must pay for their sin. As a result of the Original Sin, Eve is also the mother of the knowledge of good and evil and she provided it to her family in the Garden of Eden. The penalty for having this knowledge is expulsion from the Garden of Eden and access to the Tree of Life, which activates mankind's mortality and brings the *first-death* to all Adam and Eve's family and all their descendents.

YHWH reminds Adam and Eve that sin is death by replacing their fig leaf aprons with coats made from dead animal skins in Genesis 3:31.

Genesis 3:21
21 Unto Adam also and to his wife did the Lord God make coats of skins, and clothed them.

They are now covered by death and from this time on all mankind will be born in sin, facing the *first-death*, because all mankind is denied access to the Tree of Life.

The first major question is what did Adam, Eve, and their descendants obtain from the Tree of Knowledge of Good and Evil?

The dictionary defines Knowledge as:

1. The act, fact or state of knowing.

2. Acquaintance with facts; range of information, awareness, or understanding.

3. All that has been perceived or grasped by the mind; learning; enlightenment.

4. The body of facts, principles, etc. accumulated by mankind.

Adam and Eve and their descendents souls actually gained new knowledge! This new knowledge included.

- They have freedom to do evil, be disobedient to YHWH's commands.
- They have freedom to do good, be obedient to YHWH's commands.
- Sin is failure to comply with YHWH's commands and is evil.
- Man will now have to work for his food.
- Man will be born in sin (death) being denied access to the Tree of Life.
- They were naked.
- In the future women will have difficulty giving birth.
- Sin has consequences!

The unique property of knowledge is that once known an individual cannot erase it. The only thing an individual can do at a future time (t) is to change the magnitude of his WILL(t) associated with an item of knowledge. Lowering his WILL(t) suppresses it while increasing his WILL(t) promotes it.

Genesis 3:22-24
*22 And the <u>Lord God said, Behold</u> [**YHWH's BODY**], <u>the man</u> [**mankind**] is become as one of us, to know good and evil: and now, lest he put forth his hand, and take also of the tree of life, and eat, and live forever:*
*23 Therefore the <u>Lord God sent</u> [**YHWH's WILL**] <u>him</u> [**mankind**] forth from the garden of Eden, to till the ground from whence he was taken.*
*24 So he drove out <u>the man</u> [**mankind**]; and he placed at the east of the Garden of Eden Cherubims, and a flaming sword which turned every way, to keep the way of the tree of life.*

Note, *the man* refers to mankind (OT:120), [5] or the species of man, but not to a specific individual because more than one person was removed from the Garden of Eden.

The second major question is what did Adam, Eve, and their descendants lose after being denied access to the Garden of Eden and the Tree of Life?

Loss of access to the Tree of Life activates the mortality constraint in mankind's mortal-material body. Thus, all mankind must now experience the *first-death* and return to dust while their spirit Body, Soul, and Will will continue to exist in the pre-creation universe with YHWH. There is no indication that Adam, Eve, and their descendent's Souls and Wills will die or become totally depraved because their souls actually received more knowledge concerning sin and its consequences. This new knowledge will affect each individual's soul with respect to good and evil as a function of whose truth the individual accepts, *Satan's-seed* or the *Eve's-seed*. Once knowledge is known by the soul, it cannot be destroyed, only suppressed by lowering the magnitude of an individual's WILL(t) associated with it.

Then, what is the purpose of the period of man's life in his mortal body? The birth of an individual brings into existence a new image of YHWH only constrained in a mortal body. Therefore, after 0000 OS all people all people must die because everyone is denied access to the Tree of Life. As an individual's soul matures, it continuously acquires knowledge and the nature, or type of soul, becomes apparent. When the individual experiences the *first-death,* YHWH knows the nature of the soul that he has developed. Thus, the mortal life allows YHWH to evaluate an individual's soul and to decide or judge what will be done with it. This is analogous to an egg farmer checking or candling eggs to determine if they are acceptable to be used.

As a result of the Original Sin, every individual must experience the *first-death.* The *first-death* is the breaking of the bond between one's mortal-material body and his spirit body. The *first-death* can occur by aging or illness or accident or murder. Once the *first-death* has occurred, you are in the pre-creation universe only, and YHWH has your eternal destiny determined.

YHWH is consistent, and the Holy Bible documents all mankind's major decisions. Mankind has made many bad decisions, and if it were not for YHWH's mercy and grace, mankind would not exist today. YHWH has allowed mankind the freedom to make decisions, but He also established appointed times for reconciling mankind's decisions with respect to Him. A flowchart of mankind's major decisions starting with the Original Sin, 0000 OS, is shown in Appendix III. This flowchart will be developed further as we progress through the remainder of this book.

The previous text describes a biblical Model of the Universe based on Genesis. It is worthwhile to pause and reflect on how it compares to some of the numerous models of the universe that exist today.

All models are based on a set of assumptions, which are referred to as doctrines or laws or theories or the like. These assumptions have a very real impact with respect to how any individual relates to YHWH and events occurring in the world today. Most Christian churches today focus mainly on the state of one's soul, but do not address or teach how empirical data from today's experiments support YHWH's six day creation of the universe.

First, consider some of the various denominational assumptions with respect to how the soul was impacted as a result of the Original Sin.

1. YHWH predetermined all events in the history of the new material component of the universe before He created it. Thus, YHWH has by name established His elect and everything that has and will occur.

2. The Original Sin established the state of man's soul as totally depraved, 100 percent evil. Thus, man has no influence in his ultimate destiny, which has already been determined by YHWH.

3. YHWH lives in the world by having His Holy Spirit indwell man's soul.

4. YHWH knows all possibilities for all things at all times and gives mankind freedom to decide the course of history. Thus mankind has the freedom to accept or reject YHWH until his *first-death*. YHWH has predetermined that those who accept and follow Him will be selected to be with Him in His kingdom.

This text does not support the first assumption that YHWH predetermined by name those who shall be saved because judgment is moot for anything already determined. Neither does this text support the second and third assumptions.

Instead this text assumes the Original Sin was a specific event in history, which occurred on 0000 OS, the start of the OS calendar. Adam and Eve were real people who by their actions imparted the knowledge of good and evil to themselves, their children, and grandchildren in the Garden of Eden. This assumption is consistent with YHWH knowing all possibilities for all things at all times and that YHWH has given mankind freedom to make decisions based on the content of their souls. This freedom places on mankind the responsibility to acquire knowledge of YHWH and place YHWH's WILL above their own Will.

A baby when born has little knowledge; and its priorities are definitely survival, food, and physical comfort as anyone can attest. As a child matures and acquires more knowledge of the material universe, it should become apparent to him that he was created.

Secondly, consider some differences between today's models for the universe and the biblical Model for the Universe. As previously discussed, the material universe we observe today is not all that exists, but it is an addition to the pre-creation universe where YHWH resides today. The pre-creation universe has at least Body dimensions ($x_{body:spirit}$, $y_{body:spirit}$, $z_{body:spirit}$), Soul dimensions (i, j, k), and Will dimensions (L, F, P).

The heavens and earth, which is the material component of the post-creation universe, may not be infinite as is typically assumed today. Consider YHWH created mankind in His own image giving him a Soul with dimensions (i, j, k), a Will with dimensions (L, F, P), and a Body with dimensions ($x_{body:spirit}$, $y_{body:spirit}$, $z_{body:spirit}$, $x_{body:material}$, $y_{body:material}$, $z_{body:material}$).

Notice YHWH made mankind in His image but He also added some constraints:
1. Mankind's soul does not have an infinite capacity for knowledge like YHWH.
2. Mankind's power P is extremely small relative to YHWH's perfect WILL with P = 1.0.
3. Mankind's body has an additional constraint of a mortal-material body ($x_{body:material}$, $y_{body:material}$, $z_{body:material}$).

The author believes that it is very possible that YHWH has also constrained the material component of the post-creation of universe. For example $E = MC^2$, the accepted model for how energy relates to mass, may be constrained by the distance from the center of the universe like:

$$E = M[(d_0 - d)/d_0]C^2$$

No value for d_0 is indicated in the Holy Bible. However, if one makes the assumption that d_0 = 4000 light years then an observer on earth:

For d = 0 light years.
$$E = [M(d_0 - d)/d_0]C^2 = M[(4000 - 0)/4000]C^2 = MC^2$$

For d = 400 light years.
$$E = [M(d_0 - d)/d_0]C^2 = M[(4000 - 400)/4000]C^2 = 0.9MC^2$$

For d = 4000 light years.
$$E = [M(d_0 - d_0)/d_0]C^2 = M[(4000 - 4000)/4000]C^2 = 0$$

If one assumes the material universe as we know it is constrained to d_0, then it would have a limited spherical shape, like a ball or egg, within the pre-creation universe.

If one assumes the material universe is not constrained, $E = MC^2$, the stars would seem to be billions of light years away due to the low level of energy levels received and our sun is depicted as a speck with respect to distant stars.

Triangulation is typically used to determine the distance to a star up to about 400 light years, but beyond that limit received energy is the basis for determining a star's distance. Likewise, empirical data can support an expanding or rate constrained universe with the earth and sun near its center. Thus what appears to be an expanding universe under one set of assumptions may be a constrained universe under another set of assumptions where an observer on earth is receiving the same data.

Is the Tree of Life consistent with evolution? The answer is no. Prior to the Original Sin on 0000 OS, YHWH's creation was good and sin (death) did not exist. YHWH created plants for food for animals and mankind. Plant kinds and animal kinds are not in the image of YHWH. Sin is death because the mortal body will lose its life when denied access to the Tree of Life. The Tree of Life was available to Adam, his wife *Woman,* and all of their descendents prior to 0000 OS and there was no death. No death makes evolution impossible for the development of plant, animal, and mankind because evolution requires death to support natural selection. The various evolution models believe that life started by random chance forming a single cell, which continued to generate new genetic information, resulting in water life, reptiles, fowl, animals, apes and eventually man over a period of millions or billions of years. This type of evolution assumes male and female of each *kind* came into existence at the same time otherwise there could be no reproduction. Noah's flood also provides additional support for the biblical Model of the Universe, which will be addressed in chapter V.

Up to this point, two types of souls have been identified those who accept *Eve's-seed*, YHWH's truth, and those who accept *Satan's-seed*, overthrow of YHWH. The first murder will introduce a third type of soul.

IV YHWH During the First Murder

When the *first-death* occurs by aging or illness, it is a normal consequence of the Original Sin. When the *first-death* occurs by accident, it is caused by people's decisions that are not planned. However, when the *first-death* occurs by murder, the planned taking of another's life, it is a result of the *Premeditative Process*. [2] In YHWH's view, murder is significant because He specifically addresses this issue in Genesis 4:1-25.

Note, there is a time lapse between the Original Sin, which probably occurred about 29 AM [2] and the first murder. The first murder probably occurred before 100 AM, but not later than 130 AM because Seth was born in 130 AM after the first murder. The world's population at this time using any reasonable growth rate would yield anywhere from 1000 to over 1,000,000 people and every soul knows why the Garden of Eden is being guarded by Cherubim, with flaming swords.

Although not specifically stated in the Biblical text, as a result of the Original Sin, YHWH must have requested from the people a portion of their harvest for a peace offering. This practice would quickly separate *Satan's-seed* from *Eve's-seed*. An individual has only three possible responses to YHWH's request to bring Him a peace offering and these options are:

1. Bring no offering at all: Self is embracing *Satan's-seed*, the overthrow of YHWH. This is evil and sin.

2. Bring an offering while keeping the best for self: Self is placing YHWH second and himself first. This is evil and sin.

3. Bring an offering that is self's best: Self is embracing *Eve's-seed* by placing YHWH first and self second. This is good.

The peace offering is a direct measure of one's Will(t) to serve YHWH and it manifests itself in one's actions as we shall see in Genesis 4:1-25.

Genesis 4:1-2
*1 And **Adam** knew **Eve** his wife; and **she conceived,** and **bare Cain**, and said, I have gotten a man from the Lord.*
*2 And she **again bare his brother Abel**. And Abel was a keeper of sheep, but Cain was a tiller of the ground.*

It is interesting that Eve conceived once and bare twice. This makes Cain and Abel twins—probably identical. This means both men have nearly identical material and spirit bodies, but they do have very unique Souls and Wills. Also, this is one of many instances where this type of detail cannot be the result of oral tradition but had to come directly from YHWH.

41

Genesis 4:3-7 is a test of these identical twins souls and WILLs.

Genesis 4:3-7
> 3 And **in process of time** it came to pass, that Cain brought of the fruit of the ground an offering unto the Lord.
> 4 And Abel, he also brought of the **firstlings** of his flock and of the **fat thereof.** And the <u>Lord had respect</u> **[YHWH's SOUL]** unto Abel and to his offering:
> 5 But unto Cain and to his offering he had not respect **[because it was not his best].** And Cain was very wroth, and his countenance fell.
> 6 And the <u>Lord said</u> **[YHWH's WILL]** unto Cain, Why art thou wroth? and why is thy countenance fallen?
> 7 If thou doest well, shalt thou not be accepted? and if thou doest not well, sin lieth at the door. And unto thee shall be his desire, and thou shalt rule over him.

After the Original Sin YHWH probably established a Peace Offering, otherwise there would be no need for either Cain or Abel to bring anything to YHWH.

The question here is what is wrong with Cain's offering? Is it possible that Cain's occupation as a farmer is sinful with respect to that of a shepherd? This cannot be because nowhere has YHWH commanded mankind not to till the soil. On the contrary, YHWH told Adam that he was responsible to till the soil in the Garden of Eden, 0000 AM, and after the Original Sin this task would become more difficult. The difference between the two offerings is stated in Genesis 4:4 where Abel brought his absolute best from his flock. He is placing YHWH above himself. Whereas, the description of Cain's offering by omission tells us it was not his very best, and Cain was placing himself above YHWH. YHWH tells Cain he expects a better offering, which would place Cain's Will for YHWH above his own. However, Cain's pride will not allow him to submit to YHWH.

It is informative to examine Cain's actions in terms of the *Premeditative Process*, which was developed in the book *Self's Destiny and Self.* [2] The Premeditative Process applies to all people throughout history, and it identifies five phases of premeditation (Appreciation, Coveting, Lusting, Obsession and Reconciliation). These are the opposite of the five phases of the well known *Grieving Process* (Denial, Anger, Guilt, Rationalization and Acceptance). Biblically both the Premeditative Process and the Grieving Process are functions of the magnitude of self's Will and Anxiety. Where:

$$Will(t) = L(t) * F(t) * P(t)$$

$$Anxiety(t) = [L(t) - F(t)] * P(t)$$

Figure IV-1 illustrates the relationship between Cain's *L*ove and *F*aith for his brother Abel. The power factor *P(t)* is not included in Figure IV-1 because it only functions as a scale factor that limits the magnitude of one's Will or Anxiety.

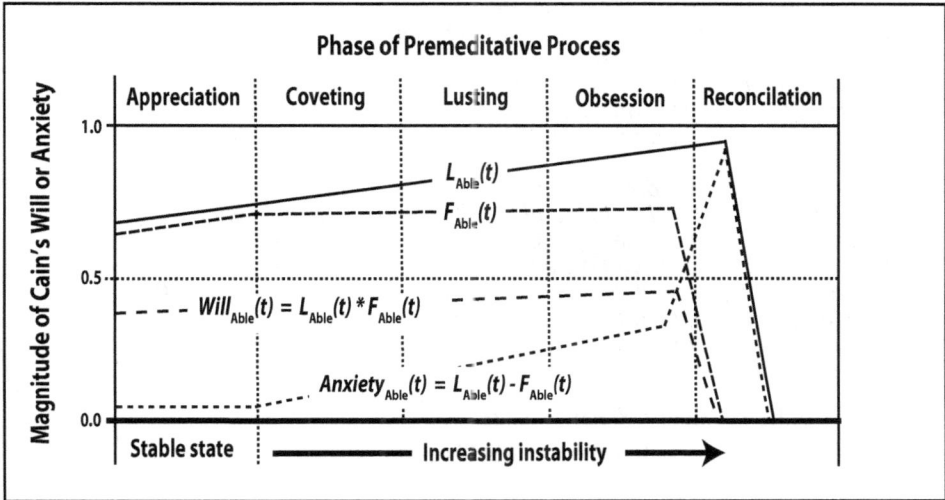

Figure IV-1 Cain and the Premeditative Process

Prior to Cain and Abel bringing their sacrifice to YHWH Cain was in the Appreciation Phase where Cain had a stable relationship with Abel. That is, in general Cain's expectations of his twin brother Abel were met and there was a low level of anxiety between them. Then YHWH accepted Abel's offering and rejected Cain's. Cain's response to YHWH is not to repent but he enters the Coveting phase where Cain begins to try an influence Abel to keep his best himself or not sacrifice to YHWH at all. Cain has a high magnitude of $L_{Abel}(t)$ that Abel reject YHWH with and high magnitude of $F_{Abel}(t)$ that he can convince Abel to do it. As Cain discusses the issue with Abel and finds Abel will not comply with his wishes Cain's $L_{Abel}(t)$ for Abel begins to increase, but his $F_{Abel}(t)$ does not and as time passes Cain enters the Lusting phase and then the Obsessive Phase over Abel's non compliance with his demands. Cain's $Will_{Abel}(t)$ and $Anxiety_{Abel}(t)$ continue to increase until Cain recognizes that Abel is not going to comply with his demands. Then Cain's $F_{Abel}(t)$ falls toward 0. The result is Cain's $Will_{Abel}(t) = L_{Abel}(t) * F_{Abel}(t)$ decreases to 0 while his $Anxiety_{Abel}(t) = L_{Abel}(t) - F_{Abel}(t)$ increases to the Premeditative Reconciliation Level where Cain must resolve his anxiety. To reduce his anxiety Cain commits the first murder as follows:

Genesis 4:8-16
> 8 And Cain talked with Abel his brother: and it came to pass, when they were in the field, that Cain rose up against Abel his brother, and slew him.
> 9 And the <u>Lord said</u> **[YHWH's WILL]** unto Cain, Where is Abel thy brother? And he said, I know not: Am I my brother's keeper?

10 And he said, What hast thou done? the voice of thy brother's <u>blood crieth unto me</u> [**YHWH's BODY**] from the ground.

11 And now art thou cursed from the earth, which hath opened her mouth to receive thy brother's blood from thy hand;

12 When thou tillest the ground, it shall not henceforth yield unto thee her strength; a fugitive and a vagabond shalt thou be in the earth.

13 And Cain said unto the <u>Lord</u> [**YHWH's BODY**], My punishment is greater than I can bear.

14 Behold, thou hast driven me out this day from the face of the earth; and from thy face shall I be hid; and I shall be a fugitive and a vagabond in the earth; and it shall come to pass, that every one that findeth me shall slay me.

15 And the <u>Lord said</u> [**YHWH's WILL**] unto him, Therefore whosoever slayeth Cain, vengeance shall be taken on him sevenfold. And the <u>Lord set</u> [**YHWH's WILL**] a mark upon Cain, lest any finding him should kill him.

16 And Cain went out from the presence of the Lord, and dwelt in the land of Nod, on the east of Eden.

What are the results of the first murder?

1. Cain's anxiety with respect to Abel is gone.

2. Cain's pride is retained.

3. Cain's relationship with YHWH is changed.

Cain's anxiety with respect to Abel is gone because the magnitude of Cain's $L_{Abel}(t)$ is now near 0.0. Thus Cain's $Will_{Abel}(t) = L_{Abel}(t) * F_{Abel}(t)$ and his $Anxiety_{Abel}(t) = L_{Abel}(t) - F_{Abel}(t)$ are both near 0.0. That is after the murder Cain no longer cares about Abel.

Once Abel is dead, Cain's priorities (*L*oves) change back to himself, and his main concern is to avoid any punishment. The arrogant Cain tells YHWH that his punishment is too severe and he must be concerned about his life. Cain has retained his pride. *Pride* can simply be defined as a state where one has a very high magnitude of $L_{self}(t)$ and $F_{self}(t)$. Cain loves and has confidence in himself above all others. Thus Cain has a very high magnitude of $Will_{Cain}(t) = L_{Cain}(t) * F_{Cain}(t)$ with a very low level of $Anxiety_{Cain}(t) = L_{Cain}(t) - F_{Cain}(t)$. This condition is characterized by an arrogant, self-centered, and over confident attitude. No one is better than Cain.

YHWH is perfectly consistent. YHWH confronts Cain and declares what he must do because of his sin. Cain will not be able to produce his own food, and YHWH tells the proud Cain to move from one place to another and beg food from other people. Cain must now make a decision. He can submit and be obedient to YHWH's commands by adjusting the magnitude of his $Will_{Cain}(t)$ to be less than his $Will_{YHWH}(t)$ and become a beggar. Cain's other option is to retain the magnitude of his $Will_{Cain}(t)$ in a state greater than his $Will_{YHWH}(t)$ and retain his pride.

Cain's response to YHWH's command is described in Genesis 4: 17-24.

Genesis 4:17-24

*17 And Cain knew his wife; and she conceived, and bare Enoch: and **he builded a city,** and called the name of the city, after the name of his son, Enoch.*

18 And unto Enoch was born Irad: and Irad begat Mehujael: and Mehujael begat Methusael: and Methusael begat Lamech.

19 And Lamech took unto him two wives: the name of the one was Adah, and the name of the other Zillah.

20 And Adah bare Jabal: he was the father of such as dwell in tents, and of such as have cattle.

21 And his brother's name was Jubal: he was the father of all such as handle the harp and organ.

22 And Zillah, she also bare Tubal-cain, an instructer of every artificer in brass and iron: and the sister of Tubal-cain was Naamah.

23 And Lamech said unto his wives, Adah and Zillah, Hear my voice; ye wives of Lamech, hearken unto my speech: for I have slain a man to my wounding, and a young man to my hurt.

24 If Cain shall be avenged sevenfold, truly Lamech seventy and sevenfold.

Cain is now in complete rebellion against YHWH. He does not wander throughout the earth and beg from other people. Instead Cain builds for himself a city to meet his needs. Cain thus controls the people in his city, and these people are required to meet his needs. Cain is no beggar now! He is also a good example of a *Son of God* who embraced evil and became a *mighty man* forcing ordinary people to serve him. Cain's subsequent descendents who are identified in Genesis 4:17-24 have actually increased their level of rebellion against YHWH.

It is important to note that Cain is not a follower of *Satan's-seed* because he did bring an offering to YHWH. Cain is full of pride and is evil because he places himself above YHWH; that is Cain's $Will_{Cain}(t) > Will_{YHWH}(t)$. This is the sin of pride. A person who is full of pride will not follow anyone including Satan. Only self is important! Cain may have been the first true atheist.

There are commonalities and differences between Cain, Satan, and Satan's followers. Both Cain and Satan will never submit to anyone else due to their personal pride. Both Cain and Satan would not hesitate to murder or enslave others for their benefit. The key difference between Cain and Satan is their personal goals. Cain's goal is personal power over other people, while Satan's goal is to destroy and replace YHWH with himself. The followers of Satan have joined Satan's army believing they will eventually over throw YHWH, and thus they are submissive to Satan. Those people who align with Cain are not real followers of his, but are more associates who place their Will for self above their Will for Cain or anyone else. Cain would be like today's atheistic dictator today.

After the first murder, it becomes apparent that men's souls have three primary types or natures which are:

1. Followers of YHWH with self's $Will_{YHWH}(t) > Will_{self}(t)$.
2. Self only with self's $Will_{self}(t) > Will_{all\ others}(t)$.
3. Followers of Satan with self's $Will_{Satan}(t) > Will_{self}(t)$.

Everyone has a soul, and every soul contains all the person's knowledge of the universe. Each item of knowledge in an individual's soul has an associated Will(t). The magnitude of Will(t) for each item of knowledge can only be consistent with either YHWH or self or Satan, and no one can be a follower of YHWH and Satan at the same time. Therefore, the total number of items of knowledge in a soul can only be; YHWH and self, or self only or Satan and self.

When the number of items of knowledge for YHWH or Satan is divided by the total number of items of knowledge the resultant ratio, or percentage, characterizes the individual's type of soul. This also compensates for the fact that all people have a different total number of items knowledge in their soul. All possible soul types are illustrated in Figure IV-2.

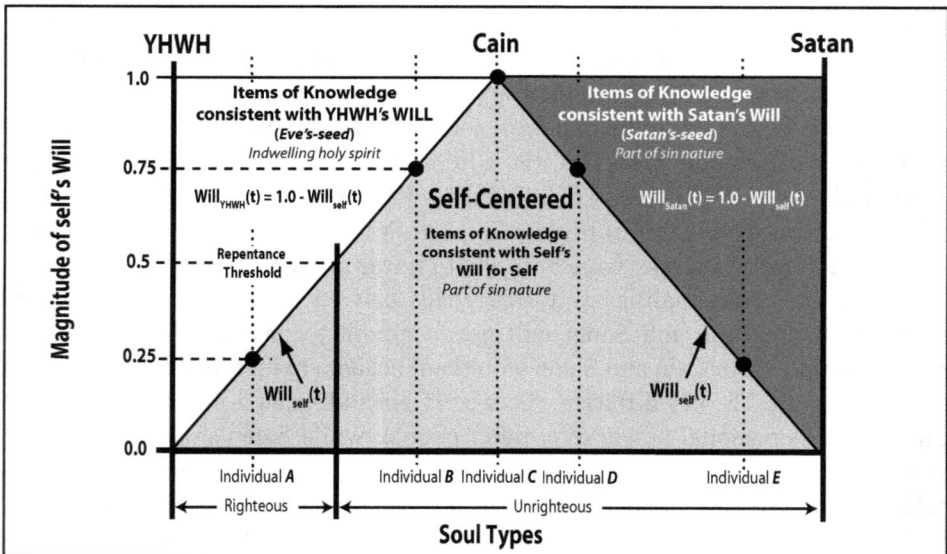

Figure IV-2 Mankind's Soul Types

The ratio, or percentage, of items of knowledge in one's soul that are devoted to YHWH versus self is referred to by theologians as one's *indwelling holy spirit*. Whereas, the ratio, or percentage, of items of knowledge in one's soul that is devoted to self or self and Satan is known as one's *sin nature*.

How an individual develops the Will associated with the each item of knowledge in his Soul determines his type of soul or character or nature.

Note, man's *indwelling holy spirit* is the part of his Soul that is consistent with YHWH's WILL, Holy Spirit. Man's *indwelling holy spirit* is not a part of or directly connected to YHWH's Holy Spirit. Throughout remainder of this book YHWH's WILL, the Holy Spirit will always be capitalized and man's *indwelling holy spirit* will always be lower case.

The white area in Figure IV-2 represents items of knowledge that are consistent with YHWH's WILL; the light gray area represents items of knowledge that are self-centered; and the dark gray area represents knowledge consistent with Satan's WILL. The line that starts at 0.0 and increases to 1.0 at the center and then decreases to 0.0 at the right hand side is equal to all possible magnitudes of $Will_{self}(t)$. An individual's sin nature is equal to $Will_{self}(t)$ and his indwelling holy spirit is computed using $Will_{YHWH}(t) = 1.0 - Will_{self}(t)$. An individual's $Will_{Satan}(t)$ is computed using $Will_{Satan}(t) = 1.0 - Will_{self}(t)$. Figure IV-2 identifies five specific individuals, which will be used to illustrate the different types of souls.

Individual *A* is a follower of YHWH with a sin nature $Will_{self}(t) = .25\ or\ 25\%$ and his indwelling holy spirit $Will_{YHWH}(t) = 1.0 - Will_{self}(t) = .75\ or\ 75\%$. That is, 75% of his decisions consistent with YHWH's WILL (Holy Spirit) making his self's $Will_{YHWH}(t) >> Will_{self}(t)$. This type of person is righteous in YHWH's sight, and he is willing to die or sacrifice for YHWH's cause.

Individual *B* is a follower of YHWH with a sin nature $Will_{self}(t) = .75\ or\ 75\%$ and his indwelling holy spirit $Will_{YHWH}(t) = 1.0 - Will_{self}(t) = .25\ or\ 25\%$. Only 25% of his decisions are consistent with YHWH's WILL (Holy Spirit) making his self's $Will_{self}(t) > Will_{YHWH}(t)$. This type of self-centered person sides with YHWH only when he can take advantage of a situation for his own benefit. Notice in Figure IV-2 that individual *B* has passed the *Repentance Threshold*, $Will_{self}(t) = Will_{YHWH}(t) = .5\ or\ 50\%$ and he must repent, change his priorities, to have a good, righteous, personal relationship with YHWH.

Individual *C* cares only about himself and will do anything to get his way—even murder like Cain. Before the first murder, Cain's soul was similar to Individual *B* because he brought a sacrifice to YHWH although it was not his best. After the first murder, Cain did not repent but placed himself first, $Will_{self}(t) = 1.0$ and $Will_{YHWH}(t) = 0.0$. Cain's soul has 0% indwelling holy spirit and is 100 % sin nature. Cain represents human perfection in being self-centered. People who are self-centered have a $Will_{self}(t) > Will_{all\ others}(t)$.

Individual D has a $Will_{self}(t) = .75\ or\ 75\%$ and is similar to individual B because both are self-centered. Only Individual D has selected to associate with Satan and comply with $Will_{Satan}(t) = 1.0 - Will_{self}(t) = .25\ or\ 25\%$ of the time. Thus, his $Will_{YHWH}(t) = 0.0$ and his $Will_{self}(t) > Will_{Satan}(t)$, which makes him a participant in the overthrow of YHWH. Individual D's soul has 0% indwelling holy spirit and is 100 % sin nature.

Individual E is a follower of Satan with $Will_{self}(t) = .25\ or\ 25\%$ and his $Will_{Satan}(t) = 1.0 - Will_{self}(t) = .75\ or\ 75\%$. Thus 75% of his decisions are consistent with Satan's WILL. His primary interest is the overthrow and destruction of YHWH by any means possible. His self's $Will_{YHWH}(t) = 0.0$ and his $Will_{Satan}(t) >> Will_{self}(t)$. This type of person will murder others or sacrifice them self for Satan's cause. He is a true servant of Satan.

The first murder is not dated in the Holy Bible, but Genesis 4:25-26, and Genesis 5:1-3 do provide a time frame.

> *Genesis 4:25-26*
> *25 And Adam knew his wife again; and she bare a son, and called his name Seth: For God, said she, hath appointed me another seed instead of Abel, whom Cain slew.*
> *26 And to Seth, to him also there was born a son; and he called his name Enos: then began men to call upon the name of the Lord.*
>
> *Genesis 5:1-3*
> *1 This is the book of the generations of Adam. In the day that God created man, in the likeness of God made he him;*
> *2 Male and female created he them; and blessed them, and called their name Adam, in the day when they were created.*
> *3 And **Adam lived an hundred and thirty years, and begat a son in his own likeness, after his image; and called his name Seth:***

Thus the three primary types of men's souls, Figure IV-2, were present at least as of the year 130 AM per Genesis 5:3 because the first murder occurred prior to the birth of Seth.

As time passes, the world population increases and each individual develops a type of soul that consists of some magnitude of *indwelling holy spirit* with some magnitude of *sin nature*. Having identified the three primary types of souls, the question becomes how are they distributed across the world's population? The Holy Bible is silent on this subject prior to Noah's Flood. However, after Noah's Flood it becomes apparent in Chapter *VIII YHWH and the Holy Nation* that the distribution of the three primary types of souls are expanded to seven types of souls. The distribution of these seven soul types across all mankind also conforms to a normal distribution. The author believes as the world population developed prior to Noah's Flood, it contained the three primary types of souls, and these souls were also distributed in accordance with a normal distribution.

Thus, it would be of interest to determine how many people have each type of soul in the developing world society.

To compute the number of people with each type of soul or nature let:

Y(z) = The number of people in the world with a given type of soul.

z = The type of soul of each individual.

Then, when one integrates the number of people with a given type of soul Y(z) over z, the area under the curve will equal the world's population. If the area under the curve is divided by the world's population, the result will be equal to 1.0 and is described by the equation:

$$\int_{-\infty}^{+\infty} Y(z)dz = 1$$

The area under the curve that is associated with a particular soul type represents the fraction of the world's population that has the soul type. The Holy Bible is self validating. That is, the specific numbers in the book of Revelation, support that the number of people a specific soul type is best mathematically expressed using the normal distribution for Y(z). Y(z) is then equal to.

$$Y(z) = 1/(2\,\pi)^{1/2}e^{-Z/2}$$

Substituting the normal distribution for Y(z) yields:

$$\int_{-\infty}^{+\infty} \left[1/(2\,\pi)^{1/2}e^{-Z/2}\right] dz = 1$$

The next step is to divided the z-axis into seven equal sections, one section for each type of soul so that the number of individuals having each soul type may be estimated as a fraction of the world population. Note that for values of z greater than +3.5 or -3.5, the number of people is equal to zero for all practical purposes. The results of the integration along z for the seven soul types are shown in Figure IV-3. The percentages of the world's population for each type of soul have been rounded to three decimal places or less for clarity.

Figure IV-3 shows that about 86 percent of the people in the world are engaged in promoting themselves. A mere 6.6 percent of the world's population is truly dedicated to either the cause of YHWH or Satan. This distribution of soul types

49

gives a disturbingly accurate description of the self-centered world society of today. It is highly probable that this is also an accurate description of the days of Noah.

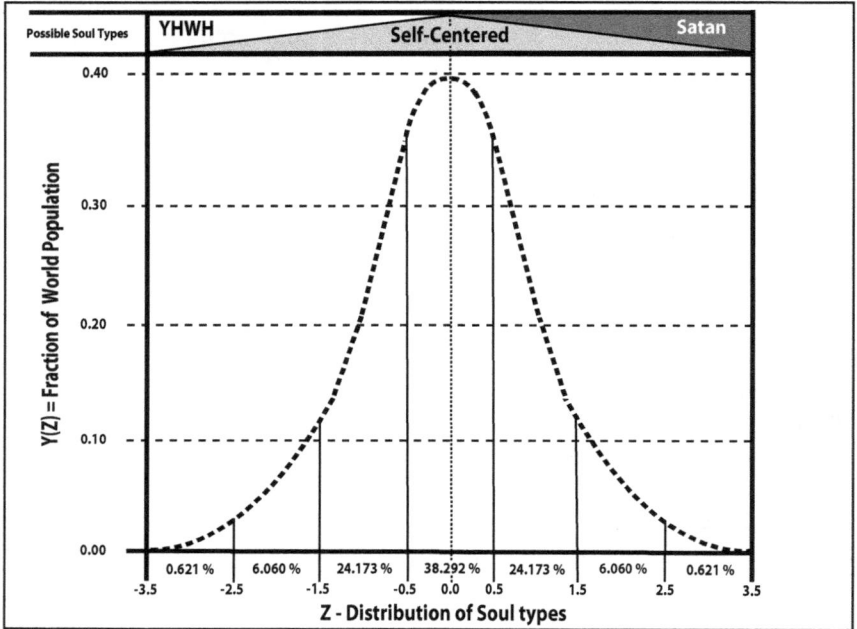

Figure IV-3 The Distribution of Soul Types

How would a normal distribution of the seven soul types impact the development of the world society after the first murder? The nature of the society that develops will reflect a societal nature that is the composite of all people's soul types that exist in the world at any particular point in time.

Hence, the nature of a society is time dependent and reflects the properties of the dominant people's soul type. With the passage of time, the self-centered people and followers of Satan, 92.6 % of the world's population, will dominate the followers of YHWH because these people will do whatever is required to get their way or eliminate any opposition. Eventually the 92.6 % will gain control over all the cities and countries in the world and establish a One-World Government. Once this occurs, the followers of YHWH would be eliminated. It is highly probable that this is what happened to bring YHWH's WRATH upon the world during Noah's Flood?

V YHWH During Noah's Flood

Development of the Pre-Flood World

After the first murder YHWH continues to describe His plan for sin reconciliation with mankind in Genesis 5:1-32. In Genesis 5:1-32 the OS and AM calendars are documented in detail through the descendents of Seth because they adhered to *Eve's-seed* and were followers of YHWH. In YHWH's plan note that the specific birth dates of Cain's descendents or any of the followers of Satan are not specified because they are in rebellion against YHWH and they are not significant in YHWH's plan for reconciliation with mankind.

Genesis 5:1-3

1 *This is the book of the generations of Adam. In the day that God created man, in the likeness of God made he him;*

2 *Male and female created he them; and blessed them, and called their name Adam, in the day when they were created.*

3 *And **Adam lived an hundred and thirty years, and begat a son in his own likeness, after his image; and called his name Seth:***

Seth is unique because he replaces Abel and is included in a specific lineage of those who embrace YHWH's truth, and more important Seth's birth establishes a maximum 130 year bound between the dates in the Original Sin (OS) calendar and dates in the AM calendar. Seth also affirms that Adam repented and was then walking with YHWH.

Genesis 5:4-32

4 *And the days of Adam after he had begotten Seth were eight hundred years: and he begat sons and daughters:*

5 *And all the days that Adam lived were nine hundred and thirty years: and he died.*

6 *And Seth lived an **hundred and five years**, and begat **Enos:***

7 *And Seth lived after he begat Enos eight hundred and seven years, and begat sons and daughters:*

8 *And all the days of Seth were nine hundred and twelve years: and he died.*

9 *And Enos lived **ninety years**, and begat **Cainan:***

10 *And Enos lived after he begat Cainan eight hundred and fifteen years, and begat sons and daughters:*

11 *And all the days of Enos were nine hundred and five years: and he died.*

12 *And Cainan lived **seventy years**, and begat **Mahalaleel:***

13 *And Cainan lived after he begat Mahalaleel eight hundred and forty years, and begat sons and daughters:*

14 *And all the days of Cainan were nine hundred and ten years: and he died.*

15 *And Mahalaleel lived **sixty and five years**, and begat **Jared:***

16 *And Mahalaleel lived after he begat Jared eight hundred and thirty years, and begat sons and daughters:*

17 *And all the days of Mahalaleel were eight hundred ninety and five years: and he died.*

18 *And Jared lived an **hundred sixty and two years**, and he begat **Enoch:***

19 And Jared lived after he begat Enoch eight hundred years, and begat sons and daughters:

20 And all the days of Jared were nine hundred sixty and two years: and he died.

21 And Enoch lived **sixty and five years**, and begat **Methuselah**:

22 And Enoch walked with God after he begat Methuselah three hundred years, and begat sons and daughters:

23 And all the days of Enoch were three hundred sixty and five years:

24 **And Enoch walked with God: and he was not; for God took him.** **[Enoch as of yet has not died. He will join Elijah as the two witnesses during the Tribulation Period.]**

25 And Methuselah lived an **hundred eighty and seven years**, and begat **Lamech:**

26 And Methuselah lived after he begat Lamech seven hundred eighty and two years, and begat sons and daughters:

27 And all the days of Methuselah were nine hundred sixty and nine years: and he died.

28 And Lamech lived an **hundred eighty and two years**, and begat a son:

29 And he called his name **Noah**, saying, This same shall comfort us concerning our work and toil of our hands, because of the ground which the Lord hath cursed.

30 And Lamech lived after he begat Noah five hundred ninety and five years, and begat sons and daughters:

31 And all the days of Lamech were seven hundred seventy and seven years: and he died.

32 And **Noah was five hundred years old: and Noah begat Shem, Ham, and Japheth.**

Genesis 5:4-32 provides a detailed accounting of the time lapse for the AM calendar up to Noah. Thus Noah was born in the year 1056 AM. Moreover, the above lineage has a particular format, which has this form:

1. The **father** lived *a number* of years and begat a **son**. This first born **son** carries the birth right.

2. The **father** lived after he begat his first **son** *a number* of years, and then he begat sons and daughters.

3. All the days of the **father** were *a number* of years and he died.

Note, in Genesis 5: 32 Noah had no children before he was 500 years old, 1556 years AM. Then in the same year when Noah was 500 years old, he had three sons Shem, Ham, and Japheth, who must be triplets. This means these brothers have nearly identical material and spirit Bodies, but have unique Souls and Wills. The birth order of these triplets makes Japheth the eldest, Shem the second, and Ham youngest. These brothers were fully aware of the culture that existed prior to Noah's flood because they were 100 years old at the start of the flood. Thus each of their Souls and Wills were strongly influenced by the pre-flood culture. We shall see that after Noah's flood that these brothers have developed very different types of Souls and Wills, which also reflect the three primary types of souls.

Now 1,656 years have passed since YHWH's creation of the material component of the universe in the year 0000 AM and at least 1,526 years since the first murder. During this period of time, mankind was fruitful and multiplied, and the pre-flood world's population probably approached one billion people [2]. These people had been influenced by *Eve's-seed*, self, and *Satan's-seed*. Satan was probably still alive and well spreading his seed of rebellion against YHWH.

In Genesis 6, YHWH begins to describe what happened to the nature of the society that developed as mankind populated the earth.

Before we examine Genesis 6, it would be beneficial to review the meaning of the term *sons of God*. What are possible meanings for this term, *sons of God*?

1. Fallen angles or aliens.

2. Men that previously walked with YHWH.

3. The kings and rulers.

The first possibility that the *sons of God* were fallen angles is improbable because Satan or fallen angels or aliens were a different kind of beast and would be unable to reproduce with human kind as stated in Genesis 3:1.

Genesis 3:1
1   Now the <u>serpent</u> **[Satan]** *was more subtil than **any beast of the field** which the Lord God had made. And he said unto the **woman**, Yea, hath God said, Ye shall not eat of every tree of the garden?*

Although during this time animals were vegetarian and companions for mankind. Animals like Satan were able to communicate with mankind. Animal kinds could not reproduce with mankind resulting in superhuman beings.

The second possibility is that the *sons of God* were people who previously walked with YHWH and subsequently rejected Him. More people were followers of YHWH, *sons of God*, than are identified by name in Genesis 5:4-32. Genesis 5:4-32 provides detailed dating of Noah's Flood as part of the AM calendar, see Appendix I, and at the same time it documents by name the lineage of Noah from Adam. Genesis 6:9 as we shall see, states that those named were faithful in their walk with YHWH, but those unnamed descendents of Seth are certainly candidates.

The third possibility is that the *sons of God* were the kings, or rulers, who were descendants of Adam, like Cain, who embraced self or those who embraced *Satan's-seed*. The word *son* is translated from the Hebrew word **ben** (OT:1121) [5] and it can imply almost any kind of descent or succession, as ben shanah, son of a year, i.e. a year old; ben kesheth, son of a bow, i.e. an arrow.

The most probable understanding is that *sons of God* are descendents of Adam, which started life following YHWH, but subsequently rejected Him because of pride like Cain or acceptance of *Satan's-seed*. When these men began to dominate and rule over ordinary people, they took whatever they wanted from them. This understanding is reinforced by YHWH referring to subsequent generations not as *sons of God* but as mighty men of renown.

Genesis 6:1-8 describes how mankind became an evil society. The comments included in the scripture reflect the above understanding of *sons of God*.

Genesis 6
1 *And it came to pass, when men began to multiply on the face of the earth, and daughters were born unto them,*
2 *That the* <u>sons of God</u> **[the rulers or dictator]** *saw the daughters of* **[ordinary]** <u>men</u> *that they were fair; and they took them wives of all which they chose.*

At this point in time, YHWH has not commanded any man to rule over any other man, but each person is responsible to be obedient to YHWH and walk with Him. Also, a man was to have one wife as stated in Genesis 1:24, "Therefore shall a man leave his father and his mother, and shall cleave unto his wife and they shall be one flesh".

Remember Satan is still alive in his mortal serpent body on earth planting his seed in men's souls. Satan tells men they should take what they want from others and do as they please for they need to practice being gods. These evil descendents of Adam, *sons of God*, were like corrupt gang leaders or dictators using violence to achieve what they desired. They dominated the entire society and were totally corrupt and evil.

Genesis 6
3 *And the* <u>Lord said</u> **[YHWH's WILL]***,* <u>My spirit</u> **[YHWH's SOUL]** *shall not always strive with man, for that he also is flesh: yet his days shall be an hundred and twenty years.*
4 *There were* <u>giants</u> **[large animals, dinosaurs, men like Goliath, etc.]** *in the earth in those days; and also after that, when the* <u>sons of God</u> **[the rulers, mighty men]** *came in unto the daughters of men, and they bare children to them, the same became* <u>mighty men</u> **[The new evil rulers did not start out walking with YHWH as *sons of God*, but were trained in rebellion from birth.]** *which were of old, men of renown.*
5 *And* <u>God saw</u> **[YHWH's BODY]** *that the wickedness of man was great in the earth, and that every imagination of the* <u>thoughts of his heart</u> **[Motives]** *was only evil continually.*
6 *And it* <u>repented the Lord</u> **[YHWH's SOUL]** *that he had made man on the earth, and it grieved him at* <u>his heart.</u> **[YHWH's SOUL]**
7 *And the* <u>Lord said</u> **[YHWH's WILL]***, I will destroy man whom I have created from the face of the earth; both man, and beast, and the creeping thing, and the fowls of the air; for it repenteth me that I have made them.*
8 *But Noah found grace in the eyes of the Lord.*
9 *These are the generations of Noah:* **Noah was a just man and perfect in his generations, and Noah walked with God.**
10 *And Noah begat three sons, Shem, Ham, and Japheth.*

11 *The earth also was corrupt before God, and the earth was filled with violence.*

12 *And* <u>*God looked*</u> **[YHWH's BODY]** *upon the earth, and, behold, it was corrupt; for all flesh had corrupted his way upon the earth.*

13 *And* <u>*God said*</u> **[YHWH's WILL]** *unto Noah, The end of all flesh is come before me; for the earth is filled with violence through them; and, behold, I will destroy them with the earth.*

What are the characteristics of this corrupt world society that YHWH was referring to?

The corruption was worldwide. The *men of renown* were no longer in local areas but were prevailing over the entire earth, which is similar to the formation of a One-World Government where the government dictates what the people can do and believe. The people were not free. This *Occult* society was based on *Satan's-seed*, and it was in complete rebellion against YHWH. Its capital city was likely Atlantis. The people were either supporters of Satan or were self-centered. These people were violent and murdered, raped, enslaved, and abused others as they desired.

However, there was a small percentage of people, probably 6.681 percent of the world's population, that still walked with YHWH embracing *Eve's-seed* and YHWH protects them. For example, Methuselah who died just before the start of Noah's flood is a foreshadow of those who are walking with YHWH and who will be raptured prior to the Tribulation Period. Noah and his family, who experience the entire flood, are a foreshadow the Remnant of Israel who will go through the entire Tribulation Period.

So the corrupt world society consisted of people whose souls embraced *Satan's-seed*, self, *Eve's-seed* or a combination of self and Satan or self and YHWH. It is probable that the distribution of these natures as the world population grew after 0000 OS took the form of a normal distribution. The key issue in determining if the world society is corrupt is establishing who is in control of all the people in the entire world. When Satan and his followers gained world control over all the people of the earth, YHWH protected His own followers and reconciles His perfect anxiety with respect to mankind's sin.

Does YHWH experience the Premeditative Process with respect to sin? The Premeditative Process will now be applied to YHWH and Noah's Flood.

The properties associated with YHWH's *WILL(t)* and *ANXIETY(t)* were developed in the book *Self's Destiny and Self.* [2] The Holy Bible refers to YHWH's *ANXIETY(t)* as His *WRATH(t).* Thus, the term *WRATH(t)* will be used when addressing YHWH.

55

Recall the equations for *WILL(t)* and *WRATH(t)* are:

$$WILL(t) = L(t) * F(t) * P(t)$$

$$WRATH(t) = [L(t) - F(t)] * P(t)$$

YHWH's Power *P(t)* and His Love for mankind $L_{mankind}(t)$ are both perfect and equal to one, but YHWH's Faith in mankind $F_{mankind}(t)$ is unique because He created mankind in His own image and gave mankind the freedom of choice. As mankind populates the earth, YHWH's $F_{mankind}(t)$ begins to decrease as just described in Genesis 6:1-8. In Genesis 6:6, YHWH's increasing *WRATH(t)* is expressed in terms like "He repented creating man" and "it grieved His SOUL". Mankind in the presence of *Satan's-seed* has accepted evil as a way of life. YHWH gives mankind every opportunity to repent and return to following Him, but when the magnitude of YHWH's $F_{mankind}(t)$ approaches 0 He enters the Reconciliation Phase and pours out His perfect $WRATH_{mankind}(t)$. YHWH's $WILL_{mankind}(t)$ and $WRATH_{mankind}(t)$ toward mankind's evil are equal to:

$$WILL_{mankind}(t) = 1 * F_{mankind}(t) * P(t) = 1 * 0 * 1 = 0$$

$$WRATH_{mankind}(t) = [1 - F_{mankind}(t)] * P(t) = [1 - 0] * 1 = 1$$

Now, mankind is about to reap the harvest of their sin by experiencing YHWH's perfect justice and *WRATH (t)*. However, Noah found grace because he was obedient giving YHWH his best for an offering. Then, YHWH starts to prepare to release His *WRATH (t)* on the world as described in Genesis 6:9 through Genesis 7:10 by having Noah build an ark.

Genesis 6

14 Make thee an ark of gopher wood; rooms shalt thou make in the ark, and shalt pitch it within and without with pitch.

15 And this is the fashion which thou shalt make it of: The length of the ark shall be three hundred cubits, the breadth of it fifty cubits, and the height of it thirty cubits.

16 A window shalt thou make to the ark, and in a cubit shalt thou finish it above; and the door of the ark shalt thou set in the side thereof; with lower, second, and third stories shalt thou make it.

17 And, behold, I, even I, do bring a flood of waters upon the earth, to destroy all flesh, wherein is the breath of life, from under heaven; and everything that is in the earth shall die.

18 But with thee will I establish my covenant; and thou shalt come into the ark, thou, and thy sons, and thy wife, and thy sons' wives with thee.

19 And of every living thing of all flesh, two of every sort shalt thou bring into the ark, to keep them alive with thee; they shall be male and female.

20 Of fowls after their kind, and of cattle after their kind, of every creeping thing of the earth after his kind, two of every sort shall come unto thee, to keep them alive.

21 And take thou unto thee of all food that is eaten, and thou shalt gather it to
thee; and it shall be for food for thee, and for them.

22 Thus did Noah; according to all that God commanded him, so did he.

Genesis 7

1 And the <u>Lord said</u> **[YHWH's WILL]** unto Noah, Come thou and all thy house
into the ark; for thee have I seen righteous before me in this generation.

2 Of every clean beast thou shalt take to thee by sevens, the male and his
female: and of beasts that are not clean by two, the male and his female.

3 Of fowls also of the air by sevens, the male and the female; to keep seed alive
upon the face of all the earth.

4 For yet seven days, and I will cause it to rain upon the earth forty days and
forty nights; and every living substance that I have made will I destroy from
off the face of the earth.

5 And Noah did according unto all that the Lord commanded him.

6 And Noah was six hundred years old when the flood of waters was upon the
earth.

7 And Noah went in, and his sons, and his wife, and his sons' wives with him,
into the ark, because of the waters of the flood.

8 Of clean beasts, and of beasts that are not clean, and of fowls, and of
everything that creepeth upon the earth,

9 There went in two and two unto Noah into the ark, the male and the female,
as God had commanded Noah.

10 And it came to pass after seven days, that the waters of the flood were upon
the earth.

The pre-flood technology was probably very sophisticated, and constructing a large boat was not a huge challenge. Particularly with YHWH's help. No one knows and the scriptures are silent on Noah's occupation, but one reason YHWH may have selected Noah from among His followers was because his trade was ship building.

Once Noah completes the ark, YHWH is ready to release His ***WRATH (t)*** upon the earth and mankind. Before we examine the actual flood, we need to review the earth's structure prior to Noah's Flood, which was much different than it is today. Before the flood the planet Earth's structure was a single dry land mass with the Garden of Eden being the highest point with four rivers emanating from it and flowing to the single sea dividing the dry land into four parts as described in Genesis 2:10-14.

Genesis 2:10-14

10 And a river went out of Eden to water the garden; and from thence it was
parted, and became into four heads.

11 The name of the first is **Pison**: that is it which compasseth the whole land of
Havilah, where there is gold;

12 And the gold of that land is good: there is bdellium and the onyx stone.

13 And the name of the second river is **Gihon**: the same is it that compasseth
the whole land of Ethiopia.

14 And the name of the third river is **Hiddekel**: that is it which goeth toward the
east of Assyria. And the fourth river is **Euphrates**.

The pre-flood world is depicted in Figure V-1. Where the white text provides pre-flood structure information, and the black text enclosed by black dashed lines reflect the names of areas one would recognize today. The exact shape and size of the single land mass is unknown. The land did have plenty of lush vegetation, metals, precious stones, and the like. The depth of the sea or the width of the water vapor canopy was not identified and remains unknown. There were no polar ice caps and it is safe to assume that only the four rivers existed. The terrain must have been quite flat because the rivers flowed into a single ocean and there is no mention of any water falls or great mountains. YHWH created the dry land to be a very people friendly environment. Eden had to be the highest point of the dry land because the four rivers descend from it. Thus, the Garden of Eden probably had the appearance of a four-sided pyramid with a river flowing down each side. This may have been the inspiration for some pyramid structures mankind built after the flood. The Garden of Eden was where YHWH came to visit mankind before the fall.

Noah's flood reflects what YHWH's perfect WRATH is like, although the Holy Bible is silent with respect to the means YHWH used to initiate the flood. Whatever the means, it had to have sufficient energy to divide the single land mass shown in Figure V-1, the pre-flood condition, into the earth's structure we know today. Some possibilities include:

1. Earthquake.

2. Water vapor canopy collapse.

3. Impact of a meteor, asteroid, or other large object.

An earthquake is a doubtful cause. An earthquake would not trigger the collapse of the water vapor canopy that resulted in forty days of rain world wide. The earth's crust cool rate might fracture the single landmass and release the abundant water in the earth's crust that formed the mist, which watered the plants per Genesis 2:6. It is extremely unlikely that an earthquake would contain sufficient energy to break the single landmass and drive the pieces a thousand miles apart.

Collapse of the water vapor canopy is also extremely doubtful. An atmospheric temperature change could have triggered the collapse of the water vapor canopy causing forty days of rain with extensive flooding. Flooding generally covers the land but would not fragment the single landmass. It is likely that the forty days of rain was not the primary cause, but only a secondary effect.

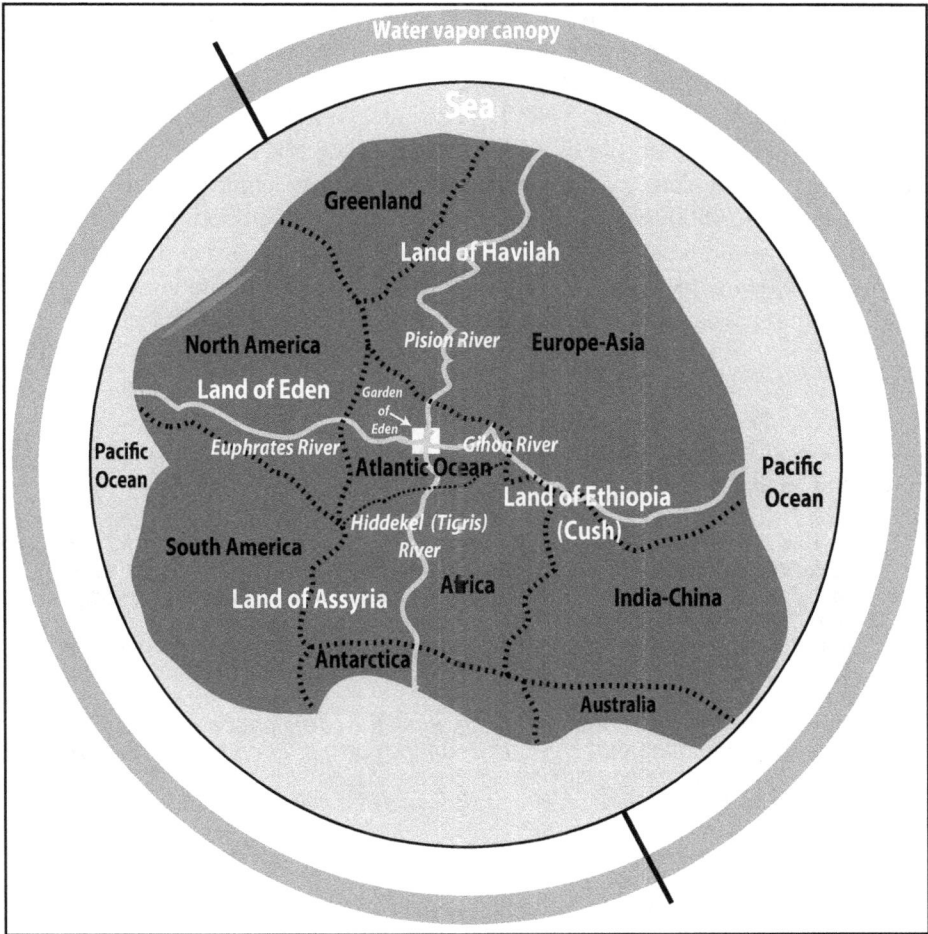

Figure V-1 Pre-flood Planet Configuration

Most likely YHWH initiated Noah's flood by using a large object such as a large meteor or asteroid to perfectly strike the pre-flood single landmass with the impact point in the area of the Garden of Eden. The meteor impact fractures and drives the pieces of the single landmass upward and apart forming large mountains and generating a world wide crater. The meteor would also trigger collapse of the water vapor canopy causing the forty days of rain. It would also release the water contained in the earth's crust, the fountains of the deep. The results of the meteor strike are discussed later in the Post-Flood World section.

The meteor strike also destroys Satan's Occult One-World Government and its capital city Atlantis. Satan's mortal-serpent body also dies leaving his spirit body imprisoned in the pre-creation universe.

It is reasonable to assume YHWH positioned Noah and the ark as far from the Garden of Eden as physically possible to achieve His objective. If the single landmass was equivalent to the surface of all today's continents, it would be approximately 57,000,000 square miles, as previously discussed. If this landmass was circular it would have a radius of 4,260 miles with the Garden of Eden near its center. Thus Noah's ark was probably over 4,000 miles from the meteor's impact area. The meteor strike also initiates Noah's flood.

The Flood

The lives of Noah and his family during the flood are documented precisely by YHWH in Genesis 7 and 8.

Genesis 7

11 **In the six hundredth year of Noah's life, in the second month, the seventeenth day of the month, the same day were all the fountains of the great deep broken up, and the windows of heaven were opened.**

12 *And the rain was upon the earth forty days and forty nights.*

13 *In the selfsame day entered Noah, and Shem, and Ham, and Japheth, the sons of Noah, and Noah's wife, and the three wives of his sons with them, into the ark;*

14 *They, and every beast after his kind, and all the cattle after their kind, and every creeping thing that creepeth upon the earth after his kind, and every fowl after his kind, every bird of every sort.*

15 *And they went in unto Noah into the ark, two and two of all flesh, wherein is the breath of life.*

16 *And they that went in, went in male and female of all flesh, as God had commanded him: and the Lord shut him in.*

17 *And the flood was forty days upon the earth; and the waters increased, and bare up the ark, and it was lift up above the earth.*

18 *And the waters prevailed, and were increased greatly upon the earth; and the ark went upon the face of the waters.*

19 *And the waters prevailed exceedingly upon the earth; and all the high hills, that were under the whole heaven, were covered.*

20 *Fifteen cubits upward did the waters prevail;* **and the mountains were covered.** **[This is the first time mountains are mentioned in the Holy Bible and it is after the meteor impact that initiated Noah's Flood.]**

21 *And all flesh died that moved upon the earth, both of fowl, and of cattle, and of beast, and of every creeping thing that creepeth upon the earth, and every man:*

22 *All in whose nostrils was the breath of life, of all that was in the dry land, died.*

23 And every living substance was destroyed which was upon the face of the ground, both man, and cattle, and the creeping things, and the fowl of the heaven; and they were destroyed from the earth: and Noah only remained alive, and they that were with him in the ark.

24 And the waters prevailed upon the earth an hundred and fifty days

Genesis 8

1 And <u>God remembered</u> [**YHWH's SOUL**] Noah, and every living thing, and all the cattle that was with him in the ark: and <u>God made</u> [**YHWH's WILL**] a wind to pass over the earth, and the waters assuaged;

2 The fountains also of the deep and the windows of heaven were stopped, and the rain from heaven was restrained;

3 And the waters returned from off the earth continually: and after the end of the hundred and fifty days the waters were abated.

4 And the ark rested in the seventh month, on the seventeenth day of the month, upon the mountains of Ararat.

5 And the waters decreased continually until the tenth month: in the tenth month, on the first day of the month, **were the tops of the mountains seen. [This is 9 months after the meteor impact]**

6 And it came to pass at the end of forty days, that Noah opened the window of the ark which he had made:

7 And he sent forth a raven, which went forth to and fro, until the waters were dried up from off the earth.

8 Also he sent forth a dove from him, to see if the waters were abated from off the face of the ground;

9 But the dove found no rest for the sole of her foot, and she returned unto him into the ark, for the waters were on the face of the whole earth: then he put forth his hand, and took her, and pulled her in unto him into the ark.

10 And he stayed yet other seven days; and again he sent forth the dove out of the ark;

11 And the dove came in to him in the evening; and, lo, in her mouth was an olive leaf pluckt off: so Noah knew that the waters were abated from off the earth.

12 And he stayed yet other seven days; and sent forth the dove; which returned not again unto him anymore.

13 **And it came to pass in the six hundredth and first year, in the first month, the first day of the month, the waters were dried up from off the earth:** and Noah removed the covering of the ark, and looked, and, behold, the face of the ground was dry.

14 **And in the second month, on the seven and twentieth day of the month, was the earth dried.**

15 And <u>God spake</u> [**YHWH's WILL**] unto Noah, saying,

16 Go forth of the ark, thou, and thy wife, and thy sons, and thy sons' wives with thee.

17 Bring forth with thee every living thing that is with thee, of all flesh, both of fowl, and of cattle, and of every creeping thing that creepeth upon the earth; that they may breed abundantly in the earth, and be fruitful, and multiply upon the earth.

18 And Noah went forth, and his sons, and his wife, and his sons' wives with him:

61

19 *Every beast, every creeping thing, and every fowl, and whatsoever creepeth upon the earth, after their kinds, went forth out of the ark.*
20 *And Noah builded an altar unto the Lord; and took of every clean beast, and of every clean fowl, and offered burnt offerings on the altar.*
21 *And the <u>Lord smelled</u> [**YHWH's BODY**], a sweet savour; and the <u>Lord said in his heart</u> [**YHWH's SOUL**], I will not again curse the ground any more for man's sake; for the imagination of man's heart is evil from his youth; neither will I again smite any more everything living, as I have done.*

Notice how precisely YHWH documents the duration of the flood. The meteor struck when Noah was 600 years old plus two months plus seventeen days, per Genesis 7:11. The flood ended when Noah and his family left the ark he was 601 years old plus two months plus seventeen days. Thus, the duration of the flood was exactly one year and ten days. The biblical chronology to this point in time is extremely precise! Dry land relative to the ark is limited by the distance a bird could fly and return to the ark, so areas of dry land in other parts of the earth could have appeared anytime after the meteor impact as the earth's crust shattered into plates and they were driven away from the impact area.

It is also important that Noah's first priority was to make an offering to YHWH to demonstrate Noah's $Will_{YHWH}(t) > Will_{self}(t)$. Noah does exactly what YHWH wants him to do and is blessed for his obedience. However, Noah and his family are now confronted with a post-flood world, which is very different from what existed just one year ago.

Post-Flood World

The pre-flood world was shown in Figure V-1 where the black text enclosed by black dashed lines identified names of areas, which are now identified in Figure V-2, the post-flood world, enclosed by solid lines. In the post-flood world after the meteor impact has occurred, both the Garden of Eden and the Occult city of Atlantis cease to exist, and they became part of the earth's magma. Now there is no need for Cherubim with flaming swords to guard the Garden of Eden. No man will ever find any artifacts of either one. YHWH's destruction was perfect!

In Figure V-2 the pre-flood Garden of Eden was probably located somewhere in the vicinity of the middle of the Atlantic Ocean because a large meteor impact there would break the earth's crust into parts forming plates. The plates would be driven with tremendous force away from the impact point as a function of the impact angle. Hence, one would expect the collision of the plates to form higher mountains on the rim of the resultant crater because the plates are being driven away from the impact point with a horizontal velocity and upward velocity that would cause them to override adjacent plates away from the impact point.

Today, the mountain ranges with larger mountains, shown as white areas in Figure V-2 , form the outer rim of the crater.

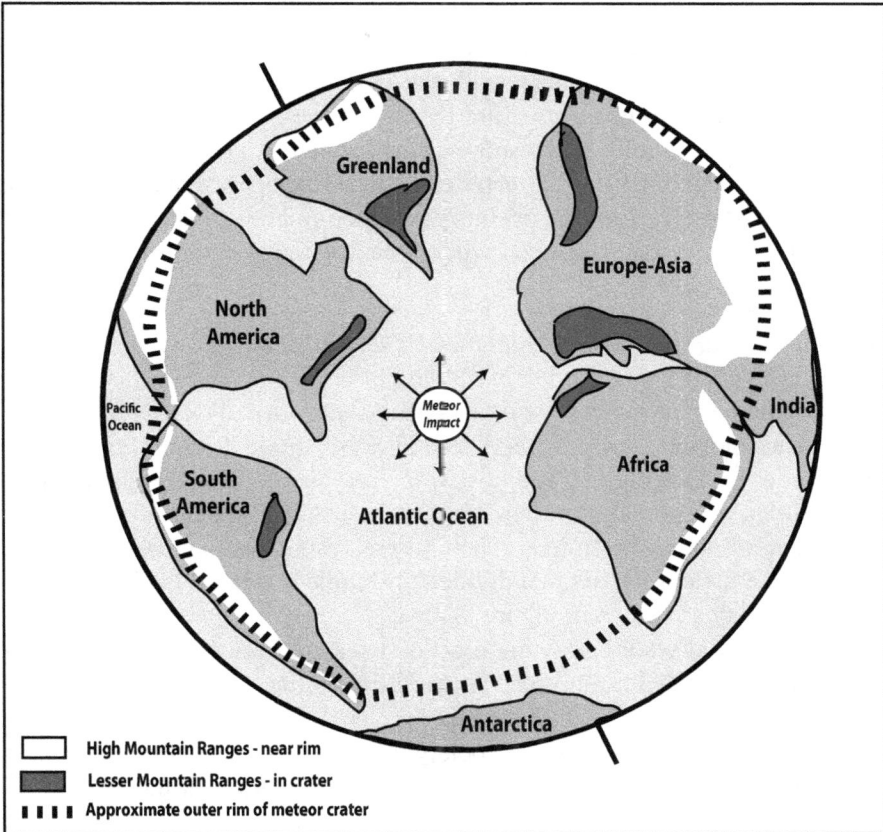

Figure V-2 Post-flood planet Configuration

The apparent outer rim of the crater is identified by the circular dashed black line in Figure V-2. Thus the outer rim of the crater is formed by North American Rockies, the South American Andes, the mountain ranges of Eastern Africa, and the Asian mountain ranges including the Great Himalaya Range. A variety of lesser mountains and mountain ranges formed closer to the center of the crater. Some of these are shown by the dark gray ares in Figure V-2. Today, we live in and around one huge crater, and the plates cf the earth's crust are still in the process of stabilizing as the study of Plate Tectonics affirms. The earth is still groaning as a result of the Original Sin.

Once the meteor's penetration stopped in the magma, the resultant hole backfilled with water from the sea forming the Atlantic Ocean. The meteor also collapsed the water vapor canopy, and it rained for forty days. The rain became part of the seas that flooded the entire earth. The waters of the new seas became extremely hot due to direct contact with the magma and the meteor. The entire earth became covered in hot water, and the protective greenhouse went away so that both poles became cold. The result was the formation a huge lake effect snow machine, which deposited the ice caps and their glaciers around the north and south poles initiating the Ice Age. [2] Thus post-flood man will now experience the four seasons spring, summer, fall and winter because the greenhouse is gone. This is affirmed by Genesis 8:22.

> Genesis 8:22
> 22 While the earth remaineth, seedtime and harvest, and cold and heat, and summer and winter, and day and night shall not cease.

The receding flood waters yields a terrain that is totally different from the pre-flood world in that the pre-flood terrain was people friendly and smooth. The post-flood world is cursed, and hostile toward people with a huge number of mountains, hills, deserts, lakes, rivers, ravines, volcanoes, and earthquakes that all impede human travel and activities. The entire earth's crust has been shaken and deformed by the meteor impact that divided the single pre-flood landmass into the continents of today as shown in Figure V-2.

Some places that were below the pre-flood sea are now above sea level so it should not be unexpected to find fossils of sea life on the top of a mountain or the remnant of the lush vegetation under the polar cap.

Some remnants of the pre-flood society such as Easter Island or the ancient people that mined the large amount of copper from the areas near the present Lake Superior, Isle Royale, and the Keweenaw Peninsula of Michigan. Noah's flood brings into question any assumptions that the ancestors of people existing in an area today were associated with any ancient activity because all the people in the pre-flood world died except for Noah and his family.

What was the impact of the flood on the world society? The pre-flood society was an Occult-based society, a society that embraced *Satan's-seed*. The society was large probably — approaching a billion people. Therefore, the collective knowledge from the souls of society's members must have been substantial. The pre-flood people were capable of building cities like Atlantis or building large boats like the ark. The pre-flood people could have been capable of sophisticated transportation, navigation, and flight. The society was violent, being dominated by dictators, men of renown, who did as they pleased. It is probable they formed a One-World Government, which was Occult-based under the direct leadership of Satan. This pre-flood society of about one billion people was decimated by YHWH's perfect WRATH to just eight people during the Noah's flood. The loss of mankind's knowledge is staggering. Just think if this were to happen today. All the sophisticated technology would be lost, and there would be no TV, cell phones, cars, airplanes, food, or any support systems. Mankind's total knowledge going forward was contained in the eight souls of Noah's family who survived.

The eight people who survived Noah's flood were Noah, Noah's wife, son Shem, Shem's wife, son Japheth, Japheth's wife, son Ham and Ham's wife. Contained in their souls is mankind's complete post-flood knowledge. They are aware of many things that existed pre-flood, but do not have the tools or materials or means or the collective knowledge to implement them.

YHWH will give them guidance in navigating their new and foreign environment. YHWH begins in Genesis 9:1-17 to tell Noah, and his sons Shem, Japheth, and Ham what they must do and He will do.

Genesis 9
1 And God blessed Noah and his sons, and said **[YHWH's WILL]** unto them, **Be fruitful, and multiply, and replenish the earth**.
2 And the fear of you and the dread of you shall be upon every beast of the earth, and upon every fowl of the air, upon all that moveth upon the earth, and upon all the fishes of the sea; into your hand are they delivered.
3 Every moving thing that liveth shall be meat for you; even as the green herb have I given you all things.
4 But flesh with the life thereof, which is the blood thereof, shall ye not eat.
5 And surely your blood of your lives will I require; at the hand of every beast will I require it, and at the hand of man; at the hand of every man's brother will I require the life of man.
6 Whoso sheddeth man's blood, by man shall his blood be shed: for in the image of God made he man.
7 And you, be ye fruitful, and multiply; bring forth abundantly in the earth, and multiply therein.
8 And God spake **[YHWH's WILL]** unto Noah, and to his sons with him, saying,
9 And I, behold, I establish my covenant with you, and with your seed after you;
10 And with every living creature that is with you, of the fowl, of the cattle, and of every beast of the earth with you; from all that go out of the ark, to every beast of the earth.
11 And I will establish my covenant with you; neither shall all flesh be cut off any more by the waters of a flood; neither shall there any more be a flood to destroy the earth.
12 And God said **[YHWH's WILL]**, This is the token of the covenant which I make between me and you and every living creature that is with you, for perpetual generations:
13 I do set my bow in the cloud, and it shall be for a token of a covenant between me and the earth.

14 *And it shall come to pass, when I bring a cloud over the earth, that the bow shall be seen in the cloud:*

15 *And I will remember* **[YHWH's SOUL]** *my covenant, which is between me and you and every living creature of all flesh; and the waters shall no more become a flood to destroy all flesh.*

16 *And the bow shall be in the cloud; and I will look* **[YHWH's BODY]** *upon it, that I may remember* **[YHWH's SOUL]** *the everlasting covenant between God and every living creature of all flesh that is upon the earth.*

17 *And God said* **[YHWH's WILL]** *unto Noah, This is the token of the covenant, which I have established between me and all flesh that is upon the earth.*

Post-flood Noah with his triplet sons Japheth, the eldest (Genesis 10:21), Shem, the second, and Ham, the youngest (Genesis 9:24), are to repopulate the earth. Also, mankind will now eat animals and plants for food, and anyone who murders another must be killed. YHWH does promise not to destroy the earth with a flood again, and the rainbow will be the symbol of this covenant. The rainbow is significant because its seven colors also represent the seven soul types of mankind.

A man's soul contains all his knowledge. Therefore, Noah and his family's souls contain the knowledge of good and evil from their pre-flood existence. A man's character is the composite of all the items of knowledge in his soul and the WILL associated with them. YHWH in Genesis 6:18-29 describes the post-flood development of the souls of Shem, Japheth, and Ham. These brothers have nearly identical bodies, being triplets, but have unique souls that represent the three primary types of souls.

Genesis 9:18-29

18 *And the sons of Noah, that went forth of the ark, were Shem, and Ham, and Japheth: and Ham is the father of Canaan.*

19 *These are the three sons of Noah: and of them was the whole earth overspread.*

20 *And Noah began to be an husbandman, and he planted a vineyard:*

21 *And he drank of the wine, and was drunken; and he was uncovered within his tent.*

22 *And Ham, the father of Canaan, saw the nakedness of his father, and told his two brethren without.*

23 *And Shem and Japheth took a garment, and laid it upon both their shoulders, and went backward, and covered the nakedness of their father; and their faces were backward, and they saw not their father's nakedness.*

24 *And Noah awoke from his wine, and knew what his younger son* **[Ham]** *had done unto him.*

25 *And he said, Cursed be Canaan; a servant of servants shall he be unto his brethren.*

26 *And he said, Blessed be the Lord God of Shem; and Canaan shall be his servant.*

27 *God shall enlarge Japheth, and he shall dwell in the tents of Shem; and Canaan shall be his servant.*

28 And Noah lived after the flood three hundred and fifty years.
29 And all the days of Noah were nine hundred and fifty years: and he died.

In Genesis 9:1 YHWH commanded Noah and his sons to be fruitful and multiply. Noah, who was always obedient to YHWH, lived 350 years after the flood without having any more children, Genesis 9:28-29. Therefore, over and above any other acts that Ham may have performed against Noah, it is probable that Ham, his youngest son, castrated his father to prevent any additional competition from more siblings. Because no sons are born to Noah after the flood in Genesis 10 that follows. Genesis 10 also gives some insight into the three primary types of souls as we look at the descendants of Noah's sons. Each of Noah's sons exhibit one of three primary types of souls, which are:

1. Sons of Japheth, who are self-centered doing what seems best for self.

2. Sons of Shem, who walk with and are obedient to YHWH.

3. Sons of Ham, who totally rejected YHWH and embraced Satan.

Japheth, the eldest triplet of Noah's, and his descendents are described in Genesis 10:1-5.

Genesis 10:1-5
1 Now these are the generations of the sons of Noah, Shem, Ham, and Japheth: and unto them were sons born after the flood.
*2 **The sons of Japheth**; Gomer, and Magog, and Madai, and Javan, and Tubal, and Meshech, and Tiras.*
3 And the sons of Gomer; Ashkenaz, and Riphath, and Togarmah.
4 And the sons of Javan; Elishah, and Tarshish, Kittim, and Dodanim.
*5 **By these were the isles of the Gentiles divided in their lands; every one after his tongue, after their families, in their nations.***

The sons of Japheth would what they believe would in their best interest. When told to do something, they might or might not do it. Their Will for self dominated any decision they make. Their religion and self, and they would align themselves with whom it was expedient at any particular time. They were unreliable and could not be trusted to keep their word. They would help others only if they believed they would ultimately benefit from their effort. Genesis 10:5 is a reference to the scattering of people throughout the earth as a result of the tower of Babel, which will be addressed shortly. In this situation, Japheth's descendents must have felt it would be in their best interest to be obedient to YHWH because they departed the area of Babel.

Ham and his descendents totally reject YHWH, and their actions are described in Genesis 10:6-20.

Genesis 10:6-10
6 **And the sons of Ham**; Cush, and Mizraim, and Phut, and Canaan.
7 And the sons of Cush; Seba, and Havilah, and Sabtah, and Raamah, and Sabtecha: and the sons of Raamah; Sheba, and Dedan.
8 And Cush begat **Nimrod: he began to be a mighty one in the earth.**
9 He was a mighty hunter before the Lord: wherefore it is said, Even as Nimrod the mighty hunter before the Lord.
10 And the beginning of **his kingdom was Babel**, and Erech, and Accad, and Calneh, in the land of Shinar.

Nimrod was a mighty-man, establishing his kingdom in the tradition of the pre-flood *mighty-men* or *men of renown* as described in Genesis 6:4. He dominated, ruled over, and took what he wanted from ordinary men. He was comparable to today's dictators, corrupt leaders, or gang bosses whose ultimate objective is to control all the people in the entire world. It is probable that Ham promoted in his family the goal to re-establish a One-World Government similar to what probably existed prior to Noah's flood only under the control of his family. The activities of the sons of Ham are described in Genesis 10:11-20.

Genesis 10:11-20
11 Out of that land went forth Asshur, and **builded Nineveh, and the city Rehoboth, and Calah,**
12 And Resen between Nineveh and Calah: **the same is a great city.**
13 And Mizraim begat Ludim, and Anamim, and Lehabim, and Naphtuhim,
14 And Pathrusim, and Casluhim, (out of whom came Philistim,) and Caphtorim.
15 And Canaan begat Sidon his firstborn, and Heth,
16 And the Jebusite, and the Amorite, and the Girgasite,
17 And the Hivite, and the Arkite, and the Sinite,
18 And the Arvadite, and the Zemarite, and the Hamathite: and afterward were the families of the Canaanites spread abroad.
19 And the border of the Canaanites was from Sidon, as thou comest to Gerar, unto Gaza; as thou goest, **unto Sodom, and Gomorrah**, and Admah, and Zeboim, even unto Lasha.
20 These are the sons of Ham, after their families, after their tongues, in their countries, and in their nations.

The sons of Ham were constantly in rebellion against YHWH by building cities, kingdoms, and structures to make names for themselves. They are greater than YHWH. They embrace the Occult, *Satan's-seed*. That is, they were obedient to Satan placing their self Will under his. The societies that developed from the descendants of Ham reflect their struggle against YHWH. Their religions included multiple gods in various states of conflict, which reflected their continuing war against YHWH. Men are often portrayed as slaves of the gods or sacrificed to appease the gods. They built temples probably trying to resemble the pyramid -shaped Garden of Eden. This reflects what the followers of Satan would consider an ongoing war with YHWH for control of the world. Nimrod continuing this war against YHWH built the tower of Babel, which caused mankind to lose their common language. These people fully embraced *Satan's-seed*.

Sons of Shem walked with and tried to be obedient to YHWH's commands. It was the lineage of Shem that continues to carry YHWH's only detailed chronology of the generations of mankind.

> Genesis 10 : 21-32
> 21 Unto Shem also, the father of all the children of Eber, the **brother of Japheth the elder**, even to him were children born.
> 22 **The children of Shem**; Elam, and Asshur, and Arphaxad, and Lud, and Aram.
> 23 And the children of Aram; Uz, and Hul, and Gether, and Mash.
> 24 And Arphaxad begat Salah; and Salah begat Eber.
> 25 And unto Eber were born two sons: **the name of one was Peleg; for in his days was the earth divided;** and his brother's name was Joktan.
> 26 And Joktan begat Almodad, and Sheleph, and Hazar-maveth, and Jerah,
> 27 And Hadoram, and Uzal, and Diklah,
> 28 And Obal, and Abimael, and Sheba,
> 29 And Ophir, and Havilah, and Jobab: all these were the sons of Joktan.
> 30 And their dwelling was from Mesha, as thou goest unto Sephar a mount of the east.
> 31 These are the sons of Shem, after their families, after their tongues, in their lands, after their nations.
> 32 These are the families of the sons of Noah, after their generations, in their nations: and by these were the nations divided in the earth after the flood.

The sons of Shem tried to be obedient to YHWH embracing *Eve's-seed*, which means the magnitude their Will places YHWH first in their lives. Sons of Shem was followers of YHWH. They tended to help other people come to know YHWH better and support other people by putting their needs before their own. They did not desire to enslave, control, or use other people.

In summary, just think about what it would be like if you and seven other family members were suddenly the only people to step out of the ark after a catastrophic flood that changed the entire earth's structure. You and your seven companion souls possess all the knowledge of your pre-flood world. You would be aware of airplanes, cars, trains, skyscrapers, cities, restaurants, books, writing, cell phones, television, governmental structure, farming, grocery stores, and the like; but this is of little or no use. The only true capability you and your companions have is your composite knowledge and your ability to apply this knowledge to your new environment. At least being from the same family, you would probably be able to communicate with each other. Your first priority would be establishing a reliable food source. After establishing yourself in the new environment and having children, what would you tell them about the pre-flood world and YHWH's disciplinary actions? Would you thank and give praise to YHWH for your new situation? Would you be angry with YHWH and just want to be left alone to survive? Would you be angry at YHWH, praise the pre-flood world, swear to get even with YHWH, and restore the pre-flood society?

Post-flood people Noah, Japheth, Shem, Ham, and their descendents exhibited all three of these primary soul types.

YHWH also used the lineage of Shem to document events relative to the AM calendar, Appendix I. Here we see the Tower of Babel, the confusing of mankind's language, occurs during the life time of Peleg in Genesis 10:25. Peleg's life is directly correlated to the AM calendar when the Tower of Babel is addressed.

VI   YHWH During the Tower of Babel

YHWH's WILL, the Holy Spirit, commanded Noah, Shem, Japheth, and Ham to be fruitful and replenish the earth in Genesis 9:1. This requires them to spread out over the face of the earth. In defiance to YHWH, the people influenced by *Satan's-seed* and led by Nimrod decide that they would prefer not to move and replenish the entire earth. Instead, they would build a tower and city for themselves per in Genesis 11:1-4.

Genesis 11:1-4
1   And the whole earth was of one language, and of one speech.
2   And it came to pass, as they journeyed from the east, that they found a plain in the land of Shinar; and they dwelt there.
3   And they said one to another, Go to, let us make brick, and burn them throughly. And they had brick for stone, and slime had they for morter.
4   And they said, Go to, let us build us a city and a tower, whose top may reach unto heaven; and let us make us a name, lest we be scattered abroad upon the face of the whole earth.

This is an attempt by those embracing *Satan's-seed* to restore the Garden of Eden from, which YHWH had banished them from. It represents a direct rejection of YHWH's WILL, the Holy Spirit, and YHWH does not ignore their sin. Again mankind is about to reap the harvest of their sin by experiencing YHWH's perfect justice and ***WRATH (t)*** as described in Genesis 11:5-9.

Genesis 11:5-9
5   And the Lord came down to see **[YHWH's BODY]** *the city and the tower, which the children of men builded.*
6   And the Lord said **[YHWH's WILL]**, *Behold, the people is one, and they have all one language; and this they begin to do: and now nothing will be restrained from them, which they have imagined to do.*
7   Go to, let us **[YHWH's SOUL, WILL and BODY]** *go down, and there confound their language, that they may not understand one another's speech.*
8   So the Lord scattered them abroad from thence upon the face of all the earth: and they left off to build the city.
9   Therefore is the name of it called Babel; because the Lord did there confound the language of all the earth: and from thence did the Lord scatter them abroad upon the face of all the earth.

When did the Tower of Babel occur? It occurred during the days of Peleg, per Genesis 10:25, and the generations between Shem and Peleg will establish the specific time period referenced to the AM calendar per Genesis 11:10-32.

Genesis 11:10-19
10   These are the generations of Shem: Shem was an hundred years old, and begat Arphaxad two years after the flood:
11   And Shem lived after he begat Arphaxad five hundred years, and begat sons and daughters.
12   And Arphaxad lived five and thirty years, and begat Salah:

13 And Arphaxad lived after he begat Salah four hundred and three years, and begat sons and daughters.
14 And Salah lived thirty years, and begat Eber:
15 And Salah lived after he begat Eber four hundred and three years, and begat sons and daughters.
16 And Eber lived four and thirty years, and begat **Peleg**:
17 And Eber lived after he begat Peleg four hundred and thirty years, and begat sons and daughters.
18 And **Peleg lived thirty years, and begat Reu:**
19 And **Peleg lived after he begat Reu two hundred and nine years**, and begat sons and daughters.

Note that during the days of Peleg, who lived a total of 239 years, the earth was divided as recorded in Genesis 10:25.

Genesis 11:20-32
20 And Reu lived two and thirty years, and begat Serug:
21 And Reu lived after he begat Serug two hundred and seven years, and begat sons and daughters.
22 And Serug lived thirty years, and begat Nahor:
23 And Serug lived after he begat Nahor two hundred years, and begat sons and daughters.
24 And Nahor lived nine and twenty years, and begat Terah:
25 And Nahor lived after he begat Terah an hundred and nineteen years, and begat sons and daughters.
26 And Terah lived seventy years, and begat Abram, Nahor, and Haran.
27 Now these are the generations of Terah: Terah begat Abram, Nahor, and Haran; and Haran begat Lot.
28 And Haran died before his father Terah in the land of his nativity, in Ur of the Chaldees.
29 And Abram and Nahor took them wives: the name of Abram's wife was Sarai; and the name of Nahor's wife, Milcah, the daughter of Haran, the father of Milcah, and the father of Iscah.
30 But Sarai was barren; she had no child.
31 And Terah took Abram his son, and Lot the son of Haran his son's son, and Sarai his daughter in law, his son Abram's wife; and they went forth with them from Ur of the Chaldees, to go into the land of Canaan; and they came unto Haran, and dwelt there.
32 And the days of Terah were two hundred and five years: and Terah died in Haran.

The period of time when YHWH spread mankind throughout the earth is computed based on the lineage from the creation of Adam, 0000 AM, via Seth to the birth of Peleg in the year 1758 AM. During the days of Peleg, the earth was divided per Genesis 10:25. Peleg lived during the 239 year period from 1758 AM to 1997 AM, which is identified by italic text in Appendix I. Before or near the beginning of the days of Peleg, Nimrod (the mighty one) dominated the society, and the people built the tower of Babel, Genesis 10:6. This was also a unique time when the polar ice caps were at their largest size and the seas were at their lowest level. Thus the newly formed continents and isles were easily populated during the 239 years of Peleg. During the days of Peleg, the world's population was dispersed physically by language group. As a result each new language group also developed a unique appearance and societal characteristics due to loss of genetic information because they did not intermarry with the other language groups.

Not only did each language group have their members' bodies impacted by the change through loss of genetic information, but each language group also experienced a loss of corporate societal knowledge. That is, each new language group when it was separated from the remainder of the world's society only contained a very limited amount of knowledge resident within the group. Remember that mankind's knowledge is just the accumulated knowledge contained in the souls of each of its members. Each new language group started with some common knowledge of the past and received additional knowledge from the environment in their new location. With the passage of time, the various language groups developed very unique societies as a direct result of their limited knowledge. Also, due to the limited genetic information, the physical characteristics of the various language groups changed due to inbreeding.

Noah died in 2007 AM after the death of Peleg, 1997 AM. The deaths of Ham and Japheth and their descendents are not dated. However, their response to YHWH's commands are identified in Genesis 10 because the days of Peleg included both Ham and Japheth generations.

Japheth and his descendents reflect a self-centered character and decided in Genesis 10:5 that it was in their best interest to get away from Ham's descendents, so they populated the isles of the gentiles, the new continents. It is possible that some of Japheth's descendents had construction, mapping. and navigational skills, which allowed them to explore and map some of the new continents and to built a city near the ocean, named Atlantis, to spite YHWH for destroying the original during Noah's flood. This would have occurred over hundreds of years while the Ice Age was at its peak and the oceans were at their lowest levels. At the end Ice Age the water level rose and destroyed the city, its society and much of its people's knowledge. This type of event could have been the mythical source of Plato's lost city of Atlantis.

Ham and his descendents, influenced by *Satan's-seed*, continued to defy YHWH, and they did not move but continued to build cities (Genesis 10:6-20). However, Shem and his descendents were influenced by the *Eve's-seed* and tried to be obedient to YHWH's commands and as such are identified specifically in the AM Calendar, Appendix I. The descendents, sons of Shem and Japheth, understood there are consequences associated with sin. Today as we look at all these ancient

73

societies around the world, we see the influence of *Satan's-seed*, *Eve's-seed* and those who rejected both and place self first. In the myths, history, and artifacts of ancient societies, we can see some of these characteristics.

The ancient societies that reflect the nature of Japheth, and embrace self populated northern Asia and America. They had lost nearly all the pre-flood knowledge, and they lost more knowledge as a result of the Tower of Babel and the rising waters as the Ice Age receded. They moved into new hostile environments where they became hunter-gatherers and reverted to primitive tools for survival. They became totally dependent upon nature and developed a reverence for it.

The ancient societies like the Egyptians, Sumerians and Incas reflect the nature of Ham who embrace *Satan's-seed.* Their artifacts include astronomy, mathematics, human sacrifice, and pyramids. The pyramids are typically four-sided, and some have large gardens. This may reflect the society's attempt to restore the Garden of Eden and overcome YHWH. In their accounts of creation, there are typically more than one god and the gods are in conflict and rebellion reflecting their struggle as gods against YHWH. They prefer cities like Babylon, Sodom, Gomorrah, and Nineveh. Like Nimrod, their leaders are dictatorial and control people by enslaving them. This is reminiscent of the men of renown before Noah's flood.

The ancient societies that reflected the nature of Shem, who embraced *Eve's-seed* are unique because it is through this line that YHWH continues to provide a detailed chronology of mankind's development. This society did not have any specific cities or nations, and many were herdsmen. Most important, is that from this society YHWH will begin to form a *Holy Nation* whose job it will be to restore all people in the world to a personal relationship with Him. Each member of this Holy Nation would individually reach out and bring others to YHWH for direct instruction.

The society that developed after 0000 OS and up to 2000 OS is referred to as the *Age of Desolation* [2] because it was during this period of time YHWH let individuals do exactly as they pleased. Those who decided to walk with YHWH He embraced. Those who rejected YHWH and lived in sin will eventually pay the consequences as Noah's flood and the Tower of Babel attest. Since the Original Sin, 0000 OS, 40 Jubilees of desolation have occurred then, 2000 OS brings the advent of a new age.

VII YHWH and 2000 OS

When YHWH brings to a close the Age of Desolation, He in His mercy initiates a new age, the *Age of the Torah*, which would provide mankind instruction about how to have a personal relationship with Him. The event that identified this point in time, 2000 OS, was Abraham's obedience to YHWH's request for him to sacrifice his son, Isaac.

The background leading up to the event marking 2000 OS started with the birth of Abram 1951 AM, Appendix I. Abram's birth occurred when both Noah and Shem were still alive.

YHWH started preparations for the new age by proceeding to test Abram with a series of requests. The first request occurred in 2026 AM when Abram was 75 years old. When YHWH appeared to Abram and told him to relocate per Genesis 12:1.

Genesis 12:1-4
1 Now the Lord had said **[YHWH's WILL]** unto Abram, Get thee out of thy country, and from thy kindred, and from thy father's house, unto a land that I will shew thee:
2 And I will make of thee a great nation, and I will bless thee, and make thy name great; and thou shalt be a blessing:
3 And I will bless them that bless thee, and curse him that curseth thee: and in thee shall all families of the earth be blessed.
4 So Abram departed, as the Lord had spoken unto him; and Lot went with him: and **Abram was seventy and five years old** when he departed out of Haran.

The history of Abram's wanderings began in 2026 AM in obedience to YHWH's command. The history of Abram's wanderings are documented in Genesis 12 through 16. In Genesis 17 YHWH counts Abram's obedience as righteousness and makes a covenant with him.

Genesis 17:1-27
1 And when **Abram was ninety years old and nine**, the Lord appeared to Abram, and said **[YHWH's BODY and WILL]** unto him, I am the Almighty God; walk before me, and be thou perfect.
2 And I will make my covenant between me and thee, and will multiply thee exceedingly.
3 And Abram fell on his face: and God talked with him, saying,
4 As for me, behold, my covenant is with thee, and thou shalt be a father of many nations.
5 **Neither shall thy name any more be called Abram, but thy name shall be Abraham; for a father of many nations have I made thee.**
6 And I will make thee exceeding fruitful, and I will make nations of thee, and kings shall come out of thee.
7 And I will establish my covenant between me and thee and thy seed after thee in their generations for an everlasting covenant, to be a God unto thee, and to thy seed after thee.

8 *And I will give unto thee, and to thy seed after thee, the land wherein thou art a stranger, all the land of Canaan, for an everlasting possession; and I will be their God.*

9 *And <u>God said</u>* **[YHWH's WILL]** *unto Abraham, Thou shalt keep my covenant therefore, thou, and thy seed after thee in their generations.*

10 *This is my covenant, which ye shall keep, between me and you and thy seed after thee; Every man child among you shall be circumcised.*

11 *And ye shall circumcise the flesh of your foreskin; and it shall be a token of the covenant betwixt me and you.*

12 *And he that is eight days* **[8 is the number that represents new beginnings]** *old shall be circumcised among you, every man child in your generations, he that is born in the house, or bought with money of any stranger, which is not of thy seed.*

13 *He that is born in thy house, and he that is bought with thy money, must needs be circumcised: and my covenant shall be in your flesh for an everlasting covenant.*

14 *And the uncircumcised man child whose flesh of his foreskin is not circumcised, that soul shall be cut off from his people; he hath broken my covenant.*

15 **And God said unto Abraham, As for Sarai thy wife, thou shalt not call her name Sarai, but Sarah shall her name be.**

16 *And I will bless her, and give thee a son also of her: yea, I will bless her, and she shall be a mother of nations; kings of people shall be of her.*

17 *Then Abraham fell upon his face, and laughed, and said in his heart,* **Shall a child be born unto him that is an hundred years old? and shall Sarah, that is ninety years old, bear?**

18 *And Abraham said unto God, O that Ishmael might live before thee!*

19 *And <u>God said</u>* **[YHWH's WILL]**, *Sarah thy wife shall bear thee a son indeed; and thou shalt call his name Isaac: and I will establish my covenant with him for an everlasting covenant, and with his seed after him.*

20 *And as for Ishmael, I have heard thee: Behold, I have blessed him, and will make him fruitful, and will multiply him exceedingly; twelve princes shall he beget, and I will make him a great nation.*

21 **But my covenant will I establish with Isaac, which Sarah shall bear unto thee at this set time in the next year.**

22 *And he left off talking with him, and God went up from Abraham.*

23 *And Abraham took Ishmael his son, and all that were born in his house, and all that were bought with his money, every male among the men of Abraham's house; and circumcised the flesh of their foreskin in the selfsame day, as God had said unto him.*

24 *And Abraham was ninety years old and nine, when he was circumcised in the flesh of his foreskin.*

25 *And Ishmael his son was thirteen years old, when he was circumcised in the flesh of his foreskin.*

26 *In the selfsame day was Abraham circumcised, and Ishmael his son.*

27 *And all the men of his house, born in the house, and bought with money of the stranger, were circumcised with him.*

Once Abraham is circumcised YHWH's covenant becomes unconditional, YHWH will make Abraham the father of many nations and give to him and his descendents all the land of Canaan for an everlasting possession. This is often referred to as the Abrahamic Covenant.

After YHWH has established His covenant with Abraham, He discusses the judgment of Sodom and Gomorrah with him and then proceeds to destroy them as described in Genesis 18 through 20.

As YHWH's appointed time of 2000 OS approaches, Isaac the son of promise, is born to Abraham and Sarah in Genesis 21:1-8.

Genesis 21:1-8
1 *And the Lord visited Sarah as he had said, and the Lord did unto Sarah as he had spoken.*
2 *For Sarah conceived, and bare Abraham a son in his old age, at the set time of which God had spoken to him.*
3 *And Abraham called the name of his son that was born unto him, whom Sarah bare to him, Isaac.*
4 ***And Abraham circumcised his son Isaac being eight days old, as God had commanded him.***
5 ***And Abraham was an hundred years old, when his son Isaac was born unto him.***
6 *And Sarah said, God hath made me to laugh, so that all that hear will laugh with me.*
7 *And she said, Who would have said unto Abraham, that Sarah should have given children suck? for I have born him a son in his old age.*
8 *And the child grew, and was weaned: and Abraham made a great feast the same day that Isaac was weaned.*

Isaac was born in the year 2051 AM when Abraham was 100 years old. Then as Isaac grows, Abraham continues to sojourn in the land for an unspecified period of time as described in Genesis 21:8-24:3. This unspecified period of time is important because it limits the ability to completely synchronize the OS and AM calendars.

The ultimate test for Abraham begins on 2000 OS at the start of the Age of the Torah and initiates the preparation of the Holy Nation, Israel. Abraham's test is described in Genesis 22.

Genesis 22
1 *And it came to pass after these things, that God did tempt Abraham, and said unto him, Abraham: and he said, Behold, here I am.*
2 *And he said, Take now thy son, thine only son Isaac, whom thou lovest, and get thee into the **land of Moriah; and offer him there for a burnt offering upon one of the mountains which I will tell thee of**.*
3 *And Abraham rose up early in the morning, and saddled his ass, and took two of his young men with him, and Isaac his son, and clave the wood for the burnt offering, and rose up, and went unto the place of which God had told him.*
4 *Then on the **third day** Abraham lifted up his eyes, and saw the place afar off.*

77

5 *And Abraham said unto his young men, Abide ye here with the ass; and I and the lad will go yonder and worship, and come again to you,*

6 *And Abraham took the wood of the burnt offering, and laid it upon Isaac his son; and he took the fire in his hand, and a knife; and they went both of them together.*

7 *And Isaac spake unto Abraham his father, and said, My father: and he said, Here am I, my son. And he said, Behold the fire and the wood: but where is the lamb for a burnt offering?*

8 *And Abraham said, My son, God will provide himself a lamb for a burnt offering: so they went both of them together.*

9 *And they came to the place which God had told him of; and Abraham built an altar there, and laid the wood in order, and bound Isaac his son, and laid him on the altar upon the wood.*

10 *And Abraham stretched forth his hand, and took the knife to slay his son.*

11 *And the angel of the Lord called unto him out of heaven, and said, Abraham, Abraham: and he said, Here am I.*

12 *And he said, Lay not thine hand upon the lad, neither do thou any thing unto him: for now I know that thou fearest God, seeing thou hast not withheld thy son, thine only son from me.*

13 *And Abraham lifted up his eyes, and looked, and behold behind him a ram caught in a thicket by his horns: and Abraham went and took the ram, and offered him up for a burnt offering in the stead of his son.*

14 *And Abraham called the name of that place Jehovah-jireh: as it is said to this day, In the mount of the Lord it shall be seen.*

15 *And the angel of the Lord called unto Abraham out of heaven the second time,*

16 *And said, By myself have I sworn, saith the Lord, for because thou hast done this thing, and hast not withheld thy son, thine only son:*

17 *That in blessing I will bless thee, and in multiplying I will multiply thy seed as the stars of the heaven, and as the sand which is upon the sea shore; and thy seed shall possess the gate of his enemies;*

18 ***And in thy seed shall all the nations of the earth be blessed; because thou hast obeyed my voice.***

19 *So Abraham returned unto his young men, and they rose up and went together to Beer-sheba; and Abraham dwelt at Beer-sheba.*

20 *And it came to pass after these things, that it was told Abraham, saying, Behold, Milcah, she hath also born children unto thy brother Nahor;*

21 *Huz his firstborn, and Buz his brother, and Kemuel the father of Aram,*

22 *And Chesed, and Hazo, and Pildash, and Jidlaph, and Bethuel.*

23 *And Bethuel begat **Rebekah**: these eight Milcah did bear to Nahor, Abraham's brother.*

24 *And his concubine, whose name was Reumah, she bare also Tebah, and Gaham, and Thahash, and Maachah.*

Abraham went to Mount Moriah, which is subsequently identified as the place where king Solomon built the Temple for YHWH in Jerusalem. Thus, Abraham was completely obedient to YHWH's request. The occurrence of 2000 OS is a very significant event that initiates a new age, the Age of the Torah, but its AM date is not given. Thus the correlation between the AM and OS calendars is bounded by

Isaac's birth in the year 2051 AM and the death of his mother Sarah. Sarah was 90 years old when Isaac was born.

Genesis 23:1-2
1 And Sarah was an hundred and seven and twenty years old: these were the years of the life of Sarah.
2 And Sarah died in Kirjath-arba; the same is Hebron in the land of Canaan: and Abraham came to mourn for Sarah, and to weep for her.

Sarah died in 2088 AM when she was 127 years old, which leaves 37 years unaccounted for. Isaac and Abraham's pilgrimage to Mount Moriah could have occurred at any time during the 37 year period. At this point in time the correlation between the AM and OS calendars is limited to 37 years. Thus the year 2000 OS would correspond to 2069 +/- 18.5 years AM.

In the year 2000 OS, YHWH begins to prepare a Holy Nation whose task it will be to bring the entire world to repentance and restore everyone's personal relationship with YHWH. This will be a huge challenge for the new nation.

From Genesis 23:3 through the remainder of the book of Genesis, YHWH constructs this Holy Nation. YHWH blesses Isaac and his wife Rebekah with twin sons, Esau and Jacob. Esau grieved Isaac and Rebekah when he married a Hittite. Rebekah then helped Jacob receive Esau's blessing from Isaac. Esau is mad, and Jacob flees to Laban, Rebekah's brother, to get a wife. Jacob is obedient, and YHWH blesses him as he served Laban 20 years for his two daughters and their handmaids. Then, YHWH told Jacob to leave the house of Laban with his family and flocks and return home. While Jacob was in route, he had a unique encounter as described in Genesis 32:24-32.

Genesis 32:24-32
24 And Jacob was left alone; and there wrestled a man with him until the breaking of the day.
25 And when he saw that he prevailed not against him, he touched the hollow of his thigh; and the hollow of Jacob's thigh was out of joint, as he wrestled with him.
26 And he said, Let me go, for the day breaketh. And he said, I will not let thee go, except thou bless me.
27 And he said unto him, What is thy name? And he said, Jacob.
28 And he said, **Thy name shall be called no more Jacob, but Israel**: for as a prince hast thou power with God and with men, and hast prevailed.
29 And Jacob asked him, and said, Tell me, I pray thee, thy name. And he said, Wherefore is it that thou dost ask after my name? And he blessed him there.
30 And Jacob called the name of the place Peniel: for I have seen God face to face, and my life is preserved.
31 And as he passed over Penuel the sun rose upon him, and he halted upon his thigh.
32 Therefore the children of Israel eat not of the sinew which shrank, which is upon the hollow of the thigh, unto this day: because he touched the hollow of Jacob's thigh in the sinew that shrank.

Jacob's name is now Israel and YHWH blesses him. YHWH also provided Israel twelve sons by four women as follows:

1st	- Reuben	- *Leah*
2nd	- Simeon	- *Leah*
3rd	- Levi	- *Leah*
4th	- Judah	- *Leah*
5th	- Dan	- *Bilhah*, Rachel's handmaid
6th	- Naphtali	- *Bilhah*, Rachel's handmaid
7th	- Gad	- *Zilpah*, Leah's handmaid
8th	- Asher	- *Zilpah,* Leah's handmaid
9th	- Issachar	- *Leah*
10th	- Zebulun	- *Leah*
11th	**- Joseph**	**- *Rachel***
12th	- Benjamin	- *Rachel*

These twelve sons of Israel and their descendants would form the twelve tribes that will form the Holy Nation of Israel.

If Israel is to be based on twelve tribes, then is there anything significant about the number twelve? Three is the number of completion, four is the number associated with creation. 4+3 = 7 implies the Holy Nation is for mankind's seven soul types. 4*3 = 12 implies Israel will be a Holy Nation. Also 6*2 = 12 where six is the number associated with mankind, and two is a number that may imply division or union depending upon its usage. 6*2 = 12 is a product and implies the Holy Nation's job is to bring mankind into unity with YHWH.

A nation includes a set of individual persons with some common beliefs and priorities that keep it together. A Holy Nation must have a set of common beliefs that makes them unique or set apart from all other nations. So, what does YHWH want the Holy Nation to be like? Everyone in the Holy Nation is to place YHWH first in their lives; their behavior should be an example to others; they need to respect and help other people to come to YHWH. A member of the Holy Nation must have the WILL associated with their soul equal to:

$$Will_{YHWH}(t) > Will_{other\,people}(t) > Will_{self}(t)$$

When this condition exists YHWH will pour out blessings upon the nation, which would make them the complete envy of all other people in the world. These overwhelming blessings would have made it much easier for the people of the Holy Nation, priests of YHWH, to bring the remaining people on earth back to YHWH. The objective of the Holy Nation is to bring every single individual in the world into a direct relationship with YHWH only. This means that no individual will rule over or take advantage of any other individual.

However, since the end of Noah's flood in 1657 AM, about 400 years have passed, and the descendants of Shem, Japheth and Ham have begun to repopulate the earth. This developing world society consists of people whose souls embraced Satan and self or self only or YHWH and self. It is probable that the distribution of these natures took the form of a normal distribution and retained it as the world population after Noah's flood 1657 AM increased. The key issue is what type of souls will control all the people in world.

Israel's twelve sons and families in the beginning have a problem with Satan and self because in their jealously ten of the brothers sold Joseph into slavery in Egypt. However, YHWH blessed Joseph in Egypt, which resulted in the relocation of Israel's entire family to Egypt in 2241 AM during the second year of the famine per Genesis 47:9. YHWH prospered the twelve tribes of Israel in Egypt. However, Egypt's government was based on *Satan's-seed* and did not recognize YHWH at all. So after the death of Joseph in 2312 AM the Egyptians became afraid of the Israelites and then enslaved them for over 300 years.

Why did YHWH place His developing Holy Nation under the rule of *Satan's-seed*? Among the Israelites were individuals having Will(t) for YHWH, self, and Satan. The Israelites who did not put YHWH first in their life and trust Him completely must change their $Will_{YHWH}(t)$ to be greater than their $Will_{self}(t)$. Living in slavery for over 300 years raises the people's $L_{YHWH}(t)$ and they call on YHWH for help. It also acquaints them with the type of people they will be required to minister to as priests of YHWH when the Holy Nation is completely formed.

After Noah's flood, followers of YHWH like all other people orally passed knowledge from one generation to the next. The twelve tribes of Israel living in slavery in Egypt have no documented historical record and have lost track of time. YHWH would restore time and their detailed history, but only after the Holy Nation is established.

YHWH raised up Moses to lead the twelve tribes of Israel out of the land of Egypt to freedom in the presence of YHWH. These people were in Egypt for a period of 430 years, Exodus 12:40-41. Moses confronted the Pharaoh with ten plagues, which resulted in the pharaoh allowing the Israelites to leave Egypt and their slavery on Passover on the fourteenth day of the first month in the year 2672 AM.

It is worthwhile at this point to pause and assess the state of the world's societies just prior to the Israelite's exodus from Egypt in 2672 AM.

81

When Noah's flood ended in 1657 AM he and his family were in the vicinity of Mesopotamia and the Tigris and Euphrates Rivers, which have pre-flood names. All the post-flood people's knowledge came from the eight souls — Noah and his family plus their subsequent experiences. Over the next 340 years, until after the Babel dispersion, they developed writing and then rapidly developed capabilities related to building sailboats, navigation, wheeled vehicles, metal smelting, irrigation systems, cities, temples with various gods, libraries, algebraic problems, geometric problems, astronomy, and medicine. This rapid societal knowledge increase must have been stimulated by their pre-flood knowledge.

The Babel dispersion was over by the time Peleg died in 1997 AM. Since then 703 years had passed and very unique societies have developed throughout the entire world. These societies reflect the loss of knowledge due to the language differences, dispersion around the world and the primary types of souls in a particular society.

Those who migrated to the Americas, northern Asia, and southern Africa were predominately descendents of Japheth and became hunter-gatherers in this harsh new environment and developed a close relationship with nature.

Those who had souls like Ham were builders of cities, pyramids, ziggurats, temples, multiple gods, and they were interested astronomy and mathematics. These societies possessed kings, or rulers, who were dictatorial. Typically these people did not relocate a great distance from Babel. They preferred warmer climates like Sumeria, India, Asia, Greece, and Egypt, and some made it as far as South America.

Egypt was the perfect example of a society that embraced *Satan's-seed*, the nature of Ham. It is in this environment that we find the Israelites in slavery learning to despise *Satan's-seed* and begging YHWH to help them.

It is important to note that <u>no society that existed in the world </u>at this point in time, 2672 AM, had any detailed precise historical records going back to the advent of mankind. Although there were various oral traditions reflecting some elements of truth, they all lacked historical detail. The detailed chronology based on the AM calendar that we have been reviewing did not even exist in 2672 AM. In fact, the Israelites who were slaves in Egypt did not even know what year it was.

However, the Holy Nation, which would become a blessing to all people was about to be born.

VIII   YHWH and the Holy Nation

Today from the examination of artifacts from ancient civilizations, it is obvious that none of them had a detailed chronology starting from the beginning of the earth's existence. A few ancient civilizations included accounts with a flood, but they all reflected oral tradition, man's limited knowledge, their type of soul and their ability to document the history accurately. The only exception is the Torah, the first five books of the Holy Bible, which is the only source of the AM calendar. However, in 2672 AM neither the Torah or the AM calendar existed.

Since 2000 OS YHWH had been preparing Abraham, Isaac, Jacob (Israel), his twelve sons, and their descendents to become the twelve tribes of Israel, which would eventually become the Holy Nation of Israel. These people were primarily herdsmen until they were forced into slavery by the Pharaoh in Egypt. The enslaved Israelites living in 2672 AM had no idea even what year it was.

In 2672 AM YHWH would intervene in history and initiate the formation of the Holy Nation, which would be under His direct leadership. YHWH began by reestablishing the AM calendar and then He established the Holy Nation on Passover as described in Exodus 12:1-44.

Exodus 12:1-44
1   And the_Lord spake_ **[YHWH's WILL]** *unto Moses and Aaron in the land of Egypt, saying,*
2   *This month shall be unto you the beginning of months: it shall be the* **first month of the year to you.**
3   *Speak ye unto all the congregation of Israel, saying, In the tenth day of this month they shall take to them every man a lamb, according to the house of their fathers, a lamb for an house:*
4   *And if the household be too little for the lamb, let him and his neighbour next unto his house take it according to the number of the souls; every man according to his eating shall make your count for the lamb.*
5   *Your lamb shall be without blemish, a male of the first year: ye shall take it out from the sheep, or from the goats:*
6   ***And ye shall keep it up until the fourteenth day of the same month: and the whole assembly of the congregation of Israel shall kill it in the evening.***
7   *And they shall take of the blood, and strike it on the two side posts and on the upper door post of the houses, wherein they shall eat it.*
8   *And they shall eat the flesh in that night, roast with fire, and unleavened bread; and with bitter herbs they shall eat it.*
9   *Eat not of it raw, nor sodden at all with water, but roast with fire; his head with his legs, and with the purtenance thereof.*
10 *And ye shall let nothing of it remain until the morning; and that which remaineth of it until the morning ye shall burn with fire.*
11 ***And thus shall ye eat it; with your loins girded, your shoes on your feet, and your staff in your hand; and ye shall eat it in haste: it is the Lord's passover.***

12 *For I will pass through the land of Egypt this night, and will smite all the firstborn in the land of Egypt, both man and beast; and against all the gods of Egypt I will execute judgment: I am the Lord.*

13 And the blood shall be to you for a token upon the houses where ye are: and when I see the blood, I will pass over you, and the plague shall not be upon you to destroy you, when I smite the land of Egypt.

14 And this day shall be unto you for a memorial; and ye shall keep it a feast to the Lord throughout your generations; ye shall keep it a feast by an ordinance for ever.

15 Seven days shall ye eat unleavened bread; even the first day ye shall put away leaven out of your houses: for whosoever eateth leavened bread from the first day until the seventh day, that soul shall be cut off from Israel.

16 And in the first day there shall be an holy convocation, and in the seventh day there shall be an holy convocation to you; no manner of work shall be done in them, save that which every man must eat, that only may be done of you.

17 And ye shall observe the feast of unleavened bread; for in this selfsame day have I brought your armies out of the land of Egypt: therefore shall ye observe this day in your generations by an ordinance for ever.

18 In the first month, on the fourteenth day of the month at even, ye shall eat unleavened bread, until the one and twentieth day of the month at even.

19 Seven days shall there be no leaven found in your houses: for whosoever eateth that which is leavened, even that soul shall be cut off from the congregation of Israel, whether he be a stranger, or born in the land.

20 Ye shall eat nothing leavened; in all your habitations shall ye eat unleavened bread.

21 Then Moses called for all the elders of Israel, and said unto them, Draw out and take you a lamb according to your families, and kill the passover.

22 And ye shall take a bunch of hyssop, and dip it in the blood that is in the bason, and strike the lintel and the two side posts with the blood that is in the bason; and none of you shall go out at the door of his house until the morning.

23 For the Lord will pass through to smite the Egyptians; and when he seeth the blood upon the lintel, and on the two side posts, the Lord will pass over the door, and will not suffer the destroyer to come in unto your houses to smite you.

24 And ye shall observe this thing for an ordinance to thee and to thy sons for ever.

25 And it shall come to pass, when ye be come to the land which the Lord will give you, according as he hath promised, that ye shall keep this service.

26 And it shall come to pass, when your children shall say unto you, What mean ye by this service?

27 That ye shall say, It is the sacrifice of the Lord's passover, who passed over the houses of the children of Israel in Egypt, when he smote the Egyptians, and delivered our houses. And the people bowed the head and worshipped.

28 And the children of Israel went away, and did as the Lord had commanded Moses and Aaron, so did they.

29 *And it came to pass, that at midnight the Lord smote all the firstborn in the land of Egypt, from the firstborn of Pharaoh that sat on his throne unto the firstborn of the captive that was in the dungeon; and all the firstborn of cattle.*

30 And Pharaoh rose up in the night, he, and all his servants, and all the Egyptians; and there was a great cry in Egypt; for there was not a house where there was not one dead.

31 And he called for Moses and Aaron by night, and said, Rise up, and get you forth from among my people, both ye and the children of Israel; and go, serve the Lord, as ye have said.

32 Also take your flocks and your herds, as ye have said, and be gone; and bless me also.

33 And the Egyptians were urgent upon the people, that they might send them out of the land in haste; for they said, We be all dead men.

34 And the people took their dough before it was leavened, their kneadingtroughs being bound up in their clothes upon their shoulders.

35 And the children of Israel did according to the word of Moses; and they borrowed of the Egyptians jewels of silver, and jewels of gold, and raiment:

36 And the Lord gave the people favour in the sight of the Egyptians, so that they lent unto them such things as they required. And they spoiled the Egyptians.

37 And the children of Israel journeyed from Rameses to Succoth, about six hundred thousand on foot that were men, beside children.

38 And a mixed multitude went up also with them; and flocks, and herds, even very much cattle.

39 And they baked unleavened cakes of the dough which they brought forth out of Egypt, for it was not leavened: because they were thrust out of Egypt, and could not tarry, neither had they prepared for themselves any victual.

40 Now the sojourning of the children of Israel, who dwelt in Egypt, was four hundred and thirty years.

41 And it came to pass at the end of the four hundred and thirty years, even the selfsame day it came to pass, that all the hosts of the Lord went out from the land of Egypt.

42 It is a night to be much observed unto the Lord for bringing them out from the land of Egypt: this is that night of the Lord to be observed of all the children of Israel in their generations.

43 And the_Lord said_ **[YHWH's WILL]** *unto Moses and Aaron, This is the ordinance of the Passover: There shall no stranger eat thereof:*

44 But every man's servant that is bought for money, when thou hast circumcised him, then shall he eat thereof.

YHWH's Holy Nation was born on Passover. Passover began at sundown with the killing of the lamb, eating, and marking the door posts with blood. Then at midnight, Exodus 12:29, all the first born of Egypt were killed by YHWH. The Pharaoh told the Israelites to leave Egypt before sunrise and they were obedient and they departed on the fourteenth day of the first month in the year 2672 AM before the end of Passover at sunset.

During their 430 year time in Egypt, the twelve sons of Israel and their families grew to over 600,000 persons. To be a Holy Nation all these people had to develop a $Will_{YHWH}(t)$, which is greater than their $Will_{self}(t)$. That is the people must completely rely on and serve YHWH. During the next three months, YHWH had to do a series of tests and miracles to improve the people's $Will_{YHWH}(t)$.

Remember that self's Will for YHWH is:

$$Will_{YHWH}(t) = L_{YHWH}(t) * F_{YHWH}(t) * P(t)$$

$$Anxiety_{YHWH}(t) = [L_{YHWH}(t) - F_{YHWH}(t)] * P(t)$$

Self's Will for self is:

$$Will_{self}(t) = L_{self}(t) * F_{self}(t) * P(t)$$

$$Anxiety_{self}(t) = [L_{self}(t) - F_{self}(t)] * P(t)$$

At the beginning of the Exodus, the soul types or natures of approximately 600,000 individuals were divided between self and YHWH or self, or self and Satan. The various soul types were probably distributed over the 600,000 people in accordance with a normal distribution. [2] The first test of the candidates for the Holy Nation occurs when they were confronted with the crossing of the Red Sea.

Exodus 14:1-31
1 *And the Lord spake unto Moses, saying,*
2 *Speak unto the children of Israel, that they turn and encamp before Pi-hahiroth, between Migdol and the sea, over against Baal-zephon: before it shall ye encamp by the sea.*
3 *For Pharaoh will say of the children of Israel, They are entangled in the land, the wilderness hath shut them in.*
4 *And I will harden Pharaoh's heart, that he shall follow after them; and I will be honoured upon Pharaoh, and upon all his host; that the Egyptians may know that I am the Lord. And they did so.*
5 *And it was told the king of Egypt that the people fled: and the heart of Pharaoh and of his servants was turned against the people, and they said, Why have we done this, that we have let Israel go from serving us?* **[YHWH sets up the test by placing Israelites in an untenable position, which will tempt the Egyptians to try and recover their slaves.]**
6 *And he made ready his chariot, and took his people with him:*
7 *And he took six hundred chosen chariots, and all the chariots of Egypt, and captains over every one of them.*
8 *And the Lord hardened the heart of Pharaoh king of Egypt, and he pursued after the children of Israel: and the children of Israel went out with an high hand.*
9 *But the Egyptians pursued after them, all the horses and chariots of Pharaoh, and his horsemen, and his army, and overtook them encamping by the sea, beside Pi-hahiroth, before Baal-zephon.*
10 *And when Pharaoh drew nigh, the children of Israel lifted up their eyes, and, behold, the Egyptians marched after them; and <u>they were sore afraid</u>* **[Anxiety$_{self}$(t) is high]** *: and the children of Israel <u>cried out unto the Lord.</u>* **[L$_{YHWH}$(t) increased]**

11 And they said unto Moses, Because there were no graves in Egypt, hast thou taken us away to die in the wilderness? wherefore hast thou dealt thus with us, to carry us forth out of Egypt?

12 Is not this the word that we did tell thee in Egypt, saying, Let us alone, that we may serve the Egyptians? For it had been better for us to serve the Egyptians, than that we should die in the wilderness. **[some Israelites Will$_{self}$(t) > Will$_{YHWH}$(t)]**

13 And Moses said unto the people, Fear ye not, stand still, and see the salvation of the Lord, which he will shew to you to day: for the Egyptians whom ye have seen to day, ye shall see them again no more for ever.

14 The Lord shall fight for you, and ye shall hold your peace.

15 And the Lord said unto Moses, Wherefore criest thou unto me? speak unto the children of Israel, that they go forward:

16 But lift thou up thy rod, and stretch out thine hand over the sea, and divide it: and the children of Israel shall go on dry ground through the midst of the sea.

17 And I, behold, I will harden the hearts of the Egyptians, and they shall follow them: and I will get me honour upon Pharaoh, and upon all his host, upon his chariots, and upon his horsemen.

18 And the Egyptians shall know that I am the Lord, when I have gotten me honour upon Pharaoh, upon his chariots, and upon his horsemen.

19 And the angel of God, which went before the camp of Israel, removed and went behind them; and the pillar of the cloud went from before their face, and stood behind them:

20 And it came between the camp of the Egyptians and the camp of Israel; and it was a cloud and darkness to them, but it gave light by night to these: so that the one came not near the other all the night.

21 And Moses stretched out his hand over the sea; and the <u>Lord caused</u> **[YHWH's WILL]** the sea to go back by a strong east wind all that night, and made the sea dry land, and the waters were divided.

22 And the children of Israel went into the midst of the sea upon the dry ground: and the waters were a wall unto them on their right hand, and on their left.

23 And the Egyptians pursued, and went in after them to the midst of the sea, even all Pharaoh's horses, his chariots, and his horsemen.

24 And it came to pass, that in the morning watch the Lord looked unto the host of the Egyptians through the pillar of fire and of the cloud, and troubled the host of the Egyptians,

25 And took off their chariot wheels, that they drave them heavily: so that the Egyptians said, Let us flee from the face of Israel; for the Lord fighteth for them against the Egyptians.

26 And the <u>Lord said</u> **[YHWH's WILL]** unto Moses, Stretch out thine hand over the sea, that the waters may come again upon the Egyptians, upon their chariots, and upon their horsemen.

27 And Moses stretched forth his hand over the sea, and the sea returned to his strength when the morning appeared; and the Egyptians fled against it; and the Lord overthrew the Egyptians in the midst of the sea.

28 And the waters returned, and covered the chariots, and the horsemen, and all the host of Pharaoh that came into the sea after them; there remained not so much as one of them.

29 But the children of Israel walked upon dry land in the midst of the sea; and the waters were a wall unto them on their right hand, and on their left.

30 Thus the Lord saved Israel that day out of the hand of the Egyptians; and Israel saw the Egyptians dead upon the sea shore.

31 And Israel saw that great work which the Lord did upon the Egyptians: and the people feared the Lord [$L_{YHWH}(t)$ **increased**], and believed the Lord, and his servant Moses [$F_{YHWH}(t)$ **increased**].

The souls of the Israelites changed with the Red Sea crossing:

1. The Israelites $Will_{YHWH}(t)$ is increased because their *L*ove and *F*aith in YHWH is increased.

2. The Israelites $Will_{Egypt}(t)$ is decreased because their *L*ove and *F*aith for Egypt is decreased.

3. The Israelites $Will_{self}(t)$ is unchanged because their *L*ove and *F*aith for themselves is unchanged.

By now nearly, all the members of this small nation have rejected Egypt, *Satan's-seed*, and the magnitude of their $F_{YHWH}(t)$ was very high. All the people knew YHWH could do anything. Now the people must deal with their own $Will_{self}(t)$, which was the focus of YHWH's second test as described in Exodus 15:22-27.

Exodus 15:22-27

22 So Moses brought Israel from the Red sea, and they went out into the wilderness of Shur; and they went three days in the wilderness, and **found no water**.

23 And when they came to Marah, they could not drink of the waters of Marah, for they were bitter: therefore the name of it was called Marah.

24 And the people murmured against Moses, saying, What shall we drink?

25 And he cried unto the Lord; and the Lord shewed him a tree, which when he had cast into the waters, **the waters were made sweet:** there he made for them a statute and an ordinance, and there he proved them,

26 And said, If thou wilt diligently hearken to the voice of the Lord thy God **[YHWH's WILL]**, and wilt do that which is right in his sight, and wilt give ear to his commandments, and keep all his statutes, I will put none of these diseases upon thee, which I have brought upon the Egyptians: for I am the Lord that healeth thee.

27 And they came to Elim, where were twelve wells of water, and threescore and ten palm trees: and they encamped there by the waters.

YHWH made it clear through Moses that to be a Holy Nation, all the people had to change so that their own $Will_{YHWH}(t) > Will_{self}(t)$. To check if the people comprehended what Moses told them, YHWH prepared a third test, which is described in Exodus 16.

Exodus 16

1 And they took their journey from Elim, and all the congregation of the children of Israel came unto the wilderness of Sin, which is between Elim and Sinai, on the **fifteenth day of the second month after their departing out of the land** of Egypt.

2 And the whole congregation of the children of Israel murmured against Moses and Aaron in the wilderness:

3 And the children of Israel said unto them, Would to God we had died by the hand of the Lord in the land of Egypt, when we sat by the flesh pots, and when we did eat bread to the full; for ye have brought us forth into this wilderness, **to kill this whole assembly with hunger.**

4 Then <u>said the Lord</u> **[YHWH's WILL]** unto Moses, Behold, I will rain bread from heaven for you; and the people shall go out and gather a certain rate every day, that I may prove them, whether they will walk in my law, or no.

5 And it shall come to pass, that on the sixth day they shall prepare that which they bring in; and it shall be twice as much as they gather daily.

6 And Moses and Aaron said unto all the children of Israel, At even, then ye shall know that the Lord hath brought you out from the land of Egypt:

7 And in the morning, then ye shall see the glory of the Lord; for that he heareth your murmurings against the Lord: and what are we, that ye murmur against us?

8 And Moses said, This shall be, when the Lord shall give you in the evening flesh to eat, and in the morning bread to the full; for that <u>the Lord heareth</u> **[YHWH's BODY] your murmurings which ye murmur against him:** and what are we? your murmurings are not against us, but against the Lord.

9 And Moses spake unto Aaron, Say unto all the congregation of the children of Israel, Come near before the Lord: for he hath heard your murmurings.

10 And it came to pass, as Aaron spake unto the whole congregation of the children of Israel, that they looked toward the wilderness, and, behold, the <u>glory of the Lord</u> **[YHWH's SOUL]** appeared in the cloud.

11 And the <u>Lord spake</u> **[YHWH's WILL]** unto Moses, saying,

12 I have heard the murmurings of the children of Israel: speak unto them, saying, At even ye shall eat flesh, and in the morning ye shall be filled with bread; and ye shall know that I am the Lord your God.

13 And it came to pass, that at even the quails came up, and covered the camp: and in the morning the dew lay round about the host.

14 And when the dew that lay was gone up, behold, upon the face of the wilderness there lay a small round thing, as small as the hoar frost on the ground.

15 And when the children of Israel saw it, they said one to another, It is manna: for they wist not what it was. And Moses said unto them, This is the bread which the Lord hath given you to eat.

16 This is the thing which the Lord hath commanded, Gather of it every man according to his eating, an omer for every man, according to the number of your persons; take ye every man for them which are in his tents.

17 And the children of Israel did so, and gathered, some more, some less.

18 And when they did mete it with an omer, he that gathered much had nothing over, and he that gathered little had no lack; they gathered every man according to his eating.

19 And Moses said, Let no man leave of it till the morning.

89

20 Notwithstanding they hearkened not unto Moses; but some of them left of it until the morning, and it bred worms, and stank: and Moses was wroth with them.
21 And they gathered it every morning, every man according to his eating: and when the sun waxed hot, it melted.
22 And it came to pass, that on the sixth day they gathered twice as much bread, two omers for one man: and all the rulers of the congregation came and told Moses.
23 And he said unto them, This is that which the Lord hath said, To morrow is the rest of the holy sabbath unto the Lord: bake that which ye will bake to day, and seethe that ye will seethe; and that which remaineth over lay up for you to be kept until the morning.
24 And they laid it up till the morning, as Moses bade: and it did not stink, neither was there any worm therein.
25 And Moses said, Eat that to day; for to day is a sabbath unto the Lord: to day ye shall not find it in the field.
26 Six days ye shall gather it; but on the seventh day, which is the sabbath, in it there shall be none.
27 And it came to pass, that there went out <u>some of the people on the seventh day for to gather, and they found none.</u> [$Will_{self}(t) > Will_{YHWH}(t)$)]
28 And the <u>Lord said</u> [YHWH's WILL] unto Moses, How long refuse ye to keep my commandments and my laws?
29 See, for that the Lord hath given you the sabbath, therefore he giveth you on the sixth day the bread of two days; abide ye every man in his place, let no man go out of his place on the seventh day.
30 So the people rested on the seventh day.
31 And the house of Israel called the name thereof Manna: and it was like coriander seed, white; and the taste of it was like wafers made with honey.
32 And Moses said, This is the thing which the Lord commandeth, Fill an omer of it to be kept for your generations; that they may see the bread wherewith I have fed you in the wilderness, when I brought you forth from the land of Egypt.
33 And Moses said unto Aaron, Take a pot, and put an omer full of manna therein, and lay it up before the Lord, to be kept for your generations.
34 As the Lord commanded Moses, so Aaron laid it up before the Testimony, to be kept.
35 And the children of Israel did eat manna forty years, until they came to a land inhabited; they did eat manna, until they came unto the borders of the land of Canaan.
36 Now an omer is the tenth part of an ephah.

What is the problem? The people now have a very high value of $F_{YHWH}(t)$. They knew YHWH could provide anything at any time he chooses. YHWH justifies one by the magnitude of their faith in Him, because the source of self's faith could only come from Him. Faith in YHWH cannot be the problem.

The people knew that they were hungry (high magnitude of $F_{self-hunger}(t)$), and they had a very high priority on themselves (very high magnitude of $L_{self}(t)$). The result was that their $L_{self}(t) > L_{YHWH}(t)$ making their $Will_{self}(t) > Will_{YHWH}(t)$. The

90

result was many of the people believed that YHWH was their servant and YHWH should have provided what they wanted when they wanted it or they had the right to complain. The problem was who was serving whom?

Now the fourth test was a repeat of the second test, but now the people were fully aware of what YHWH expected of them, so there was no excuse. The fourth test is described in Exodus 17:1-7.

Exodus 17:1-7
1 *And all the congregation of the children of Israel journeyed from the wilderness of Sin, after their journeys, according to the commandment of the Lord, and pitched in Rephidim: and* **there was no water for the people to drink***.*
2 *Wherefore the people did chide with Moses, and said, Give us water that we may drink. And Moses said unto them, Why chide ye with me?* **wherefore do ye tempt the Lord?***
3 *And the people thirsted there for water; and the people murmured against Moses, and said, Wherefore is this that thou hast brought us up out of Egypt, to kill us and our children and our cattle with thirst?*
4 *And Moses cried unto the Lord, saying, What shall I do unto this people? they be almost ready to stone me.*
5 *And the Lord said unto Moses, Go on before the people, and take with thee of the elders of Israel; and thy rod, wherewith thou smotest the river, take in thine hand, and go.*
6 *Behold, I will stand before thee there upon the rock in Horeb; and thou shalt smite the rock, and there shall come water out of it, that the people may drink. And Moses did so in the sight of the elders of Israel.*
7 *And he called the name of the place Massah, and Meribah, because of the chiding of the children of Israel, and because* **they tempted the Lord***, saying, Is the Lord among us, or not?*

Those people who were tempting YHWH knew what they should do, wait patiently for YHWH to provide for them in His time, but for these people it was not about YHWH; it was about themselves. Those who were tempting YHWH continued to place their $Will_{self}(t) > Will_{YHWH}(t)$.

YHWH had given the people the opportunity to change their priorities by performing miracles for them. However, not all the people had gotten the message so YHWH could instruct the people directly from Mount Sinai.

Exodus 19:1-20:21
1 **In the third month***, when the children of Israel were gone forth out of the land of Egypt, the same day came they into the wilderness of Sinai.*
2 *For they were departed from Rephidim, and were come to the desert of Sinai, and had pitched in the wilderness; and there Israel camped before the mount.*
3 *And Moses went up unto God, and the* <u>Lord called</u> **[YHWH's WILL]** *unto him out of the mountain, saying, Thus shalt thou say to the house of Jacob, and tell the children of Israel;*

4 *Ye have seen what I did unto the Egyptians, and how I bare you on eagles' wings, and brought you unto myself.*

5 *Now therefore, **if ye will obey my voice indeed, and keep my covenant,** then ye shall be a peculiar treasure unto me above all people: for all the earth is mine:*

6 *And ye shall be unto me **a kingdom of priests, and an holy nation**. These are the words which thou shalt speak unto the children of Israel.*

7 *And Moses came and called for the elders of the people, and laid before their faces all these words which the Lord commanded him.*

8 *And all the people answered together, and said, All that the Lord hath spoken we will do. And Moses returned the words of the people unto the Lord.*

9 *And the <u>Lord said</u> [**YHWH's WILL**] unto Moses, Lo, I come unto thee in a **thick cloud**, that the people may hear when I speak with thee, and believe thee for ever. And Moses told the words of the people unto the Lord.*

10 *And the <u>Lord said</u> [**YHWH's WILL**] unto Moses, Go unto the people, and sanctify them today and tomorrow, and let them wash their clothes,*

11 *And be ready against the **third day**: for the third day the Lord will come down in the sight of all the people upon Mount Sinai.*

12 *And thou shalt set bounds unto the people round about, saying, Take heed to yourselves, that ye go not up into the mount, or touch the border of it: whosoever toucheth the mount shall be surely put to death:*

13 *There shall not an hand touch it, but he shall surely be stoned, or shot through; whether it be beast or man, it shall not live: when the trumpet soundeth long, they shall come up to the mount.*

14 *And Moses went down from the mount unto the people, and sanctified the people; and they washed their clothes.*

15 *And he said unto the people, Be ready against the third day: come not at your wives.*

16 *And it **came to pass on the third day** in the morning, that there were thunders and lightnings, and a thick cloud upon the mount, and the voice of the trumpet exceeding loud; so that all the people that were in the camp trembled.*

17 *And Moses brought forth the people out of the camp to meet with God; and they stood at the nether part of the mount.*

18 *And Mount Sinai was altogether on a smoke, because the <u>Lord descended upon it in fire</u> [**YHWH's SOUL**]: and the smoke thereof ascended as the smoke of a furnace, and the whole mount quaked greatly.*

19 *And when the voice of the trumpet sounded long, and waxed louder and louder, Moses spake, and <u>God answered him by a voice</u> [**YHWH's WILL via His BODY**].*

20 *And the Lord came down upon Mount Sinai, on the top of the mount: and the Lord called Moses up to the top of the mount; and Moses went up.*

21 *And the Lord said unto Moses, Go down, charge the people, lest they break through unto the Lord to gaze, and many of them perish.*

22 *And let the priests also, which come near to the Lord, sanctify themselves, lest the Lord break forth upon them.*

23 *And Moses said unto the Lord, The people cannot come up to Mount Sinai: for thou chargedst us, saying, Set bounds about the mount, and sanctify it.*

24 *And the Lord said unto him, Away, get thee down, and thou shalt come up, thou, and Aaron with thee: but let not the priests and the people break through to come up unto the Lord, lest he break forth upon them.*
25 *So Moses went down unto the people, and spake unto them.*

Exodus 20:1-21

1 *And <u>God spake all these words</u> [**YHWH's WILL via His BODY**], saying,*
2 *I am the Lord thy God, which have brought thee out of the land of Egypt, out of the house of bondage.*
3 *Thou shalt have no other gods before me.*
4 *Thou shalt not make unto thee any graven image, or any likeness of any thing that is in heaven above, or that is in the earth beneath, or that is in the water under the earth:*
5 *Thou shalt not bow down thyself to them, nor serve them: for I the Lord thy God am a jealous God, visiting the iniquity of the fathers upon the children unto the third and fourth generation of them that hate me;*
6 *And shewing mercy unto thousands of them that love me, and keep my commandments.*
7 *Thou shalt not take the name of the Lord thy God in vain; for the Lord will not hold him guiltless that taketh his name in vain.*
8 *Remember the sabbath day, to keep it holy.*
9 *Six days shalt thou labour, and do all thy work:*
10 *But the seventh day is the sabbath of the Lord thy God: in it thou shalt not do any work, thou, nor thy son, nor thy daughter, thy manservant, nor thy maidservant, nor thy cattle, nor thy stranger that is within thy gates:*
11 *For in six days the Lord made heaven and earth, the sea, and all that in them is, and rested the seventh day: wherefore the Lord blessed the sabbath day, and hallowed it.*
12 *Honour thy father and thy mother: that thy days may be long upon the land which the Lord thy God giveth thee*
13 *Thou shalt not kill.*
14 *Thou shalt not commit adultery.*
15 *Thou shalt not steal.*
16 *Thou shalt not bear false witness against thy neighbour.*
17 *Thou shalt not covet thy neighbour's house, thou shalt not covet thy neighbour's wife, nor his manservant, nor his maidservant, nor his ox, nor his ass, nor any thing that is thy neighbour's.*
18 *And all the people saw the thunderings, and the lightnings, and the noise of the trumpet, and the mountain smoking: and when the people saw it, they removed, and stood afar off.*
19 ***And they said unto Moses, Speak thou with us, and we will hear: but let not God speak with us, lest we die.***
20 *And Moses said unto the people, Fear not: **for God is come to prove you, and that his fear may be before your faces, that ye sin not.***
21 *And the people stood afar off, and Moses drew near unto the thick darkness where God was.*

Exodus 19:19-20 describes a monumental event that changed history when Israel, *the Holy Nation*, became Israel, *the Rebellious Nation*, by rejecting YHWH's direct presence and leadership by asking for Moses instead. The Holy Nation began on the fourteenth day of the first month, Passover, in the year 2672 AM and fell on the third day of the third month in the year 2672 AM. The Holy Nation existed less than three months. The people of the Holy Nation were just as intelligent if not more than anyone today. These people clearly understood what YHWH was asking them do. They had to submit to YHWH and be obedient to His personal instruction. YHWH's personal instruction included the Ten Commandments, which specified how the people must set their individual soul priorities, $L(t)$s, and $Will(t)$s to become a member of the Holy Nation. To be a member of the Holy Nation, an individual had to place YHWH first as shown in Figure VIII-1.

Figure VIII-1 shows all possible ratios or percentages for composition of self's soul as a member of the Holy Nation. No one could be a member of the Holy Nation if the magnitude of their $Will_{self}(t)$ was above the *Repentance Threshold* where one's $Will_{YHWH}(t) = Will_{self}(t) = 0.5$ or 50%. When self's $Will_{self}(t)$ is above the *Repentance Threshold,* he must repent, change the composition of his soul's Wills. To do this requires altering the equation $Will(t) = L(t) * F(t) * P(t)$ for both YHWH and self. $L(t)$ is self's Love (priority) for anything and YHWH told the people at Mount Sinai that these must be in accordance with the Ten Commandments. $F(t)$ is self's Faith (confidence) in anything, and the magnitude of $F(t)$ is the reconciliation of one's expectation versus the actual result. Thus, the magnitude of $F(t)$ is a direct measure of one's confidence, faith, trust in YHWH. No wonder YHWH justifies an individual by their faith in Him. Expectations varied from YHWH is trustworthy, to YHWH must give us what we want, to YHWH is a slave master.

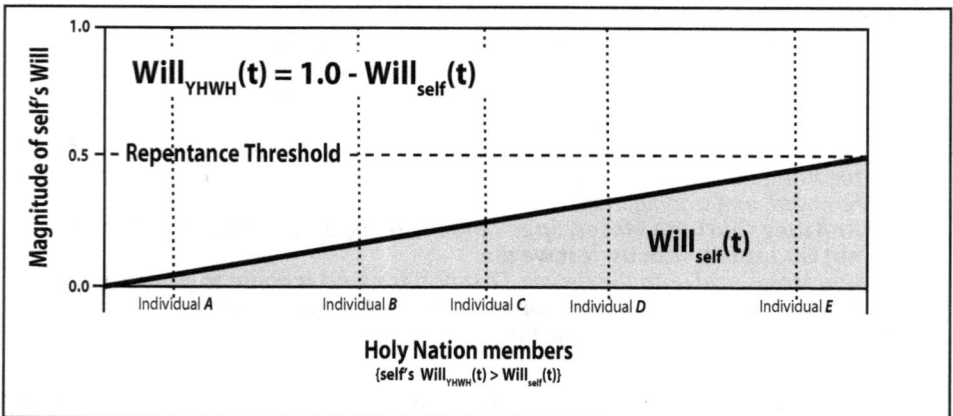

Figure VIII-1 Soul Composition for Holy Nation Members

If each individual at Mount Sinai had listened to YHWH and then placed their *F(t)* in Him and accepted personal responsibility to adjusted their *L(t)*s according to the Ten Commandments, then the entire nation would have conformed to Figure VIII-1. The entire nation would have been holy and blessed by YHWH beyond anyone's imagination. As a member of the Holy Nation each individual would have been a priest or direct representative of YHWH, like Moses. They would have served each other and eventually brought all the other people in the world to YHWH. YHWH would have showered them as individuals and as a nation with prosperity that would have made them and their converts the envy of all people and nations of the world. Their job was to be obedient to YHWH, reach out and serve others so that the world would develop into a single nation with everyone directly responsible to YHWH. That is, no individual would rule over any other person. There would be no kings or men of renown or man made governments dictating to the people.

Although all the people of the Holy Nation had experienced YHWH's great miracles during their exodus from Egypt when they stood before YHWH at Mount Sinai, the distribution of their types of souls became apparent. There were committed followers of YHWH; those who were self-centered and expected YHWH to give them what they wanted when they wanted it; and those who felt they were YHWH's slaves.

However, when the people were at the base of Mount Sinai they had to decide to directly submit to YHWH and accept Him and the Ten commandments as described in Exodus 20:3-17 or become a Rebellious Nation. The normal distribution of the people's souls caused the majority of the people to place their $Will_{self}(t) > Will_{YHWH}(t)$ and the peoples decision was to rebel. This monumental non-recoverable decision is shown in Appendix III, and it changed the character of the Age of the Torah.

YHWH's process for dealing with mankind had remained perfectly consistent since the Garden of Eden:

1. YHWH told the individual(s) what He expected them to do and the consequences for non compliance.

2. YHWH allowed individual(s) to decide what they would do.

3. YHWH would bless obedience and He would tell the individual(s) what must be done to reconcile with Him.

YHWH in dealing with His rejection was merciful, not giving the individual(s) what was deserved, but allowed them time for repentance before their time of accountability, the *first-death*. YHWH also showed His amazing grace by providing the individual(s) an alternate means to reconcile with Him.

The people's rejection of YHWH at Mount Sinai is sin and warrants death. However, YHWH is merciful and concedes to communicating with the people through Moses, which changes the course of history. The new course of history reflects two different paths:

1. In the future YHWH will take on a human body, Jesus the Messiah, and instruct and lead the people in place Moses. This future event will usher in the Age of the Messiah, which will be addressed in Chapter X, YHWH the *Son of Man*, 4000 OS.

2. YHWH will mercifully give the Rebellious Nation of Israel the Tabernacle, which is a perfect picture of a personal relationship with YHWH. The feasts also define YHWH's appointed time of reconciliation. YHWH will still provide Moses the Torah, which provides a detailed record of creation, the development of mankind, and the development of the Holy Nation. The Torah will be a blessing to all mankind.

The Tabernacle

The Rebellious Nation could no longer fulfill the mission of the Holy Nation. The Rebellious Nation could not go back in time and change its decision. It could only strive to change its members souls from YHWH-self, self, Satan-self to everyone with a nature of YHWH-self. That is, each individual's soul must reflect a $Will_{YHWH}(t) > Will_{self}(t)$, as shown in Figure VIII-1.

YHWH wanted all people to willingly submit themselves to Him. YHWH was merciful and communicates His desires and commands through Moses to the people as they had requested. YHWH also provided the people aids to help them recover from their bad decision to reject Him because they must return to the state of a Holy Nation before they could accomplish their assigned mission as priests of YHWH. YHWH mercifully gave the Rebellious Nation of Israel the Tabernacle, which was a perfect picture of a personal relationship with YHWH. The feasts and sabbaths associated with the Tabernacle picture YHWH's future appointed times that resulted from their rejection of Him at Mount Sinai.

At Mount Sinai YHWH gave the Ten Commandments to the people, which told them how they needed to align their soul's $L(t)s$, priorities, to become priests of YHWH. The Ten Commandments were open in character, which means that the people could do whatever they want as long as their priorities were consistent with them. However, when YHWH begins to speak through Moses His direction took on a closed character. That is, giving specific laws that told the people what they had to do to reconcile with Him. In Exodus 21 through 31, YHWH gave directions through Moses to the Rebellious Nation establishing how they must build the Tabernacle. Figure VIII-2 shows a functional diagram of the Tabernacle, which was developed in the book *Self's Destiny and Self.* [2] The Tabernacle was a magnificent structure that contains a physical representation of YHWH's image and how every individual must relate to Him. The feasts and Sabbaths associated with the Tabernacle point to future ages—the Age of the Messiah and the Age of the Kingdom.

How does the Tabernacle illustrate a personal relationship with YHWH? A personal relationship with YHWH, Figure VIII-2, is a circular or closed loop process. This process can be entered at any point.

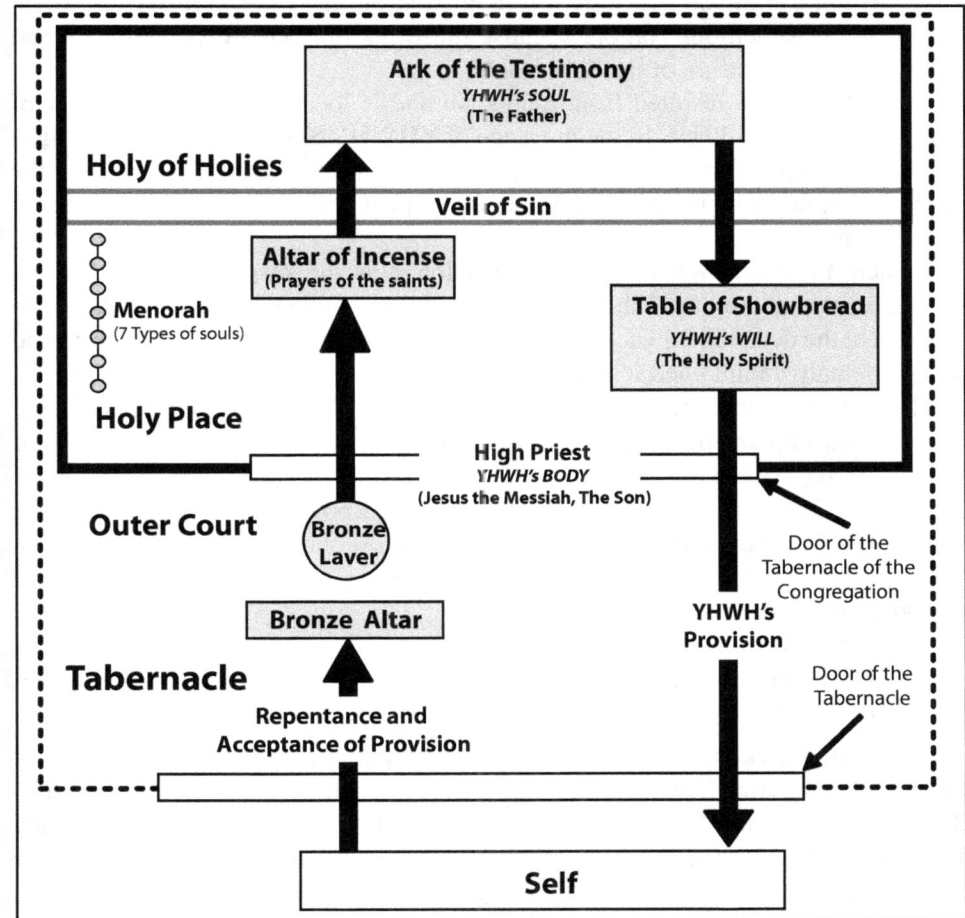

Figure VIII-2 The Tabernacle

Starting in the Holy of Holies, which contains the Ark of the Testimony that represents YHWH's SOUL, His Glory. YHWH's SOUL contains perfect knowledge, and is the source His perfect decisions, expectation, and authority. The Ark of the Testimony contains the Ten Commandments, manna and Aaron's Rod.

The Ten commandments were given by YHWH's voice to the people of the Holy Nation before they rejected Him, and later He provided a written copy on non negotiable stone, which was placed in the Ark of the Testimony. The Ten Commandments still define how YHWH expected an individual to align his priorities and Wills for a personal relationship with Him.

The Ten Commandments are different from the laws that were provided via Moses to the Rebellious Nation, because those laws directed civil activities and implement the operation of the Tabernacle.

The Veil of Sin resulted from man's sin and is located between the Holy of Holies and the Holy Place. In the presence of YHWH's SOUL, the Holy of Holies, the consequence of sin is death. The Veil of Sin protected the souls of all the people from death while giving them time to repent, and this is another symbol of YHWH's mercy and grace.

When YHWH's SOUL makes a decision it is the responsibility YHWH's WILL, represented by the Table of Showbread, to provide whatever is required to implement the decision for each individual or all mankind. The Table of Showbread was perpetually maintained with new loaves of bread, which represented YHWH's everlasting provision. YHWH's WILL also utilizes YHWH's BODY, the High Priest, when implementing speech or other actions directed to the people at their level.

Next, in Figure VIII-2 is the individual whose responsibility it was to accept or reject YHWH's provision. The individual had to respond by bringing his offering to the Bronze Altar in the outer court of the Tabernacle. The individual's possible responses were to:

- Offer their best—be a follower of YHWH.
- Offer their seconds—be a self-centered person like Cain.
- Offer nothing—be a follower of Satan.

Only an individual's bringing his best offering to the Bronze Altar in the outer court of the Tabernacle will have it inputted to the Altar of Incense by YHWH's BODY the High Priest for blessing by YHWH's SOUL. The High Priest represented YHWH's direct interface with all individuals in the world at a human level. The High Priest was like the gate keeper to a good personal relationship with YHWH, which was represented by the Holy Place.

This completes the circular path that forms the basic personal relationship between an individual and YHWH per in Figure VIII-2. This circular process implies that as an individual placed his $L(t)$ on YHWH, relied on Him, YHWH would meet his needs and the individual's $F(t)$ would increase. Thus, an individual's $Will_{YHWH}(t)$ would continuously increase. The Tabernacle literally could sort the types of souls that the people had.

The seven-branched Menorah in the Tabernacle was and is symbolic of the seven types of mankind's souls with its lamps that symbolize eternal life. The seven-branched Menorah also reflects the seven basic colors of the rainbow and each unique soul type has its own color in the spectrum. Previously there were three primary types of souls, followers of YHWH, self-centered, and followers of Satan.

The shape of the Menorah is unique with six branches attached to the center branch. Does the length of each Menorah branch reflect a particular type of soul? Consider that the length of each Menorah branch is proportional to the magnitude of self's $Will_{YHWH}(t)$ or $Will_{self}(t)$ or $Will_{Satan}(t)$ at the mid point of each soul type as shown in Figure VIII-3.

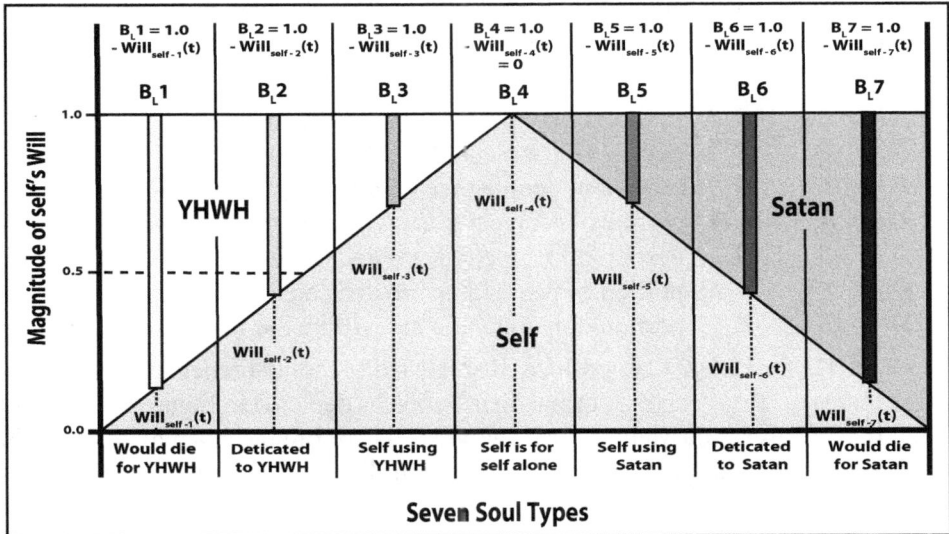

Figure VIII-3 Soul Composition versus Menorah Branch Length

Each Menorah branch has length $(B_L x)$ where $x = 1$ through 7

$B_L 1 = $ ***Will***$_{YHWH}(t) = 1.0 - $ ***Will***$_{self\ -1}(t)$ Self is willing to die for YHWH.

$B_L 2 = $ ***Will***$_{YHWH}(t) = 1.0 - $ ***Will***$_{self-2}(t)$ Self is dedicated to YHWH.

$B_L 3 = $ ***Will***$_{YHWH}(t) = 1.0 - $ ***Will***$_{self-3}(t)$ Self first, then YHWH.

$B_L 4 = $ ***Will***$_{YHWH}(t) = 1.0 - $ ***Will***$_{self-4}(t) = 0$ Self is willing kill any opposition.

$B_L 5 = $ ***Will***$_{Satan}(t) = 1.0 - $ ***Will***$_{self-5}(t)$ Self first, then Satan.

$B_L 6 = $ ***Will***$_{Satan}(t) = 1.0 - $ ***Will***$_{self-6}(t)$ Self is dedicated to Satan.

$B_L 7 = $ ***Will***$_{Satan}(t) = 1.0 - $ ***Will***$_{self-7}(t)$ Self is willing to die for Satan.

The seven-branched Menorah is made of gold, which show that mankind's seven types of souls are precious to YHWH and its lamps were kept continuously burning, which is symbolic of eternal life.

The seven-branched Menorah has another unique property, and that is when the branch length is subtracted from the center branch and the result is place on top of the branch a normal distribution appears as shown in Figure VIII-4. Note, when the center branch $B_L 4 = 0$ for either YHWH or Satan is subtracted from the center support the result is the magnitude of ***Will***$_{self}(t) = 1.0.$

It is also possible that the volume of the Menorah is equal to the world's population and when the volume of each Menorah branch (B_V) is subtracted from the volume of the center stand (B_{Vself}) reflects the portion (D) of the world population with a particular type of soul. $D1$ through $D7$ are computed as follows.

$D1 = (B_{Vself} - B_V 1)$ portion of people that are willing die for YHWH.

$D2 = (B_{Vself} - B_V 2)$ portion of people that are dedicated to YHWH.

$D3 = (B_{Vself} - B_V 3)$ portion of people that are dedicated to self then YHWH.

$D4 = (B_{Vself} - B_V 4)$ portion of people that are willing to murder their opposition.

$D5 = (B_{Vself} - B_V 5)$ portion of people that are dedicated to self then Satan

$D6 = (B_{Vself} - B_V 6)$ portion of people that are dedicated to Satan.

$D7 = (B_{Vself} - B_V 7)$ portion of people that are willing die for Satan.

When $D1$ through $D7$ are positioned atop each Menorah branch the result is an image that takes the form of a normal distribution as depicted in Figure VIII-4. The exact dimensions of the Menorah are unknown. Therefore the exact distribution is indeterminate, but it is most probably a normal distribution, which is consistent with the Book of Revelation [2]

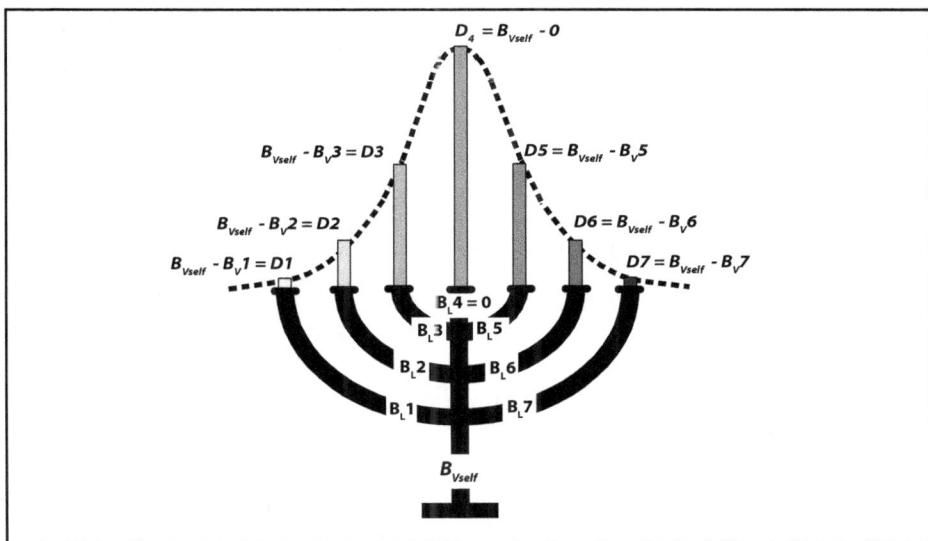

Figure VIII-4 Menorah's Distribution of Soul types

In Exodus 21 through Exodus 40 and the book of Leviticus, YHWH provides via Moses civil laws and instructions on how to build the Tabernacle. The Tabernacle was a perfect picture of what is required for a good personal relationship with YHWH where self must accept YHWH's provision via the Table of Showbread, Holy Spirit, and respond by giving his best offering to YHWH at the Bronze Altar.

The Tabernacle also had associated Sabbaths and feasts that picture future events, which will occur because the people rejected YHWH at Mount Sinai.

Exodus also documents a continuing series of bad decisions and there associated consequences. For example some people reverted to following Satan by worshiping the gold calf as described in Exodus 32:26-35.

Exodus 32:26-35
26 Then Moses stood in the gate of the camp, and said, Who is on the Lord's side? let him come unto me. And all the sons of Levi gathered themselves together unto him.
27 And he said unto them, Thus saith the Lord God of Israel, Put every man his sword by his side, and go in and out from gate to gate throughout the camp, and slay every man his brother, and every man his companion, and every man his neighbour.
28 And the children of Levi did according to the word of Moses: **and there fell of the people that day about three thousand men.**
29 For Moses had said, Consecrate yourselves to day to the Lord, even every man upon his son, and upon his brother; that he may bestow upon you a blessing this day.

101

30 And it came to pass on the morrow, that Moses said unto the people, Ye have sinned a great sin: and now I will go up unto the Lord; peradventure I shall make an atonement for your sin.

31 And Moses returned unto the Lord, and said, Oh, this people have sinned a great sin, and have made them gods of gold.

*32 Yet now, if thou wilt forgive their sin; and if not, **blot me, I pray thee, out of thy book which thou hast written.***

33 And the <u>Lord said</u> **[YHWH's WILL]** *unto Moses, Whosoever hath* <u>sinned against me, him will I</u> **[YHWH's SOUL]** *blot out of my book.*

34 Therefore now go, lead the people unto the place of which I have spoken unto thee: behold, mine Angel shall go before thee: nevertheless in the day when I visit I will visit their sin upon them.

35 And the Lord plagued the people, because they made the calf, which Aaron made.

Exodus 32:26-35 shows an individual's indwelling holy spirit is time dependent because those people who pushed Aaron into making the golden calf for them had reverted to following Satan. This event also raises a question. When is an individual's name placed into the book of life? YHWH makes it very clear this is His task only. Exodus 32:32 showed YHWH only holds the actual individuals who committed the sin accountable. Moses was not involved with the golden calf. The following are possible times when YHWH blots a name from the Book of Life.

1. YHWH starts with the book containing a list of all people who were conceived or born and during the final judgment some names will be blotted out. This is possible.

2. An individual's name never gets in or it goes in and out of the Book of Life as time goes on prior to their death. This is doubtful because if one's name never made it into the Book of Life it cannot be blotted out.

3. An individual's name is either retained or blotted out of the Book of Life when he dies and can no longer alter the magnitude of his indwelling holy spirit or repent. This would also be consistent with YHWH selecting who will be raptured. In Exodus 32:28 those who sided with Satan fell that day and had their names removed from YHWH's book of life. This is probable.

In Exodus 32:34-35 YHWH express His WRATH(t) toward the remaining people with plagues and He will no longer lead the Rebellious Nation into the Promised Land, but delegate this task to an angel.

The Tabernacle was completed and made operational on the first day, first month, of second year (2673 AM) in accordance Exodus 40:16-38

Exodus 40:16-38

16 Thus did Moses: according to all that the Lord commanded him, so did he.

17 **And it came to pass in the first month in the second year, on the first day of the month, that the tabernacle was reared up.**

18 And Moses reared up the tabernacle, and fastened his sockets, and set up the boards thereof, and put in the bars thereof, and reared up his pillars.

19 And he spread abroad the tent over the tabernacle, and put the covering of the tent above upon it; as the Lord commanded Moses.

20 And he took and put the testimony into the ark, and set the staves on the ark, and put the mercy seat above upon the ark:

21 And he brought the ark into the tabernacle, and set up the vail of the covering, and covered the ark of the testimony; as the Lord commanded Moses.

22 And he put the table in the tent of the congregation, upon the side of the tabernacle northward, without the vail.

23 And he set the bread in order upon it before the Lord; as the Lord had commanded Moses.

24 And he put the candlestick in the tent of the congregation, over against the table, on the side of the tabernacle southward.

25 And he lighted the lamps before the Lord; as the Lord commanded Moses.

26 And he put the golden altar in the tent of the congregation before the vail:

27 And he burnt sweet incense thereon; as the Lord commanded Moses.

28 And he set up the hanging at the door of the tabernacle.

29 And he put the altar of burnt offering by the door of the tabernacle of the tent of the congregation, and offered upon it the burnt offering and the meat offering; as the Lord commanded Moses.

30 And he set the laver between the tent of the congregation and the altar, and put water there, to wash withal.

31 And Moses and Aaron and his sons washed their hands and their feet thereat:

32 When they went into the tent of the congregation, and when they came near unto the altar, they washed; as the Lord commanded Moses.

33 And he reared up the court round about the tabernacle and the altar, and set up the hanging of the court gate. So Moses finished the work.

34 Then a cloud covered the tent of the congregation, and the glory of the Lord filled the tabernacle.

35 And Moses was not able to enter into the tent of the congregation, because the cloud abode thereon, and the glory of the Lord filled the tabernacle.

36 And when the cloud was taken up from over the tabernacle, the children of Israel went onward in all their journeys:

37 But if the cloud were not taken up, then they journeyed not till the day that it was taken up.

38 For the cloud of the Lord was upon the tabernacle by day, and fire was on it by night, in the sight of all the house of Israel, throughout all their journeys.

Once the Tabernacle was built and the Rebellious Nation was organized, the time to begin the journey toward the Promised Land had come. Later in the year 2673 AM YHWH had the angel lead the Rebellious Nation into the wilderness of Paran where YHWH told Moses in Numbers 13 to send spies into the Promised Land in preparation to enter and take possession of it.

Numbers 13

1 And the Lord spake unto Moses, saying,
2 Send thou men, that they may search the land of Canaan, which I give unto the children of Israel: of every tribe of their fathers shall ye send a man, every one a ruler among them.
3 And Moses by the commandment of the Lord sent them from the wilderness of Paran: all those men were heads of the children of Israel.
4 And these were their names: of the tribe of Reuben, Shammua the son of Zaccur.
5 Of the tribe of Simeon, Shaphat the son of Hori.
6 Of the tribe of Judah, Caleb the son of Jephunneh.
7 Of the tribe of Issachar, Igal the son of Joseph.
8 Of the tribe of Ephraim, Oshea the son of Nun.
9 Of the tribe of Benjamin, Palti the son of Raphu.
10 Of the tribe of Zebulun, Gaddiel the son of Sodi.
11 Of the tribe of Joseph, namely, of the tribe of Manasseh, Gaddi the son of Susi.
12 Of the tribe of Dan, Ammiel the son of Gemalli.
13 Of the tribe of Asher, Sethur the son of Michael.
14 Of the tribe of Naphtali, Nahbi the son of Vophsi.
15 Of the tribe of Gad, Geuel the son of Machi.
16 These are the names of the men which Moses sent to spy out the land. And Moses called Oshea the son of Nun Jehoshua.
17 And Moses sent them to spy out the land of Canaan, and said unto them, Get you up this way southward, and go up into the mountain:
18 And see the land, what it is; and the people that dwelleth therein, whether they be strong or weak, few or many;
19 And what the land is that they dwell in, whether it be good or bad; and what cities they be that they dwell in, whether in tents, or in strong holds;
20 And what the land is, whether it be fat or lean, whether there be wood therein, or not. And be ye of good courage, and bring of the fruit of the land. Now the time was the time of the first ripe grapes.
21 So they went up, and searched the land from the wilderness of Zin unto Rehob, as men come to Hamath.
22 And they ascended by the south, and came unto Hebron; where Ahiman, Sheshai, and Talmai, the children of Anak, were. (Now Hebron was built seven years before Zoan in Egypt.)
23 And they came unto the brook of Eshcol, and cut down from thence a branch with one cluster of grapes, and they bare it between two upon a staff; and they brought of the pomegranates, and of the figs.
24 The place was called the brook Eshcol, because of the cluster of grapes which the children of Israel cut down from thence.
25 And they returned from searching of the land after forty days.
26 **And they went and came to Moses, and to Aaron, and to all the congregation of the children of Israel, unto the wilderness of Paran, to Kadesh; and brought back word unto them, and unto all the congregation, and shewed them the fruit of the land.**
27 **And they told him, and said, We came unto the land whither thou sentest us, and surely it floweth with milk and honey; and this is the fruit of it.**

28 Nevertheless the people be strong that dwell in the land, and the cities are walled, and very great: and moreover we saw the children of Anak there.

29 The Amalekites dwell in the land of the south: and the Hittites, and the Jebusites, and the Amorites, dwell in the mountains: and the Canaanites dwell by the sea, and by the coast of Jordan.

30 And Caleb stilled the people before Moses, and said, Let us go up at once, and possess it; for we are well able to overcome it.

31 But the men that went up with him said, We be not able to go up against the people; for they are stronger than we.

32 And they brought up an evil report of the land which they had searched unto the children of Israel, saying, The land, through which we have gone to search it, is a land that eateth up the inhabitants thereof; and all the people that we saw in it are men of a great stature.

33 And there we saw the giants, the sons of Anak, which come of the giants: and we were in our own sight as grasshoppers, and so we were in their sight.

The spies report of the Promise Land, Numbers 13:26-33 above, reflects the nature of each individual's soul. Two spies, Joshua and Caleb, reported the land was like milk and honey, and YHWH will give it to us to and possess. The remaining ten spies reported the land is good, but the people living there were stronger than we were. 17% of the spies, Joshua and Caleb, were walking with YHWH knowing that nothing is impossible for Him. However, the other 83% of the spies that either relied on self and had no desire to fight a superior foe or those who relied on Satan and wanted to return to Egypt. Note, both the 17 % and 83% are consistent with a normal distribution of soul types. The people's souls reflected a similar nature as the spies and YHWH's reaction to their decision was described in Numbers 14:1-38.

Numbers 14:1-38

1 And all the congregation lifted up their voice, and cried; and the people wept that night.

2 And all the children of Israel murmured against Moses and against Aaron: and the whole congregation said unto them, Would God that we had died in the land of Egypt! or would God we had died in this wilderness!

3 And wherefore hath the Lord brought us unto this land, to fall by the sword, that our wives and our children should be a prey? were it not better for us to return into Egypt?

4 And they said one to another, Let us make a captain, and let us return into Egypt.

5 Then Moses and Aaron fell on their faces before all the assembly of the congregation of the children of Israel.

6 And Joshua the son of Nun, and Caleb the son of Jephunneh, which were of them that searched the land, rent their clothes:

7 And they spake unto all the company of the children of Israel, saying, The land, which we passed through to search it, is an exceeding good land.

8 If the Lord delight in us, then he will bring us into this land, and give it us; a land which floweth with milk and honey.

9 Only rebel not ye against the Lord, neither fear ye the people of the land; for they are bread for us: their defence is departed from them, and the Lord is with us: fear them not.

10 But all the congregation bade stone them with stones. And the glory of the Lord appeared in the tabernacle of the congregation before all the children of Israel.

11 And the Lord said unto Moses, How long will this people provoke me? and how long will it be ere they believe me, for all the signs which I have shewed among them?

12 I will smite them with the pestilence, and disinherit them, and will make of thee a greater nation and mightier than they.

13 And Moses said unto the Lord, Then the Egyptians shall hear it, (for thou broughtest up this people in thy might from among them;)

14 And they will tell it to the inhabitants of this land: for they have heard that thou Lord art among this people, that thou Lord art seen face to face, and that thy cloud standeth over them, and that thou goest before them, by day time in a pillar of a cloud, and in a pillar of fire by night.

15 Now if thou shalt kill all this people as one man, then the nations which have heard the fame of thee will speak, saying,

16 Because the Lord was not able to bring this people into the land which he sware unto them, therefore he hath slain them in the wilderness.

17 And now, I beseech thee, let the power of my Lord be great, according as thou hast spoken, saying,

18 The Lord is long suffering, and of great mercy, forgiving iniquity and transgression, and by no means clearing the guilty, visiting the iniquity of the fathers upon the children unto the third and fourth generation.

19 Pardon, I beseech thee, the iniquity of this people according unto the greatness of thy mercy, and as thou hast forgiven this people, from Egypt even until now.

20 And the Lord said, I have pardoned according to thy word:

21 But as truly as I live, all the earth shall be filled with the glory of the Lord.

22 Because all those men which have seen my glory, and my miracles, which I did in Egypt and in the wilderness, and have tempted me now these ten times, and have not hearkened to my voice;

23 Surely they shall not see the land which I sware unto their fathers, neither shall any of them that provoked me see it:

24 But my servant Caleb, because he had another spirit with him, and hath followed me fully, him will I bring into the land whereinto he went; and his seed shall possess it.

25 (Now the Amalekites and the Canaanites dwelt in the valley.) To morrow turn you, and get you into the wilderness by the way of the Red sea.

26 And the Lord spake unto Moses and unto Aaron, saying,

27 How long shall I bear with this evil congregation, which murmur against me? I have heard the murmurings of the children of Israel, which they murmur against me.

28 Say unto them, As truly as I live, saith the Lord, as ye have spoken in mine ears, so will I do to you:

29 *Your carcases shall fall in this wilderness; and all that were numbered of you, according to your whole number, from twenty years old and upward, which have murmured against me,*

30 *Doubtless ye shall not come into the land, concerning which I sware to make you dwell therein, save Caleb the son of Jephunneh, and Joshua the son of Nun.*

31 *But your little ones, which ye said should be a prey, them will I bring in, and they shall know the land which ye have despised.*

32 **But as for you, your carcases, they shall fall in this wilderness.**

33 **And your children shall wander in the wilderness forty years, and bear your whoredoms, until your carcases be wasted in the wilderness.**

34 **After the number of the days in which ye searched the land, even forty days, each day for a year, shall ye bear your iniquities, even forty years, and ye shall know my breach of promise.**

35 *I the Lord have said, I will surely do it unto all this evil congregation, that are gathered together against me: in this wilderness they shall be consumed, and there they shall die.*

36 *And the men, which Moses sent to search the land, who returned, and made all the congregation to murmur against him, by bringing up a slander upon the land,*

37 **Even those men that did bring up the evil report upon the land, died by the plague before the Lord.**

38 **But Joshua the son of Nun, and Caleb the son of Jephunneh, which were of the men that went to search the land, lived still.**

The majority of the people embraced the report of the ten spies. They were still only interested in themselves and did not want to enter the Promised Land. YHWH's response was perfectly consistent with the past. YHWH allowed the people to decide on their own and then held them to their decision and has Moses tell them what the consequences of their decision would be. Numbers 14:32-34 identifies the consequences of their current sin. The generation that made the decision not to enter the Promised Land would perish in the wilderness within forty years. The consequences for the twelve spies was described in Numbers 14:37-38 where the ten spies who were either, self-centered or followers of Satan, died immediately and only the followers of YHWH, Joshua and Caleb, survived.

After the Rebellious Nation had wandered in the wilderness thirty-nine years, Moses addressed the new generation of the Rebellious Nation just prior to their entry into the Promised Land. Moses final address to the people occurred on the first day of the eleventh month in the fortieth year (AM 2711) after the Exodus per Deuteronomy 1:3. The book of Deuteronomy documents Moses address to the people where he reviewed the history of their nation, what YHWH had done, what YHWH would do, YHWH's commandments, YHWH's civil and Levitical laws, YHWH's expectations, and YHWH's requirements for when they enter the Promised Land. Moses' final address was essentially a summary of the Torah and also its end.

The Torah

The Torah includes the books of Genesis, Exodus, Leviticus, Numbers, and Deuteronomy. These books are called the books of Moses and are the first five books in the Holy Bible. These books are extraordinary because they provide a detailed description of how the material universe came into existence; mankind's composition; how mankind is to have a good personal relationship with YHWH; a detailed calendar accurate to the year, month, and day starting from 0000 AM through 2711 AM. YHWH gave the Torah to Moses probably in sections after the Exodus in 2672 AM, but before Moses death in 2711 AM.

Moses' last actions included placing Joshua in charge and giving the final installment of the Torah to the people before he went to the top of Mount Pisgah. From the top of the mountain YHWH let Moses view part of the Promised Land without crossing the Jordan River. Then Moses, the first judge, died at 120 years of age in the land of Moab, and only YHWH knows where he is buried per Deuteronomy 34.

All the descendants of Shem, Japheth, and Ham were aware of the flood to some degree through oral tradition. Some civilizations eventually documented some of these stories that were passed on through oral tradition. For example, the Epic of Gilgamish predated the Torah, and it supported the idea of a global flood, but its source is recognized as man's oral tradition. Moreover, no civilization was present on earth prior to the Exodus in 2672 AM that possessed any known documentation of historical events from creation, 0000 AM, that identified specific people, and events with the correct dates. The Torah completely restored history and time to Israel, the Rebellious Nation, and the remainder of the world so that all people would eventually know what YHWH had done.

Figure VIII-5 shows mankind's knowledge developed by the pre-flood civilization, the subsequent loss of knowledge resulting from Noah's Flood, and the dispersion of the people as a result of the Tower of Babel. Then, YHWH mercifully gave Israel the Torah via Moses to restore the lost knowledge of Him and mankind's history.

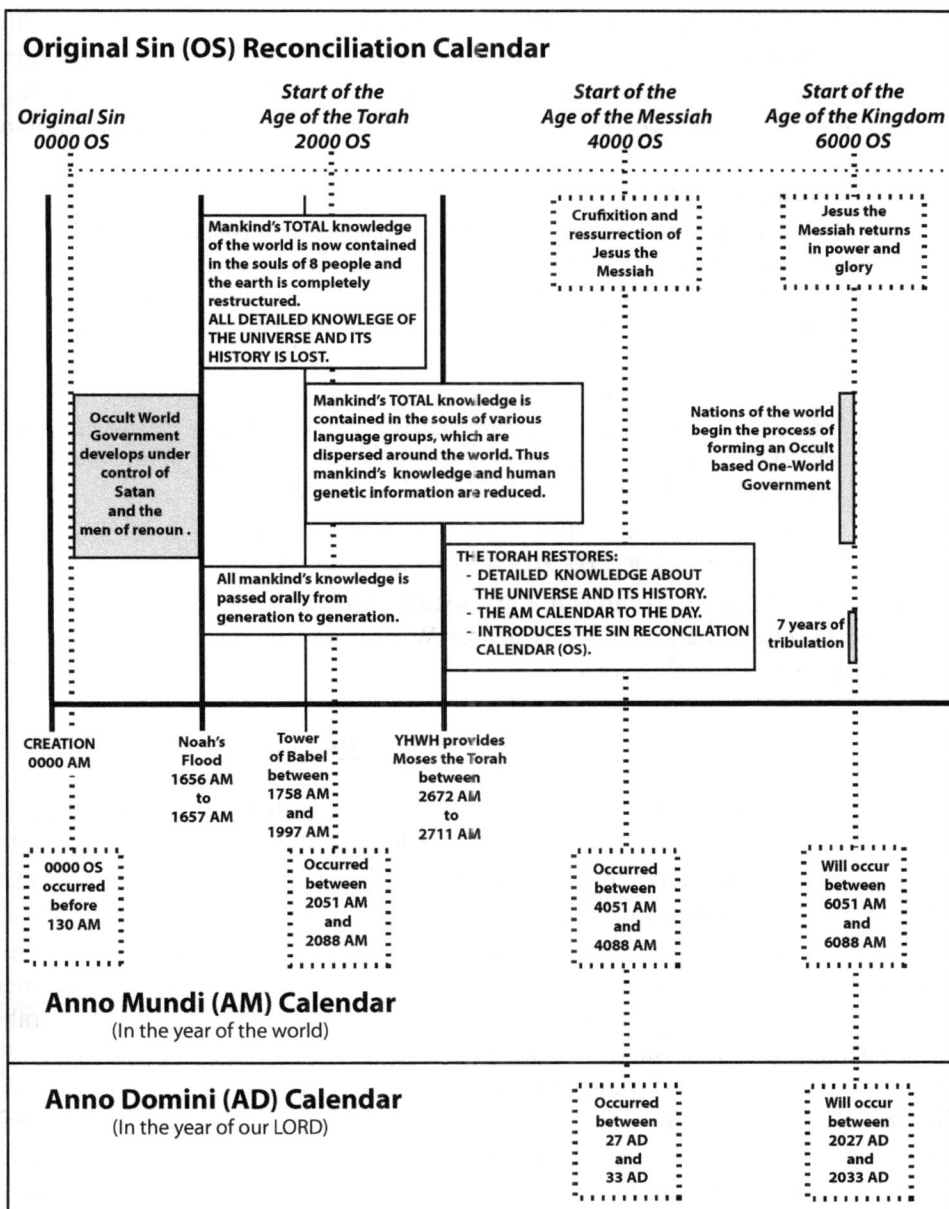

Original Sin (OS) Reconciliation Calendar

	Start of the Age of the Torah 2000 OS	Start of the Age of the Messiah 4000 OS	Start of the Age of the Kingdom 6000 OS
Original Sin 0000 OS			

Mankind's TOTAL knowledge of the world is now contained in the souls of 8 people and the earth is completely restructured. ALL DETAILED KNOWLEGE OF THE UNIVERSE AND ITS HISTORY IS LOST.

Crufixition and ressurrection of Jesus the Messiah

Jesus the Messiah returns in power and glory

Occult World Government develops under control of Satan and the men of renoun.

Mankind's TOTAL knowledge is contained in the souls of various language groups, which are dispersed around the world. Thus mankind's knowledge and human genetic information are reduced.

Nations of the world begin the process of forming an Occult based One-World Government

THE TORAH RESTORES:
- **DETAILED KNOWLEDGE ABOUT THE UNIVERSE AND ITS HISTORY.**
- **THE AM CALENDAR TO THE DAY.**
- **INTRODUCES THE SIN RECONCILATION CALENDAR (OS).**

7 years of tribulation

All mankind's knowledge is passed orally from generation to generation.

CREATION 0000 AM	Noah's Flood 1656 AM to 1657 AM	Tower of Babel between 1758 AM and 1997 AM	YHWH provides Moses the Torah between 2672 AM to 2711 AM		
0000 OS occurred before 130 AM		Occurred between 2051 AM and 2088 AM		Occurred between 4051 AM and 4088 AM	Will occur between 6051 AM and 6088 AM

Anno Mundi (AM) Calendar
(In the year of the world)

Anno Domini (AD) Calendar
(In the year of our LORD)

			Occurred between 27 AD and 33 AD	Will occur between 2027 AD and 2033 AD

Figure VIII-5 Mankind's Knowledge of the Universe versus Time

109

The Torah also documents YHWH's initial plan for His reconciliation with mankind through His Holy Nation. YHWH allowed the Holy Nation to reject Him, and YHWH gracefully deals with it by subsequently introducing a new age called the *Age of the Messiah*, which starts in 4000 OS and ends on 6000 OS as shown in Figure VIII-5.

It is very important to recognize:

1. The Torah could not be based on oral tradition because it contains detailed lineage that could not be predicted by any one generation even if they have the means to document it. Try and predict by name who in your family will be in a particular place five generations in the future.

2. It was impossible for Moses to generate the information in the Torah. Moses grew up in the Pharaoh's palace; when young he fled for his life from Egypt; took care of his father-in-law's flocks; in obedience to YHWH's request he returned to Egypt to lead the people during the Exodus. Moses had to be told by YHWH what year it was.

3. YHWH interfaced with the people through Moses. Thus the Torah was literally provided by YHWH to the people via Moses.

When one states the Torah is not historically correct or YHWH did not create the universe, one is calling YHWH a liar! What a dangerous thing to do when considering one's eternal destiny.

The Promised Land

The Rebellious Nation of Israel cannot recover the Holy Nation status because their majority decision at Mount Sinai changed history. However, YHWH will still use this Rebellious Nation to bless the entire world by providing the Torah and the future Messiah through them. Because of YHWH's grace and mercy He will bless an individual or the nation when they try to serve Him and He will discipline them when they turn away from Him. Notice YHWH will repeat this process of blessing and disciplining numerous times throughout the remainder of the Age of the Torah Now Joshua, the second judge, who replaced Moses will lead the Israelites over the Jordan River into the Promised Land in the year AM 2712 on the tenth day, of the first month after forty years in the wilderness per Joshua 4:19. The book of Joshua describes the Rebellious Nation's entry into the Promised Land. The book of Joshua ends with his death, and the book of Judges 2:6-8 begins with Joshua's death.

Judges 2:6-8
   6 *And when Joshua had let the people go, the children of Israel went every man unto his inheritance to possess the land.*
   7 And the people served the Lord all the days of Joshua, and all the days of the elders that outlived Joshua, who had seen all the great works of the Lord, that he did for Israel.
   8 *And Joshua the son of Nun, the servant of the Lord, died, being an hundred and ten years old.*

After Joshua and the elders' deaths, there are no specific AM calendar dates identified. Appendix I provides a summary of key events in the AM calendar from creation, but the period of the judges are not specifically dated by YHWH because Judges 2:10-17 states that the people were not following YHWH.

Judges 2:10-17
   10 *And also all that generation were gathered unto their fathers: and there arose another generation after them, which knew not the Lord, nor yet the works which he had done for Israel.*
   11 *And the children of Israel did evil in the sight of the Lord, and served Baalim:*
   12 *And they forsook the Lord God of their fathers, which brought them out of the land of Egypt, and followed other gods, of the gods of the people that were round about them, and bowed themselves unto them, and provoked the Lord to anger.*
   13 *And they forsook the Lord, and served Baal and Ashtaroth.*
   14 *And the anger of the Lord was hot against Israel, and he delivered them into the hands of spoilers that spoiled them, and he sold them into the hands of their enemies round about, so that they could not any longer stand before their enemies.*
   15 *Whithersoever they went out, the hand of the Lord was against them for evil, as the Lord had said, and as the Lord had sworn unto them: and they were greatly distressed.*
   16 *Nevertheless the Lord raised up judges, which delivered them out of the hand of those that spoiled them.*
   17 *And yet they would not hearken unto their judges, but they went a whoring after other gods, and bowed themselves unto them: they turned quickly out of the way which their fathers walked in, obeying the commandments of the Lord; but they did not so.*

During the period of the judges YHWH is consistent by dealing with evil whether it was from the Rebellious Nation as a whole or evil from within a tribe. YHWH would send a plague, or He would discipline the evil individual(s), or He would bless an enemy to rise up and enslave or destroy those doing evil. Once punished YHWH would raise up a judge to deliver the people.

Appendix I provides a summary of all the judges starting with Moses in 2672 AM and ending with Samuel. Notice that YHWH does not typically include evil people or events in the construction of the AM calendar, and precise dating to the day is not restored until king Solomon started to build the first Temple for YHWH.

IX   YHWH and the Kings

Samuel was the judge when the people came to him and requested that he appoint a king to rule over Israel. YHWH told Samuel the people were rejecting Him and that he was to grant the peoples' request. The desire for a king would result in the Rebellious Nation moving farther away from YHWH. This fall is described in I Samuel 8:1-22.

1 Samuel 8:1-22
1   *And it came to pass, when Samuel was old, that he made his sons judges over Israel.*
2   *Now the name of his firstborn was Joel; and the name of his second, Abiah: they were judges in Beer-sheba.*
3   *And his sons walked not in his ways, but turned aside after lucre, and took bribes, and perverted judgment.*
4   *Then all the elders of Israel gathered themselves together, and came to Samuel unto Ramah,*
5   *And said unto him, Behold, thou art old, and thy sons walk not in thy ways: now make us a king to judge us like all the nations.*
6   *But the thing displeased Samuel, when they said, Give us a king to judge us. And Samuel prayed unto the Lord.*
7   *And the <u>Lord said</u> [YHWH's WILL] unto Samuel, **Hearken unto the voice of the people in all that they say unto thee:** for they have not rejected thee, <u>but they have rejected me</u> [YHWH], that I should not reign over them.*
8   *According to all the works which they have done since the day that I brought them up out of Egypt even unto this day, wherewith they have forsaken me, and served other gods, so do they also unto thee.*
9   *Now therefore hearken unto their voice: howbeit yet protest solemnly unto them, and shew them the manner of the king that shall reign over them.*
10 *And Samuel told all the words of the Lord unto the people that asked of him a king.*
11 *And he said, This will be the manner of the king that shall reign over you: He will take your sons, and appoint them for himself, for his chariots, and to be his horsemen; and some shall run before his chariots.*
12 *And he will appoint him captains over thousands, and captains over fifties; and will set them to ear his ground, and to reap his harvest, and to make his instruments of war, and instruments of his chariots.*
13 *And he will take your daughters to be confectionaries, and to be cooks, and to be bakers.*
14 *And he will take your fields, and your vineyards, and your oliveyards, even the best of them, and give them to his servants.*
15 *And he will take the tenth of your seed, and of your vineyards, and give to his officers, and to his servants.*
16 *And he will take your menservants, and your maidservants, and your goodliest young men, and your asses, and put them to his work.*
17 *He will take the tenth of your sheep: and ye shall be his servants.*
18 ***And ye shall cry out in that day because of your king which ye shall have chosen you; and the Lord will not hear you in that day.***
19 ***Nevertheless the people refused to obey the voice of Samuel; and they said, Nay; but we will have a king over us;***
20 *That we also may be like all the nations; and that our king may judge us, and go out before us, and fight our battles.*

> 21 *And Samuel heard all the words of the people, and he rehearsed them in the ears of the Lord.*
>
> 22 *And the* <u>*Lord said*</u> **[YHWH's WILL]** *to Samuel,* **Hearken unto their voice, and make them a king.** *And Samuel said unto the men of Israel, Go ye every man unto his city.*

When the people ask Samuel to give them a king so they could be like all the other nations, YHWH's response was perfectly consistent. YHWH had Samuel tell the people what would happen if they have a king. A king essentially owns the people and would take what ever he wanted from them like Cain or Satan. When a king was a follower of YHWH the people would have better times, but when a king rejects YHWH the peoples' cry for mercy would not be heard. The people had again rejected YHWH.

The people had not learned from their previous bad decisions. The Exodus started with the Holy Nation. Then, at Mount Sinai the people rejected YHWH's direct instruction. YHWH gave the people their desire and a series of judges to aid this Rebellious Nation. YHWH requires self's $Will_{YHWH}(t) > Will_{self}(t)$ to have a good relationship with Him. Based on previous decisions and current desire for a king the people had made it clear that the majority of the people believed that YHWH should give them what they wanted when they wanted it. This placed self's $Will_{self}(t) > Will_{YHWH}(t)$. After warning the people YHWH he gave the people a king.

Now Samuel will be the last judge to serve Israel because YHWH's interface with the people changed to accommodate their decision to have a king. Having a king made Israel a *Worldly Nation* because then they were just like all the other nations in the world. YHWH selected Saul to be the first king of Israel the Worldly Nation. YHWH's perfect mercy and grace provided a series of prophets, through whom YHWH guided, warned and declared future events to the king(s) and the people.

YHWH also used the reign of king Solomon to restore the accuracy of the AM calendar to the day per I Kings 6:1 and II Chronicles 3:1-2. The synchronization of calendar was no accident, because it occurred when King Solomon started to build the Temple for YHWH that would replace the existing Tabernacle.

1 Kings 6:1

> 1 *And it came to pass in the* **four hundred and eightieth year after the children of Israel were come out of the land of Egypt,** *in the fourth year of Solomon's reign over Israel, in the month Zif, which is the second month, that he began to build the house of the Lord.*

2 Chronicles 3:1-2

> 3 *Then Solomon began to build the house of the Lord at Jerusalem in Mount Moriah, where the Lord appeared unto David his father, in the place that David had prepared in the threshing floor of Ornan the Jebusite.*

114

*2 And he began to build in the **second day** of the **second month**, in the **fourth year of his reign**.*

The reference to the start of the Exodus in the year 2672 AM plus 480 years placed the start of Solomon's Temple in the city of Jerusalem in 3152 AM. The AM calendar was again accurate to a day. The various kings of Judah were also responsible for the city of Jerusalem and the care of YHWH's Temple. The kings either tried to follow YHWH and obeyed YHWH's prophets or ignored them and did evil in the sight of YHWH. The prophets warned the kings and the people of their impending destruction, but they were ignored. Eventually the ten tribes were carried away by the Assyrians and subsequently YHWH raised up king Nebuchadnezzar of Babylon and last king of Judah, Zedekiah, watched his sons die then he was blinded and taken to Babylon in 3581 AM. At this point in time Israel, the *Worldly Nation*, ceases to exist as a nation and becomes Israel *the Desolate Nation* with no king or national government they are completely controlled by people from other nations.

YHWH through the prophet Jeremiah in Jeremiah 25:1-18 told the people what evil they had done and what was going to happen to them as a result.

Jeremiah 25:1-18
1 The word that came to Jeremiah concerning all the people of Judah in the fourth year of Jehoiakim the son of Josiah king of Judah, that was the first year of Nebuchadrezzar king of Babylon;
2 The which Jeremiah the prophet spake unto all the people of Judah, and to all the inhabitants of Jerusalem, saying,
3 From the thirteenth year of Josiah the son of Amon king of Judah, even unto this day, that is the three and twentieth year, the word of the Lord hath come unto me, and I have spoken unto you, rising early and speaking; but ye have not hearkened.
4 And the Lord hath sent unto you all his servants the prophets, rising early and sending them; but ye have not hearkened, nor inclined your ear to hear.
5 They said, Turn ye again now every one from his evil way, and from the evil of your doings, and dwell in the land that the Lord hath given unto you and to your fathers for ever and ever:
6 And go not after other gods to serve them, and to worship them, and provoke me not to anger with the works of your hands; and I will do you no hurt.
7 Yet ye have not hearkened unto me, saith the Lord; that ye might provoke me to anger with the works of your hands to your own hurt.
8 Therefore thus saith the Lord of hosts; Because ye have not heard my words,
9 Behold, I will send and take all the families of the north, saith the Lord, and Nebuchadrezzar the king of Babylon, my servant, and will bring them against this land, and against the inhabitants thereof, and against all these nations round about, and will utterly destroy them, and make them an astonishment, and an hissing, and perpetual desolations.

10 *Moreover I will take from them the voice of mirth, and the voice of gladness, the voice of the bridegroom, and the voice of the bride, the sound of the millstones, and the light of the candle.*

11 **And this whole land shall be a desolation, and an astonishment; and these nations shall serve the king of Babylon seventy years.**

12 *And it shall come to pass, when seventy years are accomplished, that I will punish the king of Babylon, and that nation, saith the Lord, for their iniquity, and the land of the Chaldeans, and will make it perpetual desolations.*

13 *And I will bring upon that land all my words which I have pronounced against it, even all that is written in this book, which Jeremiah hath prophesied against all the nations.*

14 *For many nations and great kings shall serve themselves of them also: and I will recompense them according to their deeds, and according to the works of their own hands.*

15 *For thus saith the Lord God of Israel unto me; Take the wine cup of this fury at my hand, and cause all the nations, to whom I send thee, to drink it.*

16 *And they shall drink, and be moved, and be mad, because of the sword that I will send among them.*

17 *Then took I the cup at the Lord's hand, and made all the nations to drink, unto whom the Lord had sent me:*

18 *To wit, Jerusalem, and the cities of Judah, and the kings thereof, and the princes thereof, to make them a desolation, an astonishment, an hissing, and a curse; as it is this day;*

With the carrying away of the people to Babylon, Israel had become a completely *Desolate Nation* and the variance associated with the AM Calendar, Appendix I, became many years. Israel remained a *Desolate Nation* through the remainder of the Age of the Torah and until near the end of the Age of the Messiah. In 1948 AD Israel was restored again to the Worldly Nation status.

Throughout the Age of the Torah (2000 OS to 4000 OS), YHWH continued to use various prophets to inform, warn, and help the people concerning future events. The prophets to the *Desolate Nation* included Jeremiah, Daniel, Ezekiel, Haggi, Zechariah, and Malichi. They added detail to future events to help prepare a remnant to transition back to Jerusalem to rebuild the temple in preparation for the coming of Jesus, the Messiah, the "Son of Man".

Notice their responsibility to take care of the city of Jerusalem and the temple belongs to the tribes of Judah, Benjamin, and Levi. Today these people are typically referred to as Jews.

The restoration of the Temple was the initial preparation for the initiation of the Age of the Messiah in 4000 OS. When YHWH would make a personal appearance Himself at mankind's level to give all mankind another chance to reconcile their sin to Him and establish a Moses-type personal relationship with Him.

X YHWH the Son of Man, 4000 OS

Recall from the Holy Nation of Israel that several hundred thousand people stood at the base of Mount Sinai when YHWH spoke the Ten Commandments. The Ten Commandments defined the requirements to become a member of the Holy Nation being formed by YHWH. However, the nature of every person's soul was different, and natures were distributed from those like Moses, to those concerned only about themselves, to those who followed Satan and would like to return to Egypt. At Mount Sinai the majority of the people did not want to submit to YHWH, their $Will_{self}(t) > Will_{YHWH}(t)$. Their response to YHWH was "have Moses speak to us and we will obey." Once the people made this decision there was no retracting it, and Israel became a Rebellious Nation.

Appendix III provides a flowchart of mankind's major decisions throughout history. Appendix III illustrates that YHWH mercifully dealt with people by providing an alternate path to reconcile with Him. After the people's rejection of YHWH at Mount Sinai, YHWH's response showed His perfect priority $L(t)$ for mankind. YHWH changed the course of history and in the future YHWH would modify His pre-creation universe Spirit-Body to bond with a Mortal-Material Body. Thus, YHWH would communicate with people at a totally human level just like Moses. At Mount Sinai this was a future event that would usher in the Age of the Messiah.

In Isaiah 53, the prophet describes the Messiah's youth through His resurrection. The Messiah would be despised by men, be a man of sorrows, who would give his life for reconciliation of mankind's sin, and He would live again.

During the Age of the Messiah the *Son of Man*, Jesus the Messiah, would transition through the following seven different phases:

1. *Son of Man's* birth.

2. *Son of Man's* growth.

3. *Son of Man's* ministry.

4. *Son of Man's* first-death.

5. *Son of Man's* resurrection.

6. *Son of Man's* ascension.

7. *Son of Man's* soul harvest.

Every person would be confronted with and will be required to respond in some manner to each of these seven phases. As the *Son of Man*, Jesus the Messiah, transitions through each of these phases He is the perfect teacher, perfect leader, and the perfect example for all people.

YHWH began the first phase by taking on a human mortal-material body.

Son of Man's **Birth**

How did YHWH acquire a human mortal-material body? We know that YHWH is triune from Chapter I and also from the structure of the Tabernacle. YHWH's triune structure consists of:

- SOUL, the Father, is represented by the Ark of the Testimony.
- WILL, the Holy Spirit, is represented by the Table of Show Bread.
- BODY, the Son, is represented by the High Priest.

Prior to YHWH's entrance into the material component of the universe through the birth of Jesus the Messiah, it is important to note that YHWH existed in the pre-creation universe and did not have a mortal-material body, but only had a spirit body. Before the birth of the *Son of Man*, Jesus the Messiah, YHWH typically communicated with people by voice, dreams, fire, clouds, and in the few instances when He appeared visible to man, YHWH's BODY was distinctive.

The birth of Jesus the Messiah was determined at Mount Sinai by YHWH's SOUL, the Father, when He decided to modify His own BODY to add a new mortal-material body identical to man's material body. YHWH's new body is referred to as the *Son*. The Son includes YHWH's existing spirit body with dimensions ($x_{BODY\text{-}spirit}$, $y_{BODY\text{-}spirit}$, $z_{BODY\text{-}spirit}$) with the addition of a mortal-material body with dimensions ($x_{BODY\text{-}material}$, $y_{BODY\text{-}material}$, $z_{BODY\text{-}material}$). YHWH's WILL, the Holy Spirit then implemented the change. The result is illustrated in Figure X-1. and the process YHWH used is described in Matthew 1:16-24 and Luke 1.

> *Matthew 1:16-24*
> *16 And Jacob begat Joseph the husband of Mary, of whom was born Jesus, who is called Christ.*
> *17 So all the generations from Abraham to David are fourteen generations; and from David until the carrying away into Babylon are fourteen generations; and from the carrying away into Babylon unto Christ are fourteen generations.*
> *18 Now the birth of Jesus Christ was on this wise: When as his mother Mary was espoused to Joseph, before they came together, she was found with child of the Holy Ghost* **[YHWH's WILL, Holy Spirit]**.
> *19 Then Joseph her husband, being a just man, and not willing to make her a publick example, was minded to put her away privily.*
> *20 But while he thought on these things, behold, the angel of the Lord appeared unto him in a dream, saying, Joseph, thou son of David, fear not to take unto thee Mary thy wife: for that which is conceived in her is of the Holy Ghost* **[YHWH's WILL, Holy Spirit]**.

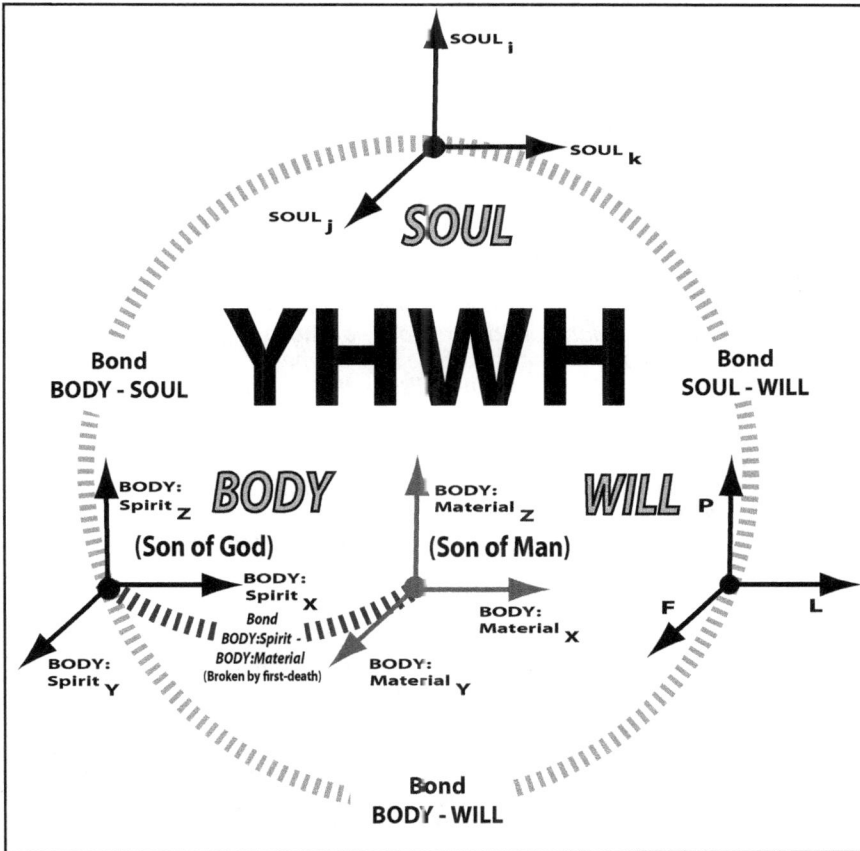

Figure X-1 YHWH's Composition with the Birth of Jesus the Messiah

21 *And she shall bring forth a son, and thou shalt call his name JESUS: for he shall save his people from their sins.*

22 *Now all this was done, that it might be fulfilled which was spoken of the Lord by the prophet, saying,*

23 *Behold, a virgin shall be with child, and shall bring forth a son, and they shall call his name Emmanuel, which being interpreted is, <u>God with us</u>* **[YHWH's BODY includes a material human body, which is literally a Son of Man.]**.

24 *Then Joseph being raised from sleep did as the angel of the Lord had bidden him, and took unto him his wife:*

119

Luke 1:1-2:1

1 Forasmuch as many have taken in hand to set forth in order a declaration of those things which are most surely believed among us,

2 Even as they delivered them unto us, which from the beginning were eyewitnesses, and ministers of the word;

3 It seemed good to me also, having had perfect understanding of all things from the very first, to write unto thee in order, most excellent Theophilus,

4 That thou mightest know the certainty of those things, wherein thou hast been instructed. 5 There was in the days of Herod, the king of Judaea, a certain priest named Zacharias, of the course of Abia: and his wife was of the daughters of Aaron, and her name was Elisabeth.

6 And they were both righteous before God, walking in all the commandments and ordinances of the Lord blameless.

7 And they had no child, because that Elisabeth was barren, and they both were now well stricken in years.

8 And it came to pass, that while he executed the priest's office before God in the order of his course,

9 According to the custom of the priest's office, his lot was to burn incense when he went into the temple of the Lord.

10 And the whole multitude of the people were praying without at the time of incense.

11 And there appeared unto him an angel of the Lord standing on the right side of the altar of incense.

12 And when Zacharias saw him, he was troubled, and fear fell upon him.

13 But the angel said unto him, Fear not, Zacharias: for thy prayer is heard; and thy wife Elisabeth shall bear thee a son, and thou shalt call his name **John**.

14 And thou shalt have joy and gladness; and many shall rejoice at his birth.

15 For he shall be great in the sight of the Lord, and shall drink neither wine nor strong drink; and <u>he shall be filled with the Holy Ghost</u> **[John's Soul and Will shall be in accordance with YHWH's WILL]**, even from his mother's womb.

16 And many of the children of Israel shall he turn to the Lord their God.

17 And he shall go before him in the spirit and power of Elias, to turn the hearts of the fathers to the children, and the disobedient to the wisdom of the just; to make ready a people prepared for the Lord.

18 And Zacharias said unto the angel, Whereby shall I know this? for I am an old man, and my wife well stricken in years.

19 And the angel answering said unto him, I am Gabriel, that stand in the presence of God; and am sent to speak unto thee, and to shew thee these glad tidings.

20 And, behold, thou shalt be dumb, and not able to speak, until the day that these things shall be performed, because thou believest not my words, which shall be fulfilled in their season.

21 And the people waited for Zacharias, and marvelled that he tarried so long in the temple.

22 And when he came out, he could not speak unto them: and they perceived that he had seen a vision in the temple: for he beckoned unto them, and remained speechless.

23 And it came to pass, that, as soon as the days of his ministration were accomplished, he departed to his own house.
24 And after those days his wife Elisabeth conceived, and hid herself five months, saying,
25 Thus hath the Lord dealt with me in the days wherein he looked on me, to take away my reproach among men.
26 And in the sixth month the angel Gabriel was sent from God unto a city of Galilee, named Nazareth,
27 To a virgin espoused to a man whose name was Joseph, of the house of David; and the virgin's name was Mary.
28 And the angel came in unto her, and said, Hail, thou that art highly favoured, the Lord is with thee: blessed art thou among women.
29 And when she saw him, she was troubled at his saying, and cast in her mind what manner of salutation this should be.
30 And the angel said unto her, Fear not, Mary: for thou hast found favour with God **[YHWH's SOUL, the Father]**.
31 And, behold, thou shalt conceive in thy womb, and bring forth a son **[YHWH's Mortal-material BODY]** and shalt call his name **JESUS**.
32 He shall be great, and shall be called the Son of the Highest: and the Lord God **[YHWH's SOUL, the Father]** shall give unto him the throne of his father David:
33 And he shall reign over the house of Jacob for ever; and of his kingdom there shall be no end.
34 Then said Mary unto the angel, How shall this be, seeing I know not a man?
35 And the angel answered and said unto her, The Holy Ghost **[YHWH's WILL]** shall come upon thee, and the power of the Highest **[YHWH's WILL]** shall overshadow thee: therefore also that holy thing which shall be born of thee shall be called the Son of God **[YHWH's BODY]**.

YHWH's WILL creates a new bond between His existing spirit BODY and His new mortal-material body that had just started to grow in Mary's womb. This bond would then be identical to that between a person's material and spirit body. This made Jesus the Messiah, YHWH's Body, **literally** the *Son of God* and also made Him **literally** the *Son of Man* because His mortal-material body was developed through Mary's womb.

This is the reason why Jesus the Messiah often referred to Himself as either *Son of God* or *Son of Man* for both terms are absolutely true. Jesus the Messiah most often referred to Himself over 85 times in the New Testament as the *Son of Man*. Typically Jesus the Messiah used the term *Son of Man* in reference to His suffering and death on the cross or to His return in power and glory. Jesus the Messiah's function was to interface with YHWH's material universe at a human level. It is also true that YHWH's BODY participated in the creation event, knew Abraham. and was also a descendent of Abraham through Mary.

The *Son of Man*, Jesus the Messiah's birth brings a baby whose name is also Emmanuel, God with us.

121

Son of Man's **Growth**

Once the *Son of Man* was born the He entered into the body maturing phase. Few details are known about Jesus the Messiah's childhood. Some insights are provided in Luke 2:39-52.

> Luke 2:39-52
> 39 And when they had performed all things according to the law of the Lord, they returned into Galilee, to their own city Nazareth.
> 40 And the child grew, and waxed strong in spirit, filled with wisdom: and the grace of God was upon him.
> 41 Now his parents went to Jerusalem every year at the feast of the passover.
> 42 And when he was **twelve years old**, they went up to Jerusalem after the custom of the feast.
> 43 And when they had fulfilled the days, as they returned, the child Jesus tarried behind in Jerusalem; and Joseph and his mother knew not of it.
> 44 But they, supposing him to have been in the company, went a day's journey; and they sought him among their kinsfolk and acquaintance.
> 45 And when they found him not, they turned back again to Jerusalem, seeking him.
> 46 And it came to pass, that after three days they found him in the temple, sitting in the midst of the doctors, both hearing them, and asking them questions.
> 47 And all that heard him were astonished at his understanding and answers.
> 48 And when they saw him, they were amazed: and his mother said unto him, Son, why hast thou thus dealt with us? behold, thy father and I have sought thee sorrowing.
> 49 And he said unto them, How is it that ye sought me? wist ye not that I must be about my Father's business?
> 50 And they understood not the saying which he spake unto them.
> 51 And he went down with them, and came to Nazareth, and was subject unto them: but his mother kept all these sayings in her heart.
> 52 And Jesus increased in wisdom and stature, and in favour with God and man.

Jesus the Messiah like all children would be completely dependent upon His parents for physical survival. This type of dependence is also an example of how all individuals need to depend upon YHWH to meet their needs.

YHWH during the maturing of His material-body protects and blesses His human family. Luke tells us His family provided for His needs and adhered to the Ten Commandments, applicable Temple Ceremonial laws and civil laws. He was responsible to His parents until He was twelve years old, which is the age of accountability, Luke 2:42-49. The age of accountability seems to be the point in time where a human individual's soul $L(t)$s, priorities, have developed to a point where he is capable of survival on his own. YHWH, the *Son of Man,* at the age of accountability challenged the men and priests in the Temple.

The activities of the *Son of Man* from the age of twelve to the start of His ministry at the age of thirty are unknown.

Son of Man's **Ministry**

YHWH's human-material body, *Son of Man*, is the perfect example of what a priest of the Most High God would have been like if the people had not rejected YHWH at Mount Sinai. The *Son of Man's* ministry is introduced by John the Baptist and is described in Matthew 3:1-17.

Matthew 3:1-17
1   *In those days came John the Baptist, preaching in the wilderness of Judaea,*
2   *And saying,* **Repent ye: for the kingdom of heaven is at hand.**
3   *For this is he that was spoken of by the prophet Esaias, saying, The voice of one crying in the wilderness, Prepare ye the way of the Lord, make his paths straight.*
4   *And the same John had his raiment of camel's hair, and a leathern girdle about his loins; and his meat was locusts and wild honey.*
5   *Then went out to him Jerusalem, and all Judaea, and all the region round about Jordan,*
6   *And were* <u>baptized of him</u> **[Declaring their allegiance to YHWH.]** *in Jordan, confessing their sins.*
7   *But when he saw many of the Pharisees and Sadducees come to his baptism, he said unto them, O generation of vipers, who hath warned you to flee from the wrath to come?*
8   *Bring forth therefore fruits meet for repentance:*
9   *And think not to say within yourselves, We have Abraham to our father: for I say unto you, that God is able of these stones to raise up children unto Abraham.*
10 *And now also the axe is laid unto the root of the trees: therefore every tree which bringeth not forth good fruit is hewn down, and cast into the fire.*
11 *I indeed baptize you with water unto repentance: but he that cometh after me is mightier than I, whose shoes I am not worthy to bear: he shall* <u>baptize you</u> **[Obtain one's allegiance.]** *with the* <u>Holy Ghost</u> **[YHWH's WILL],** *and with fire* **[tribulation]:**
12 *Whose fan is in his hand, and he will throughly purge his floor, and gather his wheat into the garner; but he will burn up the chaff with unquenchable fire.*
13 *Then cometh Jesus from Galilee to Jordan unto John, to be baptized of him.*
14 *But John forbad him, saying, I have need to be baptized of thee, and comest thou to me?*
15 *And Jesus answering said unto him, Suffer it to be so now: for thus it becometh us to* <u>fulfil all righteousness</u> **[Jesus must be the perfect example of what each man is expected to do.].** *Then he suffered him.*
16 *And Jesus, when he was baptized, went up straightway out of the water: and, lo, the heavens were opened unto him, and he saw the* <u>Spirit of God</u> **[YHWH's WILL]** *descending like a dove, and lighting upon him:*

> *17 And lo a <u>voice from heaven, saying</u>* **[YHWH's WILL]**, *This is my beloved <u>Son</u>* **[YHWH's mortal material-BODY]**, *in whom <u>I</u>* **[YHWH's SOUL]** *am well pleased.*

John the Baptist introduced the *Son of Man* by declaring each individual must repent and be baptized. Repent means to decide to change one's ways, but what did this mean with respect to the start of the *Son of Man's* ministry? Repentance meant to accept the Ten Commandments, which were rejected at Mount Sinai and resulted in the coming of the *Son of Man*. YHWH has and will not change His requirements for an individual to be with Him.

Once an individual decides to accept and adhere to the Ten Commandments he must be baptized, which is just a public declaration of his allegiance to YHWH. Note, John the Baptist helped people declare their allegiance to YHWH, but he could not authorize their salvation, eternal life. YHWH (SON, SOUL, WILL) would separate, baptize, and provide salvation for those who are in allegiance with Himself. YHWH will also destroy the chaff, those who reject Him.

The entire ministry of the *Son of Man,* Jesus the Messiah, demonstrated to the people what it is like to live face to face with YHWH. Jesus the Messiah is absolutely Emmanuel, God with us. What is the character of YHWH's face to face relationship with mankind through Jesus the Messiah?

The relationship is the same as that illustrated by the Tabernacle process; only the High Priest is now Jesus the Messiah. Thus, YHWH's BODY, Jesus the Messiah, observes and takes in information from His surroundings; passes the information to YHWH's SOUL, the Father, who decides what will be done or said; and YHWH's WILL, the Holy Spirit, then is responsible to implement the decision. The Holy Spirit's implementation of a decision can take on a variety of forms such as conveying a verbal or physical response via Jesus the Messiah, the *Son of Man*; or quieting a stormy sea; or raising the dead; or healing the sick; feeding the 5000; or any other needed response.

Then, what did Jesus the Messiah, the *Son of Man,* tell the people they had to do to have a good personal relationship with Him?

The *Son of Man* taught that everyone's ultimate goal should be to achieve a Philadelphian-type soul. The Philadelphian-type soul was and is unique among the seven types of men's souls because it is prized by YHWH. YHWH's promise to the Philadelphian is eternal life as stated in His letter to them in Revelation 3:7-11.

> *Revelation 3:7-11*
> *7 And to the angel of the <u>church in Philadelphia</u>* **[soul type]** *write; These things saith he that is holy, he that is true, he that hath the key of David, he that openeth, and no man shutteth; and shutteth, and no man openeth;*

8 I know thy works: behold, I have set before thee an open door, and no man
can shut it: for thou hast a little strength, and hast kept my word, and hast
not denied my name.

9 Behold, I will make them of the synagogue of Satan, which say they are
Jews, and are not, but do lie; behold, I will make them to come and worship
before thy feet, and to know that I have loved thee.

10 Because thou hast kept the word of my patience, I also will keep thee from
the hour of temptation, which shall come upon all the world, to try them
that dwell upon the earth.

11 Behold, I come quickly: hold that fast which thou hast, that no man take thy
crown.

Therefore, the Philadelphian-type soul will be examined in some detail. Philadelphians are dear friends of Jesus the Messiah because they place Him first in their lives and are willing to die for Him. That is their $Will_{YHWH}(t) >> Will_{self}(t)$. They will not experience the Tribulation Period, the time of temptation, because they will be the first soul type to be raptured.

The *Son of Man's* Sermon on the Mount, Matthew 5:1-6:2, was equivalent to YHWH declaring the Ten Commandments from Mount Sinai and both events conveyed what was expected of a Philadelphian-type soul. Only the Sermon on the Mount was YHWH's BODY gracefully providing instruction by replacing Moses with Himself and thus implementing what the people had requested at Mount Sinai. However, YHWH had not changed and told His disciples and the people that they needed to keep the Ten Commandments.

Matthew 5:1-6:2

1 And seeing the multitudes, he went up into a mountain: and when he was
set, his disciples came unto him: [**Philadelphians**]

2 And he opened his mouth, and taught them, saying,

3 *Blessed are the poor in spirit:* for theirs is the kingdom of heaven.
**[Philadelphians must put self last, poor in spirit, and YHWH first or
self's $Will_{YHWH}(t) >> Will_{Yself}(t)$.]**

4 *Blessed are they that mourn:* for they shall be comforted.
**[When a Philadelphian knows he has sinned he will experience
high Anxiety(t) and grieve, because he has a high $L_{YHWH}(t)$ and a low
$F_{YHWH}(t)$ that he has pleased YHWH.]**

5 *Blessed are the meek:* for they shall inherit the earth.
**[The Philadelphian will experience low Anxiety(t) when confronted
by adverse situations, because he has a high $L_{YHWH}(t)$ and a high
$F_{YHWH}(t)$ that he has pleased Him. The Philadelphian will not
compromise YHWH's truth under any circumstances. Daniel and the
apostle Paul are good examples of meek men.]**

6 *Blessed are they which do hunger and thirst after righteousness:* for they
shall be filled.
[Philadelphians truly seek YHWH's truth and they will receive it.]

7 *Blessed are the merciful:* for they shall obtain mercy.
**[Philadelphians help other people without expectation of being
repaid or their $L_{others}(t) > L_{self}(t)$.]**

125

8 *Blessed are the pure in heart:* for they shall see God.
   [Philadelphians set their L(t)s, priorities, in accordance with YHWH's Ten Commandments.]
9 *Blessed are the peacemakers:* for they shall be called the children of God.
   [Philadelphians rightly apply YHWH's truth to each situation. That is, they have wisdom.]
10 *Blessed are they which are persecuted for righteousness' sake:* for theirs is the kingdom of heaven.
11 *Blessed are ye, when men shall revile you, and persecute you, and shall say all manner of evil against you falsely, for my sake.*
12 *Rejoice, and be exceeding glad: for great is your reward in heaven: for so persecuted they the prophets which were before you.*
   [Philadelphians can expect persecution because their life reflects their absolute belief in YHWH, Jesus the Messiah, whom evil people hate, have high Anxiety(t) toward.]
13 *Ye are the salt of the earth:* but if the salt have lost his savour, wherewith shall it be salted? it is thenceforth good for nothing, but to be cast out, and to be trodden under foot of men.
   [Philadelphians preserve YHWH's truth, *Eve's-seed*, for all by not compromising it, living it as an example to others and teaching it to all people they encounter.]
14 *Ye are the light of the world.* A city that is set on an hill cannot be hid.
15 *Neither do men light a candle, and put it under a bushel, but on a candlestick; and it giveth light unto all that are in the house.*
16 *Let your light so shine before men, that they may see your good works, and glorify your Father which is in heaven.*
   [Philadelphians declare YHWH's truth, *Eve's-seed*, to all people they encounter. They shall not isolate themselves from society.]
17 *Think not that I am come to destroy the law, or the prophets:* I am not come to destroy, but to fulfil.
18 *For verily I say unto you, Till heaven and earth pass, one jot or one tittle shall in no wise pass from the law, till all be fulfilled.*
19 *Whosoever therefore shall break one of these least commandments, and shall teach men so, he shall be called the least in the kingdom of heaven: but whosoever shall do and teach them, the same shall be called great in the kingdom of heaven.*
20 *For I say unto you, That except your righteousness shall exceed the righteousness of the scribes and Pharisees, ye shall in no case enter into the kingdom of heaven.*
   [Jesus the Messiah carried out and complied with the Ten Commandments, judicial and ceremonial laws as they were intended and not as amended by the Pharisees. For example, He healed on the Sabbath. With Jesus the Messiah's death and resurrection the picture formed by the High Priest and the Bronze Altar transitions directly to Jesus the Messiah. When Jesus the Messiah, our High Priest, ascended into heaven, the Tabernacle was no longer applicable because He was not present. However, all the prophesies, the picture of a personal relationship with YHWH and the pictures of future events would remain valid until all are fulfilled after His return. Philadelphians and all mankind need to set their L(t)s, priorities, in accordance with the Ten Commandments.]

126

21 Ye have heard that it was said by them of old time, Thou shalt not kill; and whosoever shall kill shall be in danger of the judgment:

22 <u>But I say unto you, That whosoever is angry with his brother without a cause shall be in danger of the judgment:</u> and whosoever shall say to his brother, Raca, shall be in danger of the council: but whosoever shall say, Thou fool, shall be in danger of hell fire.

23 Therefore if thou bring thy gift to the altar, and there rememberest that thy brother hath ought against thee;

24 Leave there thy gift before the altar, and go thy way; first be reconciled to thy brother, and then come and offer thy gift.

25 Agree with thine adversary quickly, whiles thou art in the way with him; lest at any time the adversary deliver thee to the judge, and the judge deliver thee to the officer, and thou be cast into prison.

26 Verily I say unto thee, Thou shalt by no means come out thence, till thou hast paid the uttermost farthing.

[Being angry with a brother without a cause means that you have wronged him, he is not at fault, and you are responsible to make it right with him to restore your personal relationship with YHWH.]

27 Ye have heard that it was said by them of old time, Thou shalt not commit adultery:

28 <u>But I say unto you, That whosoever looketh on a woman to lust after her hath committed adultery with her already in his heart.</u>

29 And if thy right eye offend thee, pluck it out, and cast it from thee: for it is profitable for thee that one of thy members should perish, and not that thy whole body should be cast into hell.

30 And if thy right hand offend thee, cut it off, and cast it from thee: for it is profitable for thee that one of thy members should perish, and not that thy whole body should be cast into hell.

31 It hath been said, Whosoever shall put away his wife, let him give her a writing of divorcement:

32 <u>But I say unto you, That whosoever shall put away his wife, saving for the cause of fornication, causeth her to commit adultery:</u> and whosoever shall marry her that is divorced committeth adultery.

[YHWH is concerned with the motive behind an action, not just the action itself.]

33 Again, ye have heard that it hath been said by them of old time, Thou shalt not forswear thyself, but shalt perform unto the Lord thine oaths:

34 <u>But I say unto you, Swear not at all; neither by heaven; for it is God's throne:</u>

35 Nor by the earth; for it is his footstool: neither by Jerusalem; for it is the city of the great King.

36 Neither shalt thou swear by thy head, because thou canst not make one hair white or black.

37 But let your communication be, Yea, yea; Nay, nay: for whatsoever is more than these cometh of evil.

[YHWH will not tolerate situational ethics.]

38 Ye have heard that it hath been said, An eye for an eye, and a tooth for a tooth:

39 <u>But I say unto you, That ye resist not evil:</u> but whosoever shall smite thee on thy right cheek, turn to him the other also.

127

40 *And if any man will sue thee at the law, and take away thy coat, let him have thy cloke also.*

41 *And whosoever shall compel thee to go a mile, go with him twain.*

42 *Give to him that asketh thee, and from him that would borrow of thee turn not thou away.*
[Philadelphians must have a low magnitude of L(t) for earthly possessions.]

43 *Ye have heard that it hath been said, Thou shalt love thy neighbour, and hate thine enemy.*

44 *But I say unto you, Love your enemies, bless them that curse you, do good to them that hate you, and pray for them which despitefully use you, and persecute you;*

45 *That ye may be the children of your Father which is in heaven: for he maketh his sun to rise on the evil and on the good, and sendeth rain on the just and on the unjust.*

46 *For if ye love them which love you, what reward have ye? do not even the publicans the same?*

47 *And if ye salute your brethren only, what do ye more than others? do not even the publicans so?*

48 *Be ye therefore perfect, even as your Father which is in heaven is perfect.*
[Philadelphians must have a high L(t), priority, on their enemy as a person and high F(t) that YHWH cares about them also, but a Philadelphian cannot hate them by placing high L(t)s on what his enemy is or has with low F(t) in achieving or controlling it for themselves because the result is high Anxiety(t) toward YHWH. This desire to have what your enemy has is hate and is a rejection of YHWH. Those who hate Philadelphians have a high L(t) that the followers of Jesus the Messiah are wrong and their presence and beliefs lower their F(t) causing them high anxiety or hate toward them because of Jesus the Messiah.]

Matthew 6:1-2

1 *Take heed that ye do not your alms before men, to be seen of them: otherwise ye have no reward of your Father which is in heaven.*

2 *Therefore when thou doest thine alms, do not sound a trumpet before thee, as the hypocrites do in the synagogues and in the streets, that they may have glory of men. Verily I say unto you, They have their reward.*
[Philadelphians shall not do anything with the motive to show people how good they are.]

Currently what does YHWH expect from each individual? Just as during the previous age it is the individual who is responsible to comply with the Ten Commandments! Compliance with the Ten Commandments is the key to being a follower of YHWH and is the key to belief and an individual's salvation.

Sin is non-compliance with the Ten Commandment and is defined concisely stated in 1 John 3:4.

1 John 3:4

4 *Whosoever committeth sin transgresseth also the law: for sin is the transgression of the law.* **[The Ten Commandments]**

Thus, when anyone repents of their sin, he is confessing he has violated the Ten Commandments and is deciding not to repeat the indiscretion. The Ten Commandments define how YHWH expects an individual to set his priorities associated with the knowledge contained within his soul.

The *Son of Man's* instruction included His personal perfect example of how an individual should treat other people. YHWH, the *Son of Man*, had great compassion for other people. YHWH did not condemn the adulterous woman but told her go her way and sin no more—that is, repent. YHWH healed the sick and lame. On several occasions YHWH fed the multitudes of people when they became hungry. YHWH's example demonstrated a soul that served, helped and took care of other people. YHWH, the *Son of Man*, also demonstrated His incredible power by raising Lazarus from the dead, controlling the weather, and forgiving sins. Any individual who had been in the presence or had heard from other people about the activity of Jesus the Messiah, the *Son of Man*, had to decide to either accept YHWH's Ten Commandments or reject Him.

The *Son of Man*, Jesus the Messiah, explicitly told the rich young man he must comply with all the Ten Commandments in Matthew 19:16-30.

> *Matthew 19:16-30*
> *16 And, behold, one came and said unto him, Good Master, what good thing shall I do, that I may have eternal life?*
> *17 And he said unto him, Why callest thou me good? there is none good but one, that is, God: but <u>if thou wilt enter into life, keep the commandments.</u>* **[This is Jesus' declaration that all Ten Commandments are applicable for today. Mark 10:19 and Luke 18:20 phased it " *Thou knowest the commandments,*" that is everyone knows what is required.]**
> *18 He saith unto him, Which? Jesus said, Thou shalt do no murder, Thou shalt not commit adultery, Thou shalt not steal, Thou shalt not bear false witness,*
> *19 Honor thy father and thy mother: and, Thou shalt love thy neighbor as thyself.* **[Jesus identifies the commandments applicable to one's relationship with other people.]**
> *20 The young man saith unto him, All these things have I kept from my youth up: what lack I yet?* **[Note: Jesus does not disagree with the young man. The man's relationship with other people was acceptable. Mark 10:21 and Luke 18:22 phased it " *Then Jesus beholding him loved him, and said unto him, One thing thou lackest:* " or you were okay with respect to the other nine commandments.]**
> *21 Jesus said unto him, If thou wilt be perfect, go and sell that thou hast, and give to the poor, and thou shalt have treasure in heaven: and come and follow me.* **[The first commandment is his problem.]**
> *22 But when the young man heard that saying, he went away sorrowful: for he had great possessions.* **[Like Cain and the Pharisees, the young man decided not to change his priorities, place YHWH first in his life, and be obedient to YHWH. That is, to repent and believe.]**

23 Then said Jesus unto his disciples, Verily I say unto you, That a rich man shall hardly enter into the kingdom of heaven.
24 And again I say unto you, It is easier for a camel to go through the eye of a needle, than for a rich man to enter into the kingdom of God.
25 When his disciples heard it, they were exceedingly amazed, saying, Who then can be saved?
26 But Jesus beheld them, and said unto them, With men this is impossible; but with God all things are possible. **[YHWH' grace will provide mankind a gift of a second chance for salvation by believing in Jesus the Messiah and if you believe Jesus the Messiah, you must accept the Ten Commandments.]**
27 Then answered Peter and said unto him, Behold, we have forsaken all, and followed thee; what shall we have therefore?
28 And Jesus said unto them, Verily I say unto you, That ye which have followed me, in the regeneration when the Son of man shall sit in the throne of his glory, ye also shall sit upon twelve thrones, judging the twelve tribes of Israel.
29 And every one that hath forsaken houses, or brethren, or sisters, or father, or mother, or wife, or children, or lands, for my name's sake, shall receive an hundredfold, and shall inherit everlasting life.
30 But many that are first shall be last; and the last shall be first.

It is unknown whether the rich young ruler ever repented and complied with the *Son of Man's* command with respect to the first commandment. But it does raise a few questions.

Can anyone keep the Ten Commandments? Some assume it is impossible and the Ten Commandments are to validate how wicked sinful man's soul is. Others assume that YHWH would only give commands that an individual can keep. It is certainly difficult to keep the Ten Commandments in thought, word, and deed, yet in Chapter VIII there are seven types of souls identified that are associated with the Menorah. Two of the seven types of souls are not required to repent because they were willing to die for or were dedicated to YHWH—men like Moses, Joshua, Caleb, and Aaron. Today some people are still willing to die for YHWH.

Another question is which commandments are most important, or do they all have the same weight? The Son of Man, Jesus the Messiah was asked this question and responded in Matthew 22: 36-40

Matthew 22:36-40
36 Master, which is the great commandment in the law?

*37 Jesus said unto him, Thou shalt **love the Lord thy God** [self's $L(t)$] with all thy heart* **[motives]**, *and with all thy soul* **[knowledge]**, *and with all thy mind* **[Will].**
38 This is the first and great commandment.

39 And the second is like unto it, Thou shalt love thy neighbour as thyself.
40 On these two commandments hang all the law and the prophets.

The most important commandment is to love YHWH. One's love has three different aspects associated with it, and they will be addressed in the following order *soul*, *mind*, and *heart*.

One's soul contains all his knowledge of the universe. The Ten Commandments state one is to place high magnitudes of $L(t)$ Love, priority, on all one's knowledge relating to YHWH. However, from the Garden of Eden everyone has the knowledge that they have the responsibility to choose what items of knowledge will receive their priority, $L(t)$. Each item of knowledge has an associated $L(t)$, Love (priority), and $F(t)$, faith (confidence). An individual applies knowledge in accordance with the magnitude of his $Will(t)$, which is:

$$Will(t) = L(t) * F(t) * P(t)$$

The first commandment is the most important because without some compliance with it, the rest of the commandments do not matter. That is, if one does not care about YHWH, $L(t) = 0$, then it does not matter how confident he is in his knowledge about YHWH, $F(t) >> 0$, because his $Will_{YHWH}(t) = 0$.

An individual's *mind* consists of the WILLs associated with all one's knowledge of the universe, and the first commandment requires the highest magnitude of Wills be associated with all knowledge of YHWH. The *mind* introduces the faith factor $F(t)$. The $F(t)$ development process is unique because the individual contributes the expectation associated with the item of knowledge, but the change in magnitude of $F(t)$ only comes from the other person. For example, if one asks another person to do a task and he does it, then one's faith in the person increases, but if the person does not do the task as expected, one's faith in the person decreases. Thus with respect to YHWH, the magnitude of one's faith in YHWH can only come from one's acceptance of YHWH's provides for him. This is the reason YHWH justifies a person by his faith in Him.

The WILL associated with all items of knowledge that are for YHWH is often referred to as one's *indwelling holy spirit,* and the items of knowledge whose Will is not consistent with YHWH's WILL are referred to as one's *sin nature*.

The heart is the motive, maximum Will associated with a decision and all one's decisions should be for YHWH. When there are several items of knowledge that are relevant to a decision that must be made, the item with the maximum magnitude Will will be selected, and it is the motive for the decision. Thus what a man decides reflects his *heart,* or motives, and the result is his works. If a person's motives are for YHWH his works or actions will reflect it. All individuals have a different number and kind of items of knowledge, and the result is everyone has a different *heart* and works.

131

In the Image of YHWH

The *Son of Man* tells the parable about two sons and characterizes how their father, YHWH, deals with these two types of souls. The younger son is the prodigal and the older son is dedicated to his father as described in Luke 15:11-32.

Luke 15:11-32
11 And he said, A certain man had two sons:
12 And the younger of them said to his father, Father, give me the portion of goods that falleth to me. And he divided unto them his living.
13 And not many days after the younger son gathered all together, and took his journey into a far country, and there wasted his substance with riotous living.
14 And when he had spent all, there arose a mighty famine in that land; and he began to be in want.
15 And he went and joined himself to a citizen of that country; and he sent him into his fields to feed swine.
16 And he would fain have filled his belly with the husks that the swine did eat: and no man gave unto him.
17 And when he came to himself, he said, How many hired servants of my father's have bread enough and to spare, and I perish with hunger!
18 I will arise and go to my father, and will say unto him, Father, I have sinned against heaven, and before thee,
19 And am no more worthy to be called thy son: make me as one of thy hired servants. **[The son decided to repent without his father going to the far country to retrieve him.]**
20 And he arose, and came to his father. But when he was yet a great way off, his father saw him, and had compassion, and ran, and fell on his neck, and kissed him.
21 And the son said unto him, Father, I have sinned against heaven, and in thy sight, and am no more worthy to be called thy son.
22 But the father said to his servants, Bring forth the best robe, and put it on him; and put a ring on his hand, and shoes on his feet:
23 And bring hither the fatted calf, and kill it; and let us eat, and be merry:
24 For this my son was dead, and is alive again; he was lost, and is found. And they began to be merry. **[The father unconditionally accepts the repentant son.]**
25 Now his elder son was in the field: and as he came and drew nigh to the house, he heard music and dancing.
26 And he called one of the servants, and asked what these things meant.
27 And he said unto him, Thy brother is come; and thy father hath killed the fatted calf, because he hath received him safe and sound.
28 And he was angry, and would not go in: therefore came his father out, and intreated him.
29 And he answering said to his father, Lo, these many years do I serve thee, neither transgressed I at any time thy commandment: and yet thou never gavest me a kid, that I might make merry with my friends:
30 But as soon as this thy son was come, which hath devoured thy living with harlots, thou hast killed for him the fatted calf. **[The elder son's anger (anxiety) is a result of his high magnitude of L(t) for his father and that both he and his father were being taken advantage of by the younger son. The issue is why celebrate the prodigal's evil living?]**

132

*31 And he said unto him, Son, thou art ever with me, and all that I have
is thine.* **[The elder son was always dedicated to his father like a
Philadelphian or Smyrnan. He will also receive additional blessings
from his father.]**
*32 It was meet that we should make merry, and be glad: for this thy brother
was dead, and is alive again; and was lost, and is found.* **[The father
states that the issues is not about what he has done, but that he
has repented.]**

In this parable the father is YHWH; the younger son rejects YHWH and then
repents; while the elder son who was dedicated to YHWH does not need to repent,
and both sons will receive eternal life, salvation. Note the father did not go out and
retrieve the younger son, but waited for him to decide to return by himself. Had the
father forced the younger son to return it, would have been enslavement, Whereas,
his return by his own choice reflects his desire to serve.

Jesus the Messiah, the *Son of Man,* makes a point in Matthew 5:17-19 about
the law and prophets during His Sermon on the Mount, which bears including
again.

Matthew 5:17-19
17 Think not that I am come to destroy the law **[Ten Commandments]***,
or the prophets* **[The prophet warned the rebellious people of
impending judgment, declared the coming Messiah, and predicted
end times events.]** *: I am not come to destroy, but to fulfil.*
*18 For verily I say unto you, Till heaven and earth pass, one jot or one tittle
shall in no wise pass from the law* **[Ten Commandments]***, till all be
fulfilled.*
*19 Whosoever therefore shall break one of these least commandments, and
shall teach men so, he shall be called the least in the kingdom of heaven:
but whosoever shall do and teach them, the same shall be called great in
the kingdom of heaven.*

Matthew 5:17-19 records a clear declaration by Jesus the Messiah that the Ten
Commandments and everything declared by all the prophets would remain valid
until the end of time. Thus, what the prophets stated relative to an individual's
behavior is applicable today.

YHWH sent the prophet Ezekiel to Israel telling the people what each individual
must do to receive His acceptance and His gift of salvation. The requirements to
receive salvation from YHWH's perspective are identified in Ezekiel 18.

Ezekiel 18:1-24
1 The word of the Lord came unto me again, saying,
*2 What mean ye, that ye use this proverb concerning the land of Israel,
saying, The fathers have eaten sour grapes, and the children's teeth are set
on edge?*
*3 As I live, saith the Lord God, ye shall not have occasion any more to use this
proverb in Israel.*

4 Behold, all souls are mine; as the soul of the father, so also the soul of the son is mine: the soul that sinneth, it shall die.

5 **But if a man be just, and do that which is lawful and right**,

6 And hath not eaten upon the mountains, neither hath lifted up his eyes to the idols of the house of Israel, neither hath defiled his neighbour's wife, neither hath come near to a menstruous woman,

7 And hath not oppressed any, but hath restored to the debtor his pledge, hath spoiled none by violence, hath given his bread to the hungry, and hath covered the naked with a garment;

8 He that hath not given forth upon usury, neither hath taken any increase, that hath withdrawn his hand from iniquity, hath executed true judgment between man and man,

9 Hath walked in my statutes, and hath kept my judgments, to deal truly; he is just, **he shall surely live**, saith the Lord God.

10 **If he beget a son** that is a robber, a shedder of blood, and that doeth the like to any one of these things,

11 And that doeth not any of those duties, but even hath eaten upon the mountains, and defiled his neighbour's wife,

12 Hath oppressed the poor and needy, hath spoiled by violence, hath not restored the pledge, and hath lifted up his eyes to the idols, hath committed abomination,

13 Hath given forth upon usury, and hath taken increase: shall he then live? he shall not live: he hath done all these abominations; **he shall surely die**; his blood shall be upon him.

14 **Now, lo, if he beget a son, that seeth all his father's sins which he hath done, and considereth, and doeth not such like,**

15 That hath not eaten upon the mountains, neither hath lifted up his eyes to the idols of the house of Israel, hath not defiled his neighbour's wife,

16 Neither hath oppressed any, hath not withholden the pledge, neither hath spoiled by violence, but hath given his bread to the hungry, and hath covered the naked with a garment,

17 That hath taken off his hand from the poor, that hath not received usury nor increase, hath executed my judgments, hath walked in my statutes; **he shall not die for the iniquity of his father, he shall surely live.**

18 **As for his father**, because he cruelly oppressed, spoiled his brother by violence, and did that which is not good among his people, lo, even he **shall die in his iniquity**.

19 **Yet say ye, Why? doth not the son bear the iniquity of the father?** When the son hath done that which is lawful and right, and hath kept all my statutes, and hath done them, he shall surely live.

20 The soul that sinneth, it shall die. The son shall not bear the iniquity of the father, neither shall the father bear the iniquity of the son: the righteousness of the righteous shall be upon him, and the wickedness of the wicked shall be upon him.

21 **But if the wicked will turn from all his sins** that he hath committed, and keep all my statutes, and do that which is lawful and right, he shall surely live, he shall not die. **[This is the meaning of repentance and it is possible for him to repent until day he dies.]**

22 *All his transgressions that he hath committed, they shall not be mentioned unto him: in his righteousness that he hath done he shall live.* **[This is unconditional acceptance by YHWH.]**

23 *Have I any pleasure at all that the wicked should die? saith the Lord God: and not that he should return from his ways, and live?*

24 **But when the righteous turneth away from his righteousness,** *and committeth iniquity, and doeth according to all the abominations that the wicked man doeth, shall he live?* *All his righteousness that he hath done shall not be mentioned: in his trespass that he hath trespassed, and in his sin that he hath sinned, in them shall he die.* **[A person's bad decisions will result in loss of salvation. This is possible until the day he dies.]**

What did Ezekiel 18 establish as requirements and responsibilities for an individual with regard to his salvation? The fundamental criterion for salvation was to obey the Ten Commandments, Ezekiel 18:5. It was important for an individual to know that he is not responsible for another person's loss of salvation due to their sin, transgression of the Ten Commandments, Ezekiel 18:10-20. While an individual who has rejected YHWH and is living in sin can receive salvation by repenting of his sin. Repentance is setting one's priorities in accordance with the Ten Commandments per Ezekiel 18:21. It is reassuring that salvation is unconditional acceptance by YHWH, Ezekiel 18:22.

Some people assume that once a person had declared their allegiance to YHWH their salvation is assured regardless of what they do for the remainder of their life. However, Ezekiel 18:24 does not support this view and states that an individual who had been trying to keep the Ten Commandments and then decided to reject them and live in sin will lose his salvation. It becomes apparent that an individual is responsible for the composition of his soul, and his salvation status is time dependent and reflect the magnitude of his $Will_{YHWH}(t)$. The individual can no longer influence his salvation after he dies, and he does not know the day or hour that this will occur. Only YHWH knows the individual's soul state and the time He will harvest it.

Another picture of a good relationship with YHWH is that of a child where the child must place his priority on his parents and have faith they will provide for him because he is not capable of surviving on his own.

An acceptable relationship with YHWH requires self's soul, mind and heart to possess $Will_{YHWH}(t) >> Will_{other\ People}(t) > Will_{self}(t)$. YHWH's goal for one's life is for him to utilize YHWH's gift of freewill to conform one's soul to the image of the *Son of Man* by relying on YHWH to provide, like a child relies on his parents.

The *Son of Man's* teaching reenforces that adherence to the Ten Commandments is necessary for a good personal relationship with YHWH. Also, He is the perfect leader and example of what each person will experience when confronted with the first-death.

135

Son of Man's **First-Death**

4000 OS is the fortieth Jubilee period since 2000 OS. This Jubilee period started five months earlier on Yom Kippur, and the excitement in Jerusalem had been building ever since. Being a Jubilee period, the prophecies concerning the anticipated Messiah should be fulfilled. The people were hoping for a leader to arise and free them from the Roman rule. The most likely candidate was a man from Galilee who had been healing the sick, making the lame to walk, the blind to see and even raised Lazarus from the dead. The man from Galilee was YHWH's mortal-material body, the *Son of Man*, who had been teaching mankind YHWH's truth, demonstrating how mankind should behave, and what mankind must experience. Jesus YHWH's mortal-material body must be forsaken and then resurrected to overcome death and demonstrate to mankind what they would experience as His followers. The people laid palm branches before Jesus, the *Son of Man*, to welcome their Messiah to Jerusalem for the Passover celebration.

This situation is like Mount Sinai, and the majority of people had to accept or reject YHWH's mortal body as the prophesied Messiah. The outcome was already known because the distribution of the soul types of man has remained unchanged. Just as the prophets said, the *Son of Man* had to die.

Most of Jesus the Messiah's followers were lower class members of society, and they possessed very little composite power. There were some self-centered souls who if they accept the *Son of Man* as the expected Messiah would experience some major losses. The High Priest, Pharisees, and Sadducees had to become servants of the *Son of Man* and lose all their prestige and power. Also, they would be in rebellion against Rome, which could cost them their lives. Those who had much to lose planned to eliminate their opposition. Rome as followers of Satan would perform the requested execution.

YHWH Himself is the *Son of Man* and is the Passover lamb that would now lay down His life for His friends. The *Son of Man*, Jesus the Messiah, identified who His friends are in John 15:10-14.

John 15:10-14
10 If ye keep my commandments, ye shall abide in my love **[L(t)]**; even as I have kept my Father's commandments, and abide in his love.
11 These things have I spoken unto you, that my joy might remain in you, and that your joy might be full.
12 This is my commandment, That ye love one another, as I have loved you.
13 Greater love [L(t)] hath no man than this, that a man lay down his life for his friends.
14 Ye are my friends, if ye do whatsoever I command you.

YHWH demonstrated His perfect love *L(t)*, mercy and grace for all mankind by willingly giving up His mortal-material body, the *first-death*, to give all mankind a chance to repent, believe in Him, and become His friend. YHWH in His grace and mercy also uses His crucifixion and resurrection to help mankind understand what is expected of them.

As a consequence of sin it was appointed for all men to experience the *first-death*. As the perfect example and leader, the *Son of Man* accepted the *first-death* and was crucified by the Roman the soldiers at the request of those who placed themselves above others.

What is the *first-death*? The *first-death* is the breaking of the bond between self's mortal-material body and self's spirit body. This bond can be stretched through the use of various drugs, which can induce, sedation, hallucinations, or out of body experiences. Only when the bond can no longer be sustained does the first-death occur. The bond can be broken through accidental injury, murder, or old age. Once the first-death occurs the mortal Body returns to its physical elements, the dust of the earth, but self's spirit Body, Soul, and Will continue to exist in the pre-creation universe hopefully in the presence of YHWH.

YHWH, *Son of Man*, died on the cross for all mankind. This is a demonstration of His perfect love for mankind, John 15:13. The *first-death* was completely experienced by YHWH. YHWH's BODY, the *Son of God* (His spirit BODY) and the *Son of Man* (His mortal-material Body) together input to YHWH's SOUL everything that was occurring. YHWH's SOUL, the Father, decided every response for each input and YHWH's WILL implemented the response through the *Son of Man's* speech, body actions, and other events. Some unique events included changing daylight to darkness and ripping the Veil of Sin in the Temple from top to bottom. YHWH suffered the entire crucifixion, and when YHWH's SOUL decided to sever the bond between His Spirit Body and forsake the *Son of Man*, His mortal Body. YHWH's WILL had the *Son of Man* declare this in Matthew 27:46.

Matthew 27:45-46
45 Now from the sixth hour there was darkness over all the land unto the ninth hour. **[Probable total eclipse of the sun from Jerusalem.]**
46 And about the ninth hour Jesus cried with a loud voice, saying, Eli, Eli, lama sabachthani? that is to say, My God **[YHWH]**, my God **[YHWH]**, why hast thou forsaken me?

The bond between YHWH's Spirit BODY and His mortal-material BODY was broken causing YHWH to experience the *first-death*. The *Son of Man* was truly forsaken! YHWH's mortal-material BODY was dead and then was placed in a tomb completing the second step, the *first-death*. .

Prior to YHWH's mortal-material BODY's *first-death*, He gave comfort to His followers telling them not to fear their *first-death* in Matthew 10:28 and Luke 12:4-5.

> *Matthew 10:28*
> **28 And fear not them which kill the body, but are not able to kill the soul:** but rather fear him which is able to destroy both soul and body in hell.
>
> *Luke 12:4-6*
> **4 And I say unto you my friends, Be not afraid of them that kill the body, and after that have no more that they can do.**
> 5 But I will forewarn you whom ye shall fear: Fear_him_ **[YHWH]**, which after he hath killed hath power to cast into hell; yea, I say unto you, Fear him.

In *first-death* the mortal-material body is forsaken, thrown away, and this is a process that all mortal human beings shall experience. However, YHWH also gives a warning that if an individual places himself or Satan first in his life then he should also consider the impact *second-death*. The consequences of the *second-death* will be addressed in Chapter XII.

YHWH keeps His mortal-material BODY in the tomb for three days and nights to ensure the people recognize the *Son of Man* was truly dead. During this time YHWH's Spirit-BODY was no longer bonded to the *Son of Man* and it was truly forsaken, but why was the statement in Matthew 27:46 "My God, my God, why hast thou forsaken me?" phrased as a question? The answer to this question relates to the Resurrection from the *first-death*.

Son of Man's **Resurrection**

The *Son of Man's* Resurrection occurred when He took on or bonded to a new glorified body, which was capable of transition between pre-creation universe and the post-creation universe in accordance with YHWH's WILL. YHWH's resurrected structure was illustrated in Figure X-2. YHWH's Resurrected *Son of Man* resembled the mortal *Son of Man* except it now had an immortal bond with *Son of God* and had additional new functionality. The glorified *Son of Man* was still responsible to interface with mankind at mankind's level. For the benefit of mankind YHWH demonstrated what a glorified body could do during the period of time between His resurrection, the taking on of His glorified body, and His ascension—the transition into the pre-creation universe. A glorified body, can go between the pre-creation universe and the material component of the universe at WILL, go through material walls, move place to place in an instant, and undoubtedly has many more extraordinary capabilities that were not demonstrated.

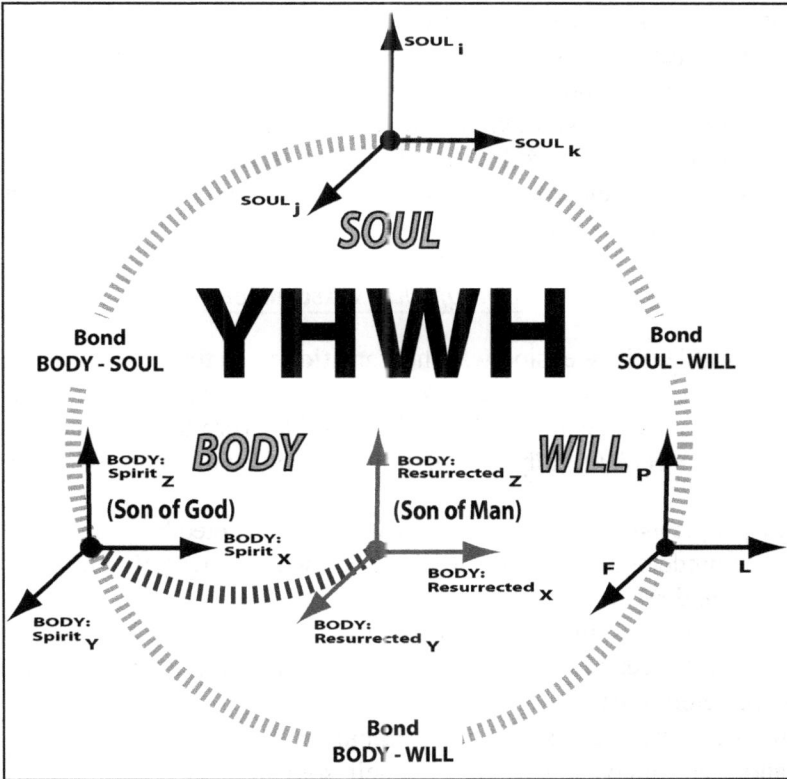

Figure X-2 YHWH's Glorified Composition after the Resurrection

The crucifixion and resurrection of YHWH's mortal BODY, Jesus the Messiah, ushered in the *Age of the Messiah* starting during the Jubilee period in the year 4000 OS, which correlates to 0030 +/- 3 AD or 4069 +/- 18.5 AM, see Appendix I and II.

There are two criteria that must be met for any individual to receive a glorified body from YHWH and they are:

1. One must have experienced the *first-death*.

2. One must be a follower of YHWH that is Self's $Will_{YHWH}(t) > Will_{self}(t)$.

The first criterion is readily met because very human since the Original Sin has been denied access to the Tree of Life, and they shall surely die. The second criteria is the problem because YHWH gave each individual the responsibility to

139

place YHWH first in his life. That is, accept the Ten Commandments. When an individual dies and he is a follower of YHWH, then YHWH's WILL, the Holy Spirit, implements a new bond to a new glorified body, which is similar to Jesus the Messiah's glorified body.

The *Son of Man's* resurrection initiated the Age of the Messiah and then He spent forty days with His followers, disciples, showing them what a glorified body is like and providing them instructions for the future. Then, the *Son of Man* concludes with His ascension.

Son of Man's **Ascension**

The *Son of Man's* ascension was the transition from the material universe into the pre-creation universe. Now the *Son of Man's* physical absence brings a new era in YHWH's relationship with mankind. What were the implications of this new era? Does YHWH totally change how He deals with an individual after His ascension?

Some people assume that the soul was totally corrupted by the original sin and YHWH has predetermined by name, the elect, who He will give faith to become His follower and receive eternal life.

Others people assume the soul was partially corrupted. The individual must chose to be a follower of YHWH, and when this decision is declared the individual has received eternal life.

While other people assume the Original Sin was an historical event where Adam and Eve gained knowledge in their soul that they had been given the responsibility by YHWH to chose to love YHWH, self, or Satan and the first-death is the event in time that determines if one will receive YHWH's gift of eternal life or not.

What did the *Son of Man* tell His disciples to do? He provides parting instructions to His disciples Luke 24:45-51 and Matthew 28:19-20.

Luke 24:45-51
45 Then opened he their understanding, that they might understand the scriptures,
46 And said unto them, Thus it is written, and thus it behoved Christ to suffer, and to rise from the dead the third day:
*47 And that **repentance** and **remission of sins** should be preached in his name [Son of Man, Jesus the Messiah, YHWH] among all nations, beginning at Jerusalem.*
48 And ye are witnesses of these things.
49 And, behold, I send the promise of my Father upon you: but tarry ye in the city of Jerusalem, until ye be endued with power from on high.

50 And he led them out as far as to Bethany, and he lifted up his hands, and blessed them.
51 And it came to pass, while he blessed them, he was parted from them, and carried up into heaven.[ascension]

Matthew 28:19-20
*19 Go ye therefore, and **teach all nations, baptizing them** in the name of the Father, and of the Son, and of the Holy Ghost:* [YHWH]
*20 Teaching them to observe **all things whatsoever I have commanded you**: and, lo, I am with you alway, even unto the end of the world. Amen.*

The disciples of Jesus the Messiah are in a unique situation because few people in the world are aware of the death and resurrection of the *Son of Man*. Thus, they must teach people about what has occurred and what it means. To teach or preach is to impart knowledge to other people. First, they must give people the knowledge of who YHWH's BODY, the *Son of Man*, Jesus the Messiah is and what He has done. This is called the gospel, good news, and it is the knowledge that:

- YHWH CAME by taking on a mortal body, Jesus the Messiah, the *Son of Man* to communicate with mankind at their level as they requested at Mount Sinai.

- YHWH TAUGHT what is required from each individual to be His disciple or follower; by being a perfect example; by demonstrating His power; by commanding acceptance of the Ten Commandments; for those rejecting YHWH, repentance is required for remission of sin and receipt of eternal life.

- YHWH DIED demonstrating the *first-death*, which all people shall experience.

- YHWH RESURRECTED to demonstrate that the *first-death* is not final, and if an individual becomes a follower of YHWH he also will be resurrected to immortality, eternal life .

- YHWH ASCENDED by transition into the pre-creation universe using His resurrected glorified body. During the time YHWH is absent every individual is to be obedient to YHWH's commands, help others, rely on YHWH to provide for his needs, and serve YHWH by telling other people about what YHWH has done and what he will do for them.

- YHWH is COMING AGAIN to earth in power and glory to establish His kingdom using His resurrected Body, Jesus the Messiah.

YHWH's expectations for each individual are also summarized in John 3:16.

John 3:16
16 For God [YHWH] so loved [perfect priority] the world, that he gave his only begotten Son [YHWH's mortal BODY - Jesus the Messiah], that whosoever believeth in him should not perish, but have everlasting life [salvation].

141

In the Image of YHWH

The question is what does it mean to believe in Jesus the Messiah? To *believe* in a person is to be his disciple or follower and this condition has several implications:

1. One must have knowledge that the person exists or existed.

2. One must understand and support what the person stands for and accept it and support it as one's truth.

The first step to *believe* is to possess knowledge about the person. Without knowledge one is ignorant of the person, and thus their soul has no WILL associated with the person. To prevent ignorance about YHWH a follower of YHWH needs to tell others who YHWH is and what He has done and will do (came, taught, died, resurrected, ascended, coming again). This is the Great Commission.

The second step to *believe* is developing the magnitude of one's Will with respect to one's knowledge about YHWH. YHWH has commanded that one set his $L(t)$s in accordance with the Ten Commandments and set one's expectations accordingly. That is, do not expect YHWH to help you violate the Ten Commandments, but depend on YHWH to provide $F(t)$ just like a child depends on his parents. The result is that one becomes a follower of YHWH and develops a $Will_{YHWH}(t) \gg Will_{self}(t)$. If one neglects YHWH's commands and depends upon himself, like Cain, the result is $Will_{self}(t) > Will_{YHWH}(t)$. Then, there is Satan and his followers who are certain, high $F(t)$, who YHWH is but they are trying to destroy Him, $L(t) = 0$ and their $Will_{YHWH}(t) = L_{YHWH}(t) * F_{YHWH}(t) = 0$.

When one believes in an item they will develop *fear* for it. *Fear* is the *Anxiety(t)* $= L_{YHWH}(t) - F_{YHWH}(t)$ associated with the knowledge of what the item requires of him and the anticipated consequences for noncompliance. For example, the student will fear the test he has not studied for. Likewise, one would fear for their life for noncompliance with regard to a dictator's commands. The anxiety experienced when one knowingly commits a sin is a result of their *fear* of YHWH, the Lord. When one knowingly makes decisions having *motives* compliant with YHWH's commands, he is known to have a *heart* for YHWH.

After the *Son of Man,* Jesus the Messiah, ascended or departs from the material universe, there were at least several thousand followers and His eleven disciples. After Pentecost the eleven disciples added a twelfth, so they could begin their primary task to preach the gospel to the twelve tribes of Israel and then to the rest of the world where knowledge of YHWH was lacking. To preach the gospel to the gentiles, YHWH placed the *fear* of YHWH in Saul by blinding him temporally to get his attention and then renaming him the apostle Paul whose job is to preach the gospel to the Gentiles throughout the world.

Paul and the other disciples only went to areas and cities that required the people to repent of their sin, and thus their preaching and letters reflected that man's soul was totally depraved. These soul types had to repent to be saved. The disciples did not go to or write letters to the souls in Philadelphia and Smyrna because these souls were already followers of YHWH.

The apostle John who wrote the Book of Revelation described the types of souls in seven cities and what they must do to receive YHWH's gift of eternal life. The seven cities physically existed in Asia Minor and were Philadelphia, Smyrna, Ephesus, Laodicea, Thyatira, Pergamos, and Sardis. The meaning of each city's name characterized the type of soul in the city. Jesus the Messiah's ascension occurred in the year 30+/- 3 AD. The apostle John documented the properties of the seven churches between 90 and 100 AD, and the following descriptions of the churches, soul types, are only applicable for this period of time. Although the cities exist today to some extent, the soul types described by John do not.

Philadelphia means "city of brotherly love" and these people are very devoted to YHWH. Exactly how this church developed is uncertain. It may have developed directly from some followers of YHWH from before His crucifixion. Note none of the apostles including Paul visited Philadelphia because the Philadelphians-type soul was already saved so there was no need. For the Philadelphian-type soul to have repented they would have had to reject YHWH. However, Philadelphians were willing to die for YHWH and they had an open door to eternal life. The members of the Philadelphia-type soul had a composite magnitude of WILL for YHWH that is $1.0 > Will_{YHWH}(t) > 0.7$.

Smyrna in ancient Greek means "Myrrh", which was highly prized. YHWH highly prizes those souls that are to dedicated to Himself. The church of Smyrna may have developed in a similar fashion as Philadelphia. Also, Smyrna did not get any attention from the apostles, and all the people needed to do to receive eternal life was the remain followers of YHWH until death. The members of this church had a composite magnitude of WILL for YHWH that is $0.7 > Will_{YHWH}(t) > 0.5$.

Ephesus means "desirable". If the Ephesian-type soul is desirable to YHWH, then why are they required to REPENT to receive the gift eternal life? Remember the majority soul type in a city represents the church. The church that the apostle John was describing was probably started in 52 AD when the apostle Paul visited the city of Ephesus. At the time of this visit, the dominate church in the city was pagan with worship centered about the Temple of Artemis. From the seed planted by Paul, the followers of YHWH began to grow and 20 years later they became the dominate soul type in the city. However, by 90 AD when the apostle John documented the church, the souls in the city of Ephesus had regressed and their soul type was the first to fall below the *Repentance Threshold*[2], $Will_{YHWH}(t) = 0.5$. The people of Ephesus were continuing to worship YHWH while rejecting the Nicolaitians or Babylonian pagan worship, but they were placing self first and YHWH second. These people had decreased their fear of YHWH and have come to the point in time where the *motive* for the majority of their decisions are placing self first and YHWH second or $Will_{self}(t) > Will_{YHWH}(t)$. The members of this church have a composite magnitude of WILL for YHWH that is $0.5 > Will_{YHWH}(t) > 0.14$. The Ephesian-type soul was unique among the seven types because it was the first type that had to REPENT to receive eternal life. The apostle Paul only went to lost souls who were required to repent, and his teaching and letters stressed that anyone who loves YHWH, (high magnitude $L_{YHWH}(t)$) was predestined before the creation of the earth to receive by YHWH's grace, a free gift, of eternal life. Paul also stressed that the gift of eternal life cannot come from the individual. Paul states this in Ephesians 2:8-9.

> *Ephesians 2:8-9*
> 8 *For by* <u>*grace*</u> [**free gift**] *are ye* <u>*saved*</u> [**receive eternal life**] *through* <u>*faith*</u>[F_{YHWH}(t)]; *and that not of yourselves: it is the* <u>*gift of God*</u> [**grace**]:
> 9 *Not of works, lest any man should boast.*

Recall that self's $Will_{YHWH}(t) = L_{YHWH}(t) * F_{YHWH}(t)$ and that:

- $Will_{YHWH}(t)$ reflects the heart or motive for one's decisions and are reflected in one's actions or works that one does.
- $L_{YHWH}(t)$, love or priority, is the responsibility of the individual.
- $F_{YHWH}(t)$, one's faith, can only come from YHWH's response to them. That is, when an individual asks YHWH for something YHWH will either provide a response that is expected or not. Thus, one's expectations of YHWH can only be reconciled by YHWH. An individual has no control over any response YHWH makes to them. Faith is the reconciliation of one's expectations to reality. The more expectations that align with received responses the greater the magnitude of one's faith.

YHWH justifies one by their faith because it directly measures their acceptance of His responses to them. Thus, as one has increases their priority, $L_{YHWH}(t)$, on YHWH and accepts His provision one's faith, $F_{YHWH}(t)$, increases resulting in increased works, $Will_{YHWH}(t)$, that are compliant with YHWH's Ten Commandments.

From Paul's letter to the Ephesians, their soul type has difficulty continuing to follow YHWH due to love of self and misplaced expectations for YHWH. They had to REPENT.

Laodicea was a very wealthy city being at the crossroads of the major trading routes. It was recognized for banking and manufacturing with a relatively high quality of life. The name Laodicea meant "rights of the people", which implied the people were in charge and self love dominated this soul type. This soul type believed the world centered about them, and they were self sufficient. The Laodicean soul type had the unique property that they were neither hot, for YHWH, or cold, for Satan. That is, the warm members have a low magnitude of $Will_{YHWH}(t)$ between $0.14 > Will_{YHWH}(t) > 0.0$ while the cool members' $Will_{YHWH}(t) = 0.0$ and their $Will_{Satan}(t)$ is between $0.0 > Will_{Satan}(t) > 0.14$. Individuals with a Laodicean soul type will align with anyone for his benefit and would not hesitate to eliminate anyone who opposed him. Cain and communist dictators are a good examples of this soul type. The majority of people in the city of Laodicea belonged to the self centered Laodicean church just described, but there was a small number people who were not. This condition was alluded to by the apostle Paul in his letter to the Colossians.

Colossians 4:13-16
13 For I bear him record, that he hath a great zeal for you, and them that are in Laodicea, and them in Hierapolis.
14 Luke, the beloved physician, and Demas, greet you.
15 Salute the brethren which are in Lacdicea, and Nymphas, and the <u>church which is in his house</u> **[This is a small group of followers of YHWH.].**
16 And when this epistle is read among you **[the house church]**, *cause that it be* <u>read also in the church of the Laodiceans</u> **[The small group of followers of YHWH were to declare to the lost Laodicean-type soul that they had to repent.];** *and that ye likewise read the epistle from Laodicea.*

YHWH sends a small number of His followers into a lost church to knock on the door of their souls with the message of repentance and they must REPENT.

Thyatira was another wealthy trade city whose name was probably associated with Jezebel and originated from the Greek thea, "a female deity, goddess," and tyrannos," a tyrant or ruler." The majority of the people in Thyatira were pagan followers of Jezebel. They were sexually immoral and ate the food of Satan, which is embracing Satan's practices. The problem with the Thyatiran-type soul was its members' $Will_{YHWH}(t) = 0.0$ and their $Will_{Satan}(t)$ was $0.14 > Will_{Satan}(t) > 0.5$. The Thyatiran-type soul promoted self and Satan for self's benefit, and they must REPENT or experience the Great Tribulation.

Pergamos in Greek means, "Married to the tower." Pergos means "tower," Gamos means "married." The pagan form of worship originated from the tower of Babel. The love of the tower of Babel was the beginning of pagan worship in Babylon, and it migrated to Pergamos after being banished from Persia. Pergamos was to represent everything the original priests in the City of Babel envisioned and instituted. The worship centered about the Altar of Zeus, the Throne of Satan, In 1910 AD archeologists relocated the Throne of Satan to the Pergamum Museum in Berlin, Germany where it resides today. The Pergamos-type souls were certainly members of the Synagogue of Satan, and embraced the Nicolaitain and Babylonian paganism. They have a $Will_{YHWH}(t) = 0.0$ and $0.5 > Will_{Satan}(t) > 0.7$. If they do not REPENT they will experience the Winepress.

Sardis was a very wealthy city noted for minting gold and silver coins. Its name comes from a blood-red colored stone "sardius", which in ancient times was obtained from Sardis. From YHWH's perspective, this Sardis soul type is dead with a $Will_{YHWH}(t) = 0.0$ and $0.7 > Will_{Satan}(t) > 1.0$. They are part of the synagogue of Satan with hearts of stone, and if they do not REPENT, they will experience the Winepress.

The Age of the Messiah started in 4000 OS with Jesus the Messiah's ascension and the subsequent ministry of the apostles. From this beginning these seven soul types have been developing in numbers, and any individual who has become a follower of YHWH has the responsibility to live for and teach the gospel of Jesus the Messiah to those he encounters. YHWH mercifully provides the Holy Bible as a guide book to tell mankind what He expects of them until He returns in 6000 OS and what future events are determined for mankind.

Son of Man's **Soul Harvest**

Before the *Son of Man* ascended into the pre-creation universe in 4000 OS, He promised to return and gather His followers to be with Him for eternity. Today 6000 OS approaches and nearly forty Jubilees have pasted since YHWH's BODY, Jesus the Messiah ascended into the pre-creation universe. What will people today experience when YHWH returns and harvests the souls of man? This is the subject of the next chapter.

XI YHWH and Today's Society, 6000 OS

How did all the different societies develop after Noah's flood to form the world societies we know today?

We have previously examined the extraordinary consequences of Noah's flood, 1656 AM. In His perfect judgment, YHWH destroyed the corrupt world that existed pre-flood, and all of mankind, both corrupt and non corrupt, died except for eight people.

Mankind's knowledge post-flood was the composite knowledge contained in eight souls that YHWH brought through the flood on the ark. The type of each of the eight souls was unchanged except for the knowledge each obtained from their flood experience. Also, the intelligence of each soul remained unchanged.

The pre-flood single land mass was friendly to human movement and communication. The post-flood land mass was fragmented, and the terrain was hostile to human movement.

After the Tower of Babel, during the days of Peleg, the world society was broken into very small language groups and compelled to disperse by YHWH among the new continents making communication and physical contact extremely difficult. For example native, Americans were unaware of the European or African cultures.

Post-flood mankind's knowledge of the pre-flood and flood was passed on orally. As time passed, oral tradition became less accurate and the source for many myths. This is like having one person start a story and telling someone, and they pass it on to someone else. After it passes through ten other people, compare the last person's story with the original, and the result is comparable to oral tradition. Oral tradition was very inaccurate and could only be stabilized once it was documented. Detailed pre and post-flood knowledge did not exist until YHWH gave the Torah to mankind via Moses.

The question becomes how does a corrupt world society develop, like the one that existed in the time of Noah, that warranted its total destruction by YHWH's perfect wrath?

The basic building block for any society is the family consisting of the male, female, and their children. When a number of families group together for a common benefit; tribes, villages, and cities are formed. When tribes, villages, and cities group together, a nation is formed; and when nations group together, empires are formed. When all empires and nations group together a One-World Government is formed.

Any group or organization will reflect the composite Will of its members and leadership and will use any unique assets, like a strong army, a unique technology, a special weapon, or the like to project their composite Will. As previously discussed, the types of souls and the number of people having a particular type soul conform to a normal distribution as shown in Figure XI-1.

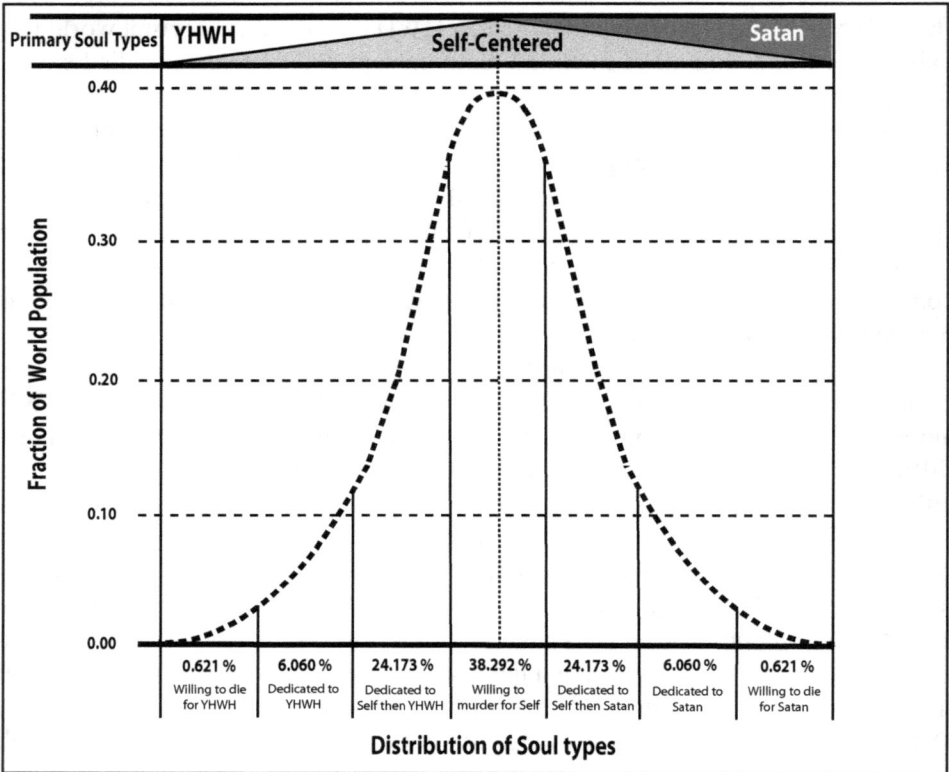

Primary Soul Types	YHWH		Self-Centered				Satan
0.621 %	6.060 %	24.173 %	38.292 %	24.173 %	6.060 %	0.621 %
Willing to die for YHWH	Dedicated to YHWH	Dedicated to Self then YHWH	Willing to murder for Self	Dedicated to Self then Satan	Dedicated to Satan	Willing to die for Satan

Distribution of Soul types

Figure XI-1 Distribution of Mankind's Soul Types

Like an individual's soul, a nation's soul is the composite of all the soul types in the nation. For example, if a nation contained 100 cities and 20 of the cities were followers of YHWH, 30 cities were devoted to themselves and 50 cities were followers of Satan. The followers of Satan controlled the government. The society would be violent because the dominate soul types would take whatever they wanted from any individual or city in the nation. This nation from YHWH's perspective is violent and corrupt.

Another example is a nation that has 100 cities and 70 of the cities were followers of YHWH, 20 cities were devoted to themselves, and 10 cities were followers of Satan; and the followers of YHWH controlled the government. The result is the majority of the cities would be helping the other cities to see the advantage of relying on YHWH to meet their needs. In this society violent acts and abuse of other people would not be tolerated. This nation from YHWH's perspective is working toward His desired goals as established by the Ten Commandments.

The nature of any society depends upon what type of souls the people have who control the society. Man's WILL is time dependent, hence the type of character a society has may change with time due to internal or external circumstances, fluctuations in the number of people, or changes in generational knowledge within the society.

How did the world's societies develop from Noah's flood to 2000 OS? By 2000 OS (2069+/- 18.5 AM) the world still contained many unique tribes, groups, cities, nations,and empires. The entire world's population had increased significantly from six people; in 1657 AM to many thousands of people by 2000 OS. The vast majority of these people were unaware that other people even existed on the continents of Africa, North America, South America, Australia/Oceania, Eurasia (Europe, Asia) and Antarctica. For example, the native Americans were unaware of the Egyptian, Asian, and African civilizations. Each independent tribe, group, nation developed their own model of the universe.

All the people in the world at this time were just as intelligent as anyone today. Their concept of the universe was based upon knowledge and WILL contained in each member's soul. Thus, the three primary types of souls, natures, can be observed in all the various universe of models that each society developed.

- Followers of YHWH are to be obedient to Him. As of yet, 2000 OS, no nation has formed that is under the control of YHWH's followers.

- Those who place self first develop models for the universe where they are an integral part it, or the sun, moon, nature are held in high regard, or an individual is a god in their own right. Their souls reflect the nature of Cain where self is the most important. Examples are the Native American religions and Vedic in Asia.

- Followers of Satan typically develop models for the universe that include multiple gods, with conflict among the gods or represent mankind as being slaves to the gods. These civilizations show a constant struggle to obtain sufficient knowledge to replace YHWH. After the tower of Babel these people tended not to move as YHWH directed because they were in direct conflict with Him. Thus, they tended to stay near the area of the Tigris and Euphrates Rivers or in the near East and liked to build cities. Examples are the Sumerian, Akkadian, Mesopotamian and Egyptian cultures.

It is very important to keep in mind that at this time, 2000 OS, no society on earth had an accurate specific calendar and detailed documents that provided the history of mankind and how the material universe came into existence. Some societies however, were beginning to document their activities.

In the Image of YHWH

Mankind's knowledge base was very limited. The technology provided stone structures, bows, arrows, wagons, chariots, armor, and use of animals such as horses to aid in work and travel. Most civilizations were hunter-gatherers or farmers while some were city dwellers; some nations were more dominate like Egypt. YHWH demonstrated what being with Satan was like by allowing the planned Holy Nation to experience evil first hand through slavery in Egypt.

After the Exodus of the Holy Nation from Egypt, 2672 AM, and prior to entering the promised land; YHWH reestablished the history and chronology of the development of the material part of the universe by giving Moses the Torah as previously discussed. The nation of Israel was to be a separate shining star that would eventually bring all nations in the world to YHWH. This lasted until the people rejected YHWH at Mount Sinai because the normal distribution of Israel's nature reflected the majority of the people who were self-centered or wanting to return to Egypt. Once rejected, YHWH in His mercy decided that in the future He would take on a mortal-material body, the Messiah, and would be the perfect example and instruct the people at their level starting in 4000 OS.

4000 OS (4069 +/- 18.5 AM) can also be correlated to the Gregorian Calendar with an even smaller variance. 4000 OS relative to the Gregorian Calendar is 0030 +/- 3.0 AD. This is based on the birth of Jesus the Messiah between 6 BC and 0 AD plus 30 years to the start of His ministry plus 3 years of ministry. Thus, 4000 OS, the time of Jesus the Messiah's crucifixion and resurrection, would have occurred between 27 AD and 33 AD. The most probable birthdate is 4 BC making 29 AD the most probable time of His crucifixion and resurrection.

By 4000 OS mankind's knowledge base was still diverse and fragmented with technology following accordingly. Antarctica remained unpopulated while Africa, North America, South America, and Australia/Oceania remained hunter-gatherers and modeled their universe with man being god or being an integral part of nature. There is still no known communication between the American continents and the rest of the world

Eurasia (Europe, Asia) being a single land mass has become the most developed part of the world. The Silk Road has enabled trade, communication between various parts of the continent from Europe to India and China. Travel still required months or years. Trade facilitated the development of communication skills, money and money standards. The Silk road and trade also facilitated the exchange of societal information.

The Roman Empire was a technologically advanced culture with more sophisticated structures from buildings, to water management systems, roads, printing on parchment and stone. The Roman Empire was based on *Satan's-seed* and it dominated a large part of the known world including Jerusalem.

The Roman Empire violently dealt with any opposition. They crucified Jesus the Messiah at the request of the High Priest and subsequently destroyed the Temple in 70 AD.

During the Age of the Messiah, the period from 4000 OS (0030 +/- 3.0 AD) to the present, it was the responsibility of each individual to help others to become followers of YHWH. This is also called the Great Commission and was described in the previous chapter. The followers of YHWH have struggled to bring all people in the world to YHWH, but just like the Holy Nation of Israel they have failed to change the distribution of the types of souls in the world's population. After nearly 2000 years of effort, today the current distribution of soul types is reflected in the world religions. When world religions are compared with the biblical distribution based on the seven churches in the book of Revelation, the result is amazing. This comparison is shown in Table XI-1 and the world religion data is based on data from *The World Almanac and Book of Facts 2013.* [3]

Those who are followers of YHWH shown in Table XI-1, are considered to include anyone who claims YHWH, Jesus the Messiah, as their savior. Thus, all Messianic Jews are included in the various religions that are followers of YHWH. The total percentage of followers of YHWH is 30.854% versus 34.200%, which tends to imply that several percent who claim YHWH are really more self-centered.

The self-centered shown in Table XI-1 are considered to include anyone who places their self above others or believes they are god or one with nature or the Remnant of Israel. The Remnant of Israel is shown as 1.500 % and this (*) indicates that 1.000 % are Atheistic and 0.500 % are Jewish because they are from the twelve tribes of Israel spread throughout the world and are currently atheistic or expecting a non divine leader as the Messiah. Today, YHWH is already protecting the Remnant of Israel. Self-centered religions often appear as dictatorial governments, or a very dominate individuals. The self-centered type religions relate self to the universe in various ways. In a political setting the self-centered people have the will to control others by whatever means seem right to them. They typically consider themselves to be the enlightened ruling class that needs to manage other people by determining what they can do, think, and if they live. Many like Cain would not hesitate to murder anyone getting in their way. Today, the self-centered type of souls are dictators, communists, socialists, gang leaders, and the like. Their goal is to dominate a group or the world.

Table XI-1 Distributions of Biblical and World Soul Types

Biblical Normal Distribution		World Religion Distribution	
Followers of YHWH	*30.854 %*		*34.200 %*
Philadelphia	0.621 %	Protestant	7.000 %
Smynra	6.060 %	Orthodox	4.500 %
Ephesus	24.173 %	Anglican	1.000 %
		Catholic	17.500 %
		Other Christian	4.200 %
Self-centered	*38.292 %*		*35.100 %*
Laodicea	38.292 %	Atheistic *	14.500 %
		Remnant of Israel *	1.500 %
		Hindu	13.000 %
		Buddhist	5.100 %
		New Age	1.000 %
Followers of Satan	*30.854 %*		*30.700 %*
Thyatira	24.173 %	Muslim	19.000 %
Pergamos	6.060 %	Other occult	2.000 %
Sardis	0.621 %	Ethnic Religions	4.500 %
		Chinese Folk	5.200 %

The followers of Satan shown in Table XI-1 are considered to include anyone who would like to overthrow YHWH. Today, the Muslim religion under Allah, Satan, is the major religion waging war against YHWH and His followers. Muslim jihad demonstrates the people's willingness to murder or die for Satan as they strive to dominate the world for Satan. Muslim Shariah law shows that followers of Satan still possesses hatred for women because of *Eve's-seed*.

Today, we are approaching 6000 OS, which corresponds to 6069 +/- 18.5 AM or 2030 +/- 3.0 AD with the most probable time being 2029 AD [2]. The type of men's souls are still distributed over the world's population in accordance with the biblical normal distribution as shown in Table XI-1.

During the current 40 Jubilee period that started with the crucifixion and resurrection of Jesus the Messiah in 4000 OS, mankind's knowledge has begun to increase exponentially. This was triggered by the invention of the Gutenberg printing press in the year 1436 AD. Since the advent of the printing press, some other key events and inventions include:

- Columbus arrives in America 1492.
- Reformation 1517-1557.
- King James Bible 1611.
- United States of America Declaration of Independence 1776.
- French Revolution 1789
- Cotton gin 1793.

- Gasoline engine 1872.
- Light bulb 1879.
- Automobile 1889.
- First flight 1903.
- Radio 1905.
- World War I 1916 - 1918.
- Television 1927.
- Radar 1940.
- World War II 1941 - 1945.
- Atomic Bomb 1945.
- **Israel restored as a nation May 15 1948.**
- Electronic computer research and development during the 1950s.
- First satellite 1957.
- First mini computer 1960.
- USA's Apollo 11 landed the first man on the Moon. 20 July 1969.
- Early net work research 1961 - 1981.
- Global Positioning System (GPS) 1973 - fully operational 1994.
- Network merging and protocol developed 1982 - 1994.
- Modern global internet 1995 - present.

Today, all the continents (Africa, North America, South America, Australia/ Oceania, Eurasia {Europe, Asia} and Antarctica) have been explored. Travel between all the continents requires only a few hours. Space exploration is just beginning. With the advent of the internet and satellite technology, worldwide communication is common place for many people in the world today. The men's souls have accumulated a huge amount of knowledge. Daniel 12:4 describes this time period.

> Daniel 12:4
> 4 But thou, O Daniel, shut up the words, <u>and seal the book, even to the time of the end:</u>[**This is a statement that the Holy Bible contains Time Dependent Revelation.**] *many shall run to and fro, and <u>knowledge shall be increased</u>.*

Today, mankind has certainly overcome the post-flood loss of his knowledge and has overcome the limitations on his the ability to travel and communicate with all the other people in the world. It is also this increase in knowledge that will open things previously hidden from previous generations.

Then, what differentiates today's society from the corrupt violent world society of Noah's day?

In the Image of YHWH

In YHWH's world society, every individual is free to decide if they will be obedient to YHWH's commands. If people were obedient, then one is to help others as needed. The result is a friendly non violent world, which is continuing to improve everyone's personal relationship with YHWH.

In a corrupt world society consisting of people who put self first, like Cain, these people would support the followers of Satan in the struggle to gain control of all the people in the world. To accomplish this, they would do anything to eliminate anyone in their way. This is just the concept that the end justifies the means. These individuals will take from other people what they desire and dictate to others what to do or think. Any opposition, or dissent is, violently suppressed.

The issue is who controls the nations of the world—the followers of YHWH, followers of Satan or the self-centered? The people of the Holy Nation of Israel were unable to overcome the normal distribution of the people's souls within their own nation. Likewise, the followers YHWH as individuals and as members of various churches have failed to overcome the normal distribution of mankind's souls around the world. This failure is validated by the percentage of the world's population who are followers of YHWH today (see Table XI-1). The distribution of the soul types has remained the same since Cain murdered Abel and today about 31 percent of the world's population claim to be followers of YHWH. Although the number of individual followers of YHWH have increased, this increase was due to the increase in the world's population and not due to conversion of the self-centered and followers of Satan because the world's population is not 100 percent followers of YHWH today! This is a mystery.

Thus, as we approach 6000 OS, we are beginning to observe worldwide the maturing dominance of the followers of Satan and self. In the days of Noah, this might be called the rising of Atlantis.

At this writing there are considered to be 206 nations states in the world. Of these nations 193 are members of the United Nations, 2 are looking at becoming members of the United Nations and 11 other nation states are not members. Of the 206 nation states the sovereignty of 190 is undisputed with 16 whose sovereignty is disputed. These numbers will change with the passage of time.

The vast majority of the 206 nations in the world are controlled by a dictator or Islamic or communist or socialist forms of government. There is only one world power, the United States of America (USA), which has attempted to comply with YHWH's freedom requirements for individuals. All other major nations in some fashion limit the freedom of speech. One other nation that is unique is Israel, which YHWH started to restore to the promised land on 15 May 1948 in preparation for YHWH's appointed time to return in power and glory in 6000 OS.

What happens when YHWH begins to pour out His WRATH?

1. YHWH gives warning to the people.

2. YHWH enables and blesses weak enemies.

3. YHWH allows economic problems.

4. YHWH allows the corrupt to prevail making the society violent.

New York City, USA is the current capital of the world. The United Nations Headquarters and the rebuilt World Trade Center are located there.

The United Nations promotes member nations to have a socialist form of government where the people are not free but belong to the state. People are to be managed by the state for the benefit of the corrupt leaders who control the state.

YHWH will allow the people of a nation to decide if they will follow Him and if they decide not to follow, there are real consequences, which history can attest too. The USA has a unique place in history today. It is the only world power that claims to follow YHWH. However, recently the United States government has removed the Holy Bible from its schools, discouraged public prayer to YHWH (Jesus the Messiah), promoted the murder of the unborn, supported rejection of YHWH's definition of marriage, and are embracing other Occult practices.

In light of the USA rejecting YHWH, He started to warn the nation to change its direction on September 11, 2001 AD by allowing the weak terrorists to succeed in their attack on the World Trade Center in the world's capital, New York City, and to partially succeed in their attack on the USA's capital in Washington DC. The response that YHWH wanted to see from the members of the government and the people was repentance! To repent means to change direction and restore those things that the nation has turned its back on. However, the national response was to build monuments, rebuild the World Trade Center and declare the nation will be stronger than before. The nation gave YHWH some lip service, but continued to retain and make new laws that reject YHWH's commandments. As a result, the character of the nation has become more corrupt and violent.

YHWH does have appointed times and a calendar that is based upon Sabbath days, Sabbath years, and Jubilee periods. After September 11, 2001 AD, the next Sabbath year was 2008 AD. 2008 AD brought the collapse of Fannie Mae and Freddie Mac that happened on September 7, 2008 AD. Then on September 11, 2008 AD Lehman Brothers collapsed, American International Group (AIG) declared it was in trouble, the stockmarket lost significant value impacting both the American and global economies. The economies have yet to recover, and the next Sabbath year is rapidly approaching in 2015 AD.

A limited nuclear war will most probably occur during 2015 AD, which will bring the intent of 11 September 2001 AD to completion with the destruction of the present world capital located in New York City, USA and the government offices in Washington DC, USA. This limited nuclear war will initiate the relocation of the world's capital from New York City, USA to Babylon, Iraq and allow the rebuilding of YHWH's Temple in Jerusalem, Israel. The duration of this war will be short, but all nations of the world will be shaken and turn to the United Nations to solve the problem.

Probably starting in 2016 AD, the United Nations will begin to develop a trilateral grouping of all the nations in the world. This was also described by the prophet Daniel as a Lion, Bear, and Leopard in Daniel 7:4-6 and is summarized in Table XI-2. The Lion, Bear, and Leopard subsequently merge to form the dreadful fourth-beast from the sea, which is the United Nations, One-World Government.

Note in Table XI-2 that the eleventh Kingdom, Israel, does not conform to the alignment of nations. Israel will not become part of the Bear because it would mean that they would have to stop construction of the Temple in Jerusalem and would cease to exist as a people and a nation.

To help stabilize the Middle East, the United Nations will make it a top priority establishing a new world capital by rebuilding United Nations headquarters in Babylon, Iraq. This would also demonstrate man's dominance over YHWH by restoring what was lost at the Tower of Babel when YHWH dispersed the nations. For the Occult, this is the equivalent to the complete restoration of Atlantis.

At this time all the United Nations efforts will be focused on forming a One-World Government that promises to bring peace to the world forever. While the United Nations and most nations of the world will be focused on forming the One-World Government and building its new world capital in Babylon, Iraq, the nation of Israel will be focused on rebuilding the Temple, which was destroyed by the Romans in 70 AD.

The prophet Daniel in Daniel 9:26 first addressed the destruction of the Temple in Jerusalem in 70 AD and subsequent turmoil and wars thereafter.

Daniel 9:26
26 And after threescore and two weeks shall Messiah be cut off, but not for himself: and the <u>people of the prince</u> **[Followers of Satan]** *that shall come shall <u>destroy the city and the sanctuary</u>* **[Roman Empire in 70 AD]***; and the end thereof shall be with a flood, and unto the end of the war desolations are determined.*

Table XI-2 The Beast from the Sea - Planned One-World Government

Beast	Kingdom Number	Nations	Scripture Reference
Beast from the Sea		**Includes all Nations of the World**	**Daniel 7:23-28**
Lion with 2 eagle's wings			*Daniel 7:4*
North American Kingdom	1	USA, Canada, Central America, West Indies	Eagle Wing #1
South American Kingdom	2	All South American nations	Eagle Wing #2
European Kingdom	3	The European Union	The Lion
Bear with 3 Ribs in mouth			*Daniel 7:5*
Northern Asian Kingdom	4	Russia, Kazakhstan, Uzbekistan	Rib #1
Central Kingdom	5	Jorden, Syria, Turkey, Turkmenistan, Iraq, Iran, Afganistan, Pakistan, Saudi Arabia, Yemen, Oman	Rib #2
	11	**Israel - assigned but will not join.**	
Southern Kingdom	6	African Nations	Rib #3
Leopard with 4 wings			*Daniel 7:6*
Southern Asian Kingdom	7	India, SriLanka, Nepal, Banglash, Burma	Wing #1
Eastern Asian Kingdom	8	Mongolia, China, Taiwan, Korea	Wing #2
Western Pacific Kingdom	9	Japan, Philippines, Malaysia, Indonesia, Vietnam, Camboida Thailand, Laos, New Guinea (part)	Wing #3
Southern Pacific Kingdom	10	Australia, New Zealand, New Guinea (part)	Wing #4

Then, in the next verse, Daniel 9:27, Daniel alludes to a future time when the leader of the One-World Government, the prince, will make a *covenant with many*.

Daniel 9:27
27 And he **[the prince, Satan]** *shall confirm the* **covenant with many** *for one week* **[seven years]**: *and in the midst of the week he* **[the prince, Satan]** *shall cause the sacrifice and the oblation to cease, and for the overspreading of abominations he* **[the prince, Satan]** *shall make it desolate, even until the consummation, and that determined shall be poured upon the desolate.*

This *covenant with many* is important because it sets the stage for 5993 OS and is the prelude to the start of the Tribulation Period. The prelude ends on the last day of Elul in 5993 OS. The *covenant with many* is made by the leader of the forming One-World Government, under the authority of Satan, with many Occult and self-centered members of the various nation states. The covenant would allow members to keep the assets of all those they eliminate who oppose the formation of a One-World Government. Who will be opposed to the One-World Government? All true followers of YHWH, Jesus the Messiah, including the Nation of Israel who will have just restored YHWH's Temple in Jerusalem and are sacrificing to Him.

It is ironic that during, Jesus the Messiah's first coming, He came in peace asking mankind to repent, place YHWH first, and love their neighbor as themselves to bring world peace. In contrast, the followers of Satan come forming the One-World Government using murder and destruction with the promise to bring world peace once they have control of the entire world.

The next Sabbath year is 2022 AD, which is the most probable time for the occurrence of 5993 OS, the start of the Tribulation Period. The Holy Bible devotes a great deal of prophetic material to the Time of Jacob's Trouble or the Tribulation Period, which is the seven year period between 5993 OS and 6000 OS. The most detailed account of the Tribulation Period is in the Holy Bible's book of Revelation. The source of the book of Revelation was YHWH who had an angel to give it to the Apostle John to record while he was imprisoned on the island of Patmos before 100 AD per Revelation 1:1-2.

The book of Revelation YHWH identifies seven churches. Each church contains people with a particular type of soul, or nature. Each church corresponds to one of the seven colors of the rainbow and one branch of the seven branched Menorah. Every person that has ever existed is a member of one of these churches. Thus, the entire world's population is represented. The book of Revelation contains YHWH's judgment that each of the seven churches will experience during the Tribulation Period. The first question becomes how many people are in each church or have a particular type of soul?

The distribution of mankind's soul types has remained the same since the first murder. The equation for the normal distribution was provided in Chapter IV. The equation for the normal distribution requires today's digital computer technology and mathematics to solve. This technology was not available until the 1960s; yet the Apostle John wrote the book of Revelation while he was imprisoned on the island of Patmos before 100 AD per Revelation 1:1-2. This was just another way that YHWH demonstrated the Holy Bible was and is directly from Him.

The second question is what will each church, soul type, experience during the Tribulation Period from YHWH's WRATH as He harvests the souls of mankind?

The souls to be harvested and what is required of each soul type is summarized in Table XI-3.

Table XI-3 Soul Type Characteristics and Salvation Requirements

Soul Type	Percent of World Population	Required Action for Salvation	Soul Type Characteristics	Soul's Magnitude of $WILL_{YHWH}(t)$
Philadelphia	0.621 %	None Open door	Believe in and are willing to die for YHWH.	$1.0 > WILL_{YHWH}(t) > 0.7$
Smynra	6.060 %	Be faithful unto death.	Believe in and are dedicated to YHWH.	$0.7 > WILL_{YHWH}(t) > 0.5$
Ephesus	24.173 %	REPENT	Promoting self and YHWH for self's benefit.	$0.5 > WILL_{YHWH}(t) > 0.14$
Laodicea	19.146 % ---------- 19.146 %	REPENT	Believe in self and willing murder for self's benefit.	$0.14 > WILL_{YHWH}(t) > 0.00$ ------------------- $WILL_{YHWH}(t) = 0$
Thyatira	24.173 %	REPENT	Promoting self and Satan for self's benefit.	$WILL_{YHWH}(t) = 0$
Pergamos	6.060 %	REPENT	Believe in and are dedicated to Satan.	$WILL_{YHWH}(t) = 0$
Sardis	0.621 %	REPENT	Believe in and are willing to die for Satan.	$WILL_{YHWH}(t) = 0$

The seven soul types are distributed across the world's population in accordance with the normal distribution. This understanding was developed in the book *Self's Destiny and Self* [2] and is summarized herein. The soul harvest is the seven year period of time known as the Tribulation Period. The soul harvest is shown by soul type in Figure XI-2 and reflects the normal distribution of mankind's souls. It is also shown as a linear function of time in Figure XI-3. These figures correlate a large amount of information. Thus, it may be useful to study them to obtain an overview of the entire Tribulation Period.

The Tribulation Period, soul harvest, includes two 3.5 year periods.

The first 3.5 year period of time is referred in the Holy Bible as the *Time of Sorrows* and by some of the Occult it is referred to as the *cleansing of Mother Earth*.

For the Occult, this is a time when Satan who is also known as the New Age Sanat Kumara, or Allah will send his personal representative(s) to enlighten the world. Some of these individual(s) include Lord Maitreya, Buddha, Krishna, and the Muslim Mahdi, or the twelfth Imam, or Mohammed. This is also a time when the unenlightened of the world, those with a lower consciousness, bad karma, and anyone who refuses to conform to the Occult doctrine will be purged. Completion of this *cleansing of Mother Earth* will usher in a new age, the Age of Aquarius.

159

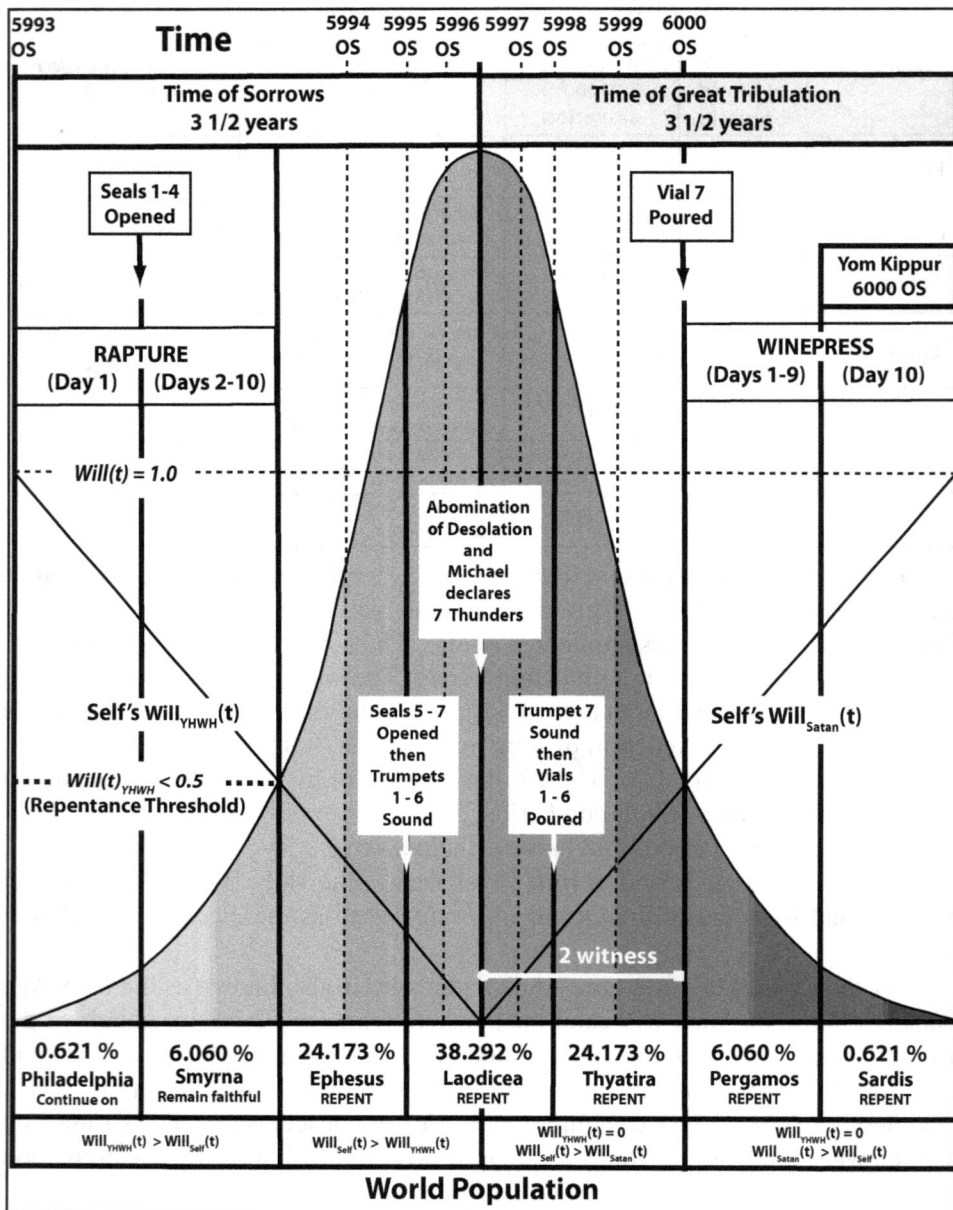

Figure XI-2 The Soul Harvest by Soul Type

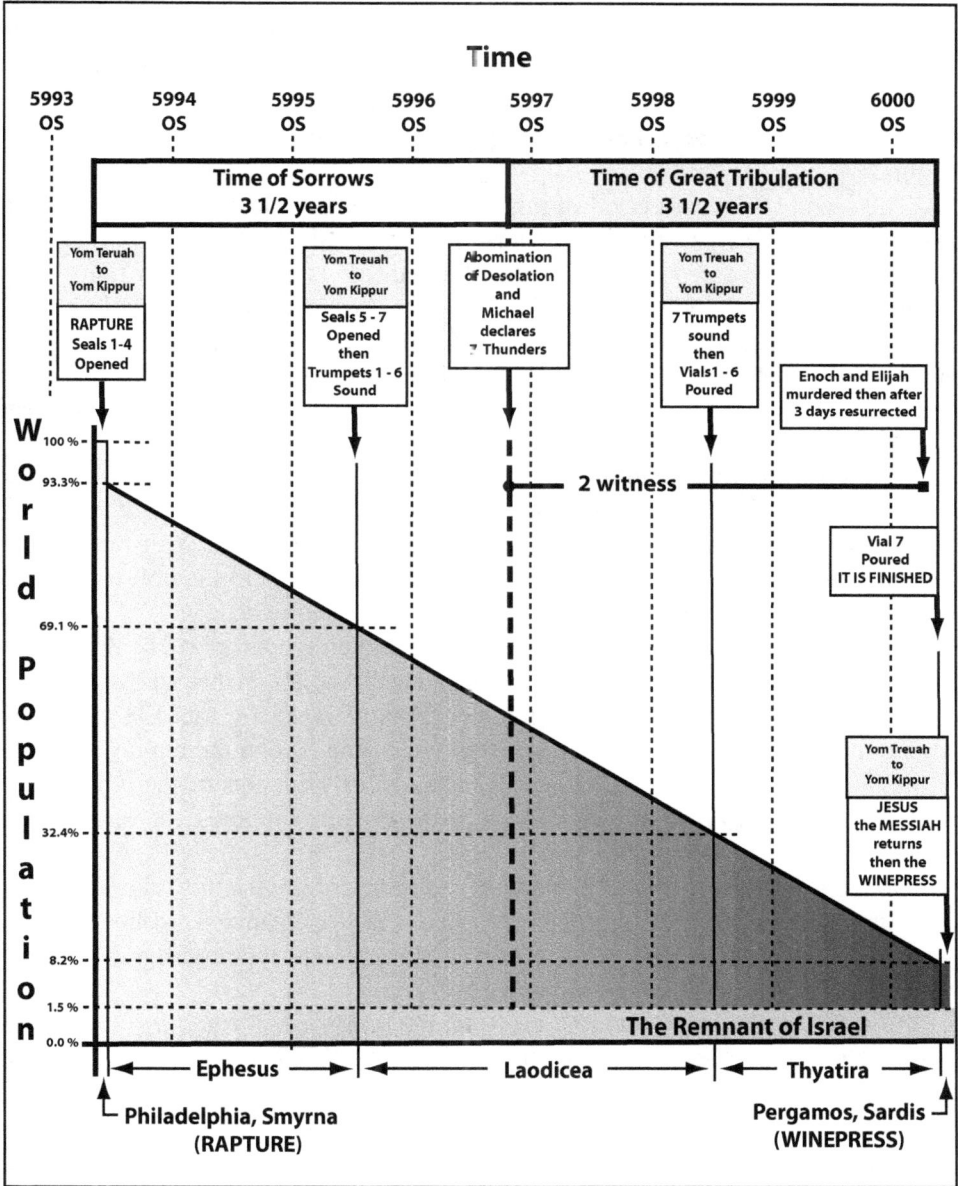

Figure XI-3 The Soul Harvest in Time

This same period time is called the *Time of Sorrows* when YHWH allows the tares (evil people) to harvest the wheat (followers of YHWH) for Him. During this time a typical dictator will murder all his opposition who, in this situation, are the followers of YHWH. However, the Rapture occurs during the first ten days of the *Time of Sorrows* where YHWH removes His devout followers before the trouble begins.

The second 3.5 year period of time is referred in the Holy Bible as the *Great Tribulation* or *Time of Vengeance*. During this time all the followers of YHWH have all been murdered except for the Remnant of Israel. This is a time when YHWH's perfect WRATH is poured out upon the followers of Satan and his self-centered associates. Also during this time YHWH places a hedge of protection over the Remnant of Israel. In 6000 OS YHWH, Jesus the Messiah, returns in power and glory and personally treads the Winepress for the last ten days of the Great Tribulation.

The most probable time that 5993 OS will occur is 2022 AD. The estimated world population in 2022 AD is 7,682,789,903 people. [2] The number of members in any one of the seven churches is distributed in accordance with the normal distribution over the world population. Therefore, the number of people associated with the judgment of each given type of soul can be computed.

During the Tribulation Period, major events will be synchronized by the Jewish feasts and Sabbaths, which occur during the seventh month, Tishri, starting on first day, Yom Teruah, and ending on the tenth day, Yom Kippur, for each OS year. This ten day period has a variety of names associated with it, like the ten *days of Awe* or the *days of admitting*. Yom Teruah is the Feast of Trumpets or the *day heaven opens* or the *day no man knows the day or hour.* Yom Kippur is the day *heaven closes* or the *day of atonement*.

Notice in Figure XI-2 that Philadelphia and Smyrna are the only churches with magnitudes of Self's $Will_{YHWH}(t)$ greater than the Repentance Threshold, which is self's $Will_{YHWH}(t) = Will_{self}(t) = 0.5$. Any church, soul type, with a magnitude self's $Will_{YHWH}(t) < 0.5$ is required to repent.

Prior to Yom Teruah 5993 OS, each individual has established the magnitude of his $Will_{YHWH}(t)$ through faith in YHWH's provision and his repentance for the sins that he has committed. Everyone in the world belongs to one of the seven soul types when the trumpet sounds on Yom Teruah 5993 OS.

From the *principle of the harvest* [2] the amount of time someone will live during the Tribulation Period is proportional to the magnitude of his $Will_{YHWH}(t)$ or his $Will_{Satan}(t)$. Where time in tribulation starts at zero, Rapture, and increases as the magnitude of self's $Will_{YHWH}(t)$ decreases to zero, it then continues to increase as

162

self's $Will_{Satan}(t)$ increases to the maximum at seven years. An individual's period of judgment starts from Yom Teruah 5993 OS and continues until he is raptured or is murdered or killed as illustrated in Figure XI-2. The *principle of the harvest* also represents a constant rate of decrease in the world's population during the Tribulation Period as shown and Figure XI-3.

Before examining the judgment of each type of soul or each church, it is worthwhile to look at the judge. Revelation 1:10-20 describes the judge!

Revelation 1:10-20

10 *I* **[Apostle John]** *was in the Spirit on the Lord's day, and heard behind me a great voice* **[YHWH]**, *as of a trumpet,*

11 *Saying, I am the Alpha and Omega, the first and the last: and, What thou seest, write in a book, and send it unto the* seven churches **[seven soul types]** *which are in Asia; unto Ephesus, and unto Smyrna, and unto Pergamos, and unto Thyatira, and unto Sardis, and unto Philadelphia, and unto Laodicea.*

12 *And I turned to see the voice that spake with me. And being turned, I saw seven golden candlesticks;*

13 *And in the midst of the* seven candlesticks **[churches, soul types]** *one like unto the* Son of man **[YHWH's resurrected BODY]**, *clothed with a garment down to the foot, and girt about the paps with a golden girdle.*

14 *His head and his hairs were white like wool, as white as snow; and his eyes were as a flame of fire;*

15 *And his feet like unto fine brass, as if they burned in a furnace; and his voice as the sound of many waters.*

16 *And he had in his right hand* seven stars **[angels]**: *and* out of his mouth went a sharp twoedged sword **[YHWH's WILL]**: *and his countenance was as the sun shineth in his strength.*

17 *And when I saw him, I fell at his feet as dead. And he laid his right hand upon me, saying unto me, Fear not; I am the first and the last:*

18 *I am he that liveth, and was dead; and, behold, I am alive for evermore, Amen; and have the keys of hell and of death.*

19 *Write the things which thou* hast seen **[Revelation 1:10-18]**, *and the* things which are **[The seven churches as described in Revelation 2 and 3.]** , *and the* things which shall be hereafter **[Starting with Revelation 4 the remainder of the book is future.]** ;

20 *The mystery of the seven stars which thou sawest in my right hand, and the seven golden candlesticks. The* **seven stars** *are the* **angels** *of the seven churches: and the seven* **candlesticks** *which thou sawest are the seven* **churches**.

Revelation 1:13-15 describes YHWH's resurrected BODY reflecting righteous judgment of all mankind. The seven candlesticks, the seven branched Menorah, and seven churches represent the soul types of all people. The colors white and gold imply righteousness. Fire, brass and keys reflect judgment.

Revelation 1:16 possesses two questions.

The first question is who are the seven stars that are under YHWH's control, in His right hand? These stars are identified as angels in Revelation 1:20. There

163

is one angel assigned to each church, soul type and the letter to each begins with "Unto the *angel* of the church of ----- write;" The seven churches are not literally organized physical Christian churches or historical church ages that one associates with the word *church* today, but are seven types of individual souls. The word *angel* is typically translated as *messenger*. Being soul types, these churches do not have unique leaders. Therefore, the *angel* is a literal angel, or a *messenger,* that is YHWH's communication manager to each soul type. For example, the angel sends a prophet to declare the gospel to a particular type of soul like Jonah to Nineveh or Paul to Ephesus. The characteristics of each church were described in the previous chapter. Every city YHWH selected has a majority of people in the physical city with a particular type of soul, which is the church that is identified and described in the letter to its assigned angel. There is a small minority of people in each physical city that are not members of the specified church. The type of souls in each church is time dependent and the seven churches are valid during the period when the book of Revelation was written sometime between 75 AD to 100 AD. All seven churches, soul types, have members with souls that have different magnitudes of WILLs for YHWH or self or Satan. The seven soul types have existed at all times since shortly after Cain murdered Abel.

The second question contained in Revelation 1:16 is, what is the twoedged sword? The answer is contained in Hebrews 4:12.

Hebrews 4:12
12 For the <u>word of God</u> **[YHWH's WILL]** *is quick, and powerful, and sharper than any* **twoedged sword,** *piercing even to the <u>dividing asunder of soul</u> <u>and spirit</u>* **[second-death],** *and of the <u>joints and marrow</u>* **[first-death],** *and is a <u>discerner of the thoughts and intents of the heart.</u>* **[YHWH knows man's soul type and his motive.]**

Hebrews 4:12 describes what YHWH's WILL is like during the judgment of mankind. YHWH knows the magnitude of everyone's $Will_{YHWH}$ *(t)* and has total authority concerning mankind's *first-death* and his *second-death.*

Chapter 2 and 3 of the Book of Revelation specifically addresses a letter to each soul type, church. Each letter has the same structure. Each letter starts with the statement *"Unto the angel of the church of --- write;".* This statement is followed by a brief introduction about YHWH's authority or who He is.

Then the statement *"I know thy works, --- "* begins a description of the type of soul that is in the specific church. It is very important to note, the indicated works relate directly to the church's soul type, which represents the of majority of people in the physical city being described. When a reference is made to those people in the city, the reference is directed to those people whose souls are not members of the church being described.

Once the soul type or church is described, a statement is made as to what the members of the church must do to overcome and have a good personal relationship with YHWH.

Then, YHWH ends each letter by telling all church members who overcome what they will receive in His Kingdom. The gift is identified by the statement *"He that hath an ear, let him hear what the Spirit saith unto the churches --- " or " And he that overcometh --- "* .

To better understand the Tribulation Period, we will start at the left side of both Figure XI-2 and Figure XI-3 in the year 5993 OS with the judgment of Philadelphia during the Rapture and conclude in the seventh month of 6000 OS with the judgment of Sardis during the Winepress. The first event during the Tribulation Period is the judgment of the Philadelphian-type soul.

The Judgment of Philadelphia - Rapture Day 1 - 5993 OS

Only the Philadelphians are raptured prior to the onset of trouble during the Tribulation Period. The day of judgment for the Philadelphian-type souls occurs on Yom Teruah (the Feast of Trumpets), which is the first day of the *10 Days of awe* in the year 5993 OS.

Before examining the Philadelphian judgment, the term *Rapture* needs to be defined. There are several common misconceptions with respect to the term Rapture. For example:

- *The idea that the Rapture will deceive people into following Satan who will later pose as Jesus the Messiah.* At the time of the Rapture, only YHWH determines who has a Philadelphian type soul and will be raptured. Self or Satan or anyone else will have no input!

- *The Rapture is a means to avoid death.* The Rapture is self's *first-death* in the twinkling of an eye; self's corrupted material body of flesh must be removed. Death is the means of that removal. It is appointed for all men once to die, Hebrews 9:27-28.

  Hebrews 9:27-28
  *27 And as **it is appointed unto men once to die**, but after this the judgment:*
  28 So Christ was once offered to bear the sins of many; and unto them that look for him shall he appear the second time without sin unto salvation.

- *The church is raptured instantaneously.* First the real "church" includes only those who are true followers of YHWH whose $Will_{YHWH}(t) >> Will_{Self}(t)$. The Rapture occurs over a period of ten days; the first day is reserved for the Philadelphians. Jesus the Messiah in Luke 21:36 tells all people to repent and pray that they be found worthy to escape the impending Tribulation Period.

Luke 21:34-36

34 And take heed to yourselves, lest at any time your hearts be overcharged with surfeiting, and drunkenness, and cares of this life, and so that day come upon you unawares.

35 For as a snare shall it come on all them that dwell on the face of the whole earth.

36 Watch ye therefore, and **pray always, that ye may be accounted worthy to escape all these things that shall come to pass, and to stand before the Son of man.**

For the Philadelphians, Luke 21:36 will be a reality and their prayers to be kept from the Tribulation Period will be answered. The Philadelphians would gladly give their lives for Jesus the Messiah, but He will not require them to experience the anxiety associated with the *first-death* because they have placed Him first in their lives.

The Philadelphian-type souls represent about 47,707,052 individuals or 0.62097% of the world population estimate of 7,682,789,903 people at the start of the Tribulation Period. Most of these 47.707 million people from all nations of the world have been persecuted for having a Philadelphian-type soul. YHWH's letter to the angel responsible for the Philadelphian-type soul is documented in Revelation 3:7-13

Revelation 3:7-13

7 **And to the angel of the church in Philadelphia write**; These things saith he that is holy, he that is true, he that hath the key of David, he that openeth, and no man shutteth; and shutteth, and no man openeth;

8 **I know thy works:** behold, I have set before thee an open door, and no man can shut it: for thou hast a little strength, and hast kept my word, and hast not denied my name.

9 Behold, I will make them of the <u>synagogue of Satan</u> **[followers of Satan]**, which <u>say they are Jews</u> **[followers of YHWH]**, and are not, but do lie; behold, I will make them to come and worship before thy feet, and to know that I have loved thee.

10 Because thou hast kept the word of my patience, **I also will keep thee from the hour of temptation, which shall come upon all the world, to try them that dwell upon the earth.**

11 Behold, I come quickly: hold that fast which thou hast, that no man take thy crown.

12 **Him that overcometh** will I make a pillar in the temple of my God, and he shall go no more out: and I will write upon him the name of my God, and the name of the city of my God, which is new Jerusalem, which cometh down out of heaven from my God: and I will write upon him my new name.

13 He that hath an ear, let him hear what the Spirit saith unto the churches.

Those of Philadelphia, like Daniel, have placed YHWH first in their lives. As a reward for their belief in and commitment to YHWH, they will be kept from the Tribulation Period with its trials and temptations. YHWH's promise to protect them is clearly stated in Revelation 3:10.

The Philadelphian type soul is unique among the seven types of souls because it is the type that is prized by YHWH, and thus this type of soul should be everyone's ultimate goal to achieve. Jesus the Messiah during the Sermon on the Mount taught what was required to develop a Philadelphian type soul. Recall Chapter X - YHWH the *Son of Man*, Jesus the Messiah included this teaching. The Sermon on the Mount is comparable to YHWH's declaration of the Ten Commandments from Mount Sinai only now YHWH was doing it at man's level using His mortal body, Jesus the Messiah. The Sermon on the Mount stresses that any Philadelphian must have the magnitude of their self Will as follows.

$$Will_{YHWH}(t) >> Will_{other\ People}(t) > Will_{self}(t)$$

Jesus the Messiah summarized these requirements in Matthew 22:36-40.

Matthew 22:36-40
36 Master, which is the great commandment in the law?
37 Jesus said unto him, Thou shalt love the Lord thy God with all thy heart, and with all thy soul, and with all thy mind. **[$Will_{YHWH}(t) >> Will_{self}(t)$]**
38 This is the first and great commandment.
39 And the second is like unto it, Thou shalt love thy neighbour as thyself. **[$Will_{other\ people}(t) > Will_{self}(t)$]**
40 On these two commandments hang all the law and the prophets.

The apostle John is an excellent example of a person who has a true Philadelphian-type soul. The apostle John describes what the Philadelphian will experience after the trumpet sounds on Yom Teruah 5993 OS calling him home to the pre-creation universe. The apostle John describes what will happen during the Rapture event in Revelation 4:1-11.

Revelation 4:1-11
*1 After this I looked, and, behold, **a door was opened in heaven**: and the first voice which **I heard was as it were of a trumpet talking with me**; which said, Come up hither, and I will shew thee things which must be hereafter.*
2 And <u>immediately I was in the spirit:</u> [in the pre-creation universe] and, behold, a throne was set in heaven, and one sat on the throne.
3 And he that sat was to look upon like a jasper and a sardine stone: and there was a rainbow round about the throne, in sight like unto an emerald.
4 And round about the throne were four and twenty seats: and upon the seats I saw four and twenty elders sitting, clothed in white raiment; and they had on their heads crowns of gold.
5 And out of the throne proceeded lightnings and thunderings and voices: and there were seven lamps of fire burning before the throne, which are the seven Spirits of God.
6 And before the throne there was a sea of glass like unto crystal: and in the midst of the throne, and round about the throne, were four beasts full of eyes before and behind.
7 And the first beast was like a lion, and the second beast like a calf, and the third beast had a face as a man, and the fourth beast was like a flying eagle.

8 And the four beasts had each of them six wings about him; and they were full of eyes within: and they rest not day and night, saying, Holy, holy, holy, Lord God Almighty, which was, and is, and is to come.

9 And when those beasts give glory and honour and thanks to him that sat on the throne, who liveth for ever and ever,

10 The four and twenty elders fall down before him that sat on the throne, and worship him that liveth for ever and ever, and cast their crowns before the throne, saying,

11 Thou art worthy, O Lord, to receive glory and honour and power: for thou hast created all things, and for thy pleasure they are and were created.

As Yom Teruah 5993 OS events continue to unfold, all the Philadelphians who have ever existed now have experienced the *first-death* and are gathered as angels before the throne waiting to see who is worthy to open the scroll in YHWH's spirit body's hand as described in Revelation 5.

Revelation 5

1 And I saw in the right hand of him **that sat on the throne a book written within and on the backside, sealed with seven seals.**

2 And I saw a strong angel proclaiming with a loud voice, Who is worthy to open the book, and to loose the seals thereof?

3 And no man in heaven, nor in earth, neither under the earth, was able to open the book, neither to look thereon.

4 And I wept much, because no man was found worthy to open and to read the book, neither to look thereon.

5 And one of the elders saith unto me, Weep not: behold, the Lion of the tribe of Juda, the Root of David, hath prevailed to open the book, and to loose the seven seals thereof.

6 And I beheld, and, lo, in the midst of the throne and of the four beasts, and in the midst of the elders, stood a Lamb as it had been slain, having seven horns and seven eyes, which are the seven Spirits of God sent forth into all the earth.

7 And he came and took the book out of the right hand of him that sat upon the throne.

8 And when he had taken the book, the four beasts and four and twenty elders fell down before the Lamb, having every one of them harps, and golden vials full of odours, which are the prayers of saints.

9 And they sung a new song, saying, Thou art worthy to take the book, and to open the seals thereof: for thou wast slain, and hast redeemed us to God by thy blood out of every kindred, and tongue, and people, and nation;

10 And hast made us unto our God kings and priests: and we shall reign on the earth.

11 And I beheld, and I heard the voice of many angels round about the throne and the beasts and the elders: **and the number of them was ten thousand times ten thousand, and thousands of thousands;**

12 Saying with a loud voice, Worthy is the Lamb that was slain to receive power, and riches, and wisdom, and strength, and honour, and glory, and blessing.

> 13 *And every creature which is in heaven, and on the earth, and under the earth, and such as are in the sea, and all that are in them, heard I saying, Blessing, and honour, and glory, and power, be unto him that sitteth upon the throne, and unto the Lamb for ever and ever.*
>
> 14 *And the four beasts said, Amen. And the four and twenty elders fell down and worshipped him that liveth for ever and ever.*

In Revelation 5 the emphasis shifts to the Book of WRATH that YHWH has. YHWH (the Lamb) is identified as the only one with the authority over the seven natures of man who is worthy to open the seven-sealed scroll. Then, YHWH (the Lamb) in Revelation 5:7 accepts the book from the right hand of YHWH's spirit body amid praise, singing, and rejoicing from those in attendance.

The number of those in attendance about the throne includes:

- 4 beasts.
- 24 elders, Philadelphians who are from the 12 tribes and the 12 apostles.
- Angels, Philadelphians from each generation since Adam.
- YHWH's BODY, SOUL and WILL.

The number of those in attendance about the throne singing praises and waiting for YHWH (the Lamb) to open the seals are all the Philadelphians since 0000 OS. This fact is very significant! The reason is the total number of Philadelphians since Adam is specifically stated in Revelation 5:11 as ten thousand times ten thousand, and thousands of thousands. This statement provides a bounded value for the total number of Philadelphians since 0000 OS. Where the minimum value is 10,000 x 10,000 = 100,000,000 and the maximum value is 19,000 x 19,000 = 361,000,000. If the number were greater than 19,000 x 19,000, then Revelation 5:11 would have read differently, such as twenty thousand times twenty thousand, and thousands of thousands. If the normal distribution of the seven types of souls is correct, then the total number of Philadelphian-type souls since 0000 OS must number between 100,000,000 and 361,000,000 people including those raptured on Yom Teruah 5993 OS.

The number of Philadelphians since 0000 OS can be estimated by accumulating 0.62097% of the world population for each generation starting from 0000 OS to 5993 OS. The first task is to prepare an estimate of the world's population as a function of time. This estimate is accomplished using pre-flood and post-flood projections.

The pre-flood projection is based on the biblical model of creation. Thus, from creation to the flood is 1656 years. Assuming the population increases about 3% for each 5 year interval, a rough estimate for the world's population at the time of Noah's flood is 1,000,000,000 people.

The post-flood projection starts after the flood with eight people (Noah and his family), continues to the present, and then projects into the future. The world population data and projections have continued to improve with the passage of time. Recent historical and projected post-flood population estimates are summarized in Table XI-4 and are based on *The World Almanac and Book of Facts* for the year 1999 AD for the years 1750 AD through 2050 AD. [3]

The number of Philadelphians about the throne is computed based on mankind's soul types having a normal distribution. That is, for each generation 0.62097% of the world's population would be Philadelphians at the time that generation existed on earth. The total number of Philadelphians at any point in time is then the sum of all the Philadelphians from previous generations and is dependent upon the length of a generation. Generations from 40 to 100 years in length were considered. Using 40 years per generation, the minimum value of 100,000,000 Philadelphians was exceeded by 1950 AD. When using 100 years per generation, the minimum value of 100,000,000 Philadelphians was exceeded before 2020 AD. [2]

Table XI-4 Post-Flood World Population Estimates

Year (AD)	Year (AM)	World Population
– – – – –	1657 +/- .005 AM	8
1750 AD	5789 +/- 21.5 AM	725,000,000
1900 AD	5939 +/- 21.5 AM	1,600,000,000
1950 AD	5989 +/- 21.5 AM	2,556,000,000
1998 AD	6037 +/- 21.5 AM	5,926,457,000
2022 AD	6061 +/- 21.5 AM	7,682,789,903
2025 AD	6064 +/- 21.5 AM	7,923,288,000
2050 AD	6089 +/- 21.5 AM	9,346,399,000

These are good estimates because the majority of Philadelphian souls were accumulated after 1750 AD when the world's population estimates started to become more reliable. Not only is it astounding that the number of Philadelphians is clearly consistent with Revelation 5:11, but this also adds scriptural validation that the seven churches are indeed seven soul types and are distributed in accordance with a normal distribution.

It also provides confirmation that the Rapture is the first event of the Tribulation Period. In addition, the number of Philadelphians about the throne are well within the bounds of 100,000,000 and 361,000,000 people during the time period from 2000 AD to 2050 AD, thus adding further support to the most probable time of the Rapture being about 2022 AD. This computation does not support any view that the content book of Revelation has already been fulfilled or has no literal understanding. YHWH's Holy Bible is self validating!

As Yom Teruah 5993 OS continues, there will be a great celebration about the throne and all the Philadelphians will attend. As the gate to heaven remains open, the voices of this great multitude can be heard praising YHWH by every living thing (Revelation 5:13). All attention turns to the Jesus the Messiah, the Lamb, who is holding the detailed judgment of mankind's sin, a seven-sealed book. The seven-sealed book is a scroll rolled in a cylinder with seven unique segments and each segment separated with a unique seal. The scene as the first four seals are opened is described in Revelation 6:1-8.

Revelation 6:1-8
1 *And I saw when the* <u>Lamb</u> **[Jesus the Messiah] opened one of the seals,** *and I heard, as it were the noise of thunder, one of the four beasts saying, Come and see.*
2 *And I saw, and behold a* **white horse:** *and he that sat on him had a bow; and a crown was given unto him: and he went forth conquering, and to conquer.*
3 *And when he had* **opened the second seal,** *I heard the second beast say, Come and see.*
4 *And there went out another* **horse that was red:** *and power was given to him that sat thereon to take peace from the earth, and that they should kill one another: and there was given unto him a great sword.*
5 *And when he had* **opened the third seal,** *I heard the third beast say, Come and see. And I beheld, and lo a* **black horse;** *and he that sat on him had a pair of balances in his hand.*
6 *And I heard a voice in the midst of the four beasts say, A measure of wheat for a penny, and three measures of barley for a penny; and see thou hurt not the oil and the wine.*
7 *And when he had* **opened the fourth seal,** *I heard the voice of the fourth beast say, Come and see.*
8 *And I looked, and behold a* **pale horse:** *and his name that sat on him was Death, and Hell followed with him. And power was given unto them* **[the Four-Horsemen]** *over the* **fourth part of the earth,** *to kill with sword, and with hunger, and with death, and with the beasts of the earth.*

The opening of the first four seals is often referred to as the ride of the *Four Horsemen of the Apocalypse, or the Four-Horsemen.* Also, the opening of the first four seals allows Satan and his followers to activate *the covenant with many* and start the cleansing of Mother Earth in their attempt to form the One-World Government.

171

Seal #1: The *white horse* and its rider imply victory and peace, but the rider is carrying a bow and wearing a crown. The bow represents military power and the crown political power. The forming One-World Government is going forth to bring world peace by conquering all its opposition. The opposition to be eliminated is all those who are true followers of Jesus the Messiah and the rebellious nation of Israel.

Seal #2: The *red horse* and its rider with a great sword represent the bloodshed that will result as the forming One-World Government proceeds to murder all its opposition.

Seal #3: The *black horse* and its rider with a balance in his hand represents the justice of the One-World Government. The justice is man's justice where all means of support are taken from the true followers of Jesus the Messiah to bring them to a state of starvation, while those who support the One-World Government are given their assets. Starvation is indicated by the extreme cost of food (wheat and barley), whereas the things belonging to the rich (oil and wine) increase and their lifestyle becomes more affluent.

Seal #4: The *pale horse* whose rider is death represents those who will be murdered, starved, or killed due to the forming One-World Government with its headquarters in Babylon.

These *Four-Horsemen* will ride for the next two years with the purpose of bringing world peace and will cause the murder of 25 percent of the world's population per Revelation 6:8. However, as Yom Teruah 5993 OS, the first day of the Tribulation Period, draws to a close, the gate to heaven remains open awaiting the judgment of Smyrna.

The Judgment of Smyrna - Rapture Days 2-10

Smyrnian-type souls have experienced the first day of the Tribulation Period with the judgment of Philadelphia. The judgment of Smyrnian-type souls will occur during the next nine days, ending on Yom Kippur 5993 OS. On Yom Kippur 5993 OS when the gate to heaven closes, the judgment of Smyrna will be complete. Smyrna's soul type is 6.05975 % of the world's population of approximately 7,682,789,903 people is equal to 465,557,861 people. YHWH's letter to the angel of Smyrna-type soul is documented in Revelation 2:8-11.

Rev elation 2:8-11
> 8 **And unto the angel of the church in Smyrna write;** *These things saith the first and the last, which was dead, and is alive;*

172

9 *I know thy works,* and tribulation, and poverty,[**When the tribulation approaches, followers of YHWH will be persecuted.**] *(but thou art rich)* and I know the blasphemy of them which say they are Jews [**followers of YHWH**], and are not, but are the synagogue of Satan [**followers of Satan**].

10 Fear none of those things which thou shalt suffer: behold, the devil shall cast some of you into prison, that ye may be tried; and **ye shall have tribulation ten days**: be thou faithful unto death, and I will give thee a crown of life.

11 **He that hath an ear, let him hear what the Spirit saith unto the churches;** He that overcometh shall not be hurt of the second death.

The Smyrian tribulation is the result of the *Four-Horsemen* going forth. They have a two-pronged approach to bring world peace by the elimination of true believers in Jesus the Messiah and the nation of Israel. Babylon's first objective is to direct the Lion, Bear, and Leopard to arrest and murder those with Smyrnian-type souls because they are dedicated to YHWH and will strongly oppose Babylon's second objective to eliminate Israel. Revelation 2:10 confirms that Smyrna's time of tribulation will be limited to a maximum of ten days. Also, the Smyrnians' ten days of tribulation will occur during the *10 days of Awe*, which are also known as *the days of admitting*. During the remaining nine days of admitting, Smyrnians around the world will be arrested, imprisoned, beaten, and brought before the courts, and some will be executed. Throughout these nine days, once an individual has given his testimony for Jesus the Messiah, he will be raptured, suddenly die. However, toward the end of the nine day period some Smyrnians, whose soul type approaches that of an Ephesian, *(Will$_{Self}$(t) > Will$_{YHWH}$(t))* will be tortured and murdered for their testimony for Jesus the Messiah, per Revelation 2:10. Under no circumstances should an individual deny YHWH, Jesus the Messiah. Just remain faithful, accept death, and accept the glory of everlasting life.

Luke 21:12-19 describes this period of trial for those of Smyrna as follows:

Luke 21:12-19

12 *But before all these, they shall lay their hands on you, and persecute you, delivering you up to the synagogues, and into prisons, being brought before kings and rulers for my name's sake.*

13 *And it shall turn to you for a testimony.*

14 *Settle it therefore in your hearts, not to meditate before what ye shall answer:*

15 *For I will give you a mouth and wisdom, which all your adversaries shall not be able to gainsay nor resist.*

16 *And ye shall be betrayed both by parents, and brethren, and kinsfolks, and friends;* **and some of you shall they cause to be put to death.**

17 *And ye shall be hated of all men for my name's sake.*

18 *But there shall not an hair of your head perish.*

19 *In your patience possess ye your souls.*

Luke adds that YHWH will provide the testimony that is to be given by each individual and also states in Luke 21:16 that some will be put to death, reaffirming Revelation 2:10.

This gathering of the true believers in Jesus the Messiah throughout the world will resemble the activities that occurred during the Holocaust of World War II or the Bolshevik Revolution; only it will be occurring simultaneously in all nations on earth.

The Smyrnians are unique because some will be raptured, and toward the end of the ten days some will be murdered. The question arises, what is the difference between being raptured and being murdered?

When one is raptured, one dies instantly, in the twinkling of an eye, that is one's mortal-material body's bond with his spirit body is broken. Of course, these Smyrnians or the previously raptured Philadelphians will not have any use for their old corrupt material body, so what will happen to them? The scriptures do not specifically tell us. However, it is probable that it will appear to people who are around a person being raptured that he just died instantly and his material body just collapses. An example might be a Smyrnian who gives his testimony for YHWH before interrogators and then falls down on the floor dead. His old mortal-material body is "forsaken," and it will return to dust of the earth.

When one is murdered, one dies from physical trauma more than likely due to torture from interrogators trying to get the names of more followers of YHWH. Whether raptured or murdered, the material body is left behind, and the all-important spirit body is in the presence of YHWH. The abundance of dead physical bodies may also provide satisfaction to those people trying to cleanse Mother Earth because the bodies would seem to affirm their initial success.

The second objective of the *Four-Horsemen* is the responsibility of the Bear. The Bear shall resolve its issues with the eleventh kingdom, Israel. It is probable that while the Smyrnians are being raptured, the Bear's army is advancing on the eleventh kingdom, Israel. From Chapter V, recall that the Bear is the second Beast formed by the coalition of the Northern Asian Kingdom, Southern Kingdom, and Arabian Kingdom. During these first ten days of the Tribulation Period, the Bear will complete his preparation to launch an attack on Israel, planned to commence on Yom Kippur 5993 OS.

During this *10 Days of Awe* when the gates to heaven are open, the Holy Bible does not describe whether those who are not Philadelphians or Smyrnians will be able to observe anything in the pre-creation universe or if there will be signs in the sky or in other parts of the material component of the universe. However, Yom Kippur 5993 OS brings the end of the Rapture with the closing of the gate to heaven. It also is the start of a great world war that brings the judgment for all those with Ephesian-type souls.

The Judgment of Ephesus

After the door to heaven closes on Yom Kippur 5993 OS, the ride of the *Four-Horsemen* will become more intense, and they will ride for the next two years bringing to the earth tremendous violence. The *Four-Horsemen*'s ride ends on Yom Teruah 5995 OS (see Figure XI-2 and Figure XI-3). The *Four-Horsemen* represent the actions of those forming One-World Government throughout the ten Kingdoms, and they will arrest and murder anyone who is found to be a follower of YHWH. For the Occult the cleansing of Mother Earth is now beginning to gain momentum, and the Bear commences its attack on the rebellious eleventh kingdom, Israel. These events and the Rapture during the previous ten days has raised the anxiety of those with Ephesian-type souls, and the result is their increased opposition to the formation of the One-World Government.

Ephesian type souls represent 24.17304 % of the world's population of approximately 7,682,789,903 people, is equal to 1,857,163,876 people. YHWH's letter to the angel of the Ephesian church, soul type, is documented in Revelation 2:1-7.

Revelation 2:1-7
1 ***Unto the angel of the church of Ephesus write;*** *These things saith he that holdeth the seven stars in his right hand, who walketh in the midst of the seven golden candlesticks;* **[YHWH makes it clear who is in charge.]**

2 ***I know thy works,*** *and thy labour, and thy patience, and how thou canst not bear them which are evil: and thou hast tried them which say they are apostles, and are not, and hast found them liars:*

3 *And hast borne, and hast patience, and for my name's sake hast laboured, and hast not fainted.*

4 *Nevertheless I have somewhat against thee, because thou hast left thy first love.*

5 *Remember therefore from whence thou art fallen, and* ***repent***, *and do the first* **works** *[*magnitude of self's Will$_{YHWH}$(t) must be greater than their Will$_{self}$(t)] ; or else I will come unto thee quickly, and will* remove thy candlestick out of his place *[*eternal life will be lost]*, except thou* ***repent.***

6 *But this thou hast, that thou hatest the deeds of the* Nicolaitans *[*followers of Satan]*, which I also hate.*

7 ***He that hath an ear, let him hear what the Spirit saith unto the churches;*** *To him that overcometh will I give to eat of the tree of life, which is in the midst of the paradise of God.*

The Apostle Paul started to preach in Ephesus 52 AD, and by 66 AD the followers of Jesus the Messiah were dominating the city, However, by 90 AD the people had placed their own interests above those of YHWH. YHWH finds this type of soul desirable because it rejects Satan, but it is still unacceptable to receive eternal life. The people with an Ephesian type soul know who YHWH is, but they love themselves more; that is, their $Will_{Self}(t) > Will_{YHWH}(t)$. The time has come when each Ephesian will be required to make a personal life or death decision. Now, YHWH's promise to the church of Ephesus in Revelation 2:5 becomes very significant. All Ephesian people to some degree have rejected YHWH, and the magnitude of their $Will_{YHWH}(t)$ falls below the Repentance Threshold. Therefore, any possibility for salvation is contingent upon their repentance!

At this point in time, the only means of repentance remaining for any individual demands that he becomes a follower of YHWH, making his $Will_{YHWH}(t) > Will_{Self}(t)$. This action requires him to claim YHWH, Jesus the Messiah, as his Savior and give testimony for YHWH, while knowing full well that these acts will cost him his physical life.

All the people who are alive at this time have one consolation and that is the promise of Jesus the Messiah in Matthew 16:24-28.

Matthew 16:24-28
24 Then said Jesus unto his disciples, If any man will come after me, let him deny himself, and take up his cross, and follow me.
*25 For whosoever will save his life shall lose it: and **whosoever will lose his life for my sake shall find it.***
26 For what is a man profited, if he shall gain the whole world, and lose his own soul? or what shall a man give in exchange for his soul?
27 For the Son of man shall come in the glory of his Father with his angels; and then he shall reward every man according to his works.
*28 Verily I say unto you, There be some standing here, which shall not taste of death, till they see the Son of man coming in his kingdom. [**Some of these people saw Jesus after His resurrection and before He ascension.**]*

Also, this is a unique point in time because during the previous several years as the One-World Government has begun to emerge, the world's birth rate probably will have decreased due to anxiety, abortion, and perversion. But now the Rapture is history, and YHWH in His mercy may close some women's wombs to protect the innocent children from the impending ride of the *Four-Horsemen* and the remainder of the Tribulation Period.

As the *Four-Horsemen* continue their ride; murder, starvation, war, and wild animals will bring death to those with an Ephesian-type soul and torment to all those who remain alive. This is a time when family, friends, and neighbors will turn on those who claim YHWH, Jesus the Messiah, and kill or turn them over to authorities. This is the time of decision for those with an Ephesian-type soul. For those who overcome, accepting torture and death while remaining true to Jesus the Messiah, there will be victory and everlasting life. The police and military throughout the ten kingdoms will murder anyone following YHWH. Their assets will be confiscated and given to loyal members of the One-World Government. The two year rampage of the *Four-Horsemen* constitutes worldwide genocide of a magnitude never before encountered by man. Revelation 6:8 states that a total of one fourth or 25 % of the world's population will lose their lives.

Revelation 6:8
8 And I looked, and behold a pale horse: and his name that sat on him was Death, and Hell followed with him. And power was given unto them [the Four-Horsemen] over the fourth part of the earth, to kill with sword, and with hunger, and with death, and with the beasts of the earth.

It is unimaginable that the *Four-Horsemen* could bring about genocide of twenty five percent, 25 %, of the world's population. This would be about 330 times greater than the holocaust of World War II. However, 25 % of the world's population is just merely the judgment of Ephesus and those with a Smyrnian-type soul who were not raptured but were murdered by the *Four-Horsemen*.

24.17304 % Ephesian type souls.

00.82696 % Smyrnians not Raptured.

25.00000 % Of the world's population.

This 25% estimate is consistent with the scriptures describing the judgment of Smyrna and Ephesus. This estimate is based on the normal distribution of the seven soul types with respect to the world's population. It is important to note that the number of Philadelphians about throne and the ride of the *Four-Horsemen* provide scripture validation that soul types conform to a normal distribution. As we proceed through the discussion of the Tribulation Period, there are several other computations, which will provide additional validation that the seven soul types conform to a normal distribution.

Jesus the Messiah describes this period of time as a *Time of Sorrows* in the following scriptures Matthew 24:3-14, Mark 13:5-13, and Luke 21:8-11.

Matthew 24:3-14
3 And as he sat upon the mount of Olives, the disciples came unto him privately, saying, Tell us, when shall these things be? and what shall be the sign of thy coming, and of the end of the world?
4 And Jesus answered and said unto them, Take heed that no man deceive you.
5 For many shall come in my name, saying, I am Christ; and shall deceive many.
6 And ye shall hear of wars and rumours of wars: see that ye be not troubled: for all these things must come to pass, but the end is not yet.

177

7 For nation shall rise against nation, and kingdom against kingdom: and there shall be famines, and pestilences, and earthquakes, in divers places.
8 All these are the beginning of sorrows.
9 Then shall they deliver you up to be afflicted, and shall kill you: and ye shall be hated of all nations for my name's sake.
10 And then shall many be offended, and shall betray one another, and shall hate one another.
11 And many false prophets shall rise, and shall deceive many.
12 And because iniquity shall abound, the love of many shall wax cold.
13 But he that shall endure unto the end, the same shall be saved.
14 And this gospel of the kingdom shall be preached in all the world for a witness unto all nations; and then shall the end come.

Mark 13:5-13
5 And Jesus answering them began to say, Take heed lest any man deceive you:
6 For many shall come in my name, saying, I am Christ; and shall deceive many.
7 And when ye shall hear of wars and rumours of wars, be ye not troubled: for such things must needs be; but the end shall not be yet.
8 For nation shall rise against nation, and kingdom against kingdom: and there shall be earthquakes in divers places, and there shall be famines and troubles: these are the beginnings of sorrows.
9 But take heed to yourselves: for they shall deliver you up to councils; and in the synagogues ye shall be beaten: and ye shall be brought before rulers and kings for my sake, for a testimony against them.
10 And the gospel must first be published among all nations.
11 But when they shall lead you, and deliver you up, take no thought beforehand what ye shall speak, neither do ye premeditate: but whatsoever shall be given you in that hour, that speak ye: for it is not ye that speak, but the Holy Ghost **[YHWH's WILL]**.
12 Now the brother shall betray the brother to death, and father the son; and children shall rise up against their parents, and shall cause them to be put to death.
13 And ye shall be hated of all men for my name's sake: but he that shall endure unto the end, the same shall be saved.

Luke 21:8-19
8 And he said, Take heed that ye be not deceived: for many shall come in my name, saying, I am Christ; and the time draweth near: go ye not therefore after them.
9 But when ye shall hear of wars and commotions, be not terrified: for these things must first come to pass; but the end is not by and by.
10 Then said he unto them, Nation shall rise against nation, and kingdom against kingdom:
11 And great earthquakes shall be in divers places, and famines, and pestilences; and fearful sights and great signs shall there be from heaven.
12 But before all these, they shall lay their hands on you, and persecute you, delivering you up to the synagogues, and into prisons, being brought before kings and rulers for my name's sake.
13 And it shall turn to you for a testimony.

14 Settle it therefore in your hearts, not to meditate before what ye shall answer:

15 For I will give you a mouth and wisdom, which all your adversaries shall not be able to gainsay nor resist.

16 And ye shall be betrayed both by parents, and brethren, and kinsfolks, and friends; and some of you shall they cause to be put to death.

17 And ye shall be hated of all men for my name's sake.

18 But there shall not an hair of your head perish.

19 In your patience possess ye your souls.

The above scriptures depict a time when magnitude of self's $Will_{YHWH}(t)$ will be tested. Some family members, friends, and neighbors who have high $L_{self}(t)$ and or $L_{Satan}(t)$ will turn on followers of YHWH, giving them over to the authorities for execution. Each individual in society will be confronted with who YHWH is. People will be separated into one of two groups (for or against), like wheat being removed from the tares. In this situation YHWH allows the tares to harvest His wheat. This separation will not be like the judgment of Philadelphia and most of Smyrna where YHWH selected people based on His knowledge of their magnitude of $Will_{YHWH}(t)$ and raptured them accordingly. Individuals during the Rapture had no input into YHWH's decision with respect to them because His decision was based on their existing $Will_{YHWH}(t)$. Recall, the length of time spent in tribulation on earth is established by the magnitude of self's $Will_{YHWH}(t)$. This principle of harvest is illustrated in Figure XI-2 and Figure XI-3. During the Tribulation Period when self's time of decision occurs, each person will be confronted with a life or death decision. Unfortunately, independent of the individual's decision for or against YHWH, the individual will die.

Not only will be this a time of persecution and execution for followers of YHWH, but it will be also the time when the Bear will attack Israel. One way the Bear may also rid himself of some known Ephesians will be to place them in his frontline to be sacrificed during the assault on Israel or executed if they fail to follow orders. The Bear's army will be large and will be referred to as the northern army. For the Bear this should be an easy conquest, but YHWH will intervene and the Bear's army will be severely beaten in its initial attack. It is not clear exactly how YHWH accomplishes this feat. The Bear's army will not be successful until the Abomination of Desolation that occurs in 5996 OS, which is 3 ½ years after the start of the Tribulation Period.

However, by Yom Teruah 5995 OS (Feast of Trumpets) we know that all Ephesians will have been murdered and the Bear's army has not conquered Israel.

On Yom Teruah 5995 OS, when heaven opens, Jesus the Messiah will open the fifth-seal (Revelation 6:9-11) and the people with Ephesian souls who stood up and gave their lives for YHWH are seen in heaven about YHWH's throne.

179

These Ephesians will be given white robes of righteousness and eternal life for their decision.

Revelation 6:9-11
*9 And when he had opened **the fifth seal**, I saw under the altar the souls of them that were slain for the word of God, and for the testimony which they held:*
10 And they cried with a loud voice, saying, How long, O Lord, holy and true, dost thou not judge and avenge our blood on them that dwell on the earth?
11 And white robes were given unto every one of them; and it was said unto them, that they should rest yet for a little season, until their fellow servants also and their brethren, that should be killed as they were, should be fulfilled.

Using a picture of a marriage, the bride consists of righteous people clothed in white robes and waiting for the Marriage Supper of the Lamb. The bridegroom is YHWH, who is waiting for His bride to be completely prepared for Him. Once the Ephesians, slain for their testimony and commitment to Jesus the Messiah, have joined the Philadelphians and the Smyrians around the throne, Jesus the Messiah will proceed to open the sixth-seal and a great earthquake occurs, punctuating the end of the Ephesians' judgment. The opening of the sixth-seal allows a large meteor to strike the earth's crust and shake the entire earth. The resultant dust and ash from the impact blocks the light of the sun and stars as it moves around the earth. Revelation 6: 12-17 describes this event.

Revelation 6:12-17
*12 And I beheld when he had opened **the sixth seal,** and, lo, there was a great earthquake; and the sun became black as sackcloth of hair, and the moon became as blood;*
13 And the stars of heaven fell unto the earth, even as a fig tree casteth her untimely figs, when she is shaken of a mighty wind.
14 And the heaven departed as a scroll when it is rolled together; and every mountain and island were moved out of their places.
15 And the kings of the earth, and the great men, and the rich men, and the chief captains, and the mighty men, and every bondman, and every free man, hid themselves in the dens and in the rocks of the mountains;
16 And said to the mountains and rocks, Fall on us, and hide us from the face of him that sitteth on the throne, and from the wrath of the Lamb:
17 For the great day of his wrath is come; and who shall be able to stand?

This great earthquake of the sixth-seal gets the attention of all those who remain alive on earth. It also demonstrates the amazing grace and mercy of YHWH. The Israelites with a Laodicean type souls are distributed among the eleven kingdoms and are now seeking and crying out to their Messiah. YHWH will pour out His spirit or reveal His truth to many and select 12,000 from each of the 12 tribes of the Remnant of Israel. These 144,000 servants will start preaching the gospel to the remainder of mankind and begin to lead the Remnant of Israel as the judgment of the Laodicean souls commences.

Mark 14:10 states the gospel will be published among all the nations, and Joel 2:28-2:29 describes this time as one where YHWH pours out His Spirit upon all flesh.

Joel 2:28-29
28 And it shall come to pass afterward, that I will pour out my spirit upon all flesh; and your sons and your daughters shall prophesy, your old men shall dream dreams, your young men shall see visions:
29 And also upon the servants and upon the handmaids in those days will I pour out my spirit.

The exact day of the anointing during this *10 days of Awe* in 5995 OS is not specified, but it is after the sixth-seal and before the seventh-seal is opened. See Figure XI-2 and Figure XI-3. Also, its exact duration is not given. However, this anointing is a unique event because YHWH in His mercy will be giving those who are still alive another chance to repent. The anointing of the 144.000 Laodicean Israelites is described in Revelation 7.

Revelation 7:1-17
*1 And after these things I saw four angels standing on the <u>four corners of the earth</u> [**North, East, West and South**], holding the four winds of the earth, that the wind should not blow on the earth, nor on the sea, nor on any tree.*
2 And I saw another angel ascending from the east, having the seal of the living God: and he cried with a loud voice to the four angels, to whom it was given to hurt the earth and the sea,
3 Saying, Hurt not the earth, neither the sea, nor the trees, till we have sealed the servants of our God in their foreheads.
*4 And I heard the number of them which were sealed: and **there were sealed an hundred and forty and four thousand of all the tribes of the children of Israel.***
5 Of the tribe of Judah were sealed twelve thousand. Of the tribe of Reuben were sealed twelve thousand. Of the tribe of Gad were sealed twelve thousand.
6 Of the tribe of Asher were sealed twelve thousand. Of the tribe of Nephthalim were sealed twelve thousand. Of the tribe of Manasses were sealed twelve thousand.
7 Of the tribe of Simeon were sealed twelve thousand. Of the tribe of Levi were sealed twelve thousand. Of the tribe of Issachar were sealed twelve thousand.
8 Of the tribe of Zabulon were sealed twelve thousand. Of the tribe of Joseph were sealed twelve thousand. Of the tribe of Benjamin were sealed twelve thousand.
*9 **After this I beheld, and, lo, a great multitude, which no man could number, of all nations, and kindreds, and people, and tongues, stood before the throne, and before the Lamb, clothed with white robes, and palms in their hands;***
*10 **And cried with a loud voice, saying, Salvation to our God which sitteth upon the throne, and unto the Lamb.***

11 And all the angels stood round about the throne, and about the elders and the four beasts, and fell before the throne on their faces, and worshipped God,

12 Saying, Amen: Blessing, and glory, and wisdom, and thanksgiving, and honour, and power, and might, be unto our God for ever and ever. Amen.

13 And one of the elders answered, saying unto me, What are these which are arrayed in white robes? and whence came they?

14 And I said unto him, Sir, thou knowest. And he said to me, These are they which came out of great tribulation, and have washed their robes, and made them white in the blood of the Lamb.

15 Therefore are they before the throne of God, and serve him day and night in his temple: and he that sitteth on the throne shall dwell among them.

16 They shall hunger no more, neither thirst any more; neither shall the sun light on them, nor any heat.

17 For the Lamb which is in the midst of the throne shall feed them, and shall lead them unto living fountains of waters: and God shall wipe away all tears from their eyes.

Revelation 7:1-8 describes the preparation of YHWH's 144,000 special servants from the Remnant of Israel, which will minister to the remaining Laodiceans throughout the world. The 144,000 are sealed with the knowledge and testimony of YHWH, and He will protect His special servants during their ministry. This will be YHWH's last call to the unsaved. Revelation 7:9-17 describes what will ultimately happen to these servants. That is, the 144,000 initially will preach to all the Laodiceans, including the Remnant of Israel, until the Abomination of Desolation in 5996 OS. Then they will lead the Remnant of Israel through the remainder of the Great Tribulation, Time of Vengeance. YHWH will give them a special position in His Kingdom as a reward for their service.

Observe the timing when YHWH pours out His Spirit,truth, upon the people and seals His 144,000 special servants. This is the first event to occur after the judgment of Philadelphia, Smyrna, and Ephesus, which ends after the completion of Seal #6 and prior to the opening of Seal #7 that brings the remainder of the Tribulation Period. The people of Philadelphia, Smyrna, and Ephesus were followers of YHWH prior to the start of the Tribulation Period, but this is not true for the Laodicean souls, who were concerned about self. The pouring out of YHWH's Spirit at this time shows His mercy toward the remainder of mankind on earth. During this time before the Abomination of Desolation in 5996 OS, anyone calling on the name of YHWH, Jesus the Messiah, and repenting will be saved. This also brings the awaking of the Remnant of Israel.

XI - YHWH and Today's Society, 6000 OS

Note the structure that is present in Revelation 7:1-17 where the text identifies a unique group of people followed by what will eventually happen to them. This structure is used in the subsequent descriptions as we turn to the seventh-seal. The seventh-seal is unique, for it contains all the remaining judgments prior to the return of YHWH, Jesus the Messiah, to the material component of the universe to personally tread the Winepress.

From YHWH's perspective, the wise are being harvested, and the foolish are being separated. From Satan's perspective, there are positives and negatives. The positives include the elimination of the majority of those who would not give up YHWH, Jesus the Messiah, as savior or acceptance of Him as just another prophet, as the united world church proclaims. The negatives include:

1. YHWH's defeat of the northern army attacking the Israel.

2. The bountiful crop growth and harvest has allowed Israel to maintain its independence.

3. The sacrifices in the tabernacle in Jerusalem are making a mockery of the One-World Church.

4. A wave of fanatical people the 144,000 have started preaching around the world and inducing more unrest toward the One-World Government. Many of those with Laodicean souls are beginning to align with YHWH.

Satan and Babylon conclude that additional cleansing will be required to achieve their desired outcome—world peace! To achieve world peace, the first three beasts the Lion, Bear, and Leopard will need to provide more support to Babylon. Daniel describes this transition in Daniel 7:7-8 and 7:19-20 as the rise of the fourth beast that subdues the power of the first three beasts. However, transferring power from the Lion, Bear, and Leopard to Babylon is a small price to pay for the prospect of perfect peace in the future.

During the first century the majority Laodiceans were considered wealthy and they were devoted believers in self like Cain. They are neither hot nor cold toward either YHWH or Satan. Their $L_{self}(t)$s is very high, but their $F_{self}(t)$s has now plummeted as they have observed the Rapture and the two-year rampage of the *Four-Horsemen*. Hence, the Laodicean anxiety is high as Jesus the Messiah prepares to open the seventh-seal and initiate their judgment.

183

The Judgment of Laodicea

Laodicean-type souls are unique because they hold the center position in the Menorah and contain the largest number of people. Laodiceans represent 38.29249% of the world's population of 7,682,789,903 people, which is equal to 2,941,932,324 people.

Revelation 3:14-22

14 **And unto the angel of the church of the Laodiceans write;** *These things saith the Amen, the faithful and true witness, the beginning of the creation of God;*

15 **I know thy works,** *that thou art neither cold nor hot: I would thou wert cold or hot.*

16 *So then because thou art lukewarm, and neither cold nor hot, I will spue thee out of my mouth.*

17 *Because thou sayest, I am rich, and increased with goods, and have need of nothing; and knowest not that thou art wretched, and miserable, and poor, and blind, and naked:*

18 *I counsel thee to buy of me gold tried in the fire, that thou mayest be rich; and white raiment, that thou mayest be clothed, and that the shame of thy nakedness do not appear; and anoint thine eyes with eyesalve, that thou mayest see.*

19 *As many as I love, I rebuke and chasten: be zealous therefore, and* **repent.**

20 **Behold, I stand at the door, and knock: if any man hear my voice, and open the door, I will come in to him, and will sup with him, and he with me.** **[Last call]**

21 **To him that overcometh** *will I grant to sit with me in my throne, even as I also overcame, and am set down with my Father in his throne.*

22 *He that hath an ear, let him hear what the Spirit saith unto the churches.*

People with a Laodicean type soul have a $Will_{Self}(t) >>> Will_{YHWH}(t)$ or $Will_{Satan}(t)$, placing themselves above all else. But even more important is the fact that it is also the transitional nature where, the magnitude of self's $Will_{YHWH}(t)$ reaches zero. During the judgment of Laodicea, the cleansing of Mother Earth ends and YHWH's Time of Vengeance begins.

On Yom Teruah 5995 OS, when Jesus the Messiah opens the seventh seal, there will be seven angels with seven trumpets waiting to sound the remaining judgments for all mankind still alive, starting with the Laodiceans.

Many of the influential Laodiceans were part of Babylon's *covenant with many* to cleanse Mother Earth of those radical supporters of YHWH and the eleventh kingdom, Israel. The Rapture and the ride of the *Four-Horsemen* have begun to awaken some of these self-centered people to their dreadful plight. YHWH's advice to the Laodicean people is to repent as revealed through Revelation 3:18-20.

During the judgment of the Laodicean souls, several major events will occur. Therefore, it may be useful to review Figure XI-2 and Figure XI-3 with regard to the Laodicean events, which include:

1. Opening of seal #7 during the *10 days of Awe* in 5995 OS.
    - Trumpet #1 through the Trumpet #4 sound initiating the destruction of a third of the earth.
    - Trumpet #5 initiates Woe #1 with Satan's return to the material component of the universe.
    - Trumpet #6 initiates Woe #2 releasing a great army that murders a third of mankind.

2. The Abomination of Desolation in 5996 OS.
    - The nation of Israel falls to Satan.
    - All people alive on earth have a $Will_{YHWH}(t) = 0.0$ except for the Remnant of Israel.
    - The seven Thunders declare YHWH's divorce indictment and verdict.
    - The two witnesses are introduced to verify the divorce and punishment of the divorced.

3. Yom Teruah 5998 OS.
    - The Judgment of Laodicea is completed.

The *10 days of Awe* starting at Yom Teruah 5995 OS and ending on Yom Kippur 5995 OS has brought the conclusion of the judgment of Ephesus with the opening of Seal #5 showing their destiny and Seal #6's great earthquake marking the end of their judgment. Then, YHWH's 144,000 servants from the twelve tribes of Israel are sealed preparing the way for opening Seal #7. These events were described in the previous section. Now, as these *10 days of Awe* continue, YHWH, Jesus the Messiah, opens the seventh-seal per Revelation 8:1-12.

Revelation 8:1-12
*1 And when he had opened the **seventh seal,** there was silence in heaven about the space of half an hour.*
2 And I saw the seven angels which stood before God; and to them were given seven trumpets.
3 And another angel came and stood at the altar, having a golden censer; and there was given unto him much incense, that he should offer it with the prayers of all saints upon the golden altar which was before the throne.
4 And the smoke of the incense, which came with the prayers of the saints, ascended up before God out of the angel's hand.
5 And the angel took the censer, and filled it with fire of the altar, and cast it into the earth: and there were voices, and thunderings, and lightnings, and an earthquake.
6 And the seven angels which had the seven trumpets prepared themselves to sound.

> 7 The **first angel sounded,** and there followed hail and fire mingled with blood, and they were cast upon the earth: and the third part of trees was burnt up, and all green grass was burnt up.
> 8 And the **second angel sounded,** and as it were a great mountain burning with fire was cast into the sea: and the third part of the sea became blood;
> 9 And the third part of the creatures which were in the sea, and had life, died; and the third part of the ships were destroyed.
> 10 And the **third angel sounded,** and there fell a great star from heaven, burning as it were a lamp, and it fell upon the third part of the rivers, and upon the fountains of waters;
> 11 And the name of the star is called Wormwood: and the third part of the waters became wormwood; **and many men died of the waters, because they were made bitter.**
> 12 And the **fourth angel sounded,** and the third part of the sun was smitten, and the third part of the moon, and the third part of the stars; so as the third part of them was darkened, and the day shone not for a third part of it, and the night likewise.

The first four trumpets unleash a series of large objects at the earth, and one is radioactive. Together these four trumpets destroy a third of the earth's surface. In addition, the radiation makes the waters deadly killing 3.43692% of the world's population or 264,050,973 people, and the impact sends so much debris into the air that the sun and moon cannot be seen in that part of the earth.

During this time YHWH is blessing Israel and their warehouses are full of food, the sun is shining, the rainbow hangs in the sky after the rains, and moonlight diminishes the darkness of the night. These are constant reminders of YHWH's protection of Israel during the initial harvest of the Laodicean souls. It is in this environment that YHWH's 144,000 servants throughout the world are providing men with an alternative, which is eternal life through repentance and faith in YHWH, Jesus the Messiah.

The rising One-World Government in Babylon views the first four trumpets as a natural disaster of monumental proportions, which is an additional item to be dealt with. The structure of the One-World Government in Babylon is still a trilateral coalition with three distinct groups. This trilateral coalition consisting of three beasts is described in Daniel 7 as the Lion, Bear, and Leopard. However, an awesome fourth beast is about to arise in Babylon. Revelation 8:13 provides a warning about this unique time when the fourth beast is released on earth.

Revelation 8:13
> 13 And I beheld, and heard an angel flying through the midst of heaven, saying with a loud voice, Woe, woe, woe, to the inhabiters of the earth by reason of the other voices of the trumpet of the three angels, which are yet to sound!

Woe unto mankind, for these three woes encompass the period of time that Satan is physically present on earth.

- Trumpet #5 (Woe # 1) is Satan's arrival in the material component of the universe.
- Trumpet #6 (Woe # 2) is Satan's reign over the world from Babylon.
- Trumpet #7 (Woe # 3) is Satan's fall.

The sounding of each of these trumpets initiates the associated Woe. All three Woes will end when Jesus the Messiah returns to earth.

Trumpet #5 (Woe # 1)

After the harvest of the Philadelphian, Smyrnian, and Ephesian souls; there is no more room in the pre-creation part of the universe for Satan. The Laodiceans and the remaining people on earth will be given the unique opportunity to experience Satan's leadership abilities firsthand. When the fifth angel sounds his trumpet, Satan is cast into the material component of the universe. Satan then releases the demons restrained in the bottomless pit as described in Revelation 9:1-12.

Revelation 9:1-12
*1 And the **fifth angel sounded,** and I saw a star [**Satan**] fall from heaven unto the earth: and to him [**Satan**] was given the key of the bottomless pit.*
*2 And he [**Satan**] opened the bottomless pit; and there arose a smoke out of the pit, as the smoke of a great furnace; and the sun and the air were darkened by reason of the smoke of the pit.*
*3 And there came out of the smoke locusts upon the earth: and unto them [**demons**] was given power, as the scorpions of the earth have power.*
*4 And it was commanded them [**demons**] that they should not hurt the grass of the earth, neither any green thing, neither any tree; **but only those men which have not the seal of God in their foreheads.***
*5 And to them [**demons**] it was given that they should not kill them, but that they should be tormented five months: and their torment was as the torment of a scorpion, when he striketh a man.*
*6 **And in those days shall men seek death, and shall not find it; and shall desire to die, and death shall flee from them.***
7 And the shapes of the locusts were like unto horses prepared unto battle; and on their heads were as it were crowns like gold, and their faces were as the faces of men.
8 And they had hair as the hair of women, and their teeth were as the teeth of lions.
9 And they had breastplates, as it were breastplates of iron; and the sound of their wings was as the sound of chariots of many horses running to battle.
10 And they had tails like unto scorpions, and there were stings in their tails: and their power was to hurt men five months.

> *11 And they had a king over them, which is the <u>angel of the bottomless pit,</u> <u>whose name in the Hebrew tongue is Abaddon, but in the Greek tongue</u> <u>hath his name Apollyon</u> [Satan].*
>
> *12 One woe is past; and, behold, there come two woes more hereafter.*

Trumpet #5 initiates Woe # 1, which is the introduction of Satan and his demons into the material component of the universe. Once Satan and his demonic spirits, previously restrained in the bottomless pit, arrive in the material component of the universe, they will go through a selection process to possess, or share, the physical bodies of those with soul types of Pergamos, Thyatira, or Sardis. These people's souls are open to demons and have no means to resist them because of the magnitude of their $L_{Satan}(t)$. The possession process is like the sting of a scorpion, and these people will want to die, but cannot because the demons want to coexist with them in their living physical bodies. The demon possession, Woe # 1, will be initiated by the sound of Trumpet #5, and it will continue to inflict people with Pergamian, Thyatiran or Sardian natures for a period of 150 days or five months, until all the demons have established their residence.

Satan's doctrine, which begins to flow from his demon-possessed followers, will affect all people who have not repented—Laodiceans in particular. No person who has repented and claimed Jesus the Messiah can be possessed by the demons for they have made the decision to die for Him. However, those who have a nature of Laodicea, Pergamos, Thyatira, or Sardis and who have not repented will experience Satan's indoctrination as taught by demons. Those who have a Laodicean nature are not familiar with the doctrines of Satan. They have focused only on what self could gain and have prospered at the expense of those previously cleansed from Mother Earth. Demon instruction will be a painful experience for these Laodiceans who do not care about Satan, but have sided with him for personal gain. Satan also sends his demons to suppress the ministry of YHWH's 144,000 servants that are ministering among the nations of the world to the Laodiceans including the Remnant of Israel.

Satan's character as the king in Babylon is described in Daniel 11:36-40.

> *Daniel 11:36-40*
>
> *36 And the <u>king shall do according to his will; and he shall exalt himself, and</u> <u>magnify himself above every god, and shall speak marvellous things against</u> <u>the God of gods, and shall prosper till the indignation be accomplished: for</u> <u>that is determined shall be done.</u> [Satan]*
>
> *37 Neither shall he regard the God of his fathers, nor the desire of women, nor regard any god: for he shall magnify himself above all.*
>
> *38 But in his estate shall he honour the God of forces: and a god whom his fathers knew not shall he honour with gold, and silver, and with precious stones, and pleasant things.*

39 Thus shall he do in the most strong holds with a strange god, whom he shall acknowledge and increase with glory: and he shall cause them to rule over many, and shall divide the land for gain.
40 And at the time of the end shall the king of the south push at him: and the king of the north shall come against him like a whirlwind, with chariots, and with horsemen, and with many ships; and he shall enter into the countries, and shall overflow and pass over.

As king of Babylon, Satan declares himself to be God, having the energy and frequency to possess the material component of the universe, to illuminate all people on earth, and to unify them with himself.

Satan and his demons have arrived to develop and control the fourth beast (Daniel 9:7, 8, 18, 20), as described in Chapter V. They overcome the humiliating defeat of the northern army at the hands of YHWH as He protects Israel. Satan is not fond of Israel, which brought Jesus the Messiah into the world in 4000 OS and is now honoring YHWH by making daily sacrifices in the temple in Jerusalem. Satan immediately plans to attack Israel again, murder any Laodicean opposition, and eliminate YHWH's 144,000 servants, who are proclaiming salvation through Jesus the Messiah to all mankind throughout the world. Satan is allowed to partially accomplish these objectives when Trumpet #6 sounds.

Trumpet #6 (Woe # 2)

As the end of the *10 days of Awe* approach in 5995 OS, Trumpet #6 sounds enabling the sequence of activities and events that will occur during Satan's reign over the One-World Government from Babylon.

Trumpet #6 initiates Woe # 2, which will introduce two events:

1. The judgment of the Laodicean nature by a 200,000,000 man army that murders one third of the world's population, or 2,560,929,968 people.

2. The Abomination of Desolation, which is the point where all people remaining on earth have a $Will_{YHWH}(t) = 0$ with the exception of YHWH's Remnant of Israel with its 144,000 servant leaders.

First, Trumpet #6 introduces the 200,000,000-man army, which over the next three years will complete the judgment of the Laodicean nature. A description of this army and the consequences of its actions are described in Revelation 9:13-21.

Revelation 9:13-21
13 And the **sixth angel sounded,** and I heard a voice from the four horns of the golden altar which is before God,
14 Saying to the sixth angel which had the trumpet, Loose the four angels which are bound in the great river Euphrates.

15 And the four angels were loosed, which were prepared for an hour, and a day, and a month, and a year, for to slay the third part of men.

*16 And the **number of the army of the horsemen were two hundred thousand thousand:** and I heard the number of them.*

17 And thus I saw the horses in the vision, and them that sat on them, having breastplates of fire, and of jacinth, and brimstone: and the heads of the horses were as the heads of lions; and out of their mouths issued fire and smoke and brimstone.

*18 **By these three was the third part of men killed,** by the fire, and by the smoke, and by the brimstone, which issued out of their mouths.*

19 For their power is in their mouth, and in their tails: for their tails were like unto serpents, and had heads, and with them they do hurt.

20 And the rest of the men which were not killed by these plagues yet repented not of the works of their hands, that they should not worship devils, and idols of gold, and silver, and brass, and stone, and of wood: which neither can see, nor hear, nor walk:

21 Neither repented they of their murders, nor of their sorceries, nor of their fornication, nor of their thefts.

At the sound of Trumpet #6 Woe # 2 starts and Satan begins to respond to the rising world anxiety by consolidating his authority over the ten kingdoms while continuing to cleanse those now claiming YHWH, Jesus the Messiah. To accomplish this, Satan demands that direct control over the military power of the Lion, Bear, and Leopard be transferred to Babylon. This is a small price to pay for the prospect of perfect peace in the future rather than assassination for noncompliance.

To ensure success, Satan's new world army must have soldiers dedicated to himself. Thus, his new army must be screened for individuals with souls from Laodicea (10%), Pergamos (24.173%), Thyatira (6.059%) and Sardis (0.621%) or approximately 40% of the world's population to draw from. Can Satan really muster a 200,000,000-man force for Babylon from 40 % of the world's population? To make a conservative estimate, the army will be assumed to be an all male force, which reduces the candidates by another 50%; and if these men are between the ages of 15 to 44 years old, the pool is reduced another 25%. Based on a projected world's population of 7,682,789,903 people at the start of the Tribulation Period, the army which could be raised is (.40 x .50 x .25 x 7,682,789,903) or 384,139,495 men between the ages of 15-44 years. This makes the 200,000,000-man army raised by Satan in Revelation 9:16 a relatively small but evil force.

Satan's new army, headquartered in Babylon, has one objective, which is to cleanse Mother Earth of any kingdom or individual that is not promoting Satan. Quickly Satan turns his attention to the completion of his first objective and that is the complete elimination of the eleventh kingdom, Israel. Satan's finest hour is at hand, as his armies surround Jerusalem. It is the winter of 5997 OS when

Satan's finest hour comes with the fall of Jerusalem. Satan has established his authority over the now ten kingdoms of the world. The world now has a single government with headquarters in Babylon, whose leader is Satan. The fourth-beast of Daniel 7, or the *beast from the sea* is now maturing. Satan has prevailed over the saints, but nothing will be as sweet as his victory over Jerusalem, because to Satan this is synonymous with great victory over YHWH. To savor the victory, Satan establishes a palace in Jerusalem for Israel's new messiah, the false prophet, as a symbol of his authority over YHWH. As the 200,000,000-man army continues the cleansing of Mother Earth, the fall of Jerusalem marks an extremely important event called the Abomination of Desolation.

Abomination of Desolation

The 200,000,000-man army, unleashed by the Trumpet #6, brings the fall of Jerusalem and the outer court of the Tabernacle to Satan during the winter of 5997 OS in the month of Kislev (November-December). This event is called the Abomination of Desolation, and it is the single most significant event to occur up to this point in time during the Tribulation Period. The Abomination of Desolation also marks the midpoint of the seven-year covenant that the One-World Government leaders made with the many influential Occult supporters from all the nations on earth to cleanse Mother Earth of the followers of YHWH. The Abomination of Desolation also marks the point where all people remaining on earth have a magnitude of $Will_{YHWH}(t) = 0$ with the exception of the Remnant of Israel.

The Abomination of Desolation is such an important event that it is described and referenced in many Scriptures. Some of these are Matthew 24:15-22, Mark 13:14-20, Luke 21:20-24, and Daniel 11:40–12:13, are included as follows.

Matthew 24:15-22
*15 When ye therefore shall see the **abomination of desolation,** spoken of by Daniel the prophet, stand in the holy place, (whoso readeth, let him understand:)*
16 Then let them which be in Judaea flee into the mountains:
17 Let him which is on the housetop not come down to take any thing out of his house:
18 Neither let him which is in the field return back to take his clothes.
19 And woe unto them that are with child, and to them that give suck in those days!
20 But pray ye that your flight be not in the winter, neither on the sabbath day:
*21 **For then shall be great tribulation,** such as was not since the beginning of the world to this time, no, nor ever shall be.*
22 And except those days should be shortened, there should no flesh be saved: but for the elect's **[followers of YHWH]** *sake those days shall be shortened.*

Mark 13:14-20

14 But when ye shall see the **abomination of desolation**, spoken of by Daniel the prophet, standing where it ought not, (let him that readeth understand,) then let them that be in Judaea flee to the mountains:

15 And let him that is on the housetop not go down into the house, neither enter therein, to take any thing out of his house:

16 And let him that is in the field not turn back again for to take up his garment.

17 But woe to them that are with child, and to them that give suck in those days!

18 And pray ye that your flight be not in the winter.

19 For in those days shall be affliction, such as was not from the beginning of the creation which God created unto this time, neither shall be.

20 And except that the Lord had shortened those days, no flesh should be saved: but for the elect's **[followers of YHWH]** sake, whom he hath chosen, he hath shortened the days. **[At this point in time YHWH has determined all who will be in His kingdom.]**

Luke 21:20-24

20 And when ye shall see Jerusalem compassed with armies, then know that the **desolation thereof is nigh**.

21 Then let them which are in Judah flee to the mountains; and let them which are in the midst of it depart out; and let not them that are in the countries enter thereinto.

22 **For these be the days of vengeance,** that all things which are written may be fulfilled.

23 But woe unto them that are with child, and to them that give suck, in those days! for there shall be great distress in the land, and wrath upon this people.

24 And they shall fall by the edge of the sword, and shall be led away captive into all nations: and Jerusalem shall be trodden down of the Gentiles, until the times of the Gentiles be fulfilled.

Daniel 11:40-45

40 And at the time of the end shall the king of the south push at him: and the king of the north shall come against him like a whirlwind, with chariots, and with horsemen, and with many ships; and he shall enter into the countries, and shall overflow and pass over.

41 He shall enter also into the glorious land, and many countries shall be overthrown: but these shall escape out of his hand, even Edom, and Moab, and the chief of the children of Ammon.

42 He shall stretch forth his hand also upon the countries: and the land of Egypt shall not escape.

43 But he shall have power over the treasures of gold and of silver, and over all the precious things of Egypt: and the Libyans and the Ethiopians shall be at his steps.

44 But tidings out of the east and out of the north shall trouble him: therefore he shall go forth with great fury to destroy, and utterly to make away many.

45 And he shall plant the tabernacles of his palace between the seas in the glorious holy mountain; yet he shall come to his end, and none shall help him.

Daniel 12:1-13

1 **And at that time shall Michael stand up, the great prince which standeth for the children of thy people: and there shall be a time of trouble,** *such as never was since there was a nation even to that same time: and at that time thy people shall be delivered, every one that shall be found written in the book.*

2 *And many of them that sleep in the dust of the earth shall awake, some to everlasting life, and some to shame and everlasting contempt.*

3 *And they that be wise shall shine as the brightness of the firmament; and they that turn many to righteousness as the stars for ever and ever.*

4 *But thou, O Daniel, shut up the words, and seal the book, even to the time of the end: many shall run to and fro, and knowledge shall be increased.*

5 *Then I Daniel looked, and, behold, there stood other two, the one on this side of the bank of the river, and the other on that side of the bank of the river.*

6 *And one said to the man clothed in linen, which was upon the waters of the river, How long shall it be to the end of these wonders?*

7 *And I heard the man clothed in linen, which was upon the waters of the river, when he held up his right hand and his left hand unto heaven, and sware by him that liveth for ever that it shall be for a time, times, and an half; and when he shall have accomplished to scatter the power of the holy people, all these things shall be finished.*

8 *And I heard, but I understood not: then said I, O my Lord, what shall be the end of these things?*

9 *And he said, Go thy way, Daniel: for the words are closed up and sealed till the time of the end.* [**YHWH will provide understanding for those facing the Tribulation Period.**]

10 *Many shall be purified, and made white, and tried; but the wicked shall do wickedly: and none of the wicked shall understand; but the wise shall understand.*

11 *And from the time that the daily sacrifice shall be taken away, and the abomination that maketh desolate set up* [**The midpoint of the Tribulation Period.**]*, there shall be a thousand two hundred and ninety days.*

12 *Blessed is he that waiteth, and cometh to the thousand three hundred and five and thirty days.*

13 *But go thou thy way till the end be: for thou shalt rest, and stand in thy lot at the end of the days.* [**The end of Tribulation Period.**]

Matthew 24:15-22 and Mark 13:14-20 call the time after the Abomination as the period of the Great Tribulation, but in Luke 21:22 it is described more simply as a *Time of Vengeance*. The Abomination of Desolation is such an important event that the book of Revelation devotes four chapters, Revelation 10-14, to this event that is initiated by the Trumpet #6 (Woe # 2).

The Abomination of Desolation marks the conclusion or initiation of the following major activities and events:

1. YHWH identifies Michael to declare the seven thunders. (Revelation 10, Daniel 12:1)

2. YHWH has completed the harvest of the saints. (Revelation 10)

3. Satan conquers Jerusalem and only the outer court of the tabernacle. (Revelation 11:1,2)

4. YHWH's cloud is over the angels within the Holy of Holies. (Revelation 11:1,2)

5. Satan introduces his messiah, the false messiah, to Israel. (Revelation 11:1,2)

6. YHWH introduces His two witnesses for the divorce process. (Revelation 11:3-13)

7. YHWH's divorce decree from Satan and his followers is read. (Revelation 12 to 14)

8. Satan breaks his seven-year *covenant with many.*

All these events could be addressed in any order because they all will occur on the same day, but for the sake of simplicity they will be addressed in the order they appear in the book of Revelation.

First, in Daniel 12:1 Michael is identified as the angel in Revelation 10.

Daniel 12
*1 And at that time shall **Michael** stand up, the great prince which standeth for the children of thy people: and there shall be a time of trouble, such as never was since there was a nation even to that same time* **[The last half of the Tribulation Period or YHWH's Time of Vengeance.]**: *and at that time thy people shall be delivered, every one that shall be found written in the book.*

The archangel Michael declares the seven Thunders at completion of the harvest of the saints and just before the start of the Great Tribulation, Time of Vengeance. Each Thunder is probably similar to YHWH's voice at Mount Sinai and everyone in the world can understand what is being said. The seven Thunders are described in Revelation 10.

Revelation 10
1 And I saw another <u>mighty angel</u> **[Michael]** *come down from heaven, clothed with a cloud: and a rainbow was upon his head, and his face was as it were the sun, and his feet as pillars of fire:*
2 And he had in his hand a little book open: and he set his right foot upon the sea, and his left foot on the earth,
*3 **And cried with a loud voice, as when a lion roareth: and when he had cried, seven thunders uttered their voices.***

4 And when the seven thunders had uttered their voices, I was about to write: and I heard a voice from heaven saying unto me, Seal up those things which the seven thunders uttered, and write them not.

5 And the angel which I saw stand upon the sea and upon the earth lifted up his hand to heaven,

6 And sware by him that liveth for ever and ever, who created heaven, and the things that therein are, and the earth, and the things that therein are, and the sea, and the things which are therein, that <u>there should be time no longer:</u> **[The time to repent has ended.]**

7 But in <u>the days of the voice of the seventh angel</u> **[5998 OS to 6000 OS]**, when he shall begin to sound, the mystery of God should be finished, as he hath declared to his servants the prophets.

8 And the voice which I heard from heaven spake unto me again, and said, Go and take the little book which is open in the hand of the angel which standeth upon the sea and upon the earth.

9 And I went unto the angel, and said unto him, Give me the little book. And he said unto me, Take it, and eat it up; and it shall make thy belly bitter, but it shall be in thy mouth sweet as honey.

10 And I took the little book out of the angel's hand, and ate it up; and it was in my mouth sweet as honey: and as soon as I had eaten it, my belly was bitter.

11 And he said unto me, Thou must prophesy again before many peoples, and nations, and tongues, and kings.

Revelation 10 pictures the archangel Michael with authority from YHWH for execution of His vengeance against the remainder of mankind on the earth. The rainbow (seven soul types) upon his head and his feet on both the sea (Gentiles) and the land (Israel) points to all the people on earth. His appearance reflects WRATH and the introduction of a time of trouble such as has never been nor will be again. Michael, with the rainbow upon his head (burden for mankind), will declare the seven Thunders shortly.

Why now does YHWH change His attitude from allowing Satan and mankind to Cleanse Mother Earth (i.e. murder the saints) to an attitude of vengeance toward those who remain alive on earth? This is because the Abomination of Desolation stops the daily sacrifice and is the event which marks the point in time where all people with any $Will_{YHWH}(t) > 0$ have been murdered with the exception of the Remnant of Israel including YHWH's 144,000 servant leaders. The remaining people with a Laodicean nature and those with natures of Pergamos, Thyatira and Sardis all possess $Will_{YHWH}(t) = 0$. YHWH has completed the harvest of the saints. Michael's declaration is sobering because the time has expired for repentance (Revelation 10:6). Prior to the Abomination of Desolation, anyone who claimed Jesus the Messiah and willingly gave their life for Him received eternal life (name written in the book on life). By now, all the people whose names are in the Book of Life have been delivered (Daniel 12:1). The harvest of the saints is complete and the Time of Vengeance, is at hand. However, the end is not yet and will not come until Trumpet #7 sounds (Revelation 10:7).

Michael is also holding a small book in his hand that contains the events that will occur during the Time of Vengeance, Great Tribulation. We know from Revelation 10:8-11 that for Satan and his followers, with the natures of Pergamos, Thyatira and Sardis, the conquering of Israel and Jerusalem has the sweet taste of victory. All too soon, this sweet taste will turn to bitterness, as they digest the wrath of YHWH during the coming Time of Vengeance. Satan has conquered Israel, the eleventh kingdom, and Jerusalem, but only the outer court of the Tabernacle is under his control as described in Revelation 11:1-2.

> *Revelation 11:1-2*
> *1 And there was given me a reed like unto a rod: and the angel stood, saying, Rise, and measure the temple of God, and the altar, and them that worship therein.*
> *2 But the **court which is without the temple leave out, and measure it not; for it is given unto the Gentiles:** and the holy city shall they tread under foot forty and two months.*

Why is the outer court of the Tabernacle, third temple, only relinquished to Satan? Recall how the temple structure represents YHWH's personal relationship with an individual. It is the outer court where an individual brings his sin offering representing his repentance and desire on his part to restore his relationship with YHWH. The bronze altar and bronze basin represent the cleansing and forgiveness by YHWH for an individual with a repentant heart. This allows the repentant individual to enter into or restore their personal relationship with YHWH as symbolized by the Holy Place and Holy of Holies. Therefore, it is truly significant that at the Abomination of Desolation, Satan is only given the outer court of the temple because when the daily sacrifices are stopped, an individual's ability to repent will be gone. As Michael said, **There is time no longer** per Revelation 10:6. All men remaining on earth from this time forth are cut off from the capability to repent and receive eternal life, and interesting enough, they are cut off by their own actions. Then, the seven Thunders are heard.

Seven Thunders - The Divorce

From YHWH's perspective Satan and his followers are an abomination. They have had time to repent but have not and their $Will_{YHWH}(t) = 0$. During the Abomination of Desolation, Michael declares the seven Thunders, which are YHWH's declaration of separation from Satan and his followers. Now, there is no chance for salvation and everlasting life There is time no longer, and the patience of the saints is at hand. The Jewish divorce process, during the Time of the Torah, illustrates the sequence of events that are about to occur. The divorce process parallels are summarized in Table XI-5.

Table XI-5 The Divorce Process

Jewish Divorce	YHWH's separation from Satan and followers
Husband	YHWH's SOUL, the Father, is wronged party.
Rabbi/Priest	Rejection of YHWH's BODY justifies the divorce.
Background for the divorce is stated.	Reason for and current state of the participants in the divorce.
Two witnesses confirm the divorce.	Two witnesses (Enoch and Elijah) confirm that the adultery occurred.
Husband says 3 times I divorce you.	YHWH's WILL, the Holy Spirit, implements the divorce.
Two witnesses supervise the punishment.	Two witnesses (Enoch and Elijah) given power to control the various plagues.
The adulterous woman is stoned.	The Great Tribulation or Time of Vengeance.
Two witnesses cast the first stones.	Two witnesses (Enoch and Elijah) provide torment.
The people stoned the adulteress.	The Remnant of Israel and the 144000 also provide torment.

The declaration of YHWH's separation from Satan and his followers starts at Revelation 12 and continues through Revelation 14. The structure of this declaration identifies who the participants are, what they did in the past, and what their present circumstances are. The participants in the divorce are:
- The woman (nation of Israel).
- The woman's seed (the remnant of Israel including the 144,000).
- The child (Jesus the Messiah).
- Satan and his followers.
- Beast from the sea (the One-World Government).
- Beast from the earth (Satan's messiah).

In Revelation 12 through 14, Jesus the Messiah's followers are often referred to as His bride, and their relationship is culminated with a wedding feast. Likewise, this divorce proceeding now separates those who reject YHWH from Him. Revelation 12 and 13 provide the background and current state of affairs that exists between the participants. Once the seven Thunders are heard and the divorce is finalized, then the Time of Vengeance begins.

The inner court of the temple is protected by YHWH's presence, a cloud over the Holy of Holies, and angels which have power to prevent anyone from entering the inner court of the Tabernacle. This is reminiscent of the cherubs guarding the entrance to the Garden of Eden. Thus, Satan is prevented from sitting on YHWH's throne in the Holy of Holies. The most Satan can do is establish a palace in Jerusalem to demonstrate his authority, but he is still denied his true desire.

Satan has a sweet taste in his mouth because he believes that he is very close to completing the cleansing of Mother Earth for Israel as a kingdom has ceased to exist and all the resistance is scattered with some escaping into the mountains of Judah. Now a very small number of people remain that oppose Satan. These people have a very high magnitude of $Will_{YHWH}(t)$. They include:

- The two witnesses.
- The Remnant of Israel including 144,000 elect.
- Angels in the Temple.

These people remain on earth for only one major reason, and that is to torment those divorced from YHWH who remain alive on earth. Satan's sweet taste turns bitter as these tormentors begin to make life miserable for Satan and his followers. The tormentors represent each lot (age) that has been subjected to *Satan's seed*. Table XI-6 identifies the tormentors by the time period they represent or their associated lot.

Table XI-6 The Tormentors

Time Period	Lot	Age	Tormentor/Witness
0000 -2000 OS	1	Tohu (Age of Desolation)	Enoch
2000 -4000 OS	2	Torah (Age of Instruction)	Elijah
4000 -6000 OS	3	Y'mot Mashiach (Age of the Messiah)	Remnant of Israel and the 144,000 elect.

Enoch (Lot #1) and Elijah (Lot #2) are the two witnesses who are introduced and given power by YHWH at the Abomination of Desolation. Enoch and Elijah qualify to be the two witnesses because they are the only men taken by YHWH without experiencing death. Recall Hebrews 9:27, "all men are appointed once to die." Enoch and Elijah will die for the first time when they are overcome by Satan. Moses does not qualify because he has died once. The two witnesses are not sheep to the slaughter, but men of vengeance and torment, dispensing the WRATH of YHWH from Jerusalem as described in Revelation 11:3-14.

Revelation 11:3-14

3 And I will give power unto my two witnesses, and they shall prophesy a thousand two hundred and threescore days, clothed in sackcloth.

4 These are the two olive trees, and the two candlesticks standing before the God of the earth.

5 And if any man will hurt them, fire proceedeth out of their mouth, and devoureth their enemies: and if any man will hurt them, he must in this manner be killed.

6 These have power to shut heaven, that it rain not in the days of their prophecy: and have power over waters to turn them to blood, and to smite the earth with all plagues, as often as they will.

7 And <u>when they shall have finished their testimony</u> **[5999 OS just before Vial #7 is poured]**, the <u>beast that ascendeth out of the bottomless pit</u> **[Satan and followers]** shall make war against them, and shall overcome them, and kill them.

8 And their dead bodies shall lie in the street of the great city, which spiritually is called <u>Sodom</u> **[Self-centered souls]** and <u>Egypt</u> **[Satan following souls]**, <u>where also our Lord was crucified</u> **[Jerusalem]**.

9 And they of the people and kindreds and tongues and nations shall see their dead bodies three days and an half, and shall not suffer their dead bodies to be put in graves.

10 And they that dwell upon the earth shall rejoice over them, and make merry, and shall send gifts one to another; because these two prophets tormented them that dwelt on the earth.

11 And after three days and an half the Spirit of life from God entered into them, and they stood upon their feet; and great fear fell upon them which saw them.

12 And they heard a great voice from heaven saying unto them, Come up hither. And they ascended up to heaven in a cloud; and their enemies beheld them.

13 And the same hour was there a great earthquake, and the tenth part of the city fell, and in the earthquake were slain of men seven thousand: and the remnant were affrighted, and gave glory to the God of heaven.

14 The second woe is past; and, behold, the third woe cometh quickly.

Revelation 11:1-2 previously identified the 42 months that Satan will control the outer court of the Tabernacle, which is also equal to the 1260 days (42*30 = 1260) duration of the two witnesses' power.

The Abomination of Desolation introduces the two witnesses in Revelation 11:3-4. Enoch and Elijah are individually described as:

- A candlestick.
- An olive tree.
- A witness.

The candlestick represents one of the seven churches, and this church is Philadelphia. Certainly, both Enoch and Elijah had Philadelphian-type souls.

The olive tree indicates these individuals were anointed by YHWH and have power to represent Him.

They are clearly identified as *witnesses*. But what are they witnesses to? The two witnesses provide testimony against and torment of those whose names are not written in the Lamb's Book of Life during their separation or divorce from salvation. Revelation 11:5-14 describes what the two witnesses are capable of doing and what will eventually happen to them. The anxiety that these two witnesses will generate in Satan and his servants during the next 1260 days will be incredible because:

- No one will be able to kill them for 1260 days (Revelation 11:5).
- They will have power to invoke all the plagues introduced by Trumpet #7 (Revelation 11:6).

Not only do Satan and his followers have Enoch, lot #1 and Elijah, lot #2, to deal with, but they must also eliminate lot #3, the remnant of the twelve tribes of Israel. Lot #3, the Remnant of Israel with its 144,000 special servants that are among the nations, go underground while those in the nation of Israel escape into the mountains of Judah. This remnant and the 144,000 are also tormentors of Satan's One-World Government because they must be eliminated to complete the cleansing of Mother Earth. Satan expends tremendous effort during the next 1260 days (3 ½ years) after the Abomination of Desolation, to kill the 144,000 and the remainder of the Remnant of Israel. YHWH protects the Remnant of Israel and none are killed. Satan's One-World Government never achieves any part of their goal to totally eliminate the Remnant of Israel.

At the Abomination of Desolation Satan's One-World Government includes:

- People with a Laodicean-type soul that are followers of Satan.
- People with a Thyatira-type soul.
- People with a Pergamos-type soul.
- People with a Sardis-type soul.

All these people possess $Will_{YHWH}(t) = 0$. Each of these natures includes some from the nation of Israel whose names are not written in the lamb's Book of Life and are expecting the Messiah to lead them into the One-World Government.

When Satan conquers Jerusalem and the outer court of the tabernacle, he was also aware that the Israelites are still expecting their Messiah. Satan's version of the messiah is described in Revelation 13:11-18 as the beast from the earth, also known as the False Messiah or False Prophet.

Revelation 13:11-18
11 *And I beheld another* <u>beast</u> **[False Messiah]** *coming up* <u>out of the earth</u> **[Nation of Israel]**; *and he had two horns like a lamb, and he spake as a dragon.*
12 *And he exerciseth all the power of the* <u>first beast</u> **[The One-World Government is the beast from the sea or world in Revelation 13:1]** *before him, and causeth the earth and them which dwell therein to worship the first beast, whose deadly wound was healed.*
13 *And he doeth great wonders, so that he maketh fire come down from heaven on the earth in the sight of men,*
14 *And deceiveth them that dwell on the earth by the means of those miracles which he had power to do in the sight of the beast; saying to them that dwell on the earth, that they should make an image to the beast, which had the wound by a sword, and did live.*
15 *And he had power to give life unto the image of the beast, that the image of the beast should both speak, and cause that as many as would not worship the image of the beast should be killed.*
16 *And he causeth all, both small and great, rich and poor, free and bond, to receive a mark in their right hand, or in their foreheads:*
17 *And that no man might buy or sell, save he that had the mark, or the name of the beast, or the number of his name.*
18 *Here is wisdom. Let him that hath understanding count the number of the beast: for it is the number of a man; and his number is Six hundred threescore and six.*

With the arrival of Satan's messiah, the beast from the earth, the Tabernacle sacrifices are declared not to be required any longer and therefore are stopped. This is fortunate for Satan because it allows him to cover up his lack of control of the Holy Place and the Holy of Holies. Satan's messiah, also known as the Antichrist, provides those who remain in conquered Israel both political and religious leadership as it enters into union with the One-World Government. Satan's messiah is accepted by those Israelites who have not kept the commandments of YHWH. Satan is now the sole world dictator and provides the power to his messiah to perform great wonders before all the people. With the installation of Satan's messiah and the cessation of daily sacrifices in the Tabernacle, the cleansing of Mother Earth is nearly complete. Revelation 13:13-17 describes the steps taken by Satan's messiah to accomplish the remaining task, to kill the remnant of the Israelites among the nations. The plan is to mark all the loyal people so that those who need to be murdered can be identified or starved to death. Satan and his followers to date have managed to murder half of the world's population in the name of peace.

After the seven Thunders are finished, the divorce is complete. The divorce consequences are summarized in Revelation 14 and then implemented during the judgment of the remainder of Laodicea followed by the judgment of Thyatira, Pergamo, and Sardis.

The seven Thunders also awaken the self-centered Laodiceans who were following Satan for their own benefit and now have a rude realization that they had been lied to. Their dissatisfaction causes Satan to break the *covenant with many* and begin murdering the Laodiceans, who once supported him.

After the occurrence of the seven Thunders, Satan has four major tasks to resolve:

1. Finish eliminating his self-centered Laodicean opposition.

2. Deal with the two witnesses.

3. Find and eliminate the Remnant of Israel.

4. Take control of the Holy of Holies and Holy Place in the Temple.

The first task will be completed when Trumpet #7 sounds on 5998 OS signaling the end of Trumpet #6 (Woe #2) where a third of mankind will have now experienced the *first-death*. This also completes the judgment of the Laodicean souls and starts the judgment of the Thyatiran-type souls.

The Judgment of Thyatira

After Satan broke his *covenant with many,* he started murdering his previous Laodicean supporters and by Yom Teruah 5998 OS, he has completed the task. Satan is now supported only by three types of souls who remain alive on earth— Thyatira, Pergamos, and Sardis. But the character of the situation is about to change. Up to this point in time, YHWH has allowed Satan and his supporters to destroy nearly two-thirds of the world's population in their quest to become god, but now it is YHWH who begins to take more direct action against Satan and his supporters starting with the nature of Thyatira.

Yom Teruah 5998 OS initiates the judgment of the Thyatiran type souls. The Thyatiran type souls represent 24.17304 % of the world's population, which is equal to 1,857,163,876 people. YHWH's letter to the Thyatiran type souls is documented in Revelation 2:18-29.

> *Revelation 2:18-29*
>
> 18 **And unto the angel of the church in Thyatira write;** *These things saith the Son of God, who hath his eyes like unto a flame of fire, and his feet are like fine brass;* **[This speaks of YHWH's anger toward the Thyatrian-type souls.]**
>
> 19 *I know thy works,* and <u>charity</u> **[L(t), Love, Priority]**, *and* <u>service</u> **[Who one serves or one's allegiance]**, *and* <u>faith</u> **[F(t), confidence]**, *and thy* <u>patience</u> **[constancy]**, *and thy* <u>works</u> **[Efforts resulting from self's Will(t)]**; *and the last to be more than the first.* **[self's Will$_{Satan}$(t) = L(t) * F(t) is increasing]**

20 <u>Notwithstanding</u> **[moreover]** *I have a few things against thee, because thou sufferest that woman Jezebel, which calleth herself a prophetess, to teach and to seduce my servants to commit fornication, and to eat things sacrificed unto idols.*

21 *And **I gave her space to repent** of her fornication; and she **repented not**.*

22 *Behold, I will cast her into a bed, and them that commit adultery with her into **great tribulation**, except they repent of their deeds.*

23 *And I will kill her children with death; and all the churches shall know that I am he which searcheth the <u>reins</u>* **[inmost mind]** *and <u>hearts</u>* **[soul's motives]**: *and I will give unto every one of you according to your works.* **[The people who are members of the church of Thyatira have souls that place self first and are aligned with Jezebel, Satan, for their benefit.]**

24 *But unto you I say, and <u>unto the rest in Thyatira</u>* **[The people in the city who are not members of the church of Thyatira.]**, *as many as have not this doctrine, and which have not known the depths of Satan, as they speak; I will put upon you none other burden.*

25 *But that which ye have already hold fast till I come.*

26 ***And he that overcometh*** **[Anyone who becomes a follower of YHWH.]**, *and keepeth my works unto the end, to him will I give power over the nations:*

27 *And he shall rule them with a rod of iron; as the vessels of a potter shall they be broken to shivers: even as I received of my Father.*

28 *And I will give him the morning star*

29 *He that hath an ear, let him hear what the Spirit saith unto the churches.*

These people are twice married—to self and to Satan. When Trumpet #7 sounds, the seven angels are introduced, and each is holding a vial containing one of the last seven plagues, Woe #3. The judgment of the Thyatiran nature will happen during the next two years, and during this time several major events will occur. Revelation 2:21-23 provided the warning to the people with a Thyatiran-type soul.

The Thyatiran-type soul is about to experience great tribulation—not from Satan's One-World Government and 200,000,000-man army, but directly from YHWH. YHWH is about to pour out His WRATH(t) and reconcile His ANXIETY(t) with respect to Satan and his Thyatiran followers. Thus, the character of the Time of Vengeance will change with the sounding of Trumpet #7 as alluded to in Revelation 10:7-11 and Revelation 11:15-19.

Revelation 10:7-11

7 **But in the days of the voice of the seventh angel, when he shall begin to sound,** *the mystery of God should be finished, as he hath declared to his servants the prophets.*

8 *And the voice which I heard from heaven spake unto me again, and said, Go and take the little book which is open in the hand of the angel which standeth upon the sea and upon the earth.*

9 *And I went unto the angel, and said unto him, Give me the little book. And he said unto me, Take it, and eat it up; and it shall make thy belly bitter, but it shall be in thy mouth sweet as honey.*

10 And I took the little book out of the angel's hand, and ate it up; and it was in my mouth sweet as honey: and as soon as I had eaten it, my belly was bitter.

11 And he said unto me, Thou must prophesy again before many peoples, and nations, and tongues, and kings.

Revelation 11:15-19

15 And the seventh angel sounded; and there were great voices in heaven, saying, The kingdoms of this world are become the kingdoms of our Lord, and of his Christ; and he shall reign for ever and ever.

16 And the four and twenty elders, which sat before God on their seats, fell upon their faces, and worshipped God,

17 Saying, We give thee thanks, O Lord God Almighty, which art, and wast, and art to come; because thou hast taken to thee thy great power, and hast reigned.

18 And the nations were angry, and thy wrath is come, and the time of the dead, that they should be judged, and that thou shouldest give reward unto thy servants the prophets, and to the saints, and them that fear thy name, small and great; and shouldest destroy them which destroy the earth.

19 And the temple of God was opened in heaven, and there was seen in his temple the ark of his testament: and there were lightnings, and voices, and thunderings, and an earthquake, and great hail.

Prior to Trumpet #7 sounding, the vast majority of life lost will have been a direct result of Lucifer's One-World Government and his 200,000,000-man army. When the great earthquake shakes the earth and the 24 elders worship at the sounding of Trumpet #7, which signals the end of the Laodicean judgment, Woe #2, and the start of Woe #3 and the Thyatira's judgment. Up to this point Satan's One-World Government seemed to be in control; but after Trumpet #7 sounds, the sweet taste of victory for the Occult turns into extreme anxiety and bitterness as the intensity of their punishment continues to increase and their control of the situation decreases. The stage for things to come is described in Revelation 15 where Trumpet #7 reveals the preparation of seven angels, each holding a vial of the wrath of YHWH.

Revelation 15

1 And I saw another sign in heaven, great and marvellous, seven angels having the seven last plagues; for in them is filled up the wrath of God.

2 And I saw as it were a sea of glass mingled with fire: and them that had gotten the victory over the beast, and over his image, and over his mark, and over the number of his name, stand on the sea of glass, having the harps of God.

3 And they sing the song of Moses the servant of God, and the song of the Lamb, saying, Great and marvellous are thy works, Lord God Almighty; just and true are thy ways, thou King of saints.

4 Who shall not fear thee, O Lord, and glorify thy name? for thou only art holy: for all nations shall come and worship before thee; for thy judgments are made manifest.

5 And after that I looked, and, behold, the temple of the tabernacle of the testimony in heaven was opened:

> 6 *And the seven angels came out of the temple, having the seven plagues, clothed in pure and white linen, and having their breasts girded with golden girdles.*
> 7 *And one of the four beasts gave unto the seven angels seven golden vials full of the wrath of God, who liveth for ever and ever.*
> 8 **And the temple was filled with smoke from the glory of God, and from his power; and no man was able to enter into the temple, till the seven plagues of the seven angels were fulfilled.**

On Yom Teruah 5998 OS after Trumpet #7 sounds initiating Woe #3, the temple fills with the glory of YHWH (Revelation 15:8). This is a major setback for Satan, for no one can enter even the outer court of the temple. The seven angels with the last seven Vials are restrained while the glory of YHWH fills the Tabernacle, but then the angels are released to pour out their vials of wrath as described in Revelation 16.

> *Revelation 16: 1-16*
> 1 *And I heard a great voice out of the temple saying to the seven angels, Go your ways, and pour out the vials of the wrath of God upon the earth.*
> 2 *And the **first** [**angel**] went, and poured out his vial upon the earth; and there fell a noisome and grievous sore upon the men which had the mark of the beast, and upon them which worshipped his image.*
> 3 *And the **second angel** poured out his vial upon the sea; and it became as the blood of a dead man: and every living soul died in the sea.*
> 4 *And the **third angel** poured out his vial upon the rivers and fountains of waters; and they became blood.*
> 5 *And I heard the angel of the waters say, Thou art righteous, O Lord, which art, and wast, and shalt be, because thou hast judged thus.*
> 6 *For they have shed the blood of saints and prophets, and thou hast given them blood to drink; for they are worthy.*
> 7 *And I heard another out of the altar say, Even so, Lord God Almighty, true and righteous are thy judgments.*
> 8 *And the **fourth angel** poured out his vial upon the sun; and power was given unto him to scorch men with fire.*
> 9 *And men were scorched with great heat, and blasphemed the name of God, which hath power over these plagues: and they repented not to give him glory.*
> 10 *And the **fifth angel** poured out his vial upon the seat of the beast; and his kingdom was full of darkness; and they gnawed their tongues for pain,*
> 11 *And blasphemed the God of heaven because of their pains and their sores, and repented not of their deeds.*
> 12 *And the **sixth angel** poured out his vial upon the great river Euphrates; and the water thereof was dried up, that the way of the <u>kings of the east</u> [**One-World Government headquartered in Babylon**] might be prepared.*
> 13 *And I saw three unclean spirits like frogs come out of the mouth of the dragon, and out of the mouth of the beast, and out of the mouth of the false prophet.*

205

14 For they are the spirits of devils, working miracles, which go forth unto the kings of the earth and of the whole world, to gather them to the battle of that great day of God Almighty.

15 Behold, I come as a thief. Blessed is he that watcheth, and keepeth his garments, lest he walk naked, and they see his shame.

16 And he gathered them together into a place called in the Hebrew tongue Armageddon.

The first five Vials, Revelation 16:2-10, unleash plagues that directly affect the welfare of Satan and all his Occult followers.

- Vial #1: Satan and all of his followers got noisome (ugly) and grievous (painful) sores.

- Vial #2: The sea became blood and all sea life died.

- Vial #3: The rivers and springs, all fresh water is turned to blood.

- Vial #4: The intensity of the sun is increased and the great heat scorched mankind.

- Vial #5: Brought darkness to Babylon and pain to Satan's followers.

It is difficult to comprehend what life would be like under these plagues. With all the fish killed, there is starvation for some. With no fresh water more illness occur like dehydration resulting in more death. Ambient temperatures would be much greater than those existing today, resulting in drought, and severe sunburn that would working difficult. The souls of Thyatira, Pergamos, or Sardis form an unstable violent, dark, society where the struggle for survival will kill more people of Thyatira. The two witnesses, the great prophets Enoch and Elijah, will begin to intensify their activity in the streets of Jerusalem. The two witnesses have the capability to invoke these and any other plague at their Will per Revelation 11:5-6. Now Satan and his One-World Government must digest the bitter taste of the last seven Vials of the wrath of YHWH and contend with the continuing torment of the two witnesses while still trying to kill the Remnant of Israel. Over the next two years, 5998 to 6000 OS, the intensity of these plagues of the wrath of YHWH will continually increase. These plagues and violence will judge and consume the lives of people with a Thyatiran nature.

Vial #6, Revelation 16:12-16, unleashes Satan's response to the previous torment by the two witnesses and the Remnant of Israel with its 144,000 special servants. The ten kingdoms of Satan's One-World Government are furious and blame Babylon and Satan for their personal health problems and persecution by YHWH. After their previous year and a half experience with the two witnesses and the present loss of the outer court of the Tabernacle, they recognize that defeating YHWH is a bigger job than originally anticipated. Satan sends out demons performing miracles to convince the influential members of the ten kingdoms to support and initiate planning to defeat YHWH. During the next two years, an army is formed and a strategy is conceived to defeat the forces of YHWH. However, by 6000 OS only Pergamos and Sardis and a small number from Thyatira remain to attack the Tabernacle in Jerusalem, which is still controlled by YHWH.

The prophet Joel 3:2-12 provides an overview of the state of some of the Remnant of Israel and the assembly of Satan's army from the ten kingdoms. Note Joel 3:1 is a reference to the Abomination of Desolation.

Joel 3:1-12
1   *For, behold, in those days, and in that time, when I shall bring again the captivity of Judah and Jerusalem,*
2   *I will also gather all nations, and will bring them down into the valley of Jehoshaphat, and will plead with them there for my people and for my heritage Israel, whom they have scattered among the nations, and parted my land.*
3   *And they have cast lots for my people; and have given a boy for an harlot, and sold a girl for wine, that they might drink.*
4   *Yea, and what have ye to do with me, O Tyre, and Zidon, and all the coasts of Palestine? will ye render me a recompence? and if ye recompence me, swiftly and speedily will I return your recompence upon your own head;*
5   *Because ye have taken my silver and my gold, and have carried into your temples my goodly pleasant things:*
6   *The children also of Judah and the children of Jerusalem have ye sold unto the Grecians, that ye might remove them far from their border.*
7   *Behold, I will raise them out of the place whither ye have sold them, and will return your recompence upon your own head:*
8   *And I will sell your sons and your daughters into the hand of the children of Judah, and they shall sell them to the Sabeans, to a people far off: for the Lord hath spoken it.*
9   *Proclaim ye this among the Gentiles; Prepare war, wake up the mighty men, let all the men of war draw near; let them come up:*
10 *Beat your plowshares into swords, and your pruninghooks into spears: let the weak say, I am strong.*
11 *Assemble yourselves, and come, all ye heathen, and gather yourselves together round about: thither cause thy mighty ones to come down, O Lord.*
12 *Let the heathen be wakened, and come up to the valley of Jehoshaphat: for there will I sit to judge all the heathen round about.*

Joel 3:9-12 is a challenge to Satan and his Occult followers to beat their plowshares into swords, their pruning hooks into spears, and come to the valley of Jehoshaphat (Armageddon) for a showdown.

As the summer of 6000 OS ends, Satan is supported by all of the people with Pergamos and Sardis natures some (600,000,000 people) and a small number that remain from Thyatira. At this time only the two witnesses and the Remnant of Israel with its 144,000 special servants are present to represent YHWH. YHWH has protected them during the past three and a half years.

For the final showdown, Satan and his One-World Government musters a huge army consisting of all his supporters. The size of the force that forms in the valley of Armageddon could approach 600,000,000 people. This huge army has very specific objectives:

1. Kill Enoch and Elijah.
2. Take the Holy of Holies in the Temple, thus defeating YHWH.

The first objective seems ridiculous! Is a 600,000,000-man army required to kill these two men (Elijah and Enoch)? Well, ever since the Abomination of Desolation of 5997 OS, Enoch and Elijah have presided over the punishment of the divorced adulterers Satan and his Occult followers. They have caused the rain to cease, killed all who have attacked them, turned the waters to blood, and have caused numerous plagues to occur at their command. Not only have they tormented the people, they are prophesying the defeat of Satan and the judgment and destruction of all those who have an Occult based soul.

All attempts to eliminate these mighty men of YHWH have ended in failure for Enoch and Elijah have killed them with the fire of judgment from their mouths. The plan is to attack them with massive and continuous assaults until their capabilities are overwhelmed. The attack on Enoch and Elijah is initiated in the city of Jerusalem and continues as planned until the first of Ab 6000 OS, which is 1260 days since the Abomination of Desolation, when Enoch and Elijah are killed.

The victors are so excited that they leave Enoch and Elijah's dead bodies in the street for all to see and say, "Satan was right, man has prevailed." It is a time to celebrate the victory, so Satan declares a world holiday for the birth of the new age. The cleansing of Mother Earth has been difficult, but now the new age is at hand. The world hails and worships Satan, who has made Babylon the most magnificent city in the world. Satan has taken the wealth from those who were cleansed from Mother Earth and given it to those who worship him. This is Satan's plan to eliminate poverty from the earth. Satan is the most enlightened, possessing the highest energy level on earth, and he will provide rapid evolution toward the godhead for all. All those on earth whose names are not written in YHWH's Book of Life give praise and honor to Satan. Enoch and Elijah's bodies are left lying in the streets of Jerusalem for all to see as a testimony to the greatness of Satan. But after three and a half days, YHWH resurrected the two witnesses' deteriorating bodies to life in front of Satan and his Occult followers. Then, a great voice from heaven calls to Enoch and Elijah, and they ascend to heaven before a watching world.

At the very same hour that Enoch and Elijah are called to heaven, an earthquake occurs which destroys a tenth of Jerusalem and kills 7000 people of Thyatira, as the Remnant of Israel give glory to YHWH, Revelation 11:7-14. The anxiety of Satan and his followers skyrocket because their $L(t)$, priority, to cleanse Mother Earth is very high, but the ascension of Enoch and Elijah has caused their $F(t)$, confidence, to achieve it to plummet toward zero. The anxiety is so great that some people of Thyatira die from sheer fright (Matthew 24:29, Mark 13:24, 25 and Luke 21:25, 26).

However, for Satan and his Occult followers, there is no turning back. By the end of the month of Ab 6000 OS, the armies of Satan and the ten kingdoms will experience the wrath contained in Vial #7.

It will have been 1290 days since the Abomination of Desolation. One might expect the final seventh-vial to be poured on the first of Tishri a month hence, but for the Remnant of Israel, the elect's, sake the time has been shortened. The first of Elul 6000 OS is very special, for it is in the fortieth Jubilee period since the crucifixion and resurrection of Jesus the Messiah in the year 4000 OS.

On the first of Elul 6000 OS, as the sound of the shofar cuts through the morning air, Satan's army is assembled in the valley of Armageddon and is prepared to take the Tabernacle. Satan's victory in this impending battle would mean the earth is cleansed and he will be God?

When the seventh angel pours his vial the dramatic consequences are described in Revelation 16:17-21, Revelation 17 and 18 as follows:

Revelation 16: 17 -21
*17 And the **seventh angel** poured out his vial into the air; and there came a great voice out of the temple of heaven, from the throne, saying, **It is done.***
18 And there were voices, and thunders, and lightnings; and there was a great earthquake, such as was not since men were upon the earth, so mighty an earthquake, and so great.
*19 And the <u>great city</u> [**Jerusalem**] was divided into three parts, and the cities of the nations fell: and great Babylon came in remembrance before God, to give unto her the cup of the wine of the fierceness of his wrath.*
20 And every island fled away, and the mountains were not found.
21 And there fell upon men a great hail out of heaven, every stone about the weight of a talent: and men blasphemed God because of the plague of the hail; for the plague thereof was exceeding great.

Revelation 17
1 And there came one of the seven angels which had the seven vials, and talked with me, saying unto me, Come hither; I will shew unto thee the judgment of the great whore that sitteth upon many waters:
2 With whom the kings of the earth have committed fornication, and the inhabitants of the earth have been made drunk with the wine of her fornication.

3 So he carried me away in the spirit into the wilderness: and I saw a woman sit upon a scarlet coloured beast, full of names of blasphemy, having seven heads and ten horns.

4 And the woman was arrayed in purple and scarlet colour, and decked with gold and precious stones and pearls, having a golden cup in her hand full of abominations and filthiness of her fornication:

5 And upon her forehead was a name written, MYSTERY, BABYLON THE GREAT, THE MOTHER OF HARLOTS AND ABOMINATIONS OF THE EARTH.

6 And I saw the woman drunken with the blood of the saints, and with the blood of the martyrs of Jesus: and when I saw her, I wondered with great admiration.

7 And the angel said unto me, Wherefore didst thou marvel? I will tell thee the mystery of the woman, and of the beast that carrieth her, which hath the seven heads and ten horns.

8 The beast that thou sawest was, and is not; and shall ascend out of the bottomless pit, and go into perdition: and they that dwell on the earth shall wonder, whose names were not written in the book of life from the foundation of the world, when they behold the beast that was, and is not, and yet is.

9 And here is the mind which hath wisdom. The seven heads are seven mountains **[Empires]**, on which the woman sitteth.

10 And there are seven kings: five are fallen **[#1 Babylonian Empire, #2 Egyptian Empire, #3 Assyrian Empire, #4 Medo/Persian Empire, #5 Grecian Empire]** , and one is **[#6 Roman Empire]**, and the other is not yet come; and when he cometh, he must continue a short space **[#7 Satan's One-World Government exists for less than 7 years]**.

11 And the beast that was **[#1 Satan's Pre-flood One-World Government]** , and is not, even he is the eighth, and is of the seven, and goeth into perdition **[#7 and #8 Satan's Post-flood One-World Government]**.

12 And the ten horns which thou sawest are ten kings, which have received no kingdom as yet; but receive power as kings one hour with the beast.

13 These have one mind, and shall give their power and strength unto the beast.

14 These shall make war with the Lamb, and the Lamb shall overcome them: for he is Lord of lords, and King of kings: and they that are with him are called, and chosen, and faithful.

15 And he saith unto me, The waters which thou sawest, where the whore sitteth, are peoples, and multitudes, and nations, and tongues.

16 And the ten horns which thou sawest upon the beast, these shall hate the whore, and shall make her desolate and naked, and shall eat her flesh, and burn her with fire.

17 For God hath put in their hearts to fulfil his will, and to agree, and give their kingdom unto the beast, until the words of God shall be fulfilled.

18 And the woman which thou sawest is that great city which reigneth over the kings of the earth.

Revelation 18
1 And after these things I saw another angel come down from heaven, having great power; and the earth was lightened with his glory.
2 And he cried mightily with a strong voice, saying, Babylon the great is fallen, is fallen, and is become the habitation of devils, and the hold of every foul spirit, and a cage of every unclean and hateful bird.
3 For all nations have drunk of the wine of the wrath of her fornication, and the kings of the earth have committed fornication with her, and the merchants of the earth are waxed rich through the abundance of her delicacies.
4 And I heard another voice from heaven, saying, Come out of her, my people, that ye be not partakers of her sins, and that ye receive not of her plagues.
5 For her sins have reached unto heaven, and God hath remembered her iniquities.
6 Reward her even as she rewarded you, and double unto her double according to her works: in the cup which she hath filled fill to her double.
7 How much she hath glorified herself, and lived deliciously, so much torment and sorrow give her: for she saith in her heart, I sit a queen, and am no widow, and shall see no sorrow.
8 Therefore shall her plagues come in one day, death, and mourning, and famine; and she shall be utterly burned with fire: for strong is the Lord God who judgeth her.
9 And the kings of the earth, who have committed fornication and lived deliciously with her, shall bewail her, and lament for her, when they shall see the smoke of her burning,
10 Standing afar off for the fear of her torment, saying, Alas, alas, that great city Babylon, that mighty city! for in one hour is thy judgment come.
11 And the merchants of the earth shall weep and mourn over her; for no man buyeth their merchandise any more:
12 The merchandise of gold, and silver, and precious stones, and of pearls, and fine linen, and purple, and silk, and scarlet, and all thyine wood, and all manner vessels of ivory, and all manner vessels of most precious wood, and of brass, and iron, and marble,
13 And cinnamon, and odours, and ointments, and frankincense, and wine, and oil, and fine flour, and wheat, and beasts, and sheep, and horses, and chariots, and slaves, and souls of men.
14 And the fruits that thy soul lusted after are departed from thee, and all things which were dainty and goodly are departed from thee, and thou shalt find them no more at all.
15 The merchants of these things, which were made rich by her, shall stand afar off for the fear of her torment, weeping and wailing,
16 And saying, Alas, alas, that great city, that was clothed in fine linen, and purple, and scarlet, and decked with gold, and precious stones, and pearls!
17 For in one hour so great riches is come to nought. And every shipmaster, and all the company in ships, and sailors, and as many as trade by sea, stood afar off,
18 And cried when they saw the smoke of her burning, saying, What city is like unto this great city!
19 And they cast dust on their heads, and cried, weeping and wailing, saying, Alas, alas, that great city, wherein were made rich all that had ships in the sea by reason of her costliness! for in one hour is she made desolate.

211

> 20 Rejoice over her, thou heaven, and ye holy apostles and prophets; for God hath avenged you on her.
> 21 And a mighty angel took up a stone like a great millstone, and cast it into the sea, saying, Thus with violence shall that great city Babylon be thrown down, and shall be found no more at all.
> 22 And the voice of harpers, and musicians, and of pipers, and trumpeters, shall be heard no more at all in thee; and no craftsman, of whatsoever craft he be, shall be found any more in thee; and the sound of a millstone shall be heard no more at all in thee;
> 23 And the light of a candle shall shine no more at all in thee; and the voice of the bridegroom and of the bride shall be heard no more at all in thee: for thy merchants were the great men of the earth; for by thy sorceries were all nations deceived.
> 24 And in her was found the blood of prophets, and of saints, and of all that were slain upon the earth.

Vial #7 describes large stones striking the earth. 100-pound, 1-talent, stones fall like rain to earth. This may be the result of Satan and his followers hitting a large meteor with a nuclear missile as they try to defend themselves from YHWH's WRATH. A meteor or fragments strike the great city of Babylon directly driving it into the magma of the earth. The impact shakes the entire earth as no other earthquake has since Noah's flood. In less than one day, the earth is so shaken that all the remaining cities of the earth lie in ruin, all man's handiwork is gone, mountains are leveled, and islands are submerged. The city of Jerusalem is divided into three parts, but the Tabernacle still stands with the cloud of the glory of YHWH hovering over it.

The relationship between the ten kingdoms, Satan, the people of earth, and the City of Babylon, and Babylon's current state are described in Revelation 17 and 18. Babylon, the great city, is described as a whore sitting on a great beast with seven heads and ten horns. The woman and the beasts are addressed previously in Chapter V, where the fourth great beast is Satan's One-World Government with its capital in Babylon, and the ten horns are the ten kingdoms that comprise it. Babylon and Satan's One-World Government are gone forever, Revelation 18:21.

After the seventh-vial was poured, the hail subsided, and a great voice from heaven declares:

<u>It is finished!</u>

But what is finished? The extraordinary conjunction of Seal #7 with Trumpet #7 and Vial #7 provides insight into what was completed. The number 3 implies complete. The number 7 implies spiritual perfection. The three sevens represents the completion of the spiritual persecution. What spiritual persecution is complete at this point in time? Jesus the Messiah's followers including the Remnant of Israel will experience no more tribulation after Vial #7. Similarly, the conjunction of the first, second, and third Woes ends Satan's time of power and ability to persecute the Remnant of Israel.

The judgment of the Thyatiran nature is also done and the cloud of the glory of YHWH still stands over the Tabernacle. Satan and his followers are defeated.

In the pre-creation universe, this is a time of rejoicing as described in Revelation 19:1-10.

Revelation 19:1-10
1 And after these things I heard a great voice of much people in heaven, saying, Alleluia; Salvation, and glory, and honour, and power, unto the Lord our God:
2 For true and righteous are his judgments: for he hath judged the great whore, which did corrupt the earth with her fornication, and hath avenged the blood of his servants at her hand.
3 And again they said, Alleluia. And her smoke rose up for ever and ever.
4 And the four and twenty elders and the four beasts fell down and worshipped God that sat on the throne, saying, Amen; Alleluia.
5 And a voice came out of the throne, saying, Praise our God, all ye his servants, and ye that fear him, both small and great.
6 And I heard as it were the voice of a great multitude, and as the voice of many waters, and as the voice of mighty thunderings, saying, Alleluia: for the Lord God omnipotent reigneth.
7 Let us be glad and rejoice, and give honour to him: for the marriage of the Lamb is come, and his wife hath made herself ready.
8 And to her was granted that she should be arrayed in fine linen, clean and white: for the fine linen is the righteousness of saints.
9 And he saith unto me, Write, Blessed are they which are called unto the marriage supper of the Lamb. And he saith unto me, These are the true sayings of God.
10 And I fell at his feet to worship him. And he said unto me, See thou do it not: I am thy fellow servant, and of thy brethren that have the testimony of Jesus: worship God: for the testimony of Jesus is the spirit of prophecy.

Note that there are two aspects associated with the rejoicing. First, rejoicing for the defeat of Satan as described in Revelation 19:1-6. The divorce proceedings are drawing to a close. Only Satan and his followers with souls from Pergamos and Sardis remain. The divorce will be finalized after the return of YHWH, Jesus the Messiah, to the material component of the universe.

The second cause for rejoicing is for the impending marriage of Jesus the Messiah (Lamb) and his betrothed bride (all true followers of Jesus the Messiah who have previously died and the Remnant of Israel who turned to Him during the Tribulation Period). His bride has been made ready. She has made good decisions demonstrating her faithfulness to Him by remaining faithful during the Tribulation Period. Now is the time for the courtship to begin as the bride prepares herself for her future husband. The first of Elul 6000 OS begins the courtship. The period is illustrated by the solemn forty-day period of preparation prior to Yom Kippur (Day of Atonement). During Elul the shofar (ram's horn) is sounded daily with the exception of each Sabbath and the morning before Yom Teruah (Feast of Trumpets). The sound of the shofar reminds men to prepare for Yom Kippur when all is restored between YHWH and mankind.

The month of Elul is also a time for the Pergamos and Sardis soul types to confront what is about to happen to them for their initiation of the cleansing of Mother Earth, which has resulted in total devastation of the earth! Except for the roaring of waves upon the sea, the earth is silent. There is a unique darkness for the sun, stars and moon are no longer clearly visible. The earth is shrouded in dust and unstable in its orbit. The morning is established by the sound of the shofar from heaven breaking through this darkness on earth to proclaim the imminent return of Jesus the Messiah to finalize the divorce from Satan, Pergamos, and Sardis by treading the Winepress.

The Judgment of Pergamos - The Winepress

As the month of Elul draws to a close and the first day of Tishri, Yom Teruah, 6000 OS draws nigh, Satan and the soul types of Pergamos and Sardis are full of anxiety because YHWH's glorified BODY, Jesus the Messiah, is about to return to the material component of the universe with the promise to tread the Winepress of YHWH's WRATH.

The Winepress is Jesus the Messiah's judgment of Pergamos and Sardis. The Winepress is a mirror image of the Rapture. That is, the first day of the Rapture included the Philadelphians followed by nine days of judgment for Smyrna. Whereas, the Winepress begins with nine days of judgment for Pergamos and concludes with one day of judgment for Sardis. The Winepress occurs during the *10 Days of Awe* starting with Yom Teruah, the Feast of Trumpets, on the first day of the seventh month in the fortieth Jubilee period since the crucifixion and resurrection of Jesus the Messiah and ending on Yom Kippur, the Day of Atonement, in the year 6000 OS.

Yom Teruah 6000 OS is known by some unique names in Jewish tradition because it is so special. Such as: "the day no man knows the day or hour" or "the one long day." The following awesome events will occur during the month of Tishri 6000 OS, starting with Yom Teruah the first day and continuing through the remainder of the month:

1. On the first day, Yom Teruah 6000 OS, Jesus the Messiah returns to the material component of the universe with all His followers.

2. During days one through nine, Jesus the Messiah judges Pergamos-type souls in the Winepress.

3. On the tenth day, Yom Kippur 6000 OS, Jesus the Messiah judges Sardis soul types in the Winepress and then binds Satan.

4. During days eleven through fourteen Jesus the Messiah constructs the Kingdom Age Temple.

5. During days fifteen through twenty one, the Feast of Tabernacles 6000 OS is celebrated, which is the marriage supper of the Lamb.

6. On day twenty-two, which was referred to as the Last Great Day, 6000 OS is the first great day of the Age of the Kingdom.

Tishri 6000 OS will be the most significant month in the history of mankind. As we progress through the remainder of this chapter, each of the above items will be addressed in the order of its occurrence.

The first event is the return of YHWH's resurrected BODY, Jesus the Messiah. Zechariah 14:4-9 describes Jesus the Messiah's return on Yom Teruah 6000 OS as follows.

Zechariah 14:4-9
*4 And <u>his</u> [**YHWH's BODY**] feet shall stand in that day upon the mount of Olives, which is before Jerusalem on the east, and the mount of Olives shall cleave in the midst thereof toward the east and toward the west, and there shall be a very great valley; and half of the mountain shall remove toward the north, and half of it toward the south.*
5 And ye shall flee to the valley of the mountains; for the valley of the mountains shall reach unto Azal: yea, ye shall flee, like as ye fled from before the earthquake in the days of Uzziah king of Judah: and the Lord my God shall come, and all the saints with thee.
6 And it shall come to pass in that day, that the light shall not be clear, nor dark:
7 But it shall be one day which shall be known to the Lord, not day, nor night: but it shall come to pass, that at evening time it shall be light.
8 And it shall be in that day, that living waters shall go out from Jerusalem; half of them toward the former sea, and half of them toward the hinder sea: in summer and in winter shall it be.
*9 And the <u>Lord</u> [**YHWH**] shall be king over all the earth: in that day shall there be one <u>Lord</u> [**YHWH**], and his name one.*

Revelation 19:11-16 also describes Jesus the Messiah's return to the material component of the universe.

Revelation 19:11-16
11 And I saw heaven opened, and behold a white horse; and he that sat upon him was called Faithful and True, and in righteousness he doth judge and make war.

12 His eyes were as a flame of fire, and on his head were many crowns; and he had a name written, that no man knew, but he himself.

13 And he was clothed with a vesture dipped in blood: and his name is called The Word of God.

14 And the armies which were in heaven followed him upon white horses, clothed in fine linen, white and clean.

*15 And out of his mouth goeth a sharp sword, that with it he should smite the nations: and he shall rule them with a rod of iron: **and he treadeth the winepress of the fierceness and wrath of Almighty God.***

16 And he hath on his vesture and on his thigh a name written, KING OF KINGS, AND LORD OF LORDS.

These scriptures picture the first day of Tishri, Yom Teruah, that one long day where it is neither light nor dark during the day or night. This condition in Jerusalem may be the result of a shift of the earth on its axis. Note that Yom Teruah is established by sighting the new moon, in Jerusalem and under the existing conditions in 6000 OS, this is impossible. Even if a person were alive at the start of the cleansing of Mother Earth in 5993 OS and kept precise track of the time, he could not know the exact time that Jesus the Messiah would return because YHWH controls the time. This one long day is the day that no man knows the day or the hour. It is YHWH's SOUL, the Father's, responsibility to know the time.

When YHWH's SOUL, the Father, decides to return, YHWH's WILL, Holy Spirit sounds the last trumpet and Yom Teruah is established. The gloom on earth is suppressed as the door to Heaven opens and the glory of YHWH's BODY, Jesus the Messiah, appears in the heavens as described in Revelation 19:11-16. As Jesus the Messiah enters the material component of the universe and His feet touch the Mount of Olives near Jerusalem, the mount cleaves in two and living waters start to flow out of Jerusalem. Jesus the Messiah's return restores stability to the earth and reestablishes day and night. His angels gather all His followers from the uttermost parts of heaven, the pre-creation universe, and earth. This event is described in Matthew 24:30-31 and Mark 13:26-27.

Matthew 24:29-31

29 Immediately after the tribulation of those days shall the sun be darkened, and the moon shall not give her light, and the stars shall fall from heaven, and the powers of the heavens shall be shaken:

*30 And then shall appear the sign of the <u>Son of man</u> **[YHWH's BODY]** in heaven: and then shall all the tribes of the earth mourn, and they shall see the <u>Son of man</u> **[YHWH's BODY]** coming in the clouds of heaven with power and great glory.*

*31 And he shall send his angels with a great sound of a trumpet, and they shall gather together his <u>elect</u> **[Those who have placed YHWH first in their lives.]** from the four winds, from one end of heaven to the other.*

Mark 13:24-27
24 But in those days, after that tribulation, the sun shall be darkened, and the moon shall not give her light,
25 And the stars of heaven shall fall, and the powers that are in heaven shall be shaken.
26 And then shall they see the Son of man [YHWH's BODY] coming in the clouds with great power and glory.
27 And then shall he send his angels, and shall gather together his elect from the four winds, from the uttermost part of the earth to the uttermost part of heaven.

Who is present on earth just after Jesus the Messiah's return to the material component of the universe?

- The Remnant of Israel from all the nations represent 1.52224 % of the world's population of 7,682,789,903 or 116,950,788 people who still have mortal-material bodies, which have survived Satan and his followers cleansing efforts.
- All followers of Jesus the Messiah, who were raptured or murdered, now have new resurrected bodies that are capable of transition between the material component of the universe and the pre-creation universe as desired.
- Satan and his followers with Pergamian and Sardian natures.

Now that Jesus the Messiah has returned as King of kings and Lord of lords, what will He do? He will keep His promises!

YHWH's first promise is to tread the Winepress, Revelation 19:15. Just the anticipation of what is about to happen in the Winepress will cause the Pergamian-type soul unimaginable fear.

Thus, the first souls impacted by the Winepress are those people with Pergamian-type souls. The Pergamian-type souls represent 6.05975 % of the world's population at the start of the Tribulation Period (7,682,789,903 people), which is equal to 465,557,861 people. YHWH's letter to the Pergamian-type souls is documented in Revelation 2:12-17.

Revelation 2:12-17
*12 **And to the angel of the church in Pergamos write;** These things saith he which hath the sharp sword with two edges; [**YHWH controls who will experience the second-death**]*
*13 **I know thy works,** and where thou dwellest, even where Satan's seat is: and thou holdest fast my name, and hast not denied my faith, even in those days wherein Antipas was my faithful martyr, who was slain among you, where Satan dwelleth. [**The Pergamos type souls know who YHWH is and what He expects, but they are followers of Satan and they are at war with YHWH.**]*
14 But I have a few things against thee, because thou hast there them that hold the doctrine of Balaam, who taught Balac to cast a stumblingblock before the children of Israel, to eat things sacrificed unto idols, and to commit fornication.

> 15 So hast thou also them that hold the doctrine of the Nicolaitans, which thing I hate. **[Not only are Pergamos-type souls dedicated followers of Satan who were trying to get followers of YHWH to commit sin.]**
>
> 16 **Repent**; or else I will come unto thee quickly, and will fight against them with the sword of my mouth. **[YHWH's will invoke the second-death.]**
>
> 17 **He that hath an ear, let him hear what the Spirit saith unto the churches;** To him that overcometh will I give to eat of the hidden manna, and will give him a white stone, and in the stone a new name written, which no man knoweth saving he that receiveth it.

Pergamos means "married to tower," and the city is historically connected to the tower of Babel because the Babylonian priests when banished moved to Pergamos and subsequently to Rome. Like those who built the tower of Babel, the vast majority of the people in Pergamos were dedicated members of the Synagogue of Satan. Many of the Pergamos-type souls that are facing the Winepress are now demon-possessed. The previous scripture, Revelation 19:15, is the implementation of the promise made to them in Revelation 2:16.

The treading of the Winepress by Jesus the Messiah will result in the death of all the people with a Pergamos-type soul during the next nine days. Zechariah 14:12 and Isaiah 63:1-10 also describe the Winepress.

Zechariah 14:12
> 12 And this shall be the plague wherewith the Lord will smite all the people that have fought against Jerusalem; Their flesh shall consume away while they stand upon their feet, and their eyes shall consume away in their holes, and their tongue shall consume away in their mouth.

Isaiah 63:1-10
> 1 Who is this that cometh from Edom, with dyed garments from Bozrah? this that is glorious in his apparel, travelling in the greatness of his strength? I that speak in righteousness, mighty to save.
>
> 2 Wherefore art thou red in thine apparel, and thy garments like him that treadeth in the winefat?
>
> 3 **I have trodden the winepress alone; and of the people there was none with me: for I will tread them in mine anger, and trample them in my fury; and their blood shall be sprinkled upon my garments, and I will stain all my raiment.**
>
> 4 For the day of vengeance is in mine heart, and the year of my redeemed is come.
>
> 5 And I looked, and there was none to help; and I wondered that there was none to uphold: therefore mine own arm brought salvation unto me; and my fury, it upheld me.
>
> 6 And I will tread down the people in mine anger, and make them drunk in my fury, and I will bring down their strength to the earth.
>
> 7 I will mention the loving kindness of the Lord, and the praises of the Lord, according to all that the Lord hath bestowed on us, and the great goodness toward the house of Israel, which he hath bestowed on them according to his mercies, and according to the multitude of his loving kindness.

218

8 *For he said, Surely they are my people, children that will not lie: so he was their Saviour.*

9 *In all their affliction he was afflicted, and the angel of his presence saved them: in his love and in his pity he redeemed them; and he bare them, and carried them all the days of old.*

10 *But they rebelled, and vexed his holy Spirit: therefore he was turned to be their enemy, and he fought against them.*

Satan and his followers are defenseless as Jesus the Messiah, King of kings and Lord of lords, treads the Winepress with perfect anger and power. Their eyes, mouths and bodies begin to rot away in front of His glory. Judgment starts with those of Pergamos with the lowest magnitude of $Will_{Satan}$ *(t)* and spreads to the others as a function of their increasing $Will_{Satan}(t)$. One cannot imagine the anxiety of those awaiting their turn before Jesus the Messiah. The Winepress is tread once a day for nine days and consumes all of the people with Pergamos-type souls.

There is another aspect of the Winepress that may seem somewhat morbid, but it must be addressed. That is, the amount of blood shed by those of Pergamos and Sardis. The blood shed in the Winepress is important because it provides another independent estimate for the world's population at the start of the Tribulation Period based upon the normal distribution of the seven soul types. This means that the volume of blood shed in the Winepress when computed based on a normal distribution must be consistent with the volume of blood stated in Revelation 14:20.

Revelation 14:20

20 *And the winepress was trodden without the city, and blood came out of the winepress, even* **unto the horse bridles, by the space of a thousand and six hundred furlongs.**

The following computation provides final scriptural validation that the distribution of the seven types of mankind's soul conforms to a normal distribution.

Jesus the Messiah treads the Winepress starting on Yom Teruah and continues for ten days. Pergamos, 6.05975 % of the world population present at the start of the Tribulation Period, is judged during the first nine days at a rate of 0.6733055556 % of the world population per day. Yom Kippur, the tenth day, is devoted entirely to the judgment of Sardis, which is 0.62097 % of the world population. The total number of people consumed during the treading of the Winepress is 6.679846 % of the world's population.

Revelation 14:20 states the amount of blood generated each time the Winepress is tread during the judgment of Pergamos and Sardis. This gives an independent means to determine the world's population at the start of the Tribulation Period.

Given the volume of blood identified in Revelation 14:20, the world population at the start of the Tribulation Period can be estimated using the following expression:

$$P * K = [V_{\text{Winepress}} / V_{\text{person}}]$$

Where:

P = The world's population at start of the Tribulation Period (people).

K = The fraction of the world's population consumed per treading (unit less).

$V_{\text{Winepress}}$ = The volume of blood from Winepress (in cubic feet).

V_{person} = The volume of blood in one person (in cubic feet/person).

The volume of blood from the Winepress can be expressed in terms of area (A) and height (H):

$$V_{\text{Winepress}} = A * H$$

Where:

A = The area of the blood (in square feet).

H = The height of the blood (in feet).

Substituting for $V_{\text{Winepress}}$ in $P * K = [V_{\text{Winepress}} / V_{\text{person}}]$ and solving for P:

$$P = [A * H] / [K * V_{\text{person}}]$$

First A must be determined by computing the area that the blood contained in the space of 1600 furlongs into square feet. The meaning of a furlong has changed over the years. The original furlong expressed length and/or width. It is an old English word describing the area of a furrow in a plowed field. The furlong had a length of approximately 1/8 mile or 660 feet with a furrow width of approximately 1.5 +/-0.5 feet. Note, tolerances are added to cover uncertainties in the various dimensions throughout this analysis. The furlong use in the King James English Bible was translated from the Greek word Stadia, which was a runner's path between the pillars at each end of the stadium located at Olympia, or a distance of approximately 630 feet of unknown width. The path width was an established Greek track standard, which was most likely less than 2.0 feet. The difference between the length of the furlong and the Stadia is 30 feet. Therefore, the nominal value selected is 645 with a +/- 15 feet variance. A 1600 furlong field represents many different shaped fields having the same area. For example a field 1600 furlongs in length and 1 furrow wide or a field 20 furlongs in length by 80 furrows in width have the same area. The nominal area for either layout will be the same and yields a area A = 645 ft * 1600 * 1.5 ft = 1,584,000 square feet.

The second factor in determining the volume is the height (H), which was defined in Revelation 14:20 as even with the horses' bridles. The bit of a horse's bridle fits into the horse's mouth. The horse's mouth is approximately the same height as the upper locks or withers (area just forward of the saddle) of the horse.

A horse's height is measured from the ground to the horse's withers in hands. A hand is 1/3 of a foot. Horses come in many different sizes. A draft horse may be as high as 20 hands, or 6.667 feet, whereas any horse under 14.2 hands, or 4.7 feet is considered a pony. This provides an average horse height $H = (6.667 + 4.733) / 2 = 5.700$ feet with a variance of +/- 0.967 feet .

The next parameter is $K = .006733055556$ or 0.6733055556 percent of world population, which is judged each day from the natures of Pergamos and Sardis by Jesus the Messiah.

The only remaining information required is V_{person}, the amount of blood in a human body. Here the amount of blood varies with respect to an individual's size and weight, but will be generally between 4 and 6 quarts per person. The nominal value is 5.0 Quarts with a variance of +/- 1 quart or $V_{person} = 0.1671$ +/- 0.03342 cubic feet per person.

Using the worst case variances; the minimum, nominal, and maximum estimates for the world's population (P) at the start of the Tribulation Period are computed as follows:

$$P = [A * H] / [K * V_{person}]$$

$P_{Minimum} = [(630*1600*1.0)*(4.733)] / [0.0067330*0.200521] = 3,533,664,698$ people.
$P_{Nominal} = [(645*1600*1.5)*(5.700)] / [0.0067330*0.167101] = 7,842,515,024$ people.
$P_{Maximum} = [(660*1600*2.5)*(6.667)] / [0.0067330*0.133681] = 19,554,825,388$ people.

The world population projections for the years from 1900 through 2100 are plotted in Figure XI-4 along with the maximum, minimum, and normal Winepress estimates for the world's population at the start of the Tribulation Period.

The world population estimates associated with the stars in Figure XI-4 are from *The World Almanac and Book of Facts* for the year 1999 AD all other data points were extrapolated by the author.

Based on the blood shed during the Winepress, the earliest start date of the Tribulation Period would be approximately 1960 AD, with the nominal start date approximately 2023 AD, and the latest start date being approximately 2090 AD. Note the nominal Tribulation Period start date of 2023 AD plus seven years of tribulation yields the year 2030 AD for the return of Jesus the Messiah. This estimate is amazingly close to the year 2029 AD, which is the most probable year corresponding to 6000 OS.

In the above computation, the blood from the Winepress is the known quantity, and it provides a totally independent computation for the world's population at the start of the Tribulation Period assuming Pergamos and Sardis conformed with a normal distribution. Whereas, the computation of the number of Philadelphians present about YHWH's throne for the opening of the first four seals at the start of

In the Image of YHWH

the Tribulation Period was the given bounded quantity and then the quantity was computed based on the world's population profile, the number of Philadelphians per generation, and the normal distribution.

How appropriate it is that the blood of the Winepress provides the final validation that the seven types of men's souls conforms to a normal distribution with a zero mean.

It is also noteworthy that Jesus the Messiah was probably crucified and resurrected during 0029 AD or 0030 AD during a Jubilee period. The number 40 is associated with trial or time in the wilderness. 40 Jubilee periods, 2000 years, have passed since Jesus the Messiah's resurrection, and thus it is probable that Jesus the Messiah will return to the material component of the universe would be expected during 2029 AD or 2030 AD.

YHWH initiated the restoration of the nation of Israel in 1948 AD, and Jerusalem became part of Israel during the 1967 AD Six Day War. Jesus the Messiah's return is anticipated within one generation. Current life expectancy is about 75 years per generation. Thus one could expect Jesus the Messiah's return anytime between 2023 AD to 2042 AD.

It is worthwhile to pause and reflect on the significance of what has just been demonstrated using Quantitative Theology to estimate the number people associated with the seven types of souls and validating the results directly in the book of Revelation.

1. First, the number of Philadelphians about the throne was computed using the world population projections shown in Figure XI-4 and 0.62097% Philadelphians per generation based on the normal distribution of souls. Revelation 5:11 states there will be 100,000,000 to 361,000,000 Philadelphians present when the Seals are opened. The earliest this 100, 000,000 number could be met was about 1950 when the world population was 2,556,000,000 people, the most probable time is about 2022 when the world population is projected to be 7,682,789,903 people, and the latest time would be the 361,000,000 number that could be meet about 2060 when the world population is projected to be 10,346,399,000 people.

2. The ride of the *Four-Horsemen* murdering 25% of the world's population, Revelation 6:8, is consistent with the judgment of the Smyrnians that were not Raptured (0.82696 %) and all the Ephesians (24.17304%).

222

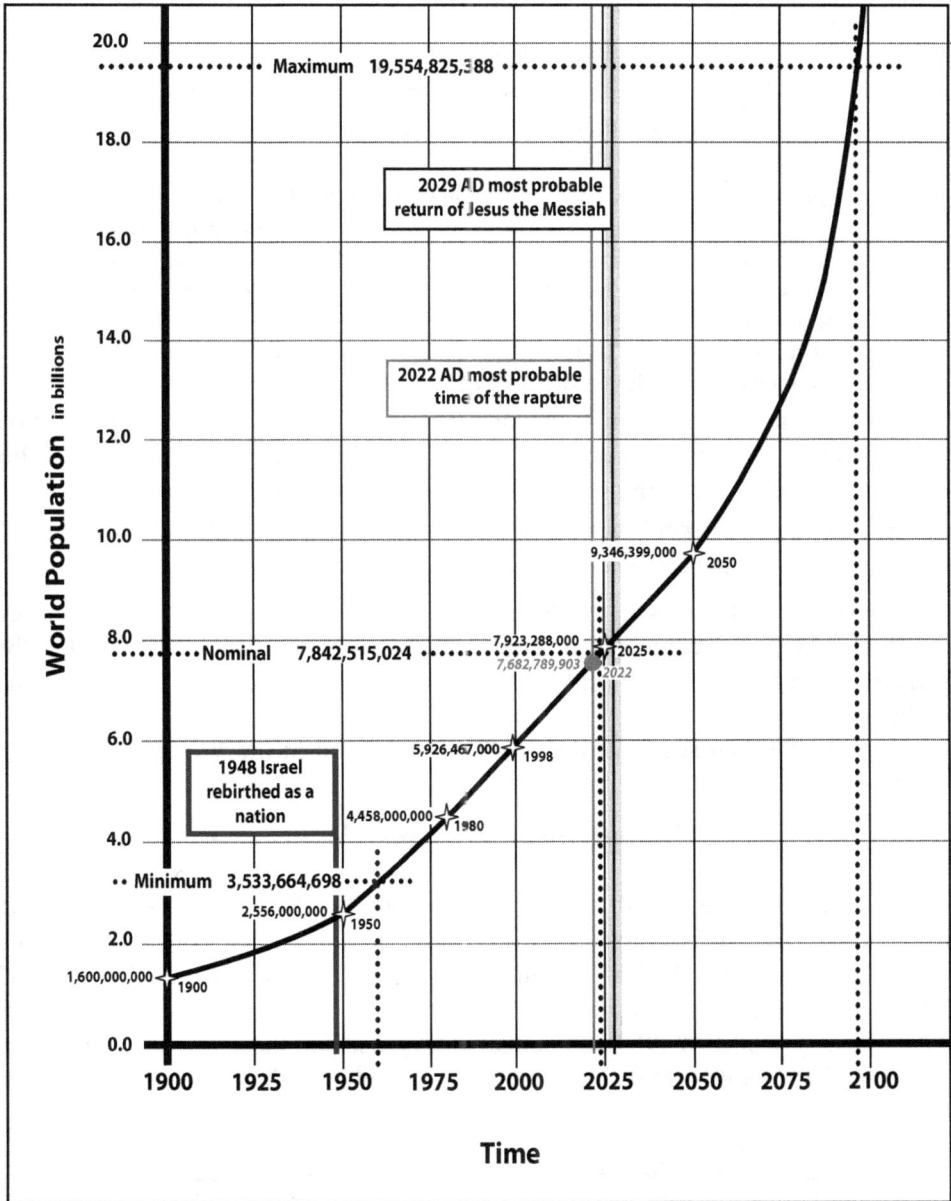

Figure XI-4 Tribulation Period versus World Population

3. The judgment of Laodicea, 38.29249% of the world's population is consistent with:
   - 3.43692 % deaths due to the bitter waters, Revelation 9:11.
   - 33.33333% due to the 200,000,000-man army, Revelation 9:18.
   - 1.52224% the Remnant of Israel that survive the entire Tribulation Period, Zechariah 13:8-9.

4. The blood of the Winepress, Revelation 14:20, is absolutely unique because the computation starts with the amount of blood that is shed by Pergamos and Sardis to estimate the world's population at the start of the Tribulation Period. The earliest time is about 1960 with a world population of 3,533,664,698. The nominal time is about 2023 with a world population of 7,842,515,024 people. The latest time is about 2090 with a world population of 19,534,825,388.

It is amazing that the nominal values for the world's population at the start of the Tribulation Period based on both the Philadelphians about the throne and the Winepress are essentially the same! The two world population estimates are:

- 7,682,789,903 people in the year 2022 based on the Philadelphians.
- 7,842,515,024 people in the year 2023 based on the Winepress.

Clearly the judgments in the book of Revelation have not been fulfilled yet and the mathematics contained in the book of Revelation requires it be literally interpreted because the numerical content cannot be addressed as allegory, fiction, or apocrypha.

Now the Sardian souls must still shed their blood in the Winepress on Yom Kippur 6000 OS.

The Judgment of Sardis - Winepress

On Yom Kippur the tenth Tishri in the year 6000 OS the time has arrived for the judgment of Sardis. Those with a Sardian nature are Satan's prized Occult followers who prospered with him and were willing to die for him, and their time of judgment has come. They represent about 0.62097% of the world's population of approximately 7,682,789,903 people that were present at the start of the cleansing of Mother Earth or 47,707,052 people. YHWH's letter to the Sardian type souls is documented in Revelation 3:1-6.

Revelation 3:1-6
*1 **And unto the angel of the church in Sardis write;** These things saith he that hath the seven Spirits of God, and the seven stars;* **[YHWH has authority over all things including Satan.]**

I know thy works, that thou hast a name that thou livest, and art dead.

2 Be watchful, and strengthen the things which remain, that are ready to die: for I have not found thy works perfect before God. **[Sardis souls are devote followers of Satan with hearts of stone. They believe they have the truth and they will replace YHWH.]**

3 Remember therefore how thou hast received and heard, and hold fast, and **repent**. If therefore thou shalt not watch, I will come on thee as a thief, and thou shalt not know what hour I will come upon thee.

4 Thou hast a _few names even in Sardis_ **[In the city, but not the church.]** which have not defiled their garments; and they shall walk with me in white: for they are worthy.

5 **He that overcometh,** the same shall be clothed in white raiment; and I will not blot out his name out of the book of life, but I will confess his name before my Father, and before his angels.

6 He that hath an ear, let him hear what the Spirit saith unto the churches.

This is the leadership of the One-World Government that initiated the destruction of the earth. During the last nine days, the people of Sardis have watched Jesus the Messiah tread the Winepress and have observed the joy of the Remnant of Israel and the host of Jesus the Messiah's followers whom they had murdered. Today, however, they face the wrath of YHWH for He has returned as promised in Revelation 3:3-4 to deal with those who never repented but continued to follow Satan.

The judgment of the Sardis type souls include the false prophet and Satan. This is so special that YHWH made Yom Kippur one of the unique appointed times that the people of Israel were required to observe. Yom Kippur is a day where self is to rest and focus on his personal relationship with YHWH because this is the day that your sin is fully reconciled to YHWH. The important events of Yom Kippur have been symbolically performed in the past during the Age of the Torah, first in the Tabernacle and then in the first and second temples in Jerusalem. It will also be observed in the third temple until the Abomination of Desolation. Recall how the daily sacrifices are a picture of an individual's personal relationship with YHWH. Yom Kippur pictures a very special time for it was the only time the High Priest, YHWH's BODY, was allowed to pass through the Veil of Sin and enter the Holy of Holies (the presence of YHWH's SOUL). The purpose of this sacrifice was to remind people that YHWH will (1) banish Satan and sin from the earth and (2) will restore His relationship with mankind.

Yom Kippur activity is described in Leviticus 16, 23:26-32, Numbers 29:7-11 and during 6000 OS Jesus the Messiah will replace the High Priest, His crucifixion will be represented the kid goat, and the Azazel goat (scapegoat) will represent Satan.

225

A summary of the Yom Kippur, the Day of Atonement, events that will be performed by the Jewish High Priest in the Tabernacle prior to Jesus the Messiah's return is contrasted those after His return as follows:

- Yom Kippur starts in the evening (sunset) when the first stars are visible from the Temple in Jerusalem. During this time the High Priest rests.

- At Yom Kippur's first light, the High Priest puts on his golden vestments and conducts the normal daily morning service representing YHWH's personal relationship with mankind. In 6000 OS, this service will be replaced by Jesus the Messiah preparing to judge Sardis.

- After the daily morning service, the High Priest puts on a special white linen garment for just this atonement service. The service consists of sacrificing one young bull (sin offering) and one ram (burnt offering) for atonement for himself and his household. He must also offer two kid goats (sin offering) and one ram (burnt offering) for the people. In 6000 OS, this service will be fulfilled when it completes the judgment of Sardis and only Satan remains alive.

- First, the High Priest casts lots for the two kid goats to be offered for the people. One goat represents YHWH's Body, Jesus the Messiah, and His authority over mankind's sin. The other goat will be the Azazel goat (scapegoat) representing the removal of Satan and sin from the earth.

- The High Priest first deals with YHWH's goat representing Jesus the Messiah by putting the blood from the sin offering, symbolic of Jesus the Messiah's blood shed on the cross, on the Altar of Incense coals, which represents the prayers of saints. Then, the High Priest enters the Holy of Holies and uses the blood of YHWH's goat to demonstrate authority over the Veil of Sin for the seven types of souls. This will be demonstrated by sprinkling the blood on the Ark of the Testimony seven times, once for each nature (soul type). The High Priest then returns to the Altar of Incense and sprinkles the blood of the YHWH's goat on the horns once for each nature of man. This demonstrates that Jesus the Messiah has answered the prayers of the saints by overcoming the Veil of Sin that separated the Holy of Holies from the Holy Place. The first objective will be complete.

- Then, High Priest addresses the second objective by taking the La Azazel goat, Satan, and attributing all the sin and wickedness in the world to him. Then, sin will be completely removed from the world by binding Satan in the bottomless pit. This binding of Satan was symbolized by banishing the La Azazel goat alive from the presence of the temple and the congregation into the wilderness (bottomless pit). This marks the utter failure of Satan.

- Once the La Azazel goat, Satan, has been banished from the presence of the camp (the world), the High Priest will then sacrifices the burnt offering that will illustrate mankind's new communion with YHWH.

- The JUBILEE TRUMPET will be sounded signaling the end of the Tribulation Period and the restoration of mankind to YHWH. Jewish tradition according to the Talmud and Mishnah Taan, iv, 8 toward the end of the day both the rich and poor maidens of Jerusalem will be given white garments to go dancing and singing in the streets of the city. It will be a joyous time!

226

However, on Yom Kippur 6000 OS, these Tabernacle activities will not done, because they will be in the process of being literally fulfilled by Jesus the Messiah, the King of kings and Lord of lords. Yom Kippur 6000 OS, the Day of Atonement, when Jesus the Messiah completes the judgment of sin and resolves YHWH's WRATH, toward those who opposed Him. The Winepress will have been tread and the Tribulation Period finished, and all people have received punishment for their sin in proportion to the magnitude of their $Will_{YHWH}(t)$.

The picture in the Scriptures depicting self's relationship with Jesus the Messiah in terms of marital status provides an interesting perspective on the current state of what will be happening on this Yom Kippur 6000 OS. The current state of self's relationship with Jesus the Messiah is described in the parable of the ten Virgins in Matthew 25:1-13. Here are some comments about the parable to keep in mind when reading its text. The parable includes ten virgins. The number ten is significant because it represents the ten kingdoms, or all the nations and people of the world. Thus, the ten virgins are all the people of the earth with each individual having the same opportunity to become a bride of Jesus the Messiah. $10 = 2*5$ where the number 2 implies division and the number 5 is associated with YHWH's grace. Notice, the five foolish virgins represent individuals who care only about themselves or those who followed Satan and lack oil (truth). Whereas, the five wise virgins have oil (truth) for they are followers of Jesus the Messiah. The bridegroom's call is the Tribulation Period where the brides are selected by their faithfulness to Jesus the Messiah.

> Matthew 25:1-13
> 1 Then shall the kingdom of heaven be likened unto <u>ten virgins</u> [**all people**], which took their lamps [**souls**], and went forth to meet the <u>bridegroom</u> [**Jesus the Messiah**].
> 2 And five of them were wise, and five were foolish.
> 3 They that were foolish took their lamps, and took no oil (truth) with them:
> 4 But the wise took <u>oil</u> [**truth**] in their vessels with their lamps.
> 5 While the <u>bridegroom</u> [**Jesus the Messiah**] tarried, they all slumbered and slept.
> 6 And at midnight there was a cry made, Behold, the <u>bridegroom</u> [**Jesus the Messiah**] cometh; go ye out to meet him.
> 7 Then all those virgins arose, and trimmed their lamps.
> 8 And the foolish said unto the wise, Give us of your oil; for our lamps are gone out.
> 9 But the wise answered, saying, Not so; lest there be not enough for us and you: but go ye rather to them that sell, and buy for yourselves.
> 10 And while they went to buy, the <u>bridegroom</u> [**Jesus the Messiah**] came; and they that were ready went in with him to the marriage: and the door was shut.
> 11 Afterward came also the other virgins, saying, Lord, Lord, open to us.
> 12 But he answered and said, Verily I say unto you, I know you not.

*13 Watch therefore, for ye know neither the day nor the hour wherein the Son of man [**Jesus the Messiah**] cometh.*

In Matthew 25:13 the *Son of Man's* coming occurs when the *Son of Man*, YHWH, determines when a person shall die. No man knows the moment he will die! Thus, one must always be ready—not like the five foolish virgins who missed their opportunity and will be separated from Jesus the Messiah forever. Whereas, the five wise virgins are brides to be on earth with Jesus the Messiah with resurrected bodies. With the binding of Satan, the soul harvest will be complete, and the five virgins, which include the Remnant of Israel, who will be waiting the call from their bridegroom. The sound of the great Jubilee Trumpet in the year 6000 OS is the bridegroom's call that will start the time of the jubilee as Jesus the Messiah begins to prepare for His marriage, the marriage supper of the Lamb.

THE JUBILEE of 6000 OS

As the sunset approaches on Yom Kippur 6000 OS, all the followers of YHWH, Jesus the Messiah, have had their souls afflicted and humbled as they have watched the judgment of Sardis and the binding of Satan. After the binding of Satan, the Winepress is complete! Let the Great Jubilee Trumpet sound for it is time for the bride, clothed in white linen, to rejoice and dance for joy. The bride includes all the followers of YHWH with glorified bodies like Jesus the Messiah's, which functions both in the pre-creation universe and also in the material component of the universe. Also included is the Remnant of Israel led by YHWH's 144,000 special servants, who have survived the entire Tribulation Period in their mortal-material bodies. The bride patiently awaits the sound of the Great Jubilee Trumpet.

The tenth of Tishri, Yom Kippur, after Satan is bound, the Great Jubilee Trumpet of 6000 OS sounds marking the start of the celebration of the restoration of the relationship between YHWH and mankind. Also, it is the time when YHWH's body, Jesus the Messiah, starts to prepare for the wedding feast. The events that remain during the month of Tishri are:

1. Building the Kingdom Temple in three days.

2. Cleansing the altar in the Kingdom Temple in two days.

3. Feast of Tabernacles, Marriage feast of the Lamb, is seven days.

4. Last great day, first day of the Kingdom is one day.

When the Great Jubilee Trumpet sounds on Yom Kippur 6000 OS among YHWH's followers dressed in the snow-white linen of righteousness, there is extraordinary joy, dancing, and excitement. Now they must patiently wait while Jesus the Messiah completes the next task, which is building the Kingdom Temple.

Jesus the Messiah literally tears down the Tribulation Temple and rebuilds a new temple that will be used during the Age of the Kingdom. He accomplishes this feat during the next three days that is, the eleventh, twelfth and thirteenth of Tishri. This is the actual physical demonstration of a capability that Jesus the Messiah alluded to in John 3:18-22, where during His first coming His body was raised from the dead in three days. However, during His second coming, 6000 OS, He will literally rebuild the Kingdom Temple in three days for the Remnant of Israel.

John 2:18-22

18 *Then answered the Jews and said unto him, What sign shewest thou unto us, seeing that thou doest these things?*

19 *Jesus answered and said unto them,* **Destroy this temple, and in three days I will raise it up.**

20 *Then said the Jews, Forty and six years was this temple in building, and wilt thou rear it up in three days?*

21 *But he spake of the temple of his body.* **[Reference to crucifixion and resurrection in 4000 OS]**

22 *When therefore he was risen from the dead, his disciples remembered that he had said this unto them; and they believed the scripture, and the word which Jesus had said.*

The new *Kingdom temple* is magnificent, and its structure is described in Ezekiel 40:1 to 43:17. It is insightful to compare the structural differences between the state of the Tabernacle and Temples during the different phases of Israel's history. The differences are summarized in Table XI-7.

In the Kingdom Temple YHWH's BODY, Jesus the Messiah is referred to as the Prince. The Prince interfaces directly with the people, and He will receive a tribute offering from each member of the Remnant of Israel, and He will sacrifice them on the altar Himself. The temple cleansing commences on the thirteenth day of Tishri when the altar of burnt offerings is completed. The cleansing will require two days and is described in Ezekiel 43:18-27.

Ezekiel 43:18-27

18 *And he said unto me, Son of man, thus saith the Lord GOD; These are the ordinances of the altar in the day* **[Day thirteen of Tishri.]** *when they shall make it, to offer burnt offerings thereon, and to sprinkle blood thereon.*

19 *And thou shalt give to the priests the Levites that be of the seed of Zadok, which approach unto me, to minister unto me, saith the Lord GOD, a young bullock for a sin offering.*

20 *And thou shalt take of the blood thereof, and put it on the four horns of it, and on the four corners of the settle, and upon the border round about: thus shalt thou cleanse and purge it.*

21 *Thou shalt take the bullock also of the sin offering, and he shall burn it in the appointed place of the house, without the sanctuary.*

22 *And on the second day* **[Day fourteen of Tishri.]** *thou shalt offer a kid of the goats without blemish for a sin offering; and they shall cleanse the altar, as they did cleanse it with the bullock.*

229

23 *When thou hast made an end of cleansing it, thou shalt offer a young bullock without blemish, and a ram out of the flock without blemish.*

24 *And thou shalt offer them before the Lord, and the priests shall cast salt upon them, and they shall offer them up for a burnt offering unto the Lord.*

25 *Seven days* **[Days fifteen through twenty one of Tishri.]** *shalt thou prepare every day a goat for a sin offering: they shall also prepare a young bullock, and a ram out of the flock, without blemish.*

26 *Seven days shall they purge the altar and purify it; and they shall consecrate themselves.*

27 *And when these days are expired, it shall be, that upon the eighth day* **[Day twenty two of Tishri.]**, *and so forward, the priests shall make your burnt offerings upon the altar, and your peace offerings; and I will accept you, saith the Lord GOD.*

Table XI-7 Structural Comparison of Tabernacle and Temples

Item	Start of the Exodus	Tabernacle, 1st, 2nd, and 3rd Temple (After Mount Sinia Fall)	Kingdom Temple (Ezekiel 40:1-43:17)
Holy of Holies			
Physical Sze	None	20 by 20 cubits	20 by 20 cubits
Gold Ark	None	Only in the Tabernacle and 1st Temple (Symbolic of YHWH's presence)	**None:** YHWH's BODY , the Prince is present.
Veil of Sin	None	Sin seperates man from YHWH.	**None:** Removed by the cross and the Tribulation Period
Holy Place			
Physical Size	None	20 by 40 cubits	20 by 40 cubits
High Priest	None	Symbolic of Jesus the Messiah.	**None:** Replace by YHWH's BODY, the Prince.
Gold Altar of Incense	None	Symbolic of the prayers of the saints.	**None:** Removed by the Tribulation Period and the Prince.
Gold Menorah	None	Symbolic of mankind's seven soul types.	**None:** Removed by the Tribulation Period.
Gold Table of Showbread	None	Symbolic of YHWH's WILL, the Holy Spirit.	**None:** Replaced by YHWH's WILL via the Prince tdirectly to the remnant of Israel.
Outer Court			
Bronze Laver	None	Symbolic of YHWH's forgiveness.	**None:** Removed by YHWH forgiviing mankind.
Altar	None	Bronze Altar with no steps is symbolic of YHWH's judgement.	Stone Altar with no steps is symbolic of YHWH's judgement.

On the first day of cleansing the Temple, a bullock is offered demonstrating YHWH's ultimate authority over sin. Then, on the second day (fourteenth day of Tishri) one bullock and one kid goat are offered demonstrating that the responsibility is now with Jesus the Messiah (kid goat). Once the altar is cleansed, that is, the responsibilities are defined, then the burnt offering is made defining who the participants are. The burnt offerings are a bullock (YHWH's SOUL) and a ram (YHWH's BODY, Jesus the Messiah) that are salted, affirming that it is a covenant of YHWH's.

Once cleansed, the seven days of purification and consecration coincide with the Feast of Tabernacles during 6000 OS. This forms a unique conjunction where the special purification and consecration burnt offering (one bullock and one ram that is salted) declares YHWH's covenant with mankind through Jesus the Messiah. The word *tabernacle* means to dwell with, and the Feast of Tabernacles, the Feast, pictures the celebration that is held by Jesus the Messiah with His followers to celebrate their return to the material component of the universe, the removal of man's sin from the earth, and the reconciliation of YHWH's WRATH with all seven soul types. The Feast will be the most joyous celebration in the history of mankind! It is the marriage supper of the Lamb when Jesus the Messiah invites all the overcomers from the seven soul types to tabernacle with Him forever. The Feast in 6000 OS is the most joyous occasion for mankind since creation because; (1) the Tribulation Period is over, (2) Satan is bound, (3) the Kingdom Temple is built and cleansed in Jerusalem, (4) Jesus the Messiah is dwelling on earth as the Prince, (5) the Remnant of Israel with mortal-material bodies will repopulate the earth, and (6) those who died for Jesus the Messiah who have resurrected eternal bodies.

The Feast starts on the fifteenth day of Tishri and continues for seven days declaring the state of reconciliation between YHWH and mankind. The picture represented by the Feast changes for the year 6000 OS and thereafter. The change reflects a new state in the relationship between YHWH and mankind as a result of the resolution of YHWH's WRATH during the Tribulation Period.

Prior to 6000 OS the specific offerings associated with the Feast includes: Burnt offerings of bullocks, rams, and lambs with a kid goat for a sin offering.

- On the first day of the Feast, thirteen bullocks are sacrificed and the number of bullocks is reduced by one each day until on the seventh day only seven bullocks are sacrificed. The bullocks indicate the status of the relationship between YHWH and mankind. This feast is a commemoration of the removal of evil from man's soul (number of man is six) from the seven types of men's souls starting with Philadelphia on the first day and ending with YHWH's expected nature of Sardis on the seventh day.

- On each day of the Feast, two rams are sacrificed representing that Jesus the Messiah is responsible to resolve the separation between YHWH and mankind.

- On each day of the Feast, $2 * 7 = 14$ lambs are sacrificed representing mankind's spiritual separation from YHWH.

231

- On each day of the Feast, the sin offering is a kid goat, which defines Jesus the Messiah as the Judge of mankind's sin.

5999 OS is the last time the Feast is performed in accordance with the above procedure. During 6000 OS the conduct of the Feast is extraordinary because it is part of the purification of the new Kingdom Temple; it is the marriage supper of the Lamb, and it is the last event in the Age of the Messiah. The Feast is performed only once using the following procedure, which is described in Ezekiel 43:24-27.

- On each day of the Feast, one bullock is sacrificed showing unity between YHWH and mankind.
- On each day of the Feast, one ram is sacrificed showing that Jesus the Messiah has resolved the separation between YHWH and mankind.
- On each day of the Feast, no lambs are sacrificed YHWH and mankind is now reconciled.
- On each day of the Feast, the sin offering is unchanged (one kid goat) retaining Jesus the Messiah as the judge of mankind's sin.

The next time the Feast is celebrated in 6001 OS, the sacrifices are adjusted again to reflect the structure that will be present during the Kingdom Age. The nature of the Feast in the Kingdom Age will be addressed in the next chapter.

The Feast is a feast of seven days. The eighth day, twenty second of Tishri, is a unique feast in itself; but when associated with the Feast, it is sometimes called the Last Great Day. However, it could be called the First Great Day of the Age of the Kingdom or the Millennium. Numbers 29:35-38 describes the special characteristics of the eighth day of the Feast.

Numbers 29:35-39
*35 On the **eighth day** [22 Tishri] ye shall have a solemn assembly: ye shall do no servile work therein:*
36 But ye shall offer a burnt offering, a sacrifice made by fire, of a sweet savour unto the Lord: one bullock, one ram, seven lambs of the first year without blemish:
37 Their meat offering and their drink offerings for the bullock, for the ram, and for the lambs, shall be according to their number, after the manner:
38 And one goat for a sin offering; beside the continual burnt offering, and his meat offering, and his drink offering.

The eight day of the Feast has significance in itself because eight is the number of new beginnings. This day is a Sabbath, no work, on the first day of the Age of the Kingdom. The eight-day is a day to focus on YHWH and what lies ahead in the next Millennium. The burnt offerings show that the state of man's relationship with YHWH is complete unity as this New Age begins. What will the Age of the Kingdom, the Millennium, bring?

232

XII   YHWH the Millennium, 7000 OS

The end of the Tribulation Period has brought the total destruction of Satan's corrupt Occult One-World Government. Then, the Age of Kingdom, the Millennium, begins with the following people present on earth:

- YHWH's resurrected BODY, Jesus the Messiah, the Prince.
- All the followers of YHWH with resurrected immortal bodies, and they will be the Prince's priests and helpers during the Millennium.
- The Remnant of Israel who have lived through the Tribulation Period and still have mortal bodies.

The souls of the Remnant of Israel now form a truly Holy Nation with all the people's *Will(t)* compliant with Figure XII-1. This is the first time in history since the Original Sin, 0000 OS, that all people in the world are submissive to YHWH by their own freewill. That is, all the people's $Will_{YHWH}(t) > 0.5 > Will_{self}(t)$ as shown in Figure XII -1.

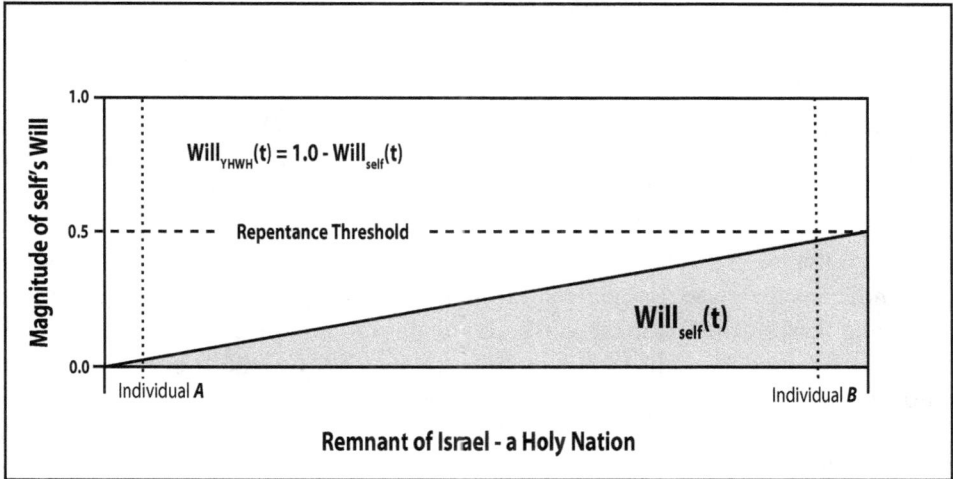

Figure XII-1 The distribution of soul types at the start of the Millennium

Also, every individual soul with a mortal body is a descendent from one of the original twelve tribes of Israel. The Remnant of Israel now speak a single language, Hebrew. Note, in Figure XII -1 individual *A* will have greater status than individual *B* because his $Will_{YHWH}(t)$ is greater. This state now reflects what society would have been like if the people had accepted YHWH at Mount Sinai. The Remnant of Israel is now a completely Holy Nation.

The Millennium starts with a new Temple in Jerusalem, which YHWH tore down and rebuilt in three days. Now all the people are directly responsible to YHWH for instruction and direction, through YHWH's BODY, Jesus the Messiah. YHWH's glorified Body will interface directly with the people, at a level like Moses, from the new Temple in Jerusalem.

Those accompanying Jesus the Messiah are all YHWH's followers as described in Revelation 20:4-6.

> *Revelation 20:4-6*
> 4 *And I saw thrones, and they sat upon them, and judgment was given unto them: and I saw the souls of them that **were beheaded** for the witness of Jesus, and for the word of God, and which had not worshipped the beast, neither his image, neither had received his mark upon their foreheads, or in their hands; and they lived and reigned with Christ a thousand years* **[Millennium]**.
> 5 *But the rest of the dead lived not again until the thousand years were finished. This is the first resurrection.*
> 6 *Blessed and holy is he that hath part in the first resurrection: on such the second death hath no power, but they shall be priests of God and of Christ, and shall reign with him a thousand years* **[Millennium]**.

These souls who are followers of Jesus the Messiah all have experienced the first-death, the breaking of the mortal body bond, and now have a new bond to a glorified body like Jesus the Messiah's. Jesus previously demonstrated what a glorified body can do. He went through walls and functioned in both the pre-creation universe and the constrained material universe we live in today. Revelation 20:6 indicates that their assignment during the Millennium will be to help instruct, guide and support the Remnant of Israel in restoration of the earth in the aftermath of the Tribulation Period. At this point in time, 6000 OS the Remnant of Israel who were 1.52224% of the world's population of 7,682,789,903 people at the start of the Tribulation Period or 116,950,788 souls with mortal bodies who are now preparing to repopulate the earth.

Some insight into the tasks confronting the Remnant of Israel may be obtained by examining the differences between Noah's flood and the Tribulation Period. A comparison of the aftermath of Noah's Flood and the Tribulation Period is summarized in Table XII-1.

The societal knowledge base of the 116,950,788 souls is very large compared to the eight souls after Noah's flood. Thus, the restoration of most of the technology and the earth's infrastructure can be accomplished much faster than after Noah's flood—particularly with the aid of Jesus the Messiah and His followers.

Table XII-1 Comparison post Noah's Flood versus post Tribulation Period

Post Noah's Flood	Post Tribulation
Destroyed the corrupt society including the physical presence of Satan.	Destroyed the corrupt society and bound all Satan's influence for the next 1000 years.
Garden of Eden and Atlantis destroyed.	Babylon destroyed.
Saved Noah and his family, eight souls.	Saved the remnant of the twelve tribes of Israel.
Reset the societies knowledge base to eight souls.	Reset the societies knowledge base to the Remnant of Israel. That is 1.52224% of the world population, 7,682,789,903 people, at the start of the Tribulation Period or 116,950,788 souls.
Man's intelligence remained unchanged.	Man's intelligence remained unchanged.
One language until the tower of Babel. Then divided into language groups and dispersed to the various new continents.	One language with no dispersion.
Three primary soul types present Shem, Japheth and Ham.	One primary soul type present, followers of YHWH.
Physical characteristics of the earth dramatically changed.	Physical structure of the earth is essentially unchanged.
Society develops with each individual doing according to his own WILL.	Society develops under YHWH's direct supervision and instruction from the Temple in Jerusalem and aided by His followers with their new resurrected, glorified, bodies.

Also, there is an issue of continuing education for the Remnant of Israel and their descendants as they repopulate the earth. The new Kingdom Temple is in place in Jerusalem, but there are some major differences between it and previous temples.

The Holy of Holies is the same size 20 by 20 cubits but the Ark of the Testimony and the Veil of Sin are not present because now the Prince, Jesus the Messiah, is physically present and the people in nation of Israel are all followers of Jesus the Messiah.

The Holy Place is the same size 20 by 40 cubits, but the room is now open to the Holy of Holies and empty. The Gold Altar of Incense, Gold Menorah, Gold Table of Showbread, and the High Priest are all gone. An individual's personal relationship with YHWH is now direct with His BODY, the Prince, Jesus the Messiah.

In the Outer Court the Bronze Laver is gone because all are now forgiven as a result of the Tribulation Period. The Bronze Altar has been replaced with a Stone Altar with steps showing that YHWH is directly approachable.

The offerings also are changed for the Age of the Kingdom. The mandatory Drink, Wave, and Heave Offerings were fulfilled by Jesus the Messiah and are no longer required. The mandatory Meat Offering, which declares the associated offering is righteous and the Sin Offering, which is a reminder that sin will be judged both remain required. A new offering has been added. The Tribute Offering to the Prince requires that all the members of the Remnant of Israel and their descendants give a portion of their very best directly to the Prince and the Prince will offer the burnt and peace offerings, Ezekiel 45:13-17.

The voluntary trespass Offering is done by the Prince to remind the people of previous sin and required repentance. The voluntary Peace, Freewill, Vow, and Thanksgiving Offerings provided by an individual as a statement of his commitment to YHWH or a promise made in YHWH's name.

During the Age of the Kingdom, YHWH's appointed times are:

- Daily offering is morning only and is a remembrance of the light of YHWH's truth and His return as Jesus the Messiah, the Prince.
- Weekly Sabbath is a day of no work, and the people worship at the east gate of the Temple.
- Monthly Sabbath, New Moon, is a day of no work, and the people worship at the east gate of the Temple.
- Sabbath year is not required because the land is no longer cursed.
- Jubilee period is not required because YHWH has restored His personal relationship with mankind.

Feasts celebrated during the Age of the Kingdom also show harmony between YHWH and mankind.

- Passover and Feast of Unleavened Bread is required and is a feast of seven days celebrating YHWH's restoration of His relationship with mankind.
- Feast of First Fruits is fulfilled and no longer required.
- Feast of Weeks, Pentacost, is fulfilled and no longer required.
- Yom Teruah and Yom Kippur are fulfilled and are no longer required.
- Feast of Tabernacles is required to celebrate that YHWH is physically present with mankind.
- Last Great Day is fulfilled and no longer required.

The Age of the Kingdom, the Millennium, begins with harmony and all people's $Will_{YHWH}(t) > Will_{self}(t)$, but as time passes how does society develop?

The Millennial Society

The Millennium is the period from 6000 OS to 7000 OS when the Remnant of Israel, with mortal bodies begin to repopulate the world. YHWH, the Prince, is perfectly consistent and His instruction from the Temple in Jerusalem would still be consistent with His sermon on the Mount and the Ten Commandments. The Prince is aided by all His followers from all the previous ages, which have resurrected bodies. The initial efforts will include restoring the earth from the destruction that occurred during the Tribulation Period. The goal of this age is to repopulate the earth with new souls who are all followers of YHWH.

During this age the Prince uses the Tribute Offering that requires that all mortal people give a portion of their very best directly to Him. Thus, YHWH continuously monitors a person's magnitude of $Will_{YHWH}(t) > Will_{self}(t)$.

YHWH will still harvest a person's soul when He determines it is the correct time, which no man knows the day or hour. The harvest process occurs anytime a person experiences the first-death, and this is a good experience for followers of YHWH. The third harvest will occur at the end of the Millennium as described in Revelation 20:7-10.

Revelation 20:7-10
7 And when the **thousand years are expired**, Satan shall be loosed out of his prison,
8 And shall go out to deceive the nations which are in the four quarters of the earth, Gog and Magog, to gather them together to battle: the number of whom is as the sand of the sea.
9 And they went up on the breadth of the earth, and compassed the camp of the saints about, and the beloved city: and fire came down from God out of heaven, and devoured them.
10 And the devil that deceived them was cast into the lake of fire and brimstone, where the beast and the false prophet are, and shall be tormented day and night for ever and ever.

In Revelation 20:7-10 Satan is released for the third and final time to spread his *seed*, knowledge of rebellion against YHWH. Many people who started under YHWH's perfect instruction in 6000 OS are found later in 7000 OS surrounding Jerusalem in an attempt to destroy YHWH and His followers per Revelation 20:9. YHWH invokes the first-death upon these people using fire. This was the third soul harvest (the number *three* means complete), and YHWH now performs the final judgment.

The Great White Throne Judgment - Second-death

At this time, everyone has experienced the first-death, but the Great White Throne Judgment will determine who will experience the second-death. The Great White Throne is the final judgment that determines if an individual is given a new glorified body that is eternal or is cast into the Lake of Fire. The Great White Throne Judgment centers about the first-resurrection and the second-resurrection and the first-death and second-death.

The Great White Throne judgment will have no effect upon those individuals who were judged in the first-resurrection as stated in Revelation 20:4-6.

Revelation 20:4-6
4   *And I saw thrones, and they sat upon them, and judgment was given unto them: and I saw the souls of them that were beheaded for the witness of Jesus, and for the word of God, and which had not worshipped the beast, neither his image, neither had received his mark upon their foreheads, or in their hands; and they lived and reigned with Christ a thousand years.*
5   *But the rest of the dead lived not again until the thousand years were finished. This is the first resurrection.*
6   *Blessed and holy is **he that hath part in the first resurrection: on such the second death hath no power, but they shall be priests of God and of Christ, and shall reign with him a thousand years.***

The first-resurrection covers the period from 0000 OS through 6000 OS and includes all Philadelphian and Smyrnian-type souls and any who repented and give up their life for Jesus the Messiah from the other five types of souls. A resurrected person's body is illustrated in Figure XII-2. The new resurrected body has access to the Tree of Life making the bond with the spirit body immortal.

Those people in the first-resurrection had already received their new resurrected, glorified bodies when they returned with Jesus the Messiah at the end of the Tribulation Period to reign with Him during the Age of the Kingdom. The people from the first-resurrection, also referred to as *the dead in Christ*, are in the image of YHWH and structured as shown in Figure XII-2.

Their resurrected bodies are capable of functioning in both the pre-creation and added material component of the universe. Resurrection is the transition from the state of being dead, the first-death, where the individual's mortal-physical body is destroyed and his existence is solely spiritual in the pre-creation universe to a new resurrected body like Jesus the Messiah. Jesus the Messiah demonstrated the resurrected body during the time between His resurrection and ascension. The resurrected body must be extraordinary!

At the end of the Age of the Kingdom (Millennium), the Remnant of Israel and their descendants who have continued to follow YHWH possess soul types like Philadelphians or Smyrnians. These people have their names written in the Lamb's Book of Life and will partake in the second-resurrection, which is part of the final judgment of mankind.

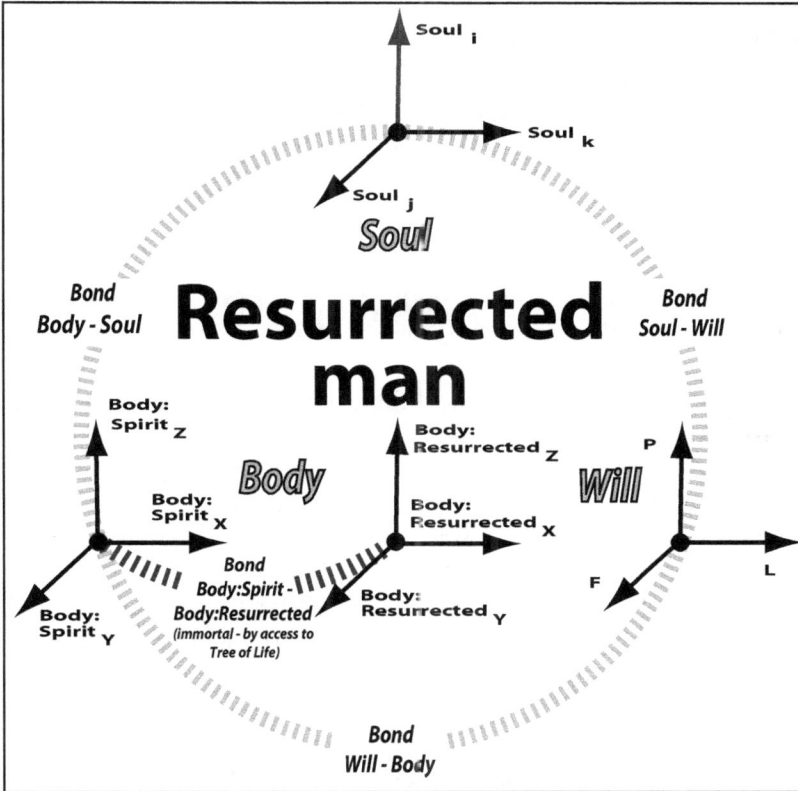

Figure XII-2 Resurrected Man

YHWH's final judgment of mankind is described in Revelation 20:11-15.

Revelation 20:11-15

11 *And I saw a **great white throne**, and him that sat on it, from whose face the earth and the heaven fled away; and there was found no place for them.*

12 *And I saw the dead, small and great, stand before God; and the books were opened: and another book was opened, which is the book of life: and the dead were judged out of those things which were written in the books, according to their works.*

13 ***And the sea gave up the dead which were in it; and death and hell delivered up the dead which were in them: and they were judged every man according to their works.***

14 ***And death and hell were cast into the lake of fire. This is the second death.***

15 *And whosoever was not found written in the book of life was cast into the lake of fire.*

Revelation 20:12 identifies the Lamb's Book of Life, which is a record of all an individual's works and actions throughout his entire life. An individual's works are a direct result of, or measure of, self's $Will(t) = L(t) * F(t) * P(t)$. Thus, the great final judgment is based on the magnitude of self's $Will_{YHWH}(t)$ with respect to self's $Will_{self}(t)$ and $Will_{Satan}(t)$.

Revelation 20:13 also identifies who will be judged. Noticeably absent are *the dead in Christ*, which are those from the first-resurrection and second-resurrection. Those to be judged include *the dead from the sea*, which correspond to those with a nature of Ephesus and part of Laodicea that did not lay down their lives for YHWH. *The dead* are Laodiceans that supported Satan and the Thyatirans while *the dead in hell* are Pergamians and Sardians.

Revelation 20:14-15 holds an ominous outlook for those souls of Laodicea, Pergamos, Thyatira and Sardis whose names are not written in the Lamb's Book of Life, for their destiny is the lake of fire. What is this lake of fire?

First, it might be useful to examine what the lake of fire and brimstone is not! It is not hell, for hell is cast into the lake of fire. It is not the state of death for it is also cast into the lake of fire. It is not the first-death. The first-death is the separation of self's Soul and spirit Body from self's mortal physical Body with the destruction of self's mortal Body.

The second-death is a mystery that YHWH has yet to reveal. However, if it has characteristics similar to the first-death, then the lake of fire may bring the destruction of the bonds that connect self's Will with self's Soul and Body or the power associated with self's Will is set to zero. These conditions are depicted in Figure XII-3.

If YHWH were to break the bond between the self's Will and Body, the individual would experience the second-death where they would be aware of what was happening but be unable to respond. This same effect is also possible if YHWH set the power $P(t) = 0$ for self's $Will(t) = L(t) * F(t) * P(t)$. If these souls are in torment, what could be worse than your body taking in information and not being able to do anything in response because self's $Will(t) = 0$ for whatever reason.

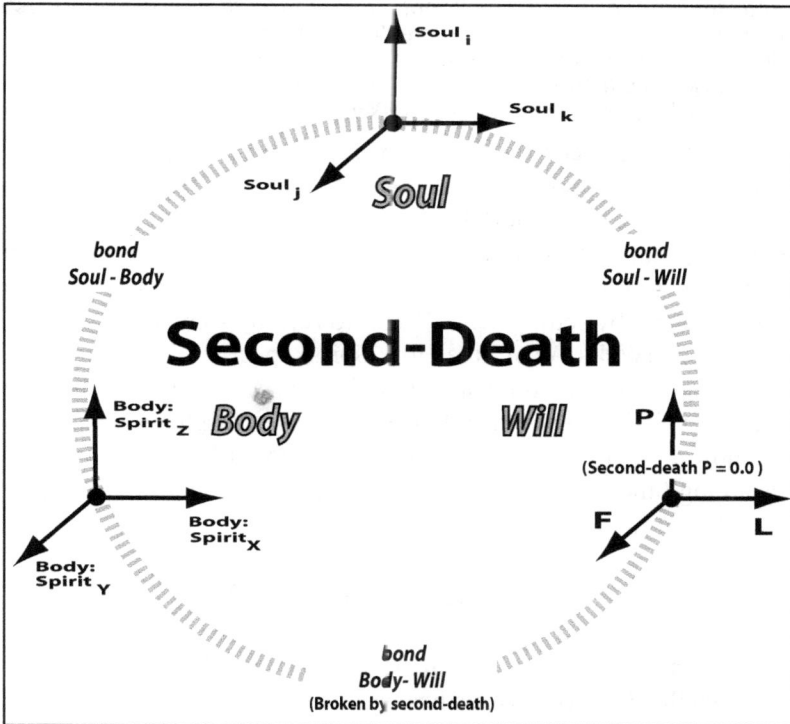

Figure XII-3 The Second-Death

YHWH warns mankind in Matthew 10:28 and Luke 12:4-5 how serious the second-death really is:

Matthew 10:28
28 And fear not them which *kill the body* [**first-death**], *but are not able to kill the soul: but rather* *fear him* [**YHWH**] *which is able to* *destroy both soul and body in hell* [**second-death and the lake of fire**].

Luke 12:4-6
4 And I say unto you my friends, Be not afraid of them that kill the body [**first-death**], and after that have no more that they can do.
5 But I will forewarn you whom ye shall fear: *Fear him* [**YHWH**], which after he hath killed hath power to *cast into hell* [**second-death and the lake of fire**]; yea, I say unto you, *Fear him* [**YHWH**].

It is clear that the second-death is a very serious condition. Matthew 10:28 and Luke 12:2-6 both support the idea that self's WILL will be disconnected from his body because to kill the mortal body (the first-death), is the breaking of the spirit body to mortal body bond; then, to kill implies the breaking or disabling a function. Thus, to kill the soul is probably disabling of the soul's capability to implement its desires by setting self's WILL to zero by some means.

Thus, when YHWH's WILL, the Holy Spirit, specifically declares what shall be done with respect to something and an individual does not do it, he is rejecting YHWH's perfect WILL. One must beware because blasphemy against the Holy Spirit is an unforgivable sin and its consequence could lead to the second-death. Eternity is a long time and self must decide between torment in the lake of fire or living with YHWH in the new heaven and earth.

New Heaven and Earth

After the great white throne judgment of 7000 OS is complete, the destiny of every individual that has ever existed has been determined and the Kingdom Age is at an end. Then comes a time referred to in Hebrew as Olam Haba, the new heaven and earth, or eternity, a time without the curse of sin. Revelation 21:10 - 22:21 introduce this new universe.

Revelation 21:10- 22:21
10 And he carried me away in the spirit to a great and high mountain, and shewed me that great city, the holy Jerusalem, descending out of heaven from God,
11 Having the glory of God: and her light was like unto a stone most precious, even like a jasper stone, clear as crystal;
12 And had a wall great and high, and had twelve gates, and at the gates twelve angels, and names written thereon, which are the names of the twelve tribes of the children of Israel:

13 On the east three gates; on the north three gates; on the south three gates; and on the west three gates.

14 And the wall of the city had twelve foundations, and in them the names of the twelve apostles of the Lamb.

15 And he that talked with me had a golden reed to measure the city, and the gates thereof, and the wall thereof.

16 And the city lieth foursquare, and the length is as large as the breadth: and he measured the city with the reed, twelve thousand furlongs. The length and the breadth and the height of it are equal.

17 And he measured the wall thereof, an hundred and forty and four cubits, according to the measure of a man, that is, of the angel.

18 And the building of the wall of it was of jasper: and the city was pure gold, like unto clear glass.

19 And the foundations of the wall of the city were garnished with all manner of precious stones. The first foundation was jasper; the second, sapphire; the third, a chalcedony; the fourth, an emerald;

20 The fifth, sardonyx; the sixth, sardius; the seventh, chrysolite; the eighth, beryl; the ninth, a topaz; the tenth, a chrysoprasus; the eleventh, a jacinth; the twelfth, an amethyst.

21 And the twelve gates were twelve pearls; every several gate was of one pearl: and the street of the city was pure gold, as it were transparent glass.

22 **And I saw no temple therein: for the Lord God Almighty and the Lamb are the temple of it.**

23 **And the city had no need of the sun, neither of the moon, to shine in it: for the glory of God** [YHWH's SOUL] **did lighten it, and the Lamb** **[YHWH's Body]** *is the light* [TRUTH] *thereof.*

24 And the nations of them which are saved shall walk in the light of it: and the kings of the earth do bring their glory and honour into it.

25 And the gates of it shall not be shut at all by day: for there shall be no night there.

26 And they shall bring the glory and honour of the nations into it.

27 And there shall in no wise enter into it any thing that defileth, neither whatsoever worketh abomination, or maketh a lie: but they which are written in the Lamb's book of life.

Revelation 22

1 **And he shewed me a pure river of water of life, clear as crystal, proceeding out of the throne of God and of the Lamb.**

2 **In the midst of the street of it, and on either side of the river, was there the tree of life, which bare twelve manner of fruits, and yielded her fruit every month: and the leaves of the tree were for the healing of the nations.**

3 And there shall be no more curse: but the throne of God and of the Lamb shall be in it; and his servants shall serve him:

4 And they shall see his face; and his name shall be in their foreheads.

5 **And there shall be no night there; and they need no candle, neither light of the sun; for the Lord God** [YHWH's SOUL] **giveth them light: and they shall reign for ever and ever.**

6 And he said unto me, These sayings are faithful and true: and the Lord God of the holy prophets sent his angel to shew unto his servants the things which must shortly be done.

7   *Behold, I come quickly: blessed is he that keepeth the sayings of the prophecy of this book.*

8   *And I John saw these things, and heard them. And when I had heard and seen, I fell down to worship before the feet of the angel which shewed me these things.*

9   *Then saith he unto me, See thou do it not: for I am thy fellow servant, and of thy brethren the prophets, and of them which keep the sayings of this book: worship God.*

10 *And he saith unto me, Seal not the sayings of the prophecy of this book: for the time is at hand.*

11 *He that is unjust, let him be unjust still: and he which is filthy, let him be filthy still: and he that is righteous, let him be righteous still: and he that is holy, let him be holy still.*

12 *And, behold, I come quickly; and my reward is with me, to give every man according as his work shall be.*

13 *I am Alpha and Omega, the beginning and the end, the first and the last.*

14 *Blessed are they that do his commandments, that they may have right to the tree of life, and may enter in through the gates into the city.*

15 *For without are dogs, and sorcerers, and whoremongers, and murderers, and idolaters, and whosoever loveth and maketh a lie.*

16 *I Jesus have sent mine angel to testify unto you these things in the churches. I am the root and the offspring of David, and the bright and morning star.*

17 *And the Spirit and the bride say, Come. And let him that heareth say, Come. And let him that is athirst come. And whosoever will, let him take the water of life freely.*

18 *For I testify unto every man that heareth the words of the prophecy of this book, If any man shall add unto these things, God shall add unto him the plagues that are written in this book:*

19 *And if any man shall take away from the words of the book of this prophecy, God shall take away his part out of the book of life, and out of the holy city, and from the things which are written in this book.*

20 *He which testifieth these things saith, Surely I come quickly. Amen. Even so, come, Lord Jesus.*

21 *The grace of our Lord Jesus Christ be with you all. Amen.*

The details of the new heaven and new earth are another mystery that YHWH has not yet fully revealed. What can be discerned from the scriptures about this incredible coming time?

YHWH remains unchanged. YHWH's SOUL, the Father or Glory, lightens the world. YHWH's BODY, Jesus the Messiah, interfaces with mankind, and YHWH's WILL, the Holy Spirit, is present as He continues to declare what will occur and implements the new heaven and earth.

The time dimension will continue to be present as indicated by the Tree of Life bearing twelve kinds of fruit each month, Revelation 22:1-2. This is like the Garden of Eden except now all the people are knowledgeable about the relationship between good and evil.

From the description of the New Jerusalem, the material and spirit dimensions of height, length, and width are also retained, Revelation 21:16. The sun and moon are present, but their light is not required because the glory of YHWH' SOUL provides the light and the result is absence of day and night as we currently experience them. YHWH's complete dimensional presence is further emphasized by the lack of a temple in New Jerusalem.

In Revelation 21 and 22, we find New Jerusalem has a unique relationship with the number 12. The number 12 is associated with governmental, or organizational perfection. The city rests on 12 foundations, one foundation for each of Jesus the Messiah's 12 apostles. This seems to be a memorial to the 12 apostles that formed the foundation of Jesus the Messiah's church. The walls of the city are $12*12 = 144$ cubits high. The walls form a square with three gates in each wall or 3 (the number of completeness)* 4 (number of created) = 12. This newly created city of Jerusalem is complete and dedicated to the 12 tribes of Israel.

The size of New Jerusalem, 12000 furlongs square and 12000 furlongs high, emphasizes the perfection and completeness of every aspect of this newly created city. 10 is the number associated with a perfect plan or order. $10^3 *12 = 12000$, implies that New Jerusalem is the completion of a perfect plan and is a city that is perfectly structured and organized. The actual shape of the city could be either a cube or a pyramid. The enormity of the New Jerusalem suggests YHWH may create a totally new universe. A furlong is 1/8 of a mile. 1/8 (mile/furlong) * 12000 (furlongs) = 1500 miles. The New Jerusalem is 1500 miles long by 1500 miles wide with a height of 1500 miles. To put this in perspective, if one corner is in Washington DC, the opposite corner would be in Brownsville, Texas, the adjacent corner would be in Reno, Nevada, and its opposite corner would be in the middle of Manitoba, Canada. The area of New Jerusalem is approximately equal to 2/3 the area of the United States of America. Moreover, if the west side of New Jerusalem were placed on Israel's Mediterranean Seacoast, the opposite side would be on the Iranian - Pakistani border; and if the north side were placed on Turkey's Black Seacoast, then the south side would be at the southern end of the Red Sea. Mount Everest is the highest mountain on earth today. It rises 5.5 miles above sea level and there is very little air at that elevation. New Jerusalem rises 1500 miles or 273 times the height of Mount Everest. New Jerusalem is a huge city!

Those from the first and second resurrections will enjoy everlasting life partaking from the Tree of Life in the presence of YHWH. In Hebrew, the time is called "Olam Haba." This completes the timeline for the AM and OS calendars that are contained in the Holy Bible.

XIII The Mystery of Soul Development

Having just reviewed the entire Holy Bible, we understand that YHWH's primary concern is the development of every individual's soul that has ever existed. YHWH is looking for a few dedicated individuals who have accepted His commandments as truth. However, there is a mystery associated with the development of new souls. Why during each age after the Fall as the population increases, do seven types of souls always develop that are distributed across the entire population in accordance with a normal distribution?

YHWH has been perfectly consistent throughout the ages.

Individuals during the Age of Desolation, 0000 OS to 2000 OS had to decide like Abel to bring YHWH an offering of their best; or like Cain to bring his second best and subsequently nothing; or support the overthrow of YHWH by following Satan's seed. The type of an individual soul becomes apparent from their decisions. Pre-flood individuals probably had developed a very sophisticated society, which could possibly include flight. However, under Satan's physical presence the government and society rejected YHWH and became corrupt. YHWH destroyed the entire society except for eight people during Noah's flood. After Noah's flood all people passed their knowledge to the next generation orally and eventually started primitive means to document it.

To help each individual better understand YHWH's requirements in 2000 OS, YHWH started to develop a Holy Nation (Israel), which was a group of people whose ultimate task was to educate all the people that existed relative to YHWH's requirements. To strengthen and to provide them an understanding of evil YHWH placed them in slavery in Egypt. Then, YHWH mercifully brought the people to Mount Sinai where YHWH stated the Ten Commandments, which were a very clear statement of the requirements for any individual to have a good personal relationship with Him and be saved from experiencing the *second-death.*

Subsequently to support all mankind in the process of developing their souls YHWH provided the Holy Bible in three increments.

The first increment was the Torah. The Torah is very special because it did not exist until between 2672 - 2711 AM. Although the Torah covers the period from 0000 AM, creation, through Noah's flood in 1656 AM, and ending with Moses death in 2711 AM. All mankind's knowledge after Noah's flood was only via oral tradition, which is very inaccurate. Only after YHWH gave the Torah to Moses was the detailed history and chronology of mankind restored. Also, the Torah reflects YHWH's responses to the decisions He allows mankind to make. These major decisions were developed in the previous chapters and a summary flowchart is provided in appendix III.

After the Holy Nation of Israel rejected YHWH's instruction at Mount Sinai by requesting YHWH to communicate with them through Moses, YHWH told the people about a coming Messiah who would instruct at mankind's level and demonstrate what must be done to participate in His Kingdom.

The second increment includes the remaining books of the Old Testament, which document YHWH's mercy, grace, and wrath with respect to the rebellious nation of Israel and provides prophecy concerning the coming Messiah and future events. During the Old Testament period, a copy of the Ten Commandments resided in the Ark of the Covenant, which declared what YHWH expected from each individual. To check a soul relative to the first commandment, YHWH required an individual to bring his best for any sacrifice to the Tabernacle. This directly measured the magnitude of the individual's $Will_{YHWH}(t)$.

The third and final increment YHWH incorporated into the Holy Bible is the New Testament. The New Testament primarily deals with the Age of the Messiah, 4000 OS to 6000 OS, which includes the first and second coming of Jesus the Messiah. It also provides some insight into the Age of the Kingdom, 6000 OS to 7000 OS and concludes with the creation of a new heaven and earth. The Age of the Messiah started with Jesus the Messiah's first coming, which is history. Today we live in the time just prior to Jesus the Messiah's second coming in 6000 OS.

Currently what does YHWH expect from each individual? Just as during the previous ages, YHWH is perfectly consistent and still requires an individual to accept or set his soul's $L(t)$, priorities in accordance with the Ten Commandments! An individual's acceptance of the Ten Commandments is the key to his salvation.

Today YHWH measures the magnitude of the individual's $Will_{YHWH}(t)$ today by the individual's compliance with the Ten Commandments. This is reminiscent of the Garden of Eden where the command was given not to eat from the Tree of Knowledge of Good and Evil, but now there are ten commands that need to be obeyed. The Ten Commandments tell each individual how his soul's $L(t)$s are to be developed so that his Wills will be acceptable to YHWH. The Ten Commandments are as valid during the New Testament period today as they were when spoken by YHWH from Mount Sinai. Recall from Chapter X that Jesus the Messiah describes the characteristics of a Philadelphian type soul during His Sermon on the Mount. The Sermon on the Mount is comparable to YHWH's giving the Ten Commandments at Mount Sinai only at mankind's level. The goal of every individual should be to develop a Philadelphian-type soul! Of the seven types of souls, churches, in the world Philadelphia is the only one with an open door to the Kingdom. The seven *churches* are best defined as those individual's with similar soul types who some times associate with each other for common support or to achieve common objectives. By the end of the Age of the Messiah, the nations of the world were controlled by soul types aligned with self and Satan. YHWH then harvests His souls during the Tribulation Period of 6000 OS, initiates the Age of the Kingdom.

During the Age of the Kingdom described in Chapter XII, YHWH provided perfect instruction supported by His followers from the previous Ages and still the seven soul types reappeared. YHWH again harvests the souls for the third and final time.

As we have seen throughout the Holy Bible, it is not the church as an organization or the nations that YHWH judges, but each individual human being as a function of the magnitude of his $Will_{YHWH}(t)$. The Holy Bible contains a fundamental theme that focuses on the mystery of soul development. Each new individual soul possess a tendency toward:

- Helping and serving other people.
- Placing self above all else and using other people for self's benefit.
- Desiring to overthrow those in power.

YHWH with perfect wisdom places these infantile souls in a mortal body, where He allows the soul to mature to the point where the type of soul is identifiable. At some point in time, every individual will experience the first-death, forsaking his mortal body, as YHWH harvests each individual soul. The first-death, the time that no man knows the day or hour, determines self's destiny. YHWH will keep those souls that love him and desire to help others, but He will impose the second-death on those individual's that are self-centered or followers of Satan, who are trying to overthrow Him.

For an individual to avoid the second-death, he must place YHWH first in his life, have faith in YHWH to provide what is best for him, and do his best to help other people also come to know YHWH. YHWH will test the magnitude of the individual's soul $Will_{YHWH}(t)$ by confronting the individual with various trials. These trials will never exceed what one can tolerate and are an aid to the individual's soul development.

YHWH is always making individuals aware of His existence and promises if any individual truly seeks Him. YHWH will accept him with the gift of eternal life. When seeking to become a follower of YHWH never trust a church or pastor or anyone else who says the Holy Bible is too complex for an individual to understand and all members must believe and do what they say. Every individual needs to regularly assess, which of the seven soul types he possess. Then, take personal responsibility to develop the soul type that will result in the destiny desired. Repent if needed, question various theological assumptions including those in this book, pray for YHWH's guidance always, and check everything out in the Holy Bible for yourself. Remember as an individual you are responsible for the content of your Soul, and YHWH will judge that content.

Keep in mind that Jesus the Messiah is divine and has never been a prophet, but He is Emmanuel (YHWH with us). As YHWH's appointed times approach, each individual follower of YHWH needs to establish a mind-set like the prophet Daniel, which is to declare YHWH's truth and have total trust in Him to provide what is best for you and the Kingdom under all circumstances.

Appendix I   - AM Calendar Events

Individual or Event	Description	Years to Event	AM Calendar	Reference
Material universe created	YHWH created the material universe and Adam and his wife Woman, which initiated a new calendar Anno Mundi (in the year of the world).	0	**0000**	Genesis 1-2
Original Sin 0000 OS	Adam and Woman sinned in the Garden of Eden initiating the Original Sin (OS) Calendar.	-	0065 +/- 65 years	Genesis 4
Seth (born)	Adam was 130 years old when he begat Seth.	130	0130	Genesis 5:3
Enos (born)	Seth was 105 years old when he begat Enos.	105	0235	Genesis 5:6
Cainan (born)	Enos was 90 years old when he begat Cainan.	90	0325	Genesis 5:9
Mahalaleel (born)	Cainan was 70 years old when he begat Mahalaleel.	70	0395	Genesis 5:12
Jared (born)	Mahalaleel was 65 years old when he begat Jared.	65	0460	Genesis 5:15
Enoch (born)	Jared was 162 years old when he begat Enoch.	162	0622	Genesis 5:18
Methuselah (born)	Enoch who (never died) was 65 years old when he begat Methuselah.	65	0687	Genesis 5:21
Lamech (born)	Methuselah was 187 years old when he begat Lamech.	187	0874	Genesis 5:25
Noah (born)	Lamech was 182 years old when he begat Noah.	182	1056	Genesis 5:28
Shem, Japheth, Ham (born)	Japheth, Shem, Ham are triplets and born when Noah was 500 years old.	500	1556	Genesis 5:32
Methuselah (died)	Methuselah was born 687 AM and died when he was 969 years old or in the year 687 + 969 = 1656. Mathuselah's death is thought to be comperable to the Rapture prior to the Tribulation Period.	-	1656	Genesis 5:27
Noah's Flood (start)	Noah was 600 years old at start of flood and Japheth, Shem, Ham were 100 years old.	100	**1656**	Genesis 7:6

251

Individual or Event	Description	Years to Event	AM Calendar	Reference
Noah's Flood (end)	Flood ended on the 1st day of the 1st month when Noah was 601 years old and Japheth, Shem and Ham were 101 years old.	1	1657	Genesis 8:13
Arphaxad (born)	Shem was 100 years old at the start of the flood and begat Arphaxad 2 years after the flood when he was 103 years old	2	1659	Genesis 11:10
Salah (born)	Arphaxad was 35 years old when he begat Salah.	35	1694	Genesis 11:12
Eber (born)	Salah was 30 years old when he begat Eber.	30	1724	Genesis 11:14
Peleg (born)	*Eber was 34 years old when he begat Peleg.*	*34*	*1758*	*Genesis 11:16*
Rue (born)	*Peleg was 30 years old when he begat Rue*	*30*	*1788*	*Genesis 11:18*
Serug (born)	*Rue was 32 years old when he begat Serug.*	*32*	*1820*	*Genesis 11:20*
Nahor (born)	*Serug was 32 years old when he begat Nahor.*	*32*	*1852*	*Genesis 11:22*
Terah (born)	*Nahor was 29 years old when he begat Terah.*	*29*	*1881*	*Genesis 11:24*
Abram (born)	*Terah was 70 years old when he begat **Abram**, Nahor, Haran.*	*70*	*1951*	*Genesis 11:26*
Peleg (died)	*Peleg lived 209 years after he begat Rue (1788 AM + 209 = 1997 AM) years and died when **Abram** was 46 years old.*	*na*	*1997*	*Genesis 11:19*
Noah (died)	Noah lived 350 years after the flood. (1657 AM + 350 = 2007 AM)	-	2007	Genesis 6:28
Abram departs Ur	Abram departed Ur when he was 75 years old. (1951 AM + 75 = 2026 AM)	-	2026	Genesis 12:4
Abrahamic covenant	Abram was 99 years YHWH made a covenant with him and changed his name to Abraham and his wife's name from Sarai to Sarah. (1951 AM + 99 = 2050 AM)	-	2050	Genesis 17:1-19
Isaac (born)	Abraham was 100 years old when he begat Isaac and Sarah was 90 years old. (1951 AM + 100 = 2051 AM)	100	2051	Genesis 17:17 Genesis 21:5

Individual or Event	Description	Years to Event	AM Calendar	Reference
2000 OS	Abraham's sacrifice of Isaac on Mount Moriah on 2000 OS starts the *Age of the Torah*. This event is bounded by Isaac's birth and Sarah's death.	na	2069 +/- 18.5 years	Genesis 22:1-2
Sarah (died)	Sarah died at 127 years of age (127 - 90 = 37) years after the birth of Isaac in 2051 AM.	na	2088	Genesis 23:1
Jacob (born)	Isaac was 60 years old when his wife Rebekah begat twins Esau and Jacob. (2051 AM + 60 = 2111 AM)	60	2111	Genesis 25:26
Abraham (died)	Abraham died at 175 years of age. (1951 AM + 175 = 2126 AM)	-	2126	Genesis 25:7
Shem (died)	Shem died 500 years after he begat Arphaxad. (1659 AM + 500 = 2159 AM)	-	2159	Genesis 11:11
Sons of **Jacob**/Israel	*Leah* (1st-Reuben, 2nd-Simeon, 3rd-Levi, 4th-Judah, 9th- Issachar, 10th-Zebulun) *Bilhah*, Rachel's handmaid, (5th-Dan, 6th-Naphtali) *Zilpah*, Leah's handmaid, (7th-Gad, 8th- Asher) *Rachel* (11th- **Joseph**, 12th- Benjamin)	-	-	Genesis 31:41
Joseph (born)	When Joseph was born Isaac asked Laban to leave. (2232 AM -30 = 2202 AM)	-	2202	Genesis 30:24 Genesis 41:46
Israel/Jacob	YHWH changed Jacob's name to Israel just after he left Laban or 6 years after Joseph's birth. (2202 AM + 6 = 2208 AM)	-	2208	Genesis 32:28 Genesis 31:41 Genesis 30:24
Isaac (died)	Isaac lived 180 years (2051 AM + 180 = 2231 AM)	-	2231	Genesis 35:28
Joseph	Joseph was 30 years when stood before the Pharaoh at the start of the 7 years of plenty. (2239 AM -7 = 2232 AM)	-	2232	Genesis 41:46 Genesis 45:6
-	Start of the years of famine (2241 AM - 2 = 2239 AM)	-	2239	-

253

Individual or Event	Description	Years to Event	AM Calendar	Reference
Israel/Jacob	Second year of famine Israel/Jacob was 130 years old when he brought his family to Egypt. (2111 AM + 130 = 2241 AM)	130	2241	Genesis 47:9
Israel/Jacob (died)	Israel lived in Egypt 17 years and was 147 years old when he died.	-	2287	Genesis 47:28
Joseph (died)	Joseph died in Egypt when he was 110 years old. (2202 AM+ 110 = 2312 AM)	-	2312	Genesis 50:26
Israelite slavery	Israelites sojourn in Egypt was 430 years. (2241 AM + 430 = 2671 AM)	430	2671	Exodus 12:40-41
Start of the Exodus	Passover 14th day of 1st month of year when Moses 80 years old and Aaron was 83 years old. (2671 AM + 1 = 2672 AM)	1	2672	Exodus 12:1-11 Exodus 7:7
YHWH Speaks	***YHWH spoke the Ten Commandments to the Holy Nation from Mount Sinai in the 3rd month on 3rd day.***	-	*2672*	***Exodus 19-20***
Moses	Tabernacle setup and operational on the 1st day, 1st month, of 2nd year. (2672 AM + 1 = 2673 AM)	-	2673	Exodus 40:17
12 Spies	Moses sent 12 spies into the promised land for 40 days and only Joshua and Caleb returned with optimism. The people rejected entering the promised land and the generation wandered in the wilderness for 40 years until they died.	-	2673	Numbers 13-14
Aaron (died)	Aaron was 123 years old and died on the 1st day, 5th month in 40th year after the start of the Exodus. (2671 AM + 40 = 2711 AM)	40	2711	Numbers 33:38-39
Moses	Moses final address to the people 1st day, 11th month in 40th year after the Exodus. He reviewed their history, YHWH's commandments, laws and the expectations when they enter the promised land.	-	2711	Deuteronomy 1:3
Moses (died)	Moses was the 1st Judge for 40 years he died when 120 years old and Israel mourned for 30 days.	-	2711	Deuteronomy 34:7

Individual or Event	Description	Years to Event	AM Calendar	Reference
Israelites into promised land	Joshua lead the Israelites over the Jordan River into the Promised Land on the 10th day of the 1st month after 40 years in the wilderness. (2711 AM + 1 = 2712 AM)	1	2712	Joshua 4:19
Joshua (died)	Joshua the 2nd judge was 110 years old when he died. The people followed YHWH all the days of Joshua and while his elders were alive. *(NOTE the exact AM dates for all the judges are not identified.)*	-	-	Joshua 24:29 Judges 2:8
Judges	When the people do evil YHWH enables their enemies and when the people call out to Him He provides a judge to restore them.	-	-	Judges 2:10-23
Servitude	Israel served Chushan-rishathaim, king of Mesopotamia 8 years.	-	-	Judges 3:8
Othniel	Othniel judged 40 years.	-	-	Judges 3:11
Servitude	Israel served Eglon the king of Moab 18 years.	-	-	Judges 3:14
Ehud and Shamgar	Ehud judged 80 years and with Shamgar 22 years.	-	-	Judges 3:15-31 I Samuel 13:19
Deborah and Barak	Deborah and Barak judged 40 years.	-	-	Judges 4-5
Gideon	Gideon (Jerrubbaal) judged 40 years.	-	-	Judges 6-8
Abimelech	Abimelech judged 3 years.	-	-	Judges 9
Tola	Tola judged 23 years.	-	-	Judges 10:1-2
Jair	Jair judged 22 years.	-	-	Judges 10: 3-5
Jephthah	Jephthah judged 6 years.	-	-	Judges 10: 6-8
Ibzan	Ibzan judged 7 years.	-	-	Judges 10:8-10
Elon	Elon judged 10 years.	-	-	Judges 12:11-12
Abdon	Abdon judged 8 years.	-	-	Judges 12:13-15
Samson	Samson judged 20 years.	-	-	Judges 13: 16
Eli	Eli judged 40 years.	-	-	I Samuel 4:18
Samuel (died)	Samuel judged Israel all the days of his life, which overlapped with king Saul.	-	-	I Samuel 7:15 I Samuel 25:1

Individual or Event	Description	Years to Event	AM Calendar	Reference
King Saul (died)	King Saul, his three sons and his armor bearer died.	-	-	I Samuel 31:1-6
King David	King David's reign lasted 40 years.	-	3108	I Kings 2:11-12 II Samuel 5:4-5
King Solomon	King Solomon's reign started 3 years before the year he started the Temple.	-	3148	II Chronicles 1:1-2
King Solomon starts Temple	In 4th year of king Solomon's reign the Temple was started on Mount Moriah. 480 years after children of Israel left Egypt. (2672 AM + 480 = 3152 AM)	480	3152	I Kings 6:1 II Chronicles 3:1-2
King Solomon (died)	King Solomon reigned 40 years or 36 years after starting the Temple. (3152 AM + 36 = 3188 AM)	36	3188	II Chronicles 9:30-31 I Kings 2:10
Rehoboam (died)	King Rehoboam reigned in Jerusalem, seventeen years. (3188 AM + 17 = 3205 AM)	17	3205	2 Chronicles 12:13
Abijam (died)	Abijah to reign over Judah for reigned three years in Jerusalem and there was war between Abijah and Jeroboam. (3205 AM + 3 = 3208 AM)	3	3208	2 Chronicles 13:1-2
Asa (died)	Asa slept with his fathers, and died in the one and fortieth year of his reign. (3208 AM + 41 = 3249 AM)	41	3249	2 Chronicles 16:13
Jehoshaphat (died)	Jehoshaphat reigned twenty and five years in Jerusalem. (3249 AM + 25 = 3274 AM)	25	3274	1 Kings 22:42
Jehoram (died)	Jehoram reigned eight years in Jerusalem and he did that which was evil in the eyes of the Lord. (3274 AM + 8 = 3282 AM)	8	3282	2 Chronicles 21:5-6
Ahaziah (died)	The inhabitants of Jerusalem made Ahaziah the son of Jehoram king of Judah because all his eldest sons had been slain. Ahaziah reigned one year in Jerusalem. He did evil in the sight of the Lord. (3282 AM + 1 = 3283 AM)	1	3283	2 Kings 8:26-27 2 Chronicles 22:1-2

256

Individual or Event	Description	Years to Event	AM Calendar	Reference
Athaliah (died)	Athaliah the mother of Ahaziah saw that her son was dead, she destroyed all the seed royal of the house of Judah. But Jehoshabeath, the daughter of the king, took Joash the son of Ahaziah, and hid him from Athaliah in the house of God six years while Athaliah reigned over the land. The people slew Athaliah with the sword. (3283 AM + 6 = 3289 AM)	6	3289	2 Kings 11:3 2 Kings 11:20-12:2 2 Chronicles 22:10-12
Jehoash (died)	Jehoash (Joash) reigned in Jerusalem forty years and did what was right in the sight of the Lord. (3289 AM + 40 = 3329 AM)	40	3329	2 Kings 11:20 - 12:2
Amaziah (died)	Amaziah reigned twenty and nine years in Jerusalem. He did that which was right in the sight of the Lord. (3329 AM + 29 = 3358 AM)	29	3358	2 Chronicles 25:1-2
Uzziah (died)	Uzziah (Azariah) reigned two and fifty years in Jerusalem. (3358 AM + 52 = 3410 AM)	52	3410	2 Kings 15:1-2
Jotham (died)	Jotham reigned sixteen years in Jerusalem. He did that which was right in the sight of the Lord. (3410 AM + 16 = 3426 AM)	16	3426	2 Chronicles 27:1-2
Ahaz (died)	Ahaz reigned sixteen years in Jerusalem. He did not do right in the sight of the Lord. (3426 AM + 16 = 3442 AM)	16	3442	2 Kings 16:1-3
Hezekiah (died)	Hezekiah reigned nine and twenty years in Jerusalem. He did that which was right in the sight of the Lord. (3442 AM + 29 = 3471 AM)	29	3471	2 Chronicles 29:1-2
Manasseh (died)	Manasseh reigned fifty and five years in Jerusalem and he did that which was evil in the sight of the Lord. (3471 AM + 55 = 3526 AM)	55	3526	2 Kings 21:1-2
Amon (died)	Amon reigned two years in Jerusalem. He did that which was evil in the sight of the Lord. The servants of Amon conspired against him, and slew the king in his own house. (3526 AM + 2 = 3528 AM)	2	3528	2 Kings 21:19-23

257

Individual or Event	Description	Years to Event	AM Calendar	Reference
Josiah (died)	Josiah reigned thirty and one years in Jerusalem and he did that which was right in the sight of the Lord. (3528 AM + 31 = 3559 AM)	31	3559	2 Kings 22:1-2
Jehoahaz (died)	Jehoahaz reigned three months in Jerusalem. He did that which was evil in the sight of the Lord.	-	3559	2 Kings 23:31-32
Jehoiakim *Taken to Babylon*	Jehoiakim reigned eleven years in Jerusalem and he did that which was evil in the sight of the Lord. Nebuchadnezzar king of Babylon took him captive to Babylon. (3559 AM + 11 = 3570 AM)	11	3570	2 Kings 23:36-37 2 Chronicles 36:5-8
Jeholachin *Taken to Babylon*	Jehoiachin reigned three months and ten days in Jerusalem: and he did that which was evil in the sight of the Lord. When the year expired, king Nebuchadnezzar brought him with the Temple vessels to Babylon.	-	3570	2 Chronicles 36:8-10
Zedekiah *Taken to Babylon*	Zedekiah was twenty and one years old when Nebuchadnezzar made Zedekiah king over Judah and Jerusalem. He reigned 11 years in Jerusalem. He did evil and would not do what the Lord asked through Jeremiah. Zedekiah rebelled against the king of Babylon, Nebuchadnezzar, and he besieged Jerusalem starting on the tenth day 10th month in the 9th year and continued until 9th day, 4th month in the eleventh year of king Zedekiah's reign when the people fled Jerusalem. They slew the sons of Zedekiah before his eyes, then put out his eyes and carried him to Babylon. (3570 AM + 11 = 3581 AM)	11	3581	2 Chronicles 36:11-13 2 Kings 24:18-25:8

258

Individual or Event	Description	Years to Event	AM Calendar	Reference
Babylonian captivity	Jerusalem, and the cities of Judah, and the kings thereof, and the princes thereof, to make them a desolation, an astonishment, an hissing, and a curse and this whole land shall be a desolation, and an astonishment; and these nations shall serve the king of Babylon seventy years. (3581 AM + 70 = 3651 AM)	70	3651	Jeremiah 25:11, 18
4000 OS	End of the *Age of the Torah* and start of the *Age of the Messiah* with the crucifixion and resurrection of YHWH's Body, Jesus the Messiah. 4000 OS is 2000 years after 2000 OS and has the same AM variance as 2000 OS. (0030 AD +/- 3.0 years)	-	4069 AM +/- 18.5 years	-
6000 OS	6000 OS ends the *Age of the Messiah with the* return of YHWH's Body, Jesus the Messiah. and starts the *Age of the Kingdom* The AM variance is the same as 2000 OS. (2030 AD +/- 3.0 years)	2000	6069 AM +/- 18.5 years	-
7000 OS	7000 OS ends the *Age of the Kingdom and* YHWH creates a new heaven and earth. The AM variance is the same as 2000 OS. (3030 AD +/- 3.0 years)	1000	7069 +/- 18.5 years	-

Notes:

a. YHWH reckons time with respect to a Lunar calendar referenced to Jerusalem.

b. No one could know who was in the detailed linage of Jesus the Messiah from 0000 AM except YHWH.

c. After the Babylonian captivity the is no precise AM date specified that correlates the AM and OS calendars better than 69 +/- 18.5 years. This variance is determined based on Abraham's "sacrifice" of Isaac at Mount Moriah on 2000 OS. This event is bounded by Isaac's birth 2051 AM and Sarah's death 2088 AM. If YHWH had provided a precise date and hour, then mankind would know the time of His return.

d. The birth of Jesus the Messiah is 0000 AD, or 4039 AM +/- 21.5 years, and 3967 OS +/- 3.0 years. 4000 OS is then 0030 AD +/- 3.0 years.

Appendix II - OS Calendar Events

OS Calendar	AM and Gregorian Calendar Variances	Event	Reference
0000	0065 +/- 65 AM 4004 +/- 800 BC	Adam and Eve's sin in the Garden of Eden started the **Original Sin (OS) Calendar** and the *Age of Desolation* where YHWH allowed all mankind to do as they desired.	Genesis 1-2
2000	2069 +/-18.5 AM 2004 +/- 800 BC	Abraham's "sacrifice" of Isaac brings an end to the *Age of Desolation* and began the *Age of the Torah*, time of instruction.	Genesis 22
4000	4069 +/-18.5 AM 0030 +/- 03.0 AD	YHWH's sacrifice of Himself, Jesus the Messiah, on the cross brought an end to the *Age of the Torah* and began the *Age of the Messiah*.	Matthew Luke
5993	6062 +/-18.5 AM 2023 +/- 03.0 AD	Start of seven year Tribulation Period to harvest men's souls.	Revelation
6000	6069 +/-18.5 AM 2030 +/- 03.0 AD	YHWH, Jesus the Messiah, returns to the material component of universe in power and glory ending the *Age of the Messiah* and ushering in the *Age of the Kingdom*.	Revelation
7000	7069 +/-18.5 AM 4030 +/- 03.0 AD	End of the *Age of the Kingdom* and the generation of a new Heaven and Earth	Revelation 22

Notes:

a.   In 0000 AM Adam and Eve were the first two people to exist. They had large family and they committed the Original Sin (OS) in 0000 OS. The original sin was the event that gave Adam and his family knowledge of good and evil.

b.   The minimum variance between the OS and the AM calendar is 69 +/- 18.5 years. This variance is determined based on Abraham's "sacrifice" of Isaac in 2000 OS, which is bounded by Isaac's birth in 2051 AM and Sarah's death in 2088 AM. See Appendix I.

c.   The minimum variance between the OS and the Gregorian calendar is 30 +/- 3.0 years and is established by YHWH's, Jesus the Messiah's crucifixion and resurrection based on His birth, ministry, and historical data.

Appendix III - Man's Decision Flowchart

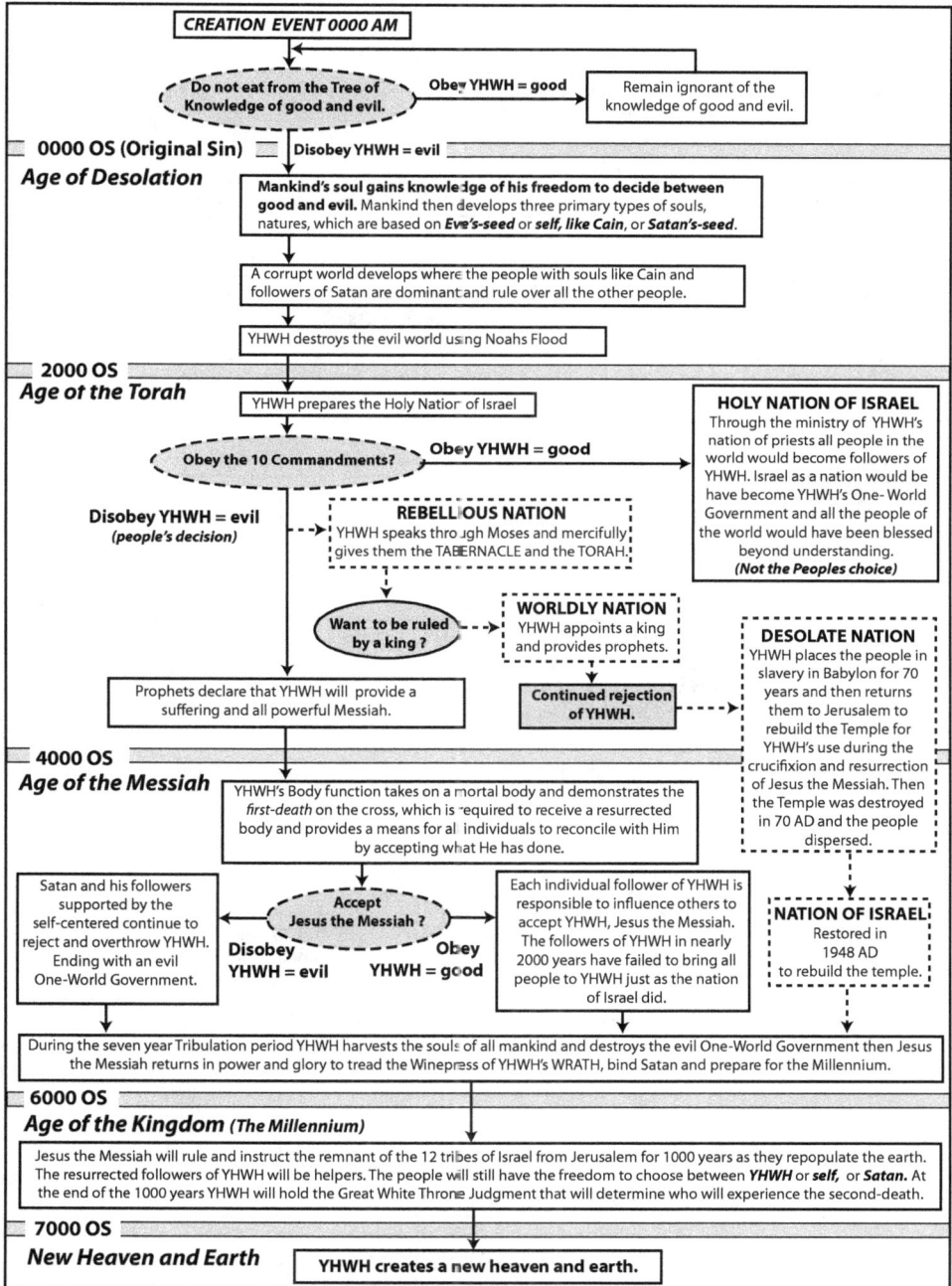

CREATION EVENT 0000 AM

Do not eat from the Tree of Knowledge of good and evil.

Obey YHWH = good → Remain ignorant of the knowledge of good and evil.

0000 OS (Original Sin)
Age of Desolation

Disobey YHWH = evil

Mankind's soul gains knowledge of his freedom to decide between good and evil. Mankind then develops three primary types of souls, natures, which are based on *Eve's-seed* or *self, like Cain*, or *Satan's-seed*.

A corrupt world develops where the people with souls like Cain and followers of Satan are dominant and rule over all the other people.

YHWH destroys the evil world using Noahs Flood

2000 OS
Age of the Torah

YHWH prepares the Holy Nation of Israel

Obey the 10 Commandments?

Obey YHWH = good

HOLY NATION OF ISRAEL
Through the ministry of YHWH's nation of priests all people in the world would become followers of YHWH. Israel as a nation would be have become YHWH's One-World Government and all the people of the world would have been blessed beyond understanding.
(Not the Peoples choice)

Disobey YHWH = evil
(people's decision)

REBELLIOUS NATION
YHWH speaks through Moses and mercifully gives them the TABERNACLE and the TORAH.

Want to be ruled by a king ?

WORLDLY NATION
YHWH appoints a king and provides prophets.

DESOLATE NATION
YHWH places the people in slavery in Babylon for 70 years and then returns them to Jerusalem to rebuild the Temple for YHWH's use during the crucifixion and resurrection of Jesus the Messiah. Then the Temple was destroyed in 70 AD and the people dispersed.

Prophets declare that YHWH will provide a suffering and all powerful Messiah.

Continued rejection of YHWH.

4000 OS
Age of the Messiah

YHWH's Body function takes on a mortal body and demonstrates the *first-death* on the cross, which is required to receive a resurrected body and provides a means for all individuals to reconcile with Him by accepting what He has done.

Satan and his followers supported by the self-centered continue to reject and overthrow YHWH. Ending with an evil One-World Government.

Accept Jesus the Messiah ?

Disobey YHWH = evil

Obey YHWH = good

Each individual follower of YHWH is responsible to influence others to accept YHWH, Jesus the Messiah. The followers of YHWH in nearly 2000 years have failed to bring all people to YHWH just as the nation of Israel did.

NATION OF ISRAEL
Restored in 1948 AD to rebuild the temple.

During the seven year Tribulation period YHWH harvests the souls of all mankind and destroys the evil One-World Government then Jesus the Messiah returns in power and glory to tread the Winepress of YHWH's WRATH, bind Satan and prepare for the Millennium.

6000 OS
Age of the Kingdom (The Millennium)

Jesus the Messiah will rule and instruct the remnant of the 12 tribes of Israel from Jerusalem for 1000 years as they repopulate the earth. The resurrected followers of YHWH will be helpers. The people will still have the freedom to choose between *YHWH* or *self*, or *Satan*. At the end of the 1000 years YHWH will hold the Great White Throne Judgment that will determine who will experience the second-death.

7000 OS
New Heaven and Earth

YHWH creates a new heaven and earth.

Appendix IV - Glossary of Terms

Term	Definition
Abomination of Desolation	The Abomination of Desolation is the point during the Tribulation Period where all people on earth have a $Will_{YHWH}(t) = 0.0$ except for the Remnant of Israel and the two witnesses. At this time YHWH has Michael declare YHWH's separation from Satan and His followers.
Age	An age is the period time when YHWH deals with mankind in a particular manner.
Age of Desolation	0000 OS to 2000 OS is the time period between the Fall of Man and the start of the Age of the Torah. During most of this time Satan was physically present on earth.
Age of the Torah	2000 OS and 4000 OS is the time period between Abraham's sacrifice of Isaac and the crucifixion and resurrection of Jesus the Messiah. During this time YHWH was going to provide personal instruction until the Holy Nation rejected Him at Mount Sinai.
Age of the Messiah	4000 OS and 6000 OS is the time period between Jesus the Messiah's crucifixion and resurrection during His first coming and His second coming in power and glory.
Age of the Kingdom (Millennium)	6000 OS to 7000 OS is the time period from the Jesus the Messiah's return in power and glory until the final judgment of mankind.
Age of Aquarius	The Occult new age that occurs when Satan's followers control the entire earth. This time period is corresponds to YHWH's Age of the Kingdom only from Satan's perspective.
AM calendar	Anno Mundi- in the year of the world. 0000 AM occurred when YHWH created the material universe.
Anxiety(t)	The amount of stress a person feels is proportional to the difference between his $L(t)$, Love, or priority for something and his $F(t)$, Faith, or confidence, in accomplishing it. $Anxiety(t) = [L(t) - F(t)]*P(t)$ P(t) is a scale factor set by YHWH to limit mankind's capability.
believe	For individual to believe in a person or YHWH: First, he must have knowledge concerning the person in his Soul or he is ignorant of the person. Second, an individual must have a high magnitude $Will(t) = L(t)*F(t)$ for items relating to the person. The magnitude of $L(t)$, priority, for these items are established by the individual. However, the magnitude of $F(t)$, confidence, is established the person's compliance with the individual's expectations of him.
Cleansing of Mother Earth	The cleansing of Mother Earth is the prelude to Age of Aquarius, new age or the new world order where the people who are unenlightened or have bad karma are purged from society. From YHWH's perspective this time is known as the Tribulation Period.
Church	The word church depending upon the context it is used in may mean: 1. A physical structure. 2. An association such as Christians, or Atheists, or Muslims or New Age. 3. A group of individuals having a specific type of soul at any point in time.
Covenant with many	During the prelude to the Tribulation Period, the leaders of the forming One-World Government make an agreement or covenant with many self-centered and Occult people throughout the world to eliminate all opposition to the One-World Government, which will include the followers of YHWH per Daniel 9:27.
Death, first	The first-death is the consequence from denial of access to the Tree of Life due to the Original Sin, rejecting of YHWH's command, and the first-death occurs when the bond between the spirt body and mortal physical body is broken.

Appendix IV - Glossary of Terms

Term	Definition
Death, second	The second-death results when one rejects YHWH and does not repent prior to their first-death. The consequence of the second-death is no resurrected body and the WILL is probably suppressed or disconnected so that one cannot implement their soul's decisions. This condition would certainly be considered a state of torment.
Elect	The elect are those people who YHWH will give the gift of eternal life, salvation. YHWH established His criteria for salvation before creating the earth and there are two different assumptions with respect to who the elect are: 1. YHWH predestined who the elect will be by specific name. 2. YHWH predestined the elect to be any person who decides to love and obey Him.
Fear	Fear is the Anxiety(t) experienced or anticipated when one has a high L(t) for someone or something and is placing a higher L(t) on another item that is in opposition to the first item. Thus, the Fear of the Lord is the Anxiety experienced or anticipated when one knowingly plans to sin.
$F(t)$	$F(t)$ is the magnitude of an individual's Faith. Faith is exactly the same word as confidence and both words project into the unseen future as hope. $F(t)$ is time dependent and reflects one's expectation for self, someone else or something. Self's faith in someone else is determined by that person's response to self's expectations. The magnitude of perfect faith = 1.0 and no faith = 0.0.
Follower of YHWH	An individual who believes in YHWH wants to know what YHWH expects of him by studying the Holy Bible and communicating with other followers. Thus, he wants to serve YHWH by trying to comply with His commands.
Follower of Satan	An individual who believes in Satan and aligns himself with Satan's goal to overthrow and destroy YHWH and His followers.
Four-Horsemen	The ride of the Four-Horsemen of the Apocalypse correspond to Seals #1 - #4 in Revelation 6:1-8. They murder 25 percent of the world's population during the judgement of the Ephesian-type soul.
Grieving process	Grieving is an anxiety resolution process triggered by a tragic event such as the death of a loved one. $Anxiety(t) = [L(t) - F(t)]*P(t)$, where the five phases of grieving are: Phase I - Denial: Both $L(t)$ and $F(t)$ are high so his $Anxiety(t)$ is low. Phase II - Anger: Recognition of the loss drops $F(t)$ resulting in high $Anxiety(t)$. Phase III - Guilt: When one's $L(t)$ begins to decrease his $Anxiety(t)$ will also. Phase IV - Rationalization: As $L(t)$ continues to decrease his $Anxiety(t)$ will also Phase V - Acceptance: Both $L(t)$ and $F(t)$ are low so his $Anxiety(t)$ has returned to a normal level. Also see reference 2.
Hate	Hate is a high state of $Anxiety(t) = [L(t) - F(t)]*P(t)$, where the magnitude of $L(t)$ is high and $F(t)$ is low, because self cannot control or possess something he loves dearly.
Indwelling holy spirit	The indwelling holy spirit is the number of items in an individual's Soul that are consistent with YHWH's WILL, Holy Spirit. Man's holy spirit is always shown in lower case in this book.
Israel, Holy Nation	In 2000 OS YHWH started to prepare the Holy Nation with Abraham's sacrifice of Isaac. The Holy Nation ended in 2672 AM at Mount Sinai when the people rejected YHWH's direct instruction and became the Rebellious Nation of Israel.
Israel, Rebellious Nation	The Rebellious Nation of Israel started in 2672 AM at Mount Sinai when the people rejected YHWH's direct instruction. YHWH provided judges to guide the people as required during this time. The Rebellious Nation of Israel ended when the people asked for a king and became a Worldly Nation.

Term	Definition
Israel, Worldly Nation	Israel became like all other nations when it received the first king, Saul. YHWH now provided prophets to warn the king and the people of the consequences of their actions and of His future appointed events. The Worldly Nation ended and became a Desolate Nation when it was carried away to Babylon by 3581 AM.
Israel, Desolate Nation	Since Babylon the Desolate Nation of Israel has had no king, no control over itself. This state ended on 15 May 1948 AD when YHWH restored Israel to a Worldly Nation with the task of rebuilding the Temple in preparation for His return.
Jubilee Period	A Jubilee Period is the period of time starting in the 49th year in the 7th month on 10th day, Yom Kippur, and ends at the end of the 50th year. During this period there is only one Passover, on the 14th day of the 1st month , and one Yom Teruah on the 1st day of the 7th month both during the 50th year.
Knowledge	All the information from the universe that is retained in an individual's Soul.
Knowledge, Item of	An item of knowledge is any unique piece of information contained in a person's soul
Knowledge, Mankind	Mankind's knowledge is the accumulated knowledge from all souls in the world.
Knowledge, Societal	Societal knowledge is the accumulated knowledge from a particular group of souls in the world. Different societies possess different quantities and types of knowledge.
$L(t)$	The magnitude of an individual's Love. Love is exactly the same word as priority and the terms are interchangeable. The magnitude of perfect love = 1.0 and no love = 0.0.
man's Body	Man's Body receives inputs from the universe, passes them to his Soul, and outputs to the universe responses as directed by his Will. Man has both a spirit Body and a mortal Body.
man's Soul	Man's Soul is the holder of all his information, it decides what will be done and then tells his Will what it needs to do.
man's Will	Man's *Will(t)* is the amount of effort, power, he expends to implement a decision and it is equal to the product of his Love, priority, for something and his Faith, confidence, in it. $Will(t) = L(t)*F(t)*P(t)$. $P(t)$ is a scale factor set by YHWH to limit mankind's capability. The composite Will associated with all the items of knowledge in a man's Soul is referred as his *mind*. The maximum Will associated with any decision is referred to as the man's *heart* or motive. See reference 2.
Occult	The Occult are people who are totally opposed to YHWH. Some Occult denominations include Satanists, Muslims, New Age, Masons, Kabbalists, Yogis, Wiccans and others.
Original Sin (OS)	An historical event that occurred when Adam and Eve, were disobedient to YHWH's command and ate from the Tree of Knowledge of Good and Evil. This event establishes a new calendar starting at 0000 OS. YHWH has established specific events using this OS calendar to reconcile mankind's sin to Himself. YHWH did not specify the exact date of the Original Sin with respect to the AM calendar so the exact timing of these events could not be known to mankind. However, as time passes the variance between the OS and AM calendars has decreased.
$P(t)$	$P(t)$, Power, is the factor that limits the maximum amount of *Will(t)* or *Anxiety(t)* that can be possessed. The magnitude of perfect power = 1.0 and no power = 0.0. YHWH's P(t) =1.0 and YHWH has set mankind's power to near 0.0 to protect the universe from man's bad decisions.

Term	Definition
Premeditative Process	Premeditative process is anxiety that occurs when one begins to increase their love for something with low or decreasing faith of possessing or controlling it. $$Anxiety(t) = [L(t) - F(t)]*P(t)$$ Phase I - Appreciation: A normal state, low $Anxiety(t)$, due to $L(t)$ and $F(t)$ having nearly the same magnitudes. YHWH's tenth Commandment protects one from going unstable by forbidding coveting. Phase II - Coveting: Increasing $L(t)$ with $F(t)$ remaining the same or decreasing. Phase III - Lusting: Continuing to increase $L(t)$ with $F(t)$ decreasing.. Phase IV - Obsession: Continuing to increase $L(t)$ with $F(t)$ decreasing.. Phase V - Reconciliation: An unstable state where one will do anything to reduce his $Anxiety(t)$ even murder. Also see reference 2.
Quantitative Theology	Quantitative Theology is the application of scientific process to the study God.
Rapture	The Rapture occurs during the first ten days of the Tribulation Period and results in the Philadelphia and Smyrna type souls experiencing the first-death in an instant.
Remnant of Israel	Members from the 12 tribes of Israel including the 144,000 all who survive the Tribulation Period and still have mortal-material bodies. These people will repopulate the world during the Age of the Kingdom.
Repentance Threshold	The Repentance Threshold is the magnitude of self's $Will_{YHWH}(t) = 0.5$. People who have self's $Will_{YHWH}(t) > 0.5$ are represented by Philadelphia and Smyrna soul types who place YHWH first in their lives. Everyone with self's $Will_{YHWH}(t) < 0.5$ must repent.
Satan	Satan's objective is to overthrow YHWH. Satan is known by a variety of names such as King of the Bottomless Pit, Devil, Great Dragon, Serpent, Abaddon, Apollyon Maitreya, Sanat Kumura, Allah, or Lucifer.
seed	Seed has several meanings but the primary two meanings used in this book are: 1. Seed of reproduction or descendents. 2. Source, origin or beginning of anything, such as the seed of revolt.
seed, Eve's or Woman's	Eve's-seed is good, which is promoting YHWH's truth and placing YHWH first in one's life.
seed, Serpent's or Satan's	Satan's-seed is evil, lying about YHWH's truth and promoting rebellion and overthrow of YHWH and His followers.
Serpent	Satan's material-body while in the Garden of Eden and until the time of Noah's flood.
Self-centered	A person who places themselves above all other people is characterized by Cain, or the Laodicean church, or Sodom and Gommorah. Their $Will_{self}(t) > Will_{others}(t)$.
Self-talk	Mankind's self-talk is silent or verbal communication between his Body, Soul, and Will. YHWH's self-talk is silent or verbal communication between His BODY, SOUL and WILL. YHWH treats His BODY, SOUL and WILL (Son, Father, Holy Spirit) as persons and uses His self-talk to illustrate their functions to mankind.
sin nature	The number of items in an individual's Soul that are consistent with Satan's-seed.
Synagogue of Satan	The Synagogue of Satan are people who are followers of Satan who have soul types of Thyatira, Pergamos, and Sardis.
(t)	Item(t) indicates the item is a variable that is time dependent.

In the Image of YHWH

Term	Definition
Time Dependent Revelation	Time Dependent Revelation occurs when an understanding can only be understood after mankind's knowledge attains a certain level after the passage of time.
Tribulation Period	Tribulation Period is the seven year period starting on Yom Teruah 5993 OS and ending on Yom Kippur in 6000 OS.
Trinity	YHWH is triune with BODY, SOUL and WILL. Following are some additional names associated with each. **Body:** Spirit of God, God saw, High Priest, The Son, Son of Man, Son of God, Jesus the Messiah, The Prince. **Soul:** Glory of God, God repented, Ark of the Testimony, The Father. **Will:** God said , God made, Table of Showbread, Holy Spirit, Holy Ghost.
Will(t)	Will(t) is the amount of effort, power, one expends to implement a decision and it is equal to the product of their Love, priority, for something and their Faith, confidence, for it. $Will(t) = L(t)*F(t)*P(t)$. P(t) is a scale factor set by YHWH to limit mankind's capability. YHWH is perfect $P(t) = 1.0$.　　　See reference 2.
Wisdom	Wisdom is an individual's application of knowledge within his Soul.
YHWH	YHWH is the Hebrew name for God. YHWH is the creator of the universe and the God of Abraham, Isaac, and Jacob. YHWH includes no vowels and when vowels are added YHWH is probably pronounced **Yahweh.**
YHWH, BODY (t)	YHWH's BODY receives inputs from the universe, passes them to YHWH's SOUL and outputs to the universe responses as directed by YHWH's WILL. Also, see the trinity.
YHWH, SOUL(t)	YHWH's SOUL is the holder of all information, it decides what will be done and tells the WILL what needs to be done. It is also known as the Glory of God, light, or Father. Also, see the trinity.
YHWH, WILL (t)	YHWH's WILL implements the desires of YHWH's SOUL. YHWH's perfect $WILL(t) = L(t)*F(t)*P(t) = 1.0*1.0*1.0 = 1.0$. YHWH's WILL is also known as God said or Holy Spirit. Also, see the trinity.
YHWH, WRATH (t)	YHWH's WRATH is His anxiety toward something or someone. YHWH's perfect $WRATH(t) = ANXIETY(t) = [L(t) - F(t)]*P(t) = [1.0 - 0.0]*1.0 = 1.0$. See Anxiety(t).

Index

267

References

1. King James version of the Holy Bible

    Public domain

2. Self's Destiny and Self by Dallas Stratman

    afjbooks.com

3. The World Almanac and Book of Facts 1999 and 2013

    Primedia Reference Inc.

4. NASA -- Measuring the Moon's Distance

    http://eclipse.gsfc.nasa.gov/SEhelp/ApolloLaser.html

5. Biblesoft's New Exhaustive Strong's Numbers and Concordance with Expanded Greek-Hebrew Dictionary

    Biblesoft, Inc. and International Bible Translators, Inc.

www.ingramcontent.com/pod-product-compliance
Lightning Source LLC
Chambersburg PA
CBHW060255100426
42742CB00011B/1762